HANDBOOK OF
Latina/o Theologies

With deep appreciation to the members of our dissertation committees:

Phillip Berryman

Katie Geneva Cannon

Justo L. González

John C. Raines

David Harrington Watt

"Iron sharpens iron, and one person sharpens the wits of another."
PROVERBS 27:17

HANDBOOK OF
Latina/o Theologies

Edwin David Aponte
Miguel A. De La Torre
EDITORS

CHALICE
PRESS
ST. LOUIS, MISSOURI

Cover art: © The Crosiers
Cover design: Elizabeth Wright
Interior design: Hui-Chu Wang

Visit Chalice Press on the World Wide Web
at www.chalicepress.com

10 9 8 7 6 5 4 3 2 1   06 07 08 09 10 11

Library of Congress Cataloging-in-Publication Data

Handbook of Latina/o theologies / Edwin David Aponte and Miguel A. De La Torre, editors.
    p. cm.
  Includes bibliographical references.
  ISBN-13: 978-0-8272-1450-7 (pbk. : alk. paper)
  ISBN-10: 0-8272-1450-2 (pbk. : alk. paper)
  1. Hispanic American theology. I. Aponte, Edwin David. II. De La Torre, Miguel A.
  BT83.575.H36 2006
  230.089'68073–dc22

                                                    2005025663

Printed in the United States of America

Contents

Contributors

Javier R. Alanís (Ph.D., Lutheran School of Theology at Chicago) is associate professor of theology, culture, and mission at the Lutheran Theological Seminary Program in the Southwest.

Edwin David Aponte (Ph.D., Temple University) is director of advanced studies and associate professor of Christianity and culture at Perkins School of Theology, Southern Methodist University.

Paul T. Barton (Ph.D., Southern Methodist University) is associate professor of Hispanic studies at the Episcopal Theological Seminary of the Southwest.

Luis E. Benavides (Th.D., Boston University) is director of the LUCE Program for New Language Immigrant Groups, and adjunct faculty in theology and New Testament at Gordon-Conwell Theological Seminary/Boston.

Teresa Chávez Sauceda (Ph.D., Graduate Theological Union) is associate for racial justice and advocacy, National Ministries Division of the Presbyterian Church (USA).

David Cortés-Fuentes (Ph.D., Northwestern University) is director of academic services and associate professor of New Testament at San Francisco Theological Seminary/Southern California.

Kenneth G. Davis, O.F.M., Conv. (D.Min., Pacific School of Theology) is associate professor of pastoral studies at Saint Meinrad School of Theology.

Miguel A. De La Torre (Ph.D., Temple University) is director of the Justice and Peace Institute and associate professor of social ethics at Iliff School of Theology.

Anita de Luna, M.C.D.P. (Ph.D., Graduate Theological Union, D.L.L., University of Notre Dame) is assistant professor of religious studies at Our Lady of the Lake University.

Miguel H. Díaz, (Ph.D., University of Notre Dame) is associate professor of theology at College of Saint Benedict/Saint John's University.

Ana María Díaz-Stevens (Ph.D., Fordham University) is professor of church & society at Union Theological Seminary in New York City.

Eduardo C. Fernández, S.J. (S.T.D., Pontifical Gregorian University) is associate professor of pastoral theology and ministry at the Jesuit School of Theology at Berkeley.

Ismael García (Ph.D., University of Chicago) is professor of Christian ethics at Austin Presbyterian Theological Seminary.

Alex García-Rivera (Ph.D., Lutheran School of Theology at Chicago) is associate professor of systematic theology at the Jesuit School of Theology at Berkeley.

Michelle A. González (Ph.D., Graduate Theological Union) is assistant professor of religious studies at the University of Miami.

Leticia A. Guardiola-Sáenz (Ph.D., Vanderbilt University) is assistant professor of New Testament at Drew University.

Alberto Hernández (Ph.D., Drew University) is assistant professor of the history of Christianity at Iliff School of Theology.

Gloria Inés Loya, P.B.V.M. (D. Min., Pacific School of Religion) is lecturer in Hispanic and ministry studies and coordinator of the Instituto Hispano, Jesuit School of Theology at Berkeley.

Nora O. Lozano (Ph.D., Drew University) is assistant professor of theological studies at the Baptist University of the Americas in San Antonio, Texas.

Juan Francisco Martínez (Ph.D., Fuller Theological Seminary) is assistant dean of Hispanic church studies and associate professor of Hispanic studies and pastoral leadership at Fuller Theological Seminary.

Manuel J. Mejido Costoya (Ph.D., Emory University) is professor titular of social theory at the Universidad Academia de Humanismo Cristiano, Santiago, Chile.

Kristy Nabhan-Warren (Ph.D., Indiana University at Bloomington) is assistant professor of American religions at Augustana College in Rock Island, Illinois.

Carmen M. Nanko-Fernández (D.Min., Catholic University of America) is assistant professor of pastoral ministry and director of field education at Catholic Theological Union.

Luis G. Pedraja (Ph.D., University of Virginia) is executive associate director of the Middle States Commission on Higher Education.

Zaida Maldonado Pérez (Ph.D., Saint Louis University) is associate professor of theological studies at Asbury Theological Seminary in Orlando, Florida.

Harold J. Recinos (D.Min., New York Theological Seminary, Ph.D., American University) is professor of church and society at Perkins School of Theology, Southern Methodist University.

Luis N. Rivera-Pagán (Ph.D., Yale University) is the Henry Winters Luce Professor of Ecumenics at Princeton Theological Seminary.

Jeanette Rodríguez (Ph.D., Graduate Theological Union) is professor of theology and religious studies at Seattle University.

Joanne Rodríguez-Olmedo (Th.M., Princeton Theological Seminary) is director of the Hispanic Theological Initiative located at Princeton Theological Seminary.

Carla E. Roland Guzmán (M.A., Graduate Theological Union) is a priest in the Episcopal Church.

Arlene M. Sánchez Walsh (Ph.D., Claremont Graduate University) is associate professor at the Haggard School of Theology, Azusa Pacific University.

Anthony M. Stevens-Arroyo (Ph.D. Fordham University) is director of the Center for Religion in Society and Culture, professor of Puerto Rican and Latino studies at Brooklyn College, distinguished scholar of the City University of New York.

Margarita M.W. Suárez (Ph.D., Northwestern University/Garrett-Evangelical Theological Seminary) is assistant professor of religion at Meredith College in Raleigh, North Carolina.

David Traverzo Galarza (Ph.D., Drew University) is instructor at Christian University in Paterson, New Jersey.

Manuel A. Vásquez (Ph.D., Temple University) is associate professor of religion at the University of Florida.

Theological and Cultural Competence *en Conjunto*

■ EDWIN DAVID APONTE

Why Latino/a Theology?

Scholars in religious studies and parishioners in the contemporary church in the United States face the reality and challenge of the varied theological, ecclesiastical, spiritual, and cultural expressions that come under the term *"Latino/a* or *Hispanic* theology." Hispanic theology can be defined as the distinct theologies that emerge out of the social and cultural contexts of Latino/a peoples, which, nonetheless, have some shared characteristics. These common traits make Latino/a theology a communal undertaking that is scholarly, pastoral, and organically connected to grassroots communities. Latino/a theology insists on doing theology in a relevant contextual way that is both in dialogue with the received dominant theological traditions as well as questioning of them and their claims of being standard. Moreover, there is no such thing as one single, unified Hispanic/Latino/a theology, but rather a multiplicity of perspectives within the diverse Latino/a communities that articulate distinctive and relevant Hispanic viewpoints for the larger endeavor of Christian theology as a whole.

Latino/a theology encompasses all subjects in all fields of theology, biblical studies, and religion; and its significance flows beyond the boundaries of Hispanic communities in an increasingly pluralistic United States. The purpose of this handbook is to introduce selected Christian theological and other religious concepts from the point of view of the Hispanic/Latino/a communities as well as providing an enhanced understanding of the Hispanic presence within overall Christian theology, thereby highlighting the diversity within the Latino/a theological discourse. This in turn will inform and challenge the traditional normative discourse held to be a self-evident "objective" orthodoxy against which everything else is measured, illustrating a great variety of approaches and positions. Simply stated, this handbook surveys how Latinos/as understand and do theology. Attention is given to the history, nature, sources, and development of the U.S. Latinos/as theological expressions and their contribution to the overall theological discourse, as well as the connection between these different theological perspectives and the identity of the individual groups that produced these perspectives. Furthermore, the correlation between religion, identity, community, context, agency, and culture in the social environment of different marginalized groups–and their impact on the development and nature on Latino/a theologies–is considered.

The first part of the handbook presents essays on many of the traditional topics in Christian theology representative both of the individual authors and various beliefs found in Latino/a communities. The second section focuses on different trends and contextual issues within the overall Hispanic/Latino/a theological conversation demonstrating the breadth, richness, and diversity of Latino/a theological and religious perspectives. There is no claim here for a unified presentation of Latino/a theologies, with all the authors espousing the same set of beliefs, approaches, and positions. Indeed, at some points it will be evident that we disagree with each other. Nevertheless, this volume does show a shared characteristic. Collectively, this *Handbook* is an expression of *teología en conjunto.*

A Word on *Teología en Conjunto*

A vital feature of Hispanic/Latino/a theology is its collaborative methodology, known as *teología en conjunto.* As a shared endeavor, Latino/a collaborative theology arises both from the historical and social contexts of Hispanics/Latinas and Latinos in the United States as well as a set of commitments, the chief of which is a commitment to community. Part of the reality of the Latino/a communities in the United Stated is that they are remarkably varied, although inaccurately classified as one homogeneous group by dominant public authorities. One dimension of the existential reality of being grouped together is discovering what it means to be part of a community that is simultaneously imagined and real, imposed and embraced. *Teología en conjunto* seeks to explore and articulate the theological dimensions of this diverse and constantly developing life together in the United States.[1]

Dominant scholarly cultural contexts stress individual academic pursuits as the epitome of scholarship while simultaneously devaluing work done in partnership as somehow less rigorous. Therefore, there is little danger of this collective approach being romanticized, given the experience of Latino/a communities in the United States where there is a continuous experience that "*estamos en la lucha*" ("we are in the struggle"). Certainly the wider Latino/a struggle engages larger social forces, including those who disparage Latino/a theology and *teología en conjunto* as a superficial, marginal activity. This communal Latino/a theological emphasis brings an alternative vision with intellectual rigor and communal connection in contrast with privatized expressions of Christian theology that are highly individualistic and increasingly removed from the contextual realities of everyday life, which are found in the United States and Europe across the theological spectrum of "liberal-conservative."

Because of its conscious commitment to Hispanic/Latino/a communities, accompanied by the goal of contextual relevance and the implementation of biblical justice in contemporary society, Hispanic theology continues to be marginalized by some in the church and the academy despite its intellectual rigor. Some theologians and church leaders dismiss Latino/a theologies as passing fads of little importance, a type of theological sideshow or distraction. Such judgments reflect arrogant dominant cultural attitudes. These de facto actions of exclusion and injustice prevail at variance with the official language of acceptance and inclusion by which Latinas and Latinos are welcomed, but only when they behave in prescribed ways that support existing patterns of control and often neglect questions of justice.

Marginality from forces outside the Latino/a community poses difficult hurdles, but there is a significant challenge from within the community as scholars of Latino/a religion and theology engage in the difficult work of collaboration. We realized that with this *Handbook* we could not produce a work that was acceptable to, or even reflected the consensus of, all the contributors on all subjects. However, we do hope that this book will give a taste of the wide ranges of theology and religion within the Hispanic/Latino/a communities within the United States as an expression of collaborative theology.

Latino/a *teología en conjunto* arises from the specific contexts of Latino religious communities in the United States, including Roman Catholic,

---

[1]For more on *teología en conjunto*, see De La Torre and Aponte, *Introducing Latino/a Theologies*, 2001:73–74; Fernández, *La Cosecha*, 2000:54, 74, 143; Goizueta, *We Are a People!*, 1992c; and Rodríguez and Martell-Otero, *Teología en Conjunto*, 1997.

Pentecostal, mainline Protestant, and evangelical groups. To varying degrees, Hispanic or Latino/a theology also explores the impact and occasional influence of alternative Latino/a religious traditions, including "older" alternatives of Indigenous beliefs and practices, African Diaspora religious traditions such as *Santería,* as well as more recent or "newer" religious movements. Moreover, some Latinos/Latinas have multiple religious involvements in several groups and traditions–sometimes concurrently–that impact contemporary beliefs and practices.

Latino/a Identity and Culture

Issues of contextual identity and multiple cultures are an inherent part of Latino/a theologies, although they do not exhaust the whole content. In the United States "Hispanics" and "Latinos/as" are peoples who have roots in Latin America, but even that shared characteristic can mask a great deal of historical and cultural diversity. Several essays explore aspects of identity and culture, so there is no need to discuss these issues in great detail here. Suffice it to say that the U.S. Census categories in 2000 did not account for all the rich racial and ethnic diversity that exists within each of these national groups. U.S. Latino/a groups maintain their connections with various ethnic and national roots and identities. Each Latino/a context and community puts its own spin on what it has received from multicultural Latin American roots, present context, and interaction with other Latino groups. The existential experience of Latinos/as includes being pilgrims, aliens, exiles, or outsiders at home (De La Torre and Aponte 2001:46–53). With its continually evolving cultural and racial identities, the population of Hispanics or Latinos/as in the United States makes this country one of the largest "Latin American" population centers in the world.

Moreover, a genuine homegrown U.S. Latino/a population beyond governmental demographic designations is developing in the United States. So there cannot be a "typical" Latina, Latino, or Hispanic. The Hispanic/Latino/a religious experience is varied in the same way, but there is an ongoing cultural *mestizaje* taking place in the United States. Commenting on the nature of *mestizaje* as part of Latino/a identity, Arturo Bañuelas states that *mestizaje:*

> is a *locus theologicus.* Furthermore, when viewed from the Latino peoples' struggles for survival, *mestizaje* is rooted in resistance against assimilationist tendencies by any oppressive, dominant culture. For this reason, Latino theology affirms *mestizaje* in the Latino's struggle for self-identity and self-determination and links it with God's plans for a new world order. While God-talk and *mestizaje* are linked in the Latino history of salvation, the issue of this relationship continues to be unsettled because

mestizaje is and will continue to be an unfinished process as the place of origin changes. (1995:1)

Additionally, some Hispanic theologians also use the term *mulatez* in conjunction with *mestizo*. Both terms are rooted in the colonial period: The first referred to a mixture of African and European; the latter referred to European and Indigenous. While there is criticism of employing *mulatez* to describe present culture, the utilization of both terms helps ensure that the racial/ethnic cultural complexity of peoples of Latin American descent is considered (Isasi-Díaz 2004:44).[2]

Identities transported from Latin America, imposed by the dominant culture, and formed in new contexts all contribute to cultural complexity within the United States and result in a self-determination that is forming and reforming, whether called "Hispanic" or "Latino/a." It is an emergent, flexible, contextual, and contested pan-ethnic identity shared among people of Latin American and Caribbean roots living in the United States while acknowledging and affirming differences. The conditions of life in the United States, including imposed racial identities, help foster this growing sense of group identity. All of this complexity of multiple identities and cultural locations is part of the context in the formulation of Latino/a theologies.

Collaboration and Theological Tradition

Although there are many collective themes, it is not yet clear if one can speak of definite schools of thought within U.S. Latino/a theologies. Certainly there is a great deal of scholarly dialogue across these various lines, and perhaps this is one of the hallmarks of Latino/a theology: a certain type of ecumenical awareness and solidarity. This is an ecumenism that, while aware of what has transpired historically in the National Council of Churches and the World Council of Churches, really developed along alternative paths, some of them located in the margins and borderlands. It also developed with a profound sense of the various Latino/a communities, to which the many theologies and scholars of religion have felt ongoing responsibility and commitment.

Some common themes have emerged despite the extreme diversity among Hispanic communities. These include the already mentioned emphasis on identity and culture, the importance of family and community, the role of experience and religious practices—especially popular religious practices, gender analysis and agency, the struggle for survival and the related agency in public life, and interreligious

---

[2]See also Valentin, *Mapping Public Theology,* 2002:69–72; De La Torre, *La Lucha for Cuba,* 2003:16–18.

dialogue.[3] One shared theme that has produced many permutations is the rubric of rereading. Justo González initially suggested the specific theme "Reading the Bible in Spanish" to discuss Hispanic/Latino/a approaches to biblical interpretation; however, this has been picked up by many others in other areas as well so that there are explorations of rereading theology in the general as well as specific areas of theology, such as christology, the history of Christianity, pastoral theology, etc. (González 1990:75–87).[4]

Latino/a theological themes include a rereading of the received traditions in dialogue with matters of concern that arise from Latino/a peoples so that the received tradition is connected to living communities of faith and comes under critical assessment in the context of the struggle for life. Assertions that the received traditions might be less than perfect and free of any cultural conditioning is a matter of concern to some contemporary theologians, historians, and ecclesiastical leaders. However, in that very challenge lies one of the great benefits of U.S. Latino/a theologies, in that all religious talk, theological formulations, and historical accounts are culturally positioned. Rereading the traditions is not necessarily a rejection of the essential claims of the tradition (although that may happen). Rereading means honestly stating what every generation does, that is, try to make sense of what has been passed on to it. Second, rereading the tradition means taking the tradition seriously. Third, rereading the tradition means a commitment to be contextual, without which any received tradition become lifeless and a museum piece.

Cultural Competence in Religious and Theological Studies

Latino/a theology is a demonstration of the need for intentional cultural competence in theology and ministry, as well as some ways this goal can be achieved. Some persons in and out of theological and religious studies argue against the need for cultural competence, saying that there is only one body of knowledge and only way of knowing. Hispanic or Latino/a theology challenges that limited way of thinking and demonstrates it to be a head-in-the-sand way of understanding the world as well as the complex history and nature of Christian theology.

Cultural competence is a commitment and orientation that encompasses a group of informed behaviors, outlooks, and policies that assists to bring about effective understanding and dialogue in cross-cultural contexts. Cultural competence involves the readiness and capacity to appreciate both the existence *and* significance of multiple

---

[3]For more on Latino/a theological themes see Aquino, Machado, and Rodríguez, *A Reader in Latina Feminist Theology,* 2002; Valentín, *New Horizons in Hispanic/Latino(a) Theology,* 2003; and Pedraja, *Teología,* 2004.

[4]For example of an application of the rereading concept see Pedraja, *Jesus Is My Uncle,* 1999b.

cultures in relationships and social interactions. It is a process of multilayered community life that involves the acquisition of skill and practices for life together. Cultural competence means the recognition and valuing of difference, and thereby accepting and respecting its importance. That does not mean one is compelled to agree with the difference or be its advocate. Cultural competence entails working toward effective cross-cultural communication, engagement with real communities, and a deeper engagement with multiple bodies of knowledge and behavior. Some people recognize difference but do not value it and, indeed, see difference as inherently destructive and a threat to the status quo, and therefore to be opposed automatically. Such opposition is ironic in that it reveals a selective view of the tradition that it seeks to protect, whitewashing the diversity that is within the received tradition itself. Christian theology has always been cross-cultural and has always involved cultural competency.

The practice of cultural competence is already occurring within Hispanic/Latino/a communities as Hispanics deal with their multicultural realities. Moreover, multicultural Latinas and Latinos daily demonstrate their cultural competence as they engage with dominant cultures at several levels and in many ways. The variety of expressions of Hispanic/Latino/a theology are yet another demonstration of the reality, need, and possibility of theological and ecclesiastical cultural competence for Christian life together and ministry in the world. With that perspective it is clear that Hispanic/Latino/a theology is not a passing fad but a needed perspective for the wider common good. It is incumbent upon the church in the United States—across denominational and jurisdictional lines—to become familiar with this evolving exciting theological and pastoral reality.

Many of the issues facing Latino/a communities are still not adequately addressed by the larger society and church, while simultaneously contributions of Latinas and Latinos in theology, history, liturgy, and pastoral ministry continue to be haphazardly and systematically ignored. *Teología en conjunto* seeks to correct this double oversight and to make positive contributions to the life, thought, and ministry of the wider Christian Church. Moreover, recognizing that all theologies arise out of some particular cultural context, *teología en conjunto* with its intentional emphasis on the value of cooperative relational work and commitment to community seeks to add its voice to wider discussions, all the while trying to be faithful to the perspectives and experiences of the diverse Hispanic or Latino/a communities in the United States. Such a scholarly approach is more than the parochial concerns of a marginalized community. Doing collaborative theology from a Latino/a perspective can then be a model and encouragement for doing theology together across the breadth of the church in the twenty-first century.

PART I

Thematic Essays

CHAPTER 1

God

■ JAVIER R. ALANÍS

Created in the Image of *Diosito*

The notion of God is a very broad metaphysical concept. To write a short chapter on this subject would not do justice to the variety of religious expressions and understandings behind this theological concept. Therefore, this chapter nuances this topic from the perspective of theological anthropology, in order to better understand notions of God from a Latino/a perspective. This chapter revisits a theological construct referred to in the dogmatic tradition as the *imago Dei*, a notion taken from the biblical reference to human beings as created in the image and likeness of God (Gen. 1:26–27). By examining the concept from the perspective of the dogmatic tradition in conversation with Hispanic popular religious expression, this chapter will elucidate how the community expresses and images its self-understanding in light of the experience of the sacred. An attempt will be made to show that God as experienced by the Hispanic/Latino/a community is not an exclusive metaphysical reality, but a personal and communal God who journeys with the people in daily life. To this end, this chapter will consult the diverse voices of both the Protestant and the Roman Catholic communities for a broader glimpse of the intimate and endearing God who is often referred to as *Diosito*.

To speak of God is to reflect on the nature or essence of God as experienced in community. When Protestant ethicist Ismael García writes that "Hispanics confess that our humanity is grounded in our being created in God's image," he is speaking about the experience of a people who understand themselves as beloved of God who is *amor*, that is, love in relationship with others and specifically with a particular community that refers to itself as the Hispanic/Latino/a people of faith (1997:130). As a Protestant theologian who has reflected deeply on the meaning of God as *amor*, I have discovered from within my own community of faith and familial relationships that the character and nature of God is to be *amoroso* and *cariñoso*. This means God is a *loving* and *affectionate* friend who is often called *Diosito*, a term of endearment for One who is known intimately. This endearing friend creates, reveals, and manifests the essence of a caring love most acutely through others. As someone who loves us, *Diosito* is both a good friend, *un Buen Amigo*, and a Lover, *un Amante*, who initiates a loving relationship with the beloved community through the life and death of the beloved Son, Jesus of Nazareth. As *Diosito*, *El Buen Amigo*, and *Amante*, God loves the beloved community and creates us with this essence and capacity for reciprocal love even as our sinful nature often mars this image of perfect love. This *amor del Amante* and *Buen Amigo* is most clearly revealed in the incarnational love and ministry of Jesus of Nazareth. This is a view poignantly expressed by Roman Catholic theologian Virgilio Elizondo in his reflections and writings on the Galilean.[1]

To better understand the construct of the *imago Dei* and the notion that we as a people have been created "in the image and likeness of *Diosito*," who is *amor*, let us briefly turn to the scriptural references. These texts are Genesis 1:26a: Then God said, "Let us make humankind in our image, according to our likeness…" and Genesis 1:27: "So God created humankind in his [*sic*] image, in the image of God he [*sic*] created them; male and female he [*sic*] created them." Biblical scholars and theologians throughout the ages have reflected on the meaning of these texts as a way of understanding the nature and essence of the human, who is a reflection of the Creator.

Biblical scholar Claus Westermann points out that human dignity and responsibility for the creation are core values conferred by God in the creation of the human and that "implicit in being created in the image of God is the capacity for language" (1987:11).[2] Westermann also observes that the succession of human generations that the early biblical writer places after the creation story in Genesis (chapters 5 and 10) is a succession of names, and in the succession of names lies the beginning of history. History, he notes, grows out of the blessing conferred on the human family through fertility and procreation.

Westermann's observations resonate with the Hispanic/Latino/a perspective on the *imago Dei* for several reasons. First, language or the

---

[1]See, for example, Elizondo, *The Galilean Journey*, 2000a.
[2]See also Alanís, *Dignity for the Foreigner*, 2002:8.

ability to speak and name the world is derivative of the *imago Dei* as a gift of *Diosito*. The language of the family of origin is a gift of a historical and theological worldview. The gift of language also confers an identity that is nurtured and affirmed through the culture and history of the family and the community. It allows us to name the world and to cocreate with *Diosito* in the language of our culture. Historically, Hispanics/Latinos/as have been chastised for speaking the Spanish language because it represents the language of a conquered people. At the same time, Hispanics/Latinos/as who speak English as their primary language have at times experienced the lament of the loss of the native language of their parents and grandparents. While the English language has provided new opportunities, they are still treated as minorities within a much larger English-speaking dominant culture that often does not appreciate or value their contributions. Since the Spanish language is considered a foreign language throughout the United States, both the governmental and educational systems have attempted to eradicate it. The community resists these efforts because it recognizes that the Spanish language is the language of the heart. It is the language of prayer and of communion with *Diosito*.

Secondly, language is history. The gift of language allows the connection to the past. It gives the Hispanic/Latino/a community its sense of history and specificity within a culture that is not its own. It nurtures the cultural memory of faith and reminds the community that it has a place of belonging in the heart of God.[3] It also provides the connection to the larger Hispanic/Latino/a community throughout the United States, so that a sense of solidarity and community arises wherever the Spanish language is heard and spoken. It helps to end the isolation that many immigrants feel when they enter this country and do not speak the English language. It reminds them that they have a common history and familiar roots. It confers dignity.

The apologists during the early church period emphasized the high value of the human being as a recurring theme in their works. This resonates with the Hispanic/Latino/a community. The early church writers appear to be in agreement with the psalmist in elevating the nature of humanity to a degree only slightly lower than the angels (Ps. 8). The noble characteristics they perceive in the human—such as dignity, purity, and virtue; moral freedom and responsibility; reason in the service of morality; the ability to commune with God; as well as the bodily nature as a reflection of the divine and royal image—are all evidence of an exalted view of humanity that was to characterize the early church movement and make it an appealing force for the community of the marginalized. These reflections were the basis for an early Christian theological anthropology that would leave its mark on the

---

[3]See, for example, Rodríguez, "Sangre llama a sangre," 1996:351–66.

Roman Empire as the Christian church continued to grow as a subversive force within the empire. This elevated view of humanity would be a dynamic force in opposing the Roman notions of conquest and subjugation of foreign peoples.

Like the early church movement, the Hispanic/Latino/a community lives with a sense of estranged otherness due to a conquest of territories dating back to the nineteenth century. For Miguel De La Torre and Edwin Aponte, most Hispanics continue to be seen by the dominant culture as exiles, aliens, and outsiders, regardless of their historical connection to U.S. lands (2001:46–53). In light of this perception, the community strives to preserve its dignity based on its understanding of the human family. For Justo González, to be fully human is to be-for-others (1990:131). In this scenario no one exercises power over others, for that would lead to the dehumanization of everyone and the loss of our for-otherness. González and other Hispanic/Latino/a scholars such as Ada María Isasi-Díaz (1993:34–54) and Ismael García (1997:130–72) affirm the human being in other ways. They express and affirm the value of the human distinctively in community and in being-for-others. Sin is the violation of that for-otherness and the violation of God's image in us, which for González is precisely the image of God's for-otherness. The Hispanic/Latino/a affirmation of the oppressed minority differs from the way the early church theologians affirmed the human being. While early theologians affirmed the capacities of humans in their abilities to be like God, their interpretation tended to focus on the physical and psychical merits of the individual as a created being. They focused less on the human as a social and relational being who, as a communal person, reflects the image of *Diosito* who cares for others in community as exemplified in the life and praxis of Jesus of Nazareth.

From the perspective of the Hispanic/Latino/a community, the Genesis texts can only be understood and interpreted from within the context of a history of conquest, exile, and diaspora. This is also the experience of the more recent immigrant community *and* the U.S. native-born Hispanic/Latino/a community. Both share a history of marginalization, exclusion, and indignity due to cultural, linguistic, and religious roots and affiliations. Reflecting on this experience, Justo González and Ismael García have interpreted the *imago Dei* construct with an understanding that to be created *in the image and likeness of God* affirms the human worth and dignity of all people and, in particular, those on the margins of society. For González, creation in the image and likeness of God means the exercise of the creative power and love of God after whom we have been created. As love, God's nature is being-for-others, and to be fully human is to be for others in a praxis of love and care.

The notion of the exiled community affirming its dignity in the face of oppressive conditions is not unlike the Hebrew writers who affirmed the dignity of their community when they constructed the Genesis texts of the *imago Dei*. They wrote those texts during or soon after the Babylonian exile and captivity as a way of affirming their God-given dignity and as a way of refuting the notion that only those in power were of divine origin. This experience closely parallels the Hispanic/Latino/a reality of exile and marginalization and the self-understanding that emerges from the encounter with the sacred. Whereas the exiled Hebrews sang the songs of Zion by the waters of Babylon, the Hispanic/Latino/a community sings songs or *coritos* (little choruses) that affirm the experience of a living and liberating God.[4]

The community interprets the biblical texts and their songs of praise in light of their experience of *Diosito* who, as being for-others, loves and cares for them. This understanding of *Diosito* is expressed most vividly through a popular *corito* known as "*Tu has venido a la orilla*" ("You have come down to the lakeshore"). The lyrics express the understanding of *Diosito* as an intimate friend who calls us by name and invites us into the service of the reign of God:

> You have come down to the lakeshore
> Seeking neither the wise nor the wealthy,
> but only asking for me to follow.
> *Refrain*
> Sweet Lord, you have looked into my eyes;
> kindly smiling, you've called out my name.
> On the sand I have abandoned my small boat;
> Now with you, I will seek other seas.
>
> You know full well what I have, Lord:
> neither treasure nor weapons for conquest;
> just these my fish nets and will for working.
>
> You need my hands, my exhaustion,
> working love for the rest of the weary
> a love that's willing to go on loving.
>
> You who have fished other waters;
> you, the longings of souls that are yearning:
> O loving Friend, you have come to call me.[5]

According to Aponte, *coritos* are concrete vehicles that express a hope, faith, and empowerment rooted in both the Bible and lived experiences of the community. They give a voice to the hope of the people and their faith in God. They allow the community the freedom to

[4]For an excellent exposition of this cultural symbol, see Aponte, "Coritos as Active Symbols," 1995:57–66.

[5] "*Tu has venido a la orilla*" by Cesáreo Gabarain; translated from the original Spanish by Medeleine Forell Marshall.

give voice to their understanding of *Diosito* in their own language. They allow us to cross denominational barriers and racial and language boundaries as we recognize that we serve the same Lord and *Diosito* of all.

In summary, Hispanics/Latinos/as understand themselves to be created in the image and likeness of *Diosito*. This self-understanding is most clearly revealed through the gift of language by which they know and name themselves in light of their experience of a loving *Diosito*. The popular *coritos* capture this sense of the sacred Other who knows them intimately and calls them by name. The Hispanic/Latino/a people proclaim in many and diverse ways that in the community of the beloved all people are welcome and no one is a stranger before *Diosito* who is both *Amigo* and *Amante*. Their faith in *Diosito* expressed through their own cultural and religious symbols affirms and celebrates their understanding of God who calls all people into a loving relationship with others.

CHAPTER 2

Jesus

■ MICHELLE A. GONZÁLEZ

At 10:00 a.m., a loud trumpet signals the entrance of Pilate onto the stage to confront Jesus of Nazareth. From this point on, the words and actions follow the gospel passion narratives, with San Fernando parishioners playing the parts of the different characters in the passion story. Pilate sends Jesus to Herod, who in turn returns him to Pilate for judgment. After the crowd calls for the release of Barrabas, Jesus is flogged and crowned with thorns. Pilate presents the beaten and broken Nazarene to the people—that is to the assembled crowd in San Fernando/Jerusalem—who cry out for his crucifixion. The scene can only be described as eerie: this is not an event that happened two thousand years ago, but an event taking place today and in which we are actively participating (Goizueta,1995:34).

With this haunting description of the Good Friday reenactment at San Fernando Cathedral in San Antonio, Texas, Cuban American theologian Roberto S. Goizueta enters into the popular rituals surrounding one of the most powerful images in Latino/a religiosity: the crucified Jesus. The Jesus of Good Friday is a central christological symbol within Latino/a theology. This stems from a theological worldview that strongly emphasizes Jesus' humble origins, his prophetic message, and his active presence in the present-day lives of Christians, in particular his solidarity with the oppressed and marginalized. This strong emphasis on Jesus' suffering and passion distinguishes Latinos/as from other Catholic ethnic groups in the United States. As noted by Goizueta, "If, among Euro-Americans, nominal Catholics are referred to as 'Christmas and Easter Catholics,' their U.S. Hispanic counterparts are often called 'Ash Wednesday and Good Friday Catholics'" (1998:2–3). The theological significance of this distinctive Latino/a understanding of Jesus is the subject of Latino/a christologies.

Latino/a christologies emphasize Jesus' concrete historical reality and its implications for our understandings of Jesus today, a crucified Jesus who reveals God's love for humanity and God's presence with an advocacy for the poor. The Latino/a faith in the crucified Jesus cannot be found in the dogmas, official teachings, or theological treatises of academic theology, but instead is situated in the concrete faith and lives of Latino/a communities. As noted by Ada María Isasi-Díaz, "What Latinas believe about Christ is not a matter of an applied doctrine, an application of what the churches teach" (2003:158). This leads Marina Herrera to conclude, "There is no dogma, no creed, no law that can surpass the power of a suffering man-God, who had assumed his powerlessness to show the extent of God's mercy and love" (1993:76). The popular faith expressions of Latino/a communities thus play a fundamental role in Latino/a christologies, the starting point of Latino/a theological reflection.

Several voices within the Latino/a community have examined the crucified Jesus. I begin by examining the *mestizo* Jesus, perhaps the most prevalent image found in Latino/a theology, which reveals a fundamental connection between the historical particularity of the incarnate Christ and the contemporary reality of U.S. Latinos/as. A second important image is the Jesus of justice, depicted in solidarity with the marginalized, where his prophetic message denounces hierarchical structures of domination. Third, there is the image of Jesus who accompanies Latino/a communities in their daily lives.

Mestizo Jesus

The groundbreaking contribution of the category of *mestizaje* within Latino/a theology cannot be underestimated. Born in a doctoral dissertation written by Virgilio Elizondo, this theme is one of the central theological loci within Latino/a theology. For Elizondo, *mestizaje* is representative of the border reality that characterizes the Latino/a experience of being people "in between." The *mestizo/a* must not see her or his racial and cultural mixing as a source for feelings of inadequacy. Instead, Elizondo asserts, the *mestizo/a* reality, on the borders between cultures, must be seen as the privileged place of God's revelation. *Mestizaje*, as the lens through which Latinos/as experience reality, becomes a methodological, anthropological, and christological category within Latino/a theology.

The major themes in Elizondo's christology are outlined in his text, *Galilean Journey: The Mexican American Promise*, in which he grounds his christological reflection on Jesus' Galilean identity, giving Jesus' social, cultural, and political particularity theological value. For Elizondo, Jesus' identity as a Galilean is not accidental; it is revelatory of his life and ministry: "Like every other man and woman, he was culturally situated and conditioned by the time and space in which he lived…Jesus was not simply a Jew, he was a Galilean Jew; throughout his life he and his disciples were identified as Galileans"(1983:49). A Galilean, Jesus was not born at the center of Jewish life and society, namely Jerusalem, but on the border. Elizondo connects this marginal, border reality to the contemporary context of Latinos/as, more specifically Mexican-Americans. As a *mestizo* figure, Elizondo contends, Jesus reveals the border as the site of God's revelation so that the ambiguity and pluralism that characterize *mestizaje* become key dimensions of God's revelation. The hybridity of Galilee calls us to a new understanding of community and consequently of church. Roberto S. Goizueta sees Elizondo's christology as representative of a global Christianity that is no longer centered in Europe—at the heart of which is the *mestizo* Christ and, consequently, the *mestizo* church. In an increasingly globalized world, the church must turn to the borders, not the centers of power, in an effort to discover the true church (2000:150).

Jesus the Liberator

For Latino/a theology, Jesus' *mestizo* and border identity exemplifies his solidarity with the marginalized, his liberative message for the poor and oppressed, and the calling for Christians to be critical of dominant sectors of society and power. Christian churches, however, have not always embraced this central dimension of Jesus' memory. As Marina Herrera notes, "The message of Jesus has been dissected, expounded on with clarity, eloquence and power; it has not been practiced with justice, nor with love" (1993:73).

For Eliseo Pérez Álvarez, Jesus is depicted as a liberator who overcomes the walls and barriers that divide us. "One of the many barriers that he brought down was the one separating the rich from the poor…Christ was incarnate in a poor person (Lk. 2:24) to avoid legitimizing the system that produced such social and economic disparities" (1997:34). Jesus, incarnate in a poor man, takes the side of those who are economically marginalized and denounces the systems and structures that create this unjust society. Denouncing spiritualized christologies that downplay his prophetic message, the christology of Latino/a communities emphasizes Jesus' taking the flesh of a marginalized person.

Within Elizondo's study of Jesus as *mestizo*-Galilean, two methodological principles arise that inform a liberationist christology. The first, entitled the Galilee principle, reads, "what human beings reject, God chooses as his own" (1983:91). This, in turn, is linked with the Jerusalem principle, "God chooses an oppressed people, not to bring them comfort in their oppression, but to enable them to comfort, transcend, and transform whatever in the oppressor society diminishes and destroys the fundamental nature of human dignity" (Ibid.:103). The symbolic marginality of Galilee is linked to God's option for the powerless.

Luis Pedraja's christology examines the complexity of language, identity, and concrete experience. Pedraja's Jesus is one who stands in solidarity with the oppressed. "Instead of a God who identifies with those who seek to dominate us, we find a God who identifies with those who suffer—who does not dominate but works with tenderness to empower everyone" (1999b:45). Emphasizing the importance of language and how the Spanish language shapes the Latino/a worldview, Pedraja highlights the intimacy of Latino/a understandings of Jesus and their relationship with God. This is linked, in turn, to the Latino/a experience of God's love, where God is seen in solidarity with oppressed communities. "Since Jesus came from a place at the margin of society and because he identified with those who were rejected and marginalized by society, we feel that God understands us" (Ibid.:50). Popular religious practices exemplify the significance of this solidarity and love for Latino/a communities. Through the incarnation God transforms human history, where God's love and justice prevail.

Marina Herrera has offered a sustained reflection on christology in light of Latina issues and concerns asserting that the starting point of a Latina christology is the concrete faith experiences of Latinas. A Latina christology must then move to a strong critique of the Western tradition that accompanied the evangelization of the Americas. "An 'Americanist critique'—done by the people of this continent, men and women, young and old, Natives, European, African, and Asian descendents—*must be a critique of all things European,* including the Westernization of Jesus and his message and the assumption that such Westernization is the only valid interpretation of the salvific event of his life and death" (1993:82). A Latino/a christology must thus begin from the underside of Latin American history, privileging the voices of those who were victims of European powers.

Following in the spirit of earlier quests for the historical Jesus, in his *The Quest for the Cuban Christ: A Historical Search,* Miguel De La Torre offers a new quest, one framed by the contours and traditions of historical and contemporary Cuban and Cuban-American cultures. De La Torre's quest attempts to unearth the Cuban Christ, one shaped by various important figures and movements within the Cuban ethos. De La Torre concludes by elaborating his *Ajiaco* Christ, a vision of Jesus grounded in the Cuban location and justice-oriented communities of faith, expressed in Cuban art from a variety of artists. Again, the Jesus of justice plays a prominent role. Linked to this understanding of Jesus is the belief that Jesus accompanies the oppressed throughout their struggles, never abandoning them in their times of need.

Ada María Isasi-Díaz represents *mujerista* theology's first attempt to offer a christological reflection. Isasi-Díaz's christology is inextricably linked to social justice, placing an emphasis on a praxiological and ethical understanding of *Jesucristo*, in which discipleship requires our active participation in the kin-dom of God as it is realized here and now. "All who commit themselves to proclaim with their lives and deeds the kingdom of God are mediators of the kingdom" (2003:162). This mediation is grounded in humanity's *imago Dei* and calls followers of *Jesucristo* to realize God's kingdom concretely here on earth, though never in its fullness. This commitment is informed by the concrete struggles of the poor and oppressed. As highlighted by Goizueta, "In Jesus' own cry of abandonment, and his intractable hope against hope, we hear our own cry and discover our own hope" (1995:184). Jesus walks with those who suffer, and so must Christians today.

Jesus Who Accompanies

A key theme in Latino/a christology is that the crucified Jesus accompanies the Latino/a community in their struggles and suffering (Elizondo 2000c:288–89). The crucified, victimized Jesus reveals his solidarity with marginalized peoples throughout history. The suffering on the cross is present in the contemporary suffering of crucified peoples.

Roberto S. Goizueta holds that the foundation of the crucified Christ of Latino/a popular Catholicism is a relational anthropology that sees the human, and consequently Jesus, as essentially social in nature. The image of the *Via Crucis* is exemplary of this point. "In the *Via Crucis*, Latinos and Latinas affirm the truth of the Resurrection not as an event that, subsequent to the Crucifixion, 'overcomes' or 'cancels out' the death of Jesus, but as the indistinguishable love and solidarity that defines the *Via Crucis* itself, as the act of 'accompaniment' that constitutes and empowers us as persons and as a community of faith" (1998:3). The Latino/a emphasis on the crucifixion is not over and against the resurrection, but is instead the active, communal confrontation of suffering. The resurrection is thus mediated through solidarity in suffering, in which humanity is affirmed in the face of injustice. The very accompaniment of Jesus in the face of death affirms the resurrection, an eternal life after death. The organic unity of the crucifixion and resurrection, in which one does not surpass the other, is exemplified in the resurrected Jesus who bears the wounds of his crucifixion. "The apostles acknowledge the reality of the Resurrection, *but only as a reality that remains marked by the Crucifixion*" (Ibid.:7). Latinos/as, as they accompany Jesus to the cross on Good Friday, affirm the communal nature of our humanity and the promise of life in the face of suffering and death.

Conclusion

The image of the crucified Jesus best embodies the spirituality and theology of Latino/a communities throughout the United States. This *mestizo* Jesus, one who has a preferential option for the oppressed and accompanies them throughout their struggles, calls Christians to be concrete disciples, ones who follow in Jesus' footsteps. "To walk with Jesus and with the poor is to walk *where* Jesus walks and *where* the poor walk" (Goizueta 1995:191). The crucified Jesus calls all Christians to a fellowship with the victims of society. Having examined the foundational contours of Latino/a christologies, I would like to conclude with three areas for future scholarship. These are spaces where Latino/a theologians can build on the work of their colleagues.

The first area is a critical analysis of Latino/a christology in light of New Testament scholarship. The relationship between theologians and scripture scholars is tenuous at best, yet a strong christology must be grounded in biblical scholarship. While the popular faith expressions of Latino/a communities should remain a central locus for Latino/a christological reflection, the New Testament witness of Jesus must also play a pivotal role. The need for this type of dialogue is most clearly seen when one reexamines the nature of Jesus' Galilean identity in light of recent New Testament scholarship.

In his 2003 Catholic Theology Society of America presentation, "Good Fences and Good Neighbors? Biblical Scholars and Theologians," New Testament scholar Jean-Pierre Ruiz explores the influence of Elizondo's *Galilean Journey* on Latino/a systematic theology.[1] Ruiz critiques Elizondo's construction of Galilee, and Latino/a systematic theology's uncritical acceptance of it, for drawing broad generalizations that are at times embellished. Citing Elizondo's depiction of Galileans as having a "warmer, more optimistic outlook on life," and a faith that was "personal, purer, simpler, and more spontaneous," Ruiz notes that, "Whether intentionally or otherwise, in these lines Elizondo lapses into a ruralist romanticism verging on anti-intellectualism—a rare and unfortunate combination for a volume that began as a doctoral dissertation." Ruiz also highlights that, through Elizondo's uncritical use of Western European biblical scholarship, sections of *Galilean Journey* border on anti-Judaism. While not discarding Elizondo's *mestizo* Jesus, Ruiz does call for a closer examination of the biblical notions underlying this christology, and for more explicit collaborations between theologians and biblical scholars. On this note I agree with Ruiz wholeheartedly.

A second area that is in need of critical development is the area of Latino/a christology itself. While the centrality of the crucified Christ in the faith and religious practices of Latino/a communities is clear, the

---

[1]Paper presented at the 2003 Annual Convention of the Catholic Theological Society of America. Unpublished paper cited with the permission of the author.

centrality of christology within Latino/a theology is not. This is seen, for example, in the absence of a christological article in the Latino/a introduction to Roman Catholic systematic theology: *From the Heart of Our People* (Espín and Díaz 1999). In their emphasis on the concrete faith experiences of Latino/a communities, Latino/a christologies have avoided some of the "classic" christological themes, such as atonement, the scandal of particularity, triumphalism, and the question of redemptive suffering. While some would argue that the language and discourse of these christological themes are couched in a Western European theological construction (and thus inconsequential to a *Latino/a* theology), I disagree. Latino/a theologians are still theologians, ones that—for better or worse—are steeped in the Western European theological tradition. To ignore central christological concepts that have shaped the discourse of systematics is to isolate the theological impact of Latino/a christologies.

A final area for future scholarship is christological reflection from a Latina perspective. Indeed, ever since Rosemary Radford Ruether asked, "Can a male savior save women?" (1993:116), christology has been a fundamental dialogue point between feminist theologians. Indeed, even Ada María Isasi-Díaz, who once articulated that Jesus does not hold a central place in the beliefs of Latinas, has recently recanted, arguing for more christological reflection.[2] "We need to develop a Christology that is related to the historical Jesus more than to the ecclesial Christ, that is not so much related to the past but rather grounded in the present" (2001b:142). Isasi-Díaz then recognizes the need for a christology within her theology, not only because of its role in traditional theology, but also for those Latinas who are familiar with and use the Bible in their faith traditions.

"To walk with Jesus is thus to walk with the wrong persons in the wrong places" (Goizueta 1995:203). The crucified Jesus of Latino/a religiosity reminds Christians of the dangerous memory of Jesus' ministry, life, and death. This Jesus calls us to be in solidarity with oppressed communities, following in his footsteps and accompanying the downtrodden. For Latinos/as the importance of popular religious practices demonstrates the active dimension of this faith, in which one does not only believe, one also acts. "The Christ of Latino passion symbolism is a tortured, suffering human being...In his passion and death he has come to be in solidarity with all those throughout history who have also innocently suffered at the hands of evildoers" (Espín

---

[2]In her first book she stated that, "A noticeable number of Hispanic Women either do not believe that Jesus was divine, or they do not consider him or his divinity something relevant in their lives." In her footnote to that rather shocking statement, Isasi- Díaz continues, "The Hispanic Women whose Christianity is simply part of their culture know very little about Jesus and do not pray to him" (Isasi-Díaz and Tarango, 1988:68). The shift in her thought is clearly seen in the above-cited christological essay.

1997:72). As disciples, Christians are therefore called to follow Jesus to those marginalized spaces. On Good Friday, as Latinos/as accompany Jesus to his crucifixion, they are reminded and comforted by the fact that they do not suffer alone. The symbolic accompaniment of the *Via Crucis* is a reminder of the constant accompaniment of Jesus in their lives and struggles.

CHAPTER 3

The Spirit

■ LUIS E. BENAVIDES

Pneumatological Foundations for Latinos/as in the U.S. Urban Context

In the history of Western theology, the doctrine of the Spirit has been characteristically neglected. Its first references early in the second century are sporadic and indirect.[1] From Augustine to later medieval scholars the doctrine of the Trinity provides a general framework for christological concern and pneumatology remains unnoticed (Rusch 1984:8–28; Olson and Hall 2002:15–52). The Councils of Nicea (325 C.E.), Constantinople (381), Ephesus (431), Chalcedon (451), and Toledo (589) function as witnesses of such christological and Trinitarian proclivities.

During the Reformation the major theological concern was God's saving grace, in which the Spirit appeared as aiding in the individual's salvation process. From the Enlightenment to the late nineteenth century, German idealism and Liberal theology brought new interpretations of the Spirit.[2] For instance, G. W. F. Hegel (1770–1831) abstracted the Spirit to the point of establishing the Spirit as a pantheist principle upon which

---

[1]References to the Spirit are found in the writings of the apostolic fathers such as Clement of Rome, Pseudo-Clement, Ignatius of Antioch, Polycarp of Smyrna, the Didache, and the Epistle of Barnabas (Burgess, 1984:16–24).

[2]Americas, ed., *German Idealism* (2000); Heron, *A Century of Protestant Theology* (1980); Welch, *Protestant Thought in the Nineteenth Century* (1972); and Pannenberg, *Systematic Theology*, vol. 1 (1988).

Christians are to unveil both God and human history. Spirit, and not substance as was claimed by Spinoza, is the key to understand the unfolding human history.

Theological luminaries such as Karl Barth (1886–1968) and Paul Tillich (1886–1965) reoriented the academic discourse about the Spirit in the twentieth century by referring to the Spirit as the giver and sustainer of life. At the congregational level, the pneumatology of the twentieth century is associated with the development of the Pentecostal and Charismatic churches in the Third World, though the root is located in the United States. This movement has been (a) identified with people who are socially poor, (b) resisted by the academy, and (c) focused on possessing the Spirit rather than defining it (Heron 1983:130–36; Hollenweger 1988:457–92). Notwithstanding, this research recognizes that the ministry of the Spirit is not circumscribed to this movement.

It seems to me much more plausible in terms of formulating a coherent perspective of the Spirit for today, to open up a new pneumatological discussion and advance the subject from a Latino/a viewpoint by identifying the ministry of the Spirit among Latinos/as in the U.S. urban context. No church or movement can claim ownership of the Spirit, because pneumatology is relational. That is shown in biblical references such as John 4:23, 24; 14:17; 15:26; 16:5–15; and Romans 8:16–26. In other words, the Spirit works in both God and human sides. In this sense, a functional pneumatology can be applied to Latino/a context so that it may be asked how Latinos/as can profit from the Spirit's ministry.

Latino/a theologians have been discussing the plight of Latinos/as in the U.S. urban context from social, political, ethical, and theological viewpoints. The contributions of Latino/a Protestant and Catholic theologians have been numerous, but a cohesive doctrine of the Spirit has been missing in Latino/a theology.[3] This study of the Spirit proposes a pneumatological approach to the Latino/a in order to renew the understanding of the Spirit and the Spirit's ministry among Latino/a Christians in the U.S. urban context. In the light of the above, this research relies on Tillich's *Systematic Theology* (1963) to develop a relational pneumatology because his categories are congruent with much Latino/a Christian life experience and address questions such as: Why are Latinos/as in need of the Spirit within the U.S. urban context? And how can Latinos/as identify and employ the Spirit in the U.S. urban context?

---

[3]For instance, see González and Maldonado Pérez, *Introduction to Christian Theology*, 2003. In it, the doctrine of the Spirit is absent; there is no concern at all to address either historically or doctrinally the Spirit.

The Spirit and the Latino/a Christian as a Social Being

We cannot deny the fact that human beings were created to exist in social contexts, but humans dialectically exist in a sociological tension between the self and the social context. The self and the social context coexist; and even though the context influences the self, the self is not bound to but rather participates in the social context. The self exists as an individual within, and separated from, the context at the same time. This tension is heightened in the urban context where Latino/a Christians experience this situation in the oppressive and challenging urban context. Amidst this situation, Latino/a Christians face society with the expectation that they will be recognized, have a position, and be accepted in the U.S. urban contexts in which they interact and reside.

Latino/a Christians are living under what Tillich calls "radical doubt," seeking for existential meaning while experiencing ontological anxiety as they live (1963:227–28). They want to experience social presence. Tillich predicted what Latinos/as want and expect from the urban context many years ago in his view of the three functions of life, which establish the role of difference in community—or otherness. These functions are self-integration, self-creativity, and self-transcendence, and can be applied to the Latino/a's expectation of recognition, position, and acceptance. The understanding of these three functions of life is fundamental to the understanding of the Latino/a's dependence on the Spirit for survival, resistance, and liberation in the U.S. urban context. Such functions of life not only make possible the realization of individual centers but also are a prerequisite for communal participation. They establish the Latino/a Christian as a social being.

First, the Latino/a Christian's recognition has to do with self-integration, which is related to the polarity of individualization and participation (Ibid.:174–77, 198).[4] In this function of life, the Latino/a Christian is established apart from the world but concurrently having a personal world. This, Tillich claims, "liberates the self from the bondage to the environment," and when "life integrates itself in the dimension of spirit," a moral act occurs and then we have a "personality within a society" (Ibid.:38). In this way a self is differentiated from other selves and this becomes the basis for morality and social ethics. In this differentiation every Latino/a Christian is recognized as another moral individual possessing an internal world but belonging to an external world or to a community of selves. Tillich confirms this when he points out that a person lives within a setting but possesses a world (Ibid.:38). This web of social relationships must be enacted with a sense of love (*agape*) that enables the whole community to unite with a sense of justice that recognizes other selves.

---

[4]In this context, polarity means that both elements are interrelated and interdependent; that is to say, one functions to determine the other.

Second, the Latino/a Christian's acceptance has to do with self-creativity, which is related to the polarity of dynamics and form (Ibid.:178–82). In this function of life, the Latino/a Christian is accepted or rejected by a culture as long as the Latino/a Christian finds meaning in participation in his or her own culture or another culture. In this context, meaning is found in art, language, concepts, images, symbols, and tools. For instance, Tillich remarks that "[a] culture live[s] in such meanings. The meaning-creating power of the word depends on the different ways in which the mind encounters reality...All this is continuous activity of the self-creation of life in producing a universe of meaning" (Ibid.:69). If the Latino/a Christian does not make an effort to grow and employ the meaning-creating power in the urban context, he or she will be prevented from growing and be dominated by a monocultural view of reality. The Latino/a Christian's acceptance or rejection lies in his/her ability to function as a bicultural being in a context in which the meaning of his/her own culture and the Anglo culture are present at the same time without dissolving one into the other.

The Latino/a Christian can transcend both cultures when new meanings are integrated. When they abandon their own culture, Latinos/as face uprooting or separation from their nurturing networks, resulting in cross-cultural shock. But when Latinos/as arrive in a new culture they face a language barrier, segregation, dearth of support systems, and competing ultimate concerns. This change demands that Latinos/as develop new cultural meanings paralleled to their own through self-creativity without abandoning the Latino/a cultural traits and values.[5] When this change is achieved with a balance between old and new cultures, Latinos/as are integrated into the U.S. urban context. When the cultures are unbalanced, the Latino/a Christian experiences a lack of a sense of belonging, with accompanying frustration, alienation, racial conflict, mistrust, suspicion, impotence, and burnout. The language of self-creativity must be integrated into the Latino/a Christian's theological literacy.

Third, the Latino/a Christian's position has to do with self-transcendence, which is related to the polarity of freedom and destiny (Ibid.:182–86). In this function of life, the Latino/a Christian is positioned in relation to self, the urban context, and God. Tillich claims that "to be aware of one's self is a way of being beyond one's self" (Ibid.:9) and refers to pleasure and pain as characterizing "the state of being beyond one's self in terms of self-awareness" (Ibid.:92). In pleasure, the Latino/a Christian is the subject leading to creative *eros,* but in pain the Latino/a

---

[5]Eldin Villafañe elaborates a Hispanic profile to determine the Hispanic being, called the "Homos Hispanicus." Such a profile is characterized by eight culture traits and value orientations, namely: passion, personalism, paradox of the soul, community, *romerías,* musical élan, "fiesta," and family. See Villafañe, *The Liberating Spirit,* 1993.

Christian is an object. Therefore, pain is of relevance for Latino/a Christians. Tillich points out that pain is "the awareness of one's self made into an object deprived of self-determination" (Ibid.:92). When the Latino/a Christian is deprived of self-determination, this results in pain. This pain emerges as a result of objectification: the Latino/a Christian is prevented from being somebody. Sometimes, however, Latinos/as have the opportunity for self-determination, but because of their inability to create a new cultural meaning they do not develop such a position within the urban context. They remain invisible and without identity, degenerating self-transcendence into self-deception.

Because all scriptural pneumatology is a relationship between the Spirit and the human spirit, the Latino/a Christians' self-integration, self-creation, and self-transcendence are made possible solely through the Spirit. At the same time, under the dimension of the human spirit, the three functions of life impact the Latino/a self, the U.S. urban context, and history (Ibid.:266, 274, 346). Ultimately, the three functions of life establish existential individuality as a precondition to functioning in U.S. urban contexts and are preparatory for experiencing transcendence and unity with the Spirit. Conversely, an inadequate understanding of these functions of life can result in a false individuality characterized by escapism in which the particulars, ways of being, and abstractions of our social existence are avoided or repelled.

The Spirit's Ministry among Latino/a Christians

Latino/a Christians seek more than survival, resistance, and liberation. They require an identity as individuals and as a community that Tillich calls a "search for Spiritual Presence" (Ibid.:260). For this reason, only the Spiritual Presence enables true liberation and identity. How can the Spiritual Presence affect the Latino/a Christians, and how can they identify the Spirit's work among them? The answer comes in four statements.

First, the Spiritual Presence is the carryover of God's relatedness with the creation. The impact of the Spirit or the Presence of God is what fulfills creation (Ibid.:283), but must not be understood as coming from outside, leaving certain effects within human beings. This impact is one of mutual immanence (Ibid.:114, 276) and means that whatever is held in Latino/a Christian existence is held concurrently with the Spiritual Presence. Latinos/as can experience such impact "ecstatically" when they are "being grasped by the Spiritual Presence" (Ibid.:112). Because all human beings are in some degree related to God, all Latino/a Christians are equally in some degree impacted by the Spiritual Presence. Since, as Tillich asserts, "the Spirit grasps the spirit," the act of being grasped does not depend on Latinos/as but on the Spiritual Presence (Ibid.:276). The Spirit's impact is active upon religion, culture, and morality in such a way that Latinos/as are included even when they are unaware of the Spiritual

Presence. The Spirit does not come and go capriciously as an abnormal disoriented force, but dwells and remains within the Latino/a Christian.

Second, the Spiritual Presence is the carryover of transformation. Tillich interprets the impact of the Spirit as "inspiration" (breathing) and as "infusion" (pouring) in order to emphasize that the Spirit is the "meaning-bearing power" (Ibid.:115). If this is true, Latino/a Christians have a powerful tool for survival, resistance, and liberation. Each encounter with the Spiritual Presence in ecstatic experiences is transformative. Old patterns of behavior can be reinforced, dismissed, or replaced by new meanings. This transformation occurs to individuals and to groups such as the Latino/a Christian community (Ibid.:115). Tillich's approach supports this idea by describing how the Jewish prophets acted under the impact of the Spirit to prevent the corruption of the Jewish religion. Likewise, the impact of the Spirit can stimulate the rise of prophetic voices that change the destiny of the Latino/a communities in the United States.

Third, the Spiritual Presence is the carryover of sanctification. Something happens once the Spiritual Presence has grasped the Latino/a Christian's spirit. A process toward maturity or sanctification in Christian life occurs that affirms that there are no perfect human beings and that our liberation is "fragmentary" in existential life. Four principles characterize this process of maturation or sanctification under the influence of the Spirit (Ibid.:231, 237, 269). The first principle is an increasing awareness that compels the Latino/a Christian to grow by evaluating the conflicts around him/her and finding ways to resolve them. Through this principle the Latino/a Christian is called to face life situations with courage (Ibid.). The second principle is an increasing freedom that results from a reunion with the Spiritual Presence. This facilitates increasing means of survival, resistance, and liberation as the Latino/a Christian is released from imposed statutes that diminish human freedom (Ibid.:232). The third principle is increasing relatedness where the Latino/a Christian is called to strengthen relations toward him/herself and others with maturity. Here "self-elevation," "self-humiliation," and "self-seclusion" must be eschewed (Ibid.:233). The fourth principle is an increasing self-transcendence that causes the Latino/a Christian to approach his or her ultimate concern (God) devotionally (Ibid.:235). When the Latino/a Christian is determined by the Spirit and not by the values of society, a movement toward maturity takes place. In self-transcendence the Latino/a Christian is called to acknowledge that the Spirit works in both sides of the divine-human relationship. There is an immediate presence of God in which the Spirit is for the human spirit. Once the Latino/a Christian gains knowledge about the immediate Spirit presence, such knowledge will empower the Latino/a Christian with endurance and hope for the future and a justification for a struggle in the present. Fourth, the Spiritual Presence has a soteriological role as the carryover of salvation. Tillich conceives of the Spiritual Presence as the one that "conquers the ambiguities of life under the dimensions of the spirit" (Ibid.:109). This also means that salvation, or healing, affects the human spirit that he describes as the "first fruits" of the New Being, which is Jesus as the Christ. Although life under the impact of the Spirit is an unambiguous life, the Latino/a Christian is still an existential being; and the impact of the Spirit does not suspend either sickness, death, or the presence of evil in the world (Ibid.:277).

In summary, Latino/a Christians must realize that no one can live by dispensing with the Spirit in a multicultural and multiethnic inner city. The three functions of life (self-integration, self-creativity, and self-transcendence) are part of the human condition and are brought to meaning by the Spirit. They are the pneumatological foundation of Latino/a Christians' way of being in the U.S. urban context. Each one of them is construed dialectically between the self and the world to achieve identity in spite of the negativities we find in society. The Spirit gives courage, meaning, and value through a relationship with the Latino/a's spirit, which always longs for a more holistic way of living.

As recipients of the impact of the Spirit, Latino/a Christians must realize that they are not alone in overcoming the problems they face daily in the U.S. urban context. The Spirit is still at work today—as vivifier, liberator, and even as judge—aiming to provide power and enable the Latino/a Christian to change him/herself and society at large. The Spirit provides the foundation for being in the world and is the divine help for liberation, resistance, and survival in the U.S. urban context.

CHAPTER 4

The Trinity

■ ZAIDA MALDONADO PÉREZ

Introduction

Focus on the meaning of the Godhead from a Latina/o perspective is a fairly recent undertaking. The Person of Christ, especially understood as the Galilean or *mestizo* Christ, has dominated the theological arena. Among Latino/a charismatic and Pentecostal faith communities, the person and function of the Holy Spirit has been given a more prevalent role. Mary, or, more specifically, the *Virgen Guadalupe* (or *La Virgen de la Caridad del Cobre, La Inmaculada Concepción* among others), has played a critical role within Roman Catholicism.[1] Liberation theology's refocus on

---

[1]Sixto García, a Roman Catholic theologian, identifies Latino/a focus on Christ as one of the three markers of a (U.S.) Hispanic Trinitarian theology in his essay, "United States Hispanic and Mainstream Trinitarian Theologies." The other two distinguishing marks are, in his words, "the difficulties in profiling and imaging the Spirit in them [the theologies]" and, "the seminal hermeneutical datum represented by the Marian dimension in Hispanic theology and prayer." The first marker bridges doctrinal divides between faith communities. The other two markers, however, are particularly representative of a Hispanic Roman Catholic perspective–especially as practiced and believed through popular religion (1992:94).

the Trinity as the God of *history*[2] and of *lo cotidiano*[3] can be given some credit for the recent Latina/o discussion on the *Santa Trinidad.* The reappropriation of this often neglected early church understanding of the Trinity as the one God who is thrice present in the world provides an important corrective both to modernity's overemphasis on a triumphalist Christ of faith and to philosophy's emphasis on a Godhead that is transcendent and therefore distant or aloof. In addition, U.S. Latino/a theologians have challenged U. S. Latinos/as and non-Latinos/as alike to reread the Bible through "Hispanic eyes."

This drive to reclaim the Latino/a experience as a valid and even critical contribution to the church's theological discourse and mission shook the foundations of a "one size fits all" theology that, for too long, had been suffering from hermeneutical scotosis.[4] Hence, advancing scholarship beyond modernity's grip has not been the ultimate drive behind Latino/a theological emphases on christology, the Virgin Mary, and the Trinitarian God of history. Lurking behind this impulse is the need to rediscover, uncover, and recover a gospel that empowers and liberates us beyond merely otherworldly hopes. This gospel invites and challenges us to participate in the present epiphanies of a Trinitarian grace that includes *lo cotidiano,* and addresses our situation and our so-called "mundane" *luchas* in the here and now. This essay will consider Latino/a reflection on the Trinity and its ramifications for ministry and for daily living—or *lo cotidiano*—especially through the Latino/a concept of *familia.*

---

[2]That God is a God of history is especially affirmed through the incarnation, life, and death of the Son, Jesus. While God's own self-revelation in human flesh is seminal to all mainstream Trinitarian theologies, their emphasis on the life, death, and suffering of Christ—over against mainstream emphasis on the divine and resurrected Christ or the "empty cross"—is axiomatic in Latino communities. Sixto García points especially to the passion plays wherein God's suffering and death reveal not only the presence of God in Christ in "sacred time" and "sacred space" but the very basis for a community's ability to relate to God. "The broken humanity of Jesus stands as a sacrament of the brokenness of the body of the Hispanic communities. Jesus the Christ is our brother in sorrow and oppression, and we can touch him, mourn with him, die with him, and yes, also hope with him" (Ibid.:94).

[3]The role of "*lo cotidiano*" as a paradigm for doing theology has especially been developed and emphasized by María Pilar Aquino 1999:39, and Ada María Isasi-Díaz, 1992:41–52. I will be using the term *lo cotidiano* in the broader sense to include our engagement in the daily nitty-gritty of existence and the synergy between that engagement and its impact upon the daily life.

[4]"Scotosis" (scotoma) refers to a blind or dark spot in the visual field. I am using the term "scotosis" here as that blind spot or "bias" that narrows our view and therefore, also, our interpretation.

The Trinity for Understanding Existence

"Trinitarian" theology professes that God is God the Father (Mother/Parent),[5] God the Son, and God the Holy Spirit; they are three in one, "one essence, distinguished in three persons." Trinitarians, for instance, believe with Gregory of Nazianzus that the triune God is "divided indivisibly…and [that] they are conjoined dividedly. For the Godhead is one in three, and the three are one" (Lossky 1976:44–67, passim). This triadic formula goes against the tritheistic and modalist teachings that developed, especially, during the second and third centuries.[6] It addressed the critical need to explain and defend the Christian faith against charges of polytheism hurled at Christians by early church critics and detractors. The writers of the creeds, borrowing from the philosophical language of their time, affirmed the worship of one God while proclaiming the full divinity of each of the three persons of the Godhead.[7] Unlike the early church, however, Latino/a focus on the Trinity does not have an apologetical aim.[8] Our focus is not on defending the faith, but rather in understanding its meaning from the perspective of what it means to be *familia* (family), from *lo cotidiano* and our *luchas* (struggles, battles). Hence, it is an existential aim with practical considerations for life and ministry. Latino/a theologians turn to the nature of God as Trinity because we believe it offers us some clear directives—as well as challenges—for understanding who we are, and how we are to live and relate to each other and the world. We want to know not "how" God is "three persons in one" but what it means that the "three act as one," or, to posit it differently, what it means that "the one acts as three." How does this tri-personal unity empower our communities? What might be some of the theological, ecclesiological, sociopolitical,

---

[5]Like many cultures influenced and/or defined by patriarchy, most Latinos/as also have problems referring to God as "Mother." It has also to do with a literal reading of scripture, even when a literal hermeneutic is not uniformly employed. When referring to the work of the early church, I will be true to the era and use "Father." However, in other instances, I will use "Parent" or "God the Parent" to refer to the relational aspect of the Trinity.

[6]Tritheism teaches that there are three separate beings in the Godhead, three separate gods. Modalism holds that there is only one person in the Godhead who revealed itself in three modes, as Father, Son, and Holy Spirit. There were various forms of modalism (also called Sabellianism).

[7]The Nicene Creed (325 C.E.), in the form of a confession, affirms the church's belief in the divinity of Christ and, therefore, also in a Trinitarian God. Hence, against the Arian belief that Jesus had been created by God before time and is subordinate to God, the Nicene Creed professed that Jesus Christ is "from the same substance of the Father, God from God, Light from Light, true God from true God, begotten, not made, of one substance *[homoousios]* with the Father."

[8]Christians found themselves having to give warrant for their belief that the Son is co-equal, and co-eternal with God and is God. Borrowing a term from philosophy, they argued that Christ is "of the same substance" (*homoousios*) with God. This they argued especially against the Arians in the fourth century. The Arians argued that Christ was "of like substance" (*homoiousios*) with God.

economic ramifications of serving and imitating a God whose very essence is diversity in unity and unity in diversity? What does it mean that in the communion of the persons of the Trinity each abides in, abides with, and works through one another? Or, put in other terms, how does the *perichoretic* life of the Trinity address the need for solidarity among, with, and through those who seek justice and peace for all?

Although focus on understanding the meaning of the Trinity stems from present, existential concerns, Latinas/os glean from the insights we have inherited. We appropriate this legacy, though not uncritically, as an important heuristic tool. The eternal *perichoretic* life of the Trinity, to which we will refer below, is one such legacy from which Latino/a theologians have drawn important analogies for ministry among, and with, Latinos/as. Scripture, as the primary source of Trinitarian revelation, is read through the Hispanic notion of *familia,* our experience of *mestizaje*[9] (or *santidad*), *lucha,* and the daily nitty gritty of life that we call *lo cotidiano* or *el meollo.* These will be explained further.

The Trinity as *La Santa Familia*

One of the ways the early church sought to explain the Trinity was through apophatic language, that is, by stating what God was not. Thus, the Son was not the Father, the Father was not the Son, the Holy Spirit was neither, and so on. While this helped to distinguish the persons from each other, it also implied a unity based on a filial relationship between them. Thus, the Father is related to the Son as Father, the Son as begotten of the Father, and the Holy Spirit as common to both and uniting the three as the bond of love.[10] Among Latina/o Christianity, this emphasis on the Trinity as *familia* is attributed largely to Roman Catholic spirituality. Indeed, to refer to the Trinity as *La Sagrada* or *Santa Familia* among Protestants already distinguishes one as *católico/a.* Protestant reticence in referring to the Trinity as *La Santa Familia* reflects the age-old theological tension between the faith communions over the role of Mary. Although official Roman Catholic doctrine refers to the composition of the Trinity as "Father, Son, and Holy Spirit," "popular" Latina/o Roman Catholicism's[11] representation of *La Sagrada Familia* also

---

[9]See Elizondo, *The Future Is Mestizo*, 1988. See also my essay, "U.S. Hispanic/Latino Identity and Protestant Experience," 2003.

[10]Augustine believed that the concept of love, for instance, not only provided the way to understanding God, who is love, but also pointed to the existence of some trace of the Trinity.

[11]See Sixto García's definition of popular religion or religiosity as "the set of experiences, beliefs and rituals which more-or-less peripheral human groups create, assume and develop...to find an access to God and salvation which they feel they cannot find in what the church and society present as normative" (1992:30).

tends to include Mary.[12] Other references to Mary as "co-redemptrix," for instance, are problematic for Protestants. Nevertheless, the model of the Trinity as *La Santa Familia* has great theological potential for theology and ministry. For instance, the Trinity as *familia* resonates with a Latino/a sociocentric organic (versus an "egocentric contractual"[13]) understanding of itself. This category, from cultural anthropology, describes a society in which individuals, by and large, "find their meaning through their place in a complicated network of relations." Latinos/as are born not just to their immediate family, but to an extended *familia* of *tias, primos, comadres, compadres,* and a *pueblo*–all of whom are expected to play a critical role in the socialization of the individual. Indeed, *familia* and *pueblo* are often used synonymously.[14] These relations are not only "prior to the individual," they define her/him (González, 2001:67). The significance of a pueblo and *familia* identity becomes even more pronounced in the U. S., where our struggle for self-definition as individuals and as a people becomes an incessant, and often exasperating, duel between what others say we are and what we understand to be true of ourselves.

But, emphasis on the familial relations in the Trinity does more than just provide Latinas/os with a familiar or "colloquial" way of understanding and conceiving *la Santa Trinidad*. The Trinity as *La Santa Familia* affirms and renders *holy* the Latino/a conception of being as *being-in-familia*. Being as *being-in-familia* means that we perceive life through the lens of relationships. This lens is far-reaching and embraces more than those of the same bloodline, race, and/or ethnicity. The invitation to be *familia* extends to anyone with a common experience of *conquista*, marginalization, *lucha,* and, especially, the desire and need to be in solidarity. One does not need to be Latina/o to be deemed a part of *la familia*. One does, however, need to be in solidarity with its goals for

---

[12]In *Trinity and Society,* Leonardo Boff refers to Mary as having been "pneumatized" by the Holy Spirit. Having come down on Mary, the Holy Spirit "'pneumatized' her, taking on human form in her, in the same manner as the Son who, in a personal and unmistakable manner, set up his tent amongst us in the figure of Jesus of Nazareth (cf. John 1:18). "To the Spirit who pneumatized Mary," he continues, "be honour, glory and everlasting adoration now and forever!" (1986: 210–12).

[13]In contradistinction with the "sociocentric organic" model of society is the "egocentric contractual model." This refers to the way of understanding and of engaging in society and is used by some cultural anthropologists to describe, among others, the Anglo or U.S. culture. In such societies the "individual finds meaning by defining his or her own strengths and weaknesses vis-à-vis others in the group, and then joins the group–or forms a group–in what amounts to a contractual arrangement on the basis of those strengths and weaknesses. Thus, while in an egocentric contractual society maturity is a process of individuation, in sociocentric organic societies' maturity is a process of socialization.

[14]*Pueblo* means more than "town." It means a people drawn together not only geographically and ethnically, but also through a common *lucha* and desire to belong. While Latinos can, and often do, refer to the *pueblo* as *familia,* they may not often refer to their *familia* as *pueblo*. *Pueblo* has a wider connotation beyond the immediate and extended family to the wider *familia* of Latinas/os and those that are in solidarity with Latinos/as.

wholeness at all levels of existence. This, like *La Santa Trinidad,* is considered good and holy.

If being is *being-in-familia,* then it also affirms and sanctifies what has been deemed unsophisticated, simplistic, and, therefore, devalued: the daily nitty-gritty of family life—*lo cotidiano, la lucha, el meollo.* An understanding of the Trinity as *familia* causes sociopolitical and economic structures that define us by what we do and not by whose we are to suffer divine reproof. Such divine affirmation of our understanding of existence as *being-in-familia* is vital to a people whose economic and sociopolitical survival requires the support and advocacy of a *pueblo;* it requires responsible (as well as critical!) *convivencia*—living as active engagement with the other.[15]

But all social constructs, built as they are by fallible humanity, are flawed. Latino/a sociocentric organic concept as *being-in-familia* also has its downside. Because we are socialized to understand ourselves as part of a larger whole to which we owe loyalty, honor, and support, *individuos*[16] who want to find and claim their own unique voice are often frowned upon. This is especially true of Latinas who operate outside cultural norms regarding the role and place of women. The model of the Trinity as *familia* provides an important corrective to what can often become an extreme in our sociocentric organic communities, that is, an overemphasis on the needs of the *familia* to the detriment of the needs and particularities of the individual. Thus, we are reminded that while the Trinity is one, it is also *three.* Although each participates, interpenetrates, or indwells the others *(perichoresis),* they are still *three* distinct substances; Parent, Son and Holy Spirit. They are, as stated earlier, "divided indivisibly" and "conjoined dividedly"; they are three yet one. We must ask then, what does this mean for the way we treat others outside of our denominations, cultural norms, and expectations? *La Santa Familia* reminds us that we are not our own center. In their isolation, centers become self-serving and their vision distorted. In *La Santa Familia* the Holy Spirit, for instance, is "neither of the Father alone, nor of the Son alone but of both."[17] What does this mean for how we understand who is included and excluded in our *familia?* The great challenge—to Latinos/as and to all who call themselves Christians—is to live out the diversity in unity and unity in diversity modeled in *La Santa Familia.* Neither is mutually exclusive. To be divine is to be unified in diversity and diverse in unity.

---

[15]To *convivir* means more than just "living with" *(vivir con)* someone or some people who are sharing the same space. *Conviviendo* is engaging actively with the other. As an example of this emphasis, the term is also used to refer to group activities where the intention is to get to know the other and engage the other as if "living together."

[16]The term *individuo* tends to have a pejorative sense in Spanish.

[17]Augustine, *On the Trinity,* book 15, chap. 17.

Lastly, though so much more can be said, in *La Santa Familia* each of the persons are also eternally equal. The Father is not greater than the Son, who is not greater than the Holy Spirit, who is not greater than either. There is no hierarchy of beings. This is a difficult concept to grasp, especially for cultures that, admittedly or not, operate on the basis of socioeconomic hierarchies. Whether in the family or in the marketplace, a person's worth becomes intricately tied to production and, especially, to *what* is being produced. Focus on the economic and ontological Trinity—that is, on the functions of each of the Persons in our redemption or "salvation history"—and on their nature or essence is often used to reflect or affirm such hierarchies. The statement, for instance, that God is *Creator, Source* of the other two Persons of the Trinity, *Father* (the "male" component becomes significant here) and the *First* Person of the Trinity, takes on more than conceptual significance; it serves to deify a social ideology of being that argues for subordination on the basis of production. If God the Father is the Source, then the Son and the Holy Spirit can be thought of (and indeed have been thought of) as subordinate to the Father.

Because the Latino is often seen as the *macho de la casa* (the "macho" of the house), the one who sets and determines the "law" in the home, one is justified in asking whether *La Santa Familia* is an adequate model. I would argue that it is precisely *because* it is a *familia* that it becomes the perfect model for Latino/a (and non-Latino/a) families. In *La Santa Familia* the persons of the Trinity are equal because of what they share together—their divinity, their essence. Their "function," or "production," in the Trinity does not elevate one over the others. They are also equal because their work is not done apart from each other. Though we tend to separate the persons by function or production, basic orthodox understanding says that each Person of the Trinity functions in and through the others so that no work is said to be better than, or to belong solely to, either the Parent, the Son, or the Holy Spirit. It is thus why we can glorify the Son for sanctifying, the Parent for redeeming, and the Holy Spirit for creating. This emphasis, on the other hand, does not blur the "distinctiveness" and "gifts" of each. Thus, by the same token, we also glorify the Parent as Creator, the Son as Redeemer and the Holy Spirit as Sanctifier.

The Trinity "To Be Continued"

There is much more to be said that cannot be accomplished in this brief chapter. In that sense, the Trinity is "to be continued." But, the Trinity is also "to be continued" in another very real and concrete form. The Trinity as family provides us with a rich countercultural model for being and doing that moves us beyond just otherworldly hopes to the promise of the fruition of God's familial reign in the here and now. As such, it becomes not only the "stuff" from which we formulate doctrines and grand theological schemas. The dynamism of the Trinity as relationship is to be lived out; it is "to be continued" in our very existence, in our *luchas,* in the *meollo* of life and the joy and pains of *being-in-familia.* What's more, this model of, or reference to, *La Santa Familia* does not belong to any denomination. To overlook it because of racial or interchurch prejudices that continue to hold our minds and hearts captive is to miss out on a critical heuristic tool and gift that models what we are and what we are called to be. That is, a *santa familia* that honors each member because of Christ in us, working in and through us through the Holy Spirit to bring about God's reign. Further, we must not overlook this model because of the risk and challenge it poses to church hierarchies, familial systems, and/or ethnic prejudices that oppress a great many of God's *familia.* To do so is to run the risk of falling short of God's calling for living and ministry that is holy, perfect, faithful.

It is not enough to say that one believes in the Trinity. It is not just about "orthodoxy." If we are to believe and love God for what God has done in Christ through the power of the Holy Spirit, then we are to live as *La Santa Familia*—in complete intimacy with each other. We must remember that intimacy does not mean that one is free from struggle. The very nature of living implies struggle. This ought not, however, be its foundation and neither should a member of *la familia* struggle alone. As *familia* we are responsible and accountable to God and to each other. This too is evident from the action of God the Parent in raising Christ the Son from the dead through the power of the Holy Spirit. This *ad-intra* nurturing among the Trinity erupts *ad-extra* through creation and through God's own self-giving for that creation.

As children of the one *Santa Familia,* we are called to recognize our family resemblance, to honor our loyalties to God and thus also to the *pueblo,* even as we honor its individual members. If we love, we are also to honor. When we honor we not only accept the "other"—we challenge, and journey with, the other toward wholeness. Thus, God the Parent becomes incarnate through the Son who sends his Holy Spirit to challenge and journey with us in and toward the fulfillment of God's reign, as none other than *familia.*

CHAPTER 5

Church

A Roman Catholic Perspective

■ JEANETTE RODRÍGUEZ

Community Called Church: Cada Pequeña Comunidad Es la Iglesia

The subject of ecclesiology is multilayered, complex, and demonstrates both a creative and conflicted history. Mediated through culture, language, symbols, and ritual, individuals forming communities have gathered to express their understanding and commitment to the teachings and the person of Jesus Christ. This chapter reflects on a particular model of church as lived and experienced in the Roman Catholic U.S. Latino/a community. The United States Conference of Catholic Bishops' *Renewed Pastoral Framework for Hispanic Ministry* recognized that U.S. Latinos/as have "a profound ecclesial vocation that leads them to work hard at belonging to the church in a more meaningful way" (2002:4). In reading the Acts of the Apostles, one realizes that the earliest form of ecclesial experience manifested itself in community meetings, held for the most part in the homes of families. The small-base Christians that have emerged in Latin America and are emerging in North America reflect and reclaim this early manifestation of church seen in the house church communities of Acts. Upon close examination of today's small-base communities within the U.S. and in particular among Hispanics or Latinos/as, we find similarity with the early Christian way of being church.

According to Eduardo Hoornaert:

As early as the second chapter of Acts we find an outline of the elements of these meetings: the "teaching" (or memory) of the apostles; mutual union, particularly in the financial area; the breaking of bread; concern for the poor; and in a broader scope, communion with the other communities—Acts 4:32; 5:12ff. (1988:166)

Small-base Christian communities began to have a face in the early 1980s within the U.S. Catholic Church experience. Small group life is a phenomenon in many Protestant traditions as well and more frequently visible in evangelical traditions.

This "phenomenon," small-base Christian communities, also known as "base communities, basic ecclesial communities, basic Christian communities," has many different traditions and histories. In Latin America these church communities first arose out of catechumenal efforts in Brazil in the 1950s (Lee 2000:7). Realizing their success, U.S. Catholic bishops made a commitment in 1986 and 1987 to help foster the growth of small church communities within Latino populations in the U.S. Within the Spanish-American Roman Catholic church there always has been tension between the hierarchical church, generally representing the powerful, dominant society's church, and the more popular community church, formed by the masses and led by pastors who "have ministered at the very edge of disobedience" (González 1990:62).

Small-base Christian communities among the Latino population also reflect a methodology that emerged from the Latin American experience in the 1970s, the focus of which is to reflect on people's lives in light of their faith. Originally, the methodology identified three steps – *Ver, Juzgar, Actuar* –that is to see, to judge (this is not a judgment, but rather a guide of criteria in making decisions), and to act. More recently, this methodology has been expanded and changed to add *Evaluar* and *Celebrar* and to include *Pensar* rather than *Juzgar*. *Ver* (which includes an analysis of reality), is to highlight a particular news event; *Pensar*, to think and reflect on the Bible as a way of illuminating our understanding of the situation; *Actuar*, to recognize what each member of the community needs to commit him- or herself to do; *Evaluar*, to evaluate the meeting and commit to an action; and last, *Celebrar*, to celebrate and socialize.[1]

The "seeing" part of this methodology allows one to move into critical reflection, which aspires to lead participants to a response and/or

---

[1]It is interesting to note that they change the term *juzgar* to *pensar*, perhaps because *juzgar* sounds too critical and *pensar* is inviting and asks people to think through and analyze. *Ver* names the reality and includes an analysis, but it really means "to see."

action that these faith communities identify as a calling and is expressed in the following way by a member of one such community:

> A sense of being called to something bigger, a call to really be faithful and committed...I got called by my community, called to do things, I didn't think, didn't know there was a way of doing...And as important, you network with all of these people who feel the same way, so it is a whole new way of ministry.[2]

Members of such small-base Christian communities view their calling as one of faith, supported by a community that motivates them to act. The proceedings of the *"Encuentros"* (consultative gatherings) articulate the most significant, participatory consequence of U.S. Latinos/as reflecting on their understanding of church. The reflections from these *"Encuentros"* contributed to the development of what is now known as the National Pastoral Plan for Hispanic Ministry. What was significant in this process was that it was consultative, it was grass roots, and the people themselves articulated their understanding of what it meant to be church.[3]

According to the United States' National Conference of Catholic Bishops, Latino communities—during their theological reflection process (*Encuentros*)—articulated their lived experience and shared faith in community this way:

> Cada pequeña comunidad es la iglesia. Esas pequeñas comunidades anunciarán con hechos y palabras. Lo que Cristo quiere es liberarnos de todas las miserias y opresiones, espirituales y materiales. [Each small community is church. These small communities announce through acts and words what Christ desires, liberation from all misery and oppression, spiritual and material.] (Secretariat for Hispanic Affairs 1985:14)

A report from the Third *Encuentro* in particular announced "a model of Church that is open to the people's needs, placing its buildings at the disposal of the people and recognizing the reality of Hispanics as a poor community. The communities affirmed a model of priesthood that is more in contact with the people it serves, and the desire to exercise leadership in smaller communities" (Ibid.:77).

This model of church is deeply rooted in the reality of U.S. Latinos/as and seeks to respond to the needs and aspirations of the poor, in particular the undocumented, the migrant workers, and the

---

[2]Quote is based on unpublished fieldwork conducted by author, based on interviews with member of a small-based Christian Community in Santa Rose, between 1997–1999.

[3]The first National Hispanic *Encuentro* was in 1972, followed by *Encuentros* celebrated in 1977 and 1985. *Encuentros* were grounded in key biblical reference for the purpose of leading to a deeper understanding of one's faith.

incarcerated. A strong commitment to social justice for advocacy for the most vulnerable is hailed as the highest value in this prophetic model of church. When Latinos/as speak of the liberation that Jesus calls us to it is a *liberación integral*—integral liberation. This includes but is not limited to political, social, economic, religious, cultural, sexual, and interior freedom.

We know in faith that each period of history, as conflictive and creative as it may be, reflects life of the Spirit. Throughout each period of historical change people have sought to create a model and a way of being and acting that reflects their ecclesial experience. Generations of communities of faith have struggled to understand "mission" as it approximately corresponds to the reality of the specific age with the inspiration of the Spirit. Today, the world is undergoing rapid global changes that appear at times to outpace our capacities to respond. The documents that emerged from Vatican Council II (1962–1965) launched the Roman Catholic world into an understanding and typology of church that encouraged dialogue, creative evangelization, service, consultation, lay participation, call to action, and transformation of leadership. The model of church shifted from a fortress-like, perfect society—a hierarchical, universal, and Eurocentric model—to a transcultural community of sinners and saints journeying with Jesus; a community of people living out their faith in the context of the everyday, life-challenging rhythm of the world.

The task of culture is to provide meaning. It holistically integrates the vast experience of a people, including such elements as sense of the physical world, sense of order, basic institutions, roles, and a sense of self. The work of culture is to bring meaning to values that are lived out in community. Cultures are always interested in the healthy sustenance of their people committed to the survival of the whole. Past cultural studies have looked at religion as an add-on to culture, as a part of the technological, economic, and social matrix. Recent studies of deep structure in human culture have seen, on the one hand, that language is not an add-on but is part of the deep structure of being human. People desire to communicate, and words provide us a means to both create and articulate our immediate cultural worldview. In the same vein, reflecting on the whole span of being human, we find that religion is a way that we have always understood our way in the world. To be *homo sapiens* is to be creatures who are aware of themselves—their past, present, and future. When we become self-reflective we realize there is something beyond us. It is not something that has been handed to us, or given to us, but something that is deep within us. It is the contact with this deep structure that connects us with the wonder of our own existence. This makes us truly human and sustains this wonder. The first evidence we have of ritual behavior has to do with religious behavior: e.g., the burying of the dead, and the honoring of sacred objects. Religion, therefore, is intrinsically human and is the vehicle by which we express our deepest hopes and identify our most urgent questions (Boff 1991:20).

The church is that community that comes together and reflects on the presence of Jesus in their daily life. While the church has articulated a number of different models of itself, the overarching paradigm of church has its roots in the mission and teachings of Jesus. These roots are in the Mosaic tradition. In this tradition, God saves a people. God is God for a community –the community that journeys, reflects, and seeks God. Jesus is part of the messianic tradition, in which God continues to visit God's people and brings them together. The Latino/a church provides for us strong schemas: emotionally laden images that further underline this message of the good news. They show us, for example, the strong images of the consequences of sustaining injustices: peasants crucified to the dollar bill of neo-liberalism and the Argentine mothers of the disappeared walking the governor's plaza. The strong images remind us of our responsibility to others and challenge us to be faithful to the word of God.

The church as a social/cultural institution has a task of forming bonds among people. How a person is brought into a community, how they are understood in a community, and how they understand their community is fostered through images and models. How does the church community form the desires of love, compassion, commitment, etc., through those bonds? How is the community in the person then empowered to bring about change, to bring about personal and communal integrity in that community? These basic human desires continue to be addressed by church as community.

They include our affectivity, our emotions, our intuition, as well as our intellect. Images integrate our perceptions. Images can alter, redirect, and inspire us to go forth with fresh aspirations. They seek to capture what is most important to a given community and yet tap into that which is so profoundly human that it may transcend its original, mediated cultural context. José Marins, an expert in Latin American small-base Christian communities, stated in one of his visits to the United States that behind every pastoral attitude lies an image of the church and a theological point of view. This image determines the spirituality as well as the pastoral spirit of an ecclesial community. It directs the particular community's course of action. The theology that emerges out of this image extends to all the activities, symbols, and structures of church life, thus transforming what was one's image into a model. The church model then is a consequence for a way of being. It has consequences, often for the community's way of being, and its model of church is the result of this way of being!

The church is not a building, the church is not only bishops, priests and sisters. The church is those who believe in Christ and follow him.[4]

The general objective of the U.S. National Pastoral Plan was the common vision that Latinos/as had of church; this was to be done as a *pastoral de conjunto*–the interplay between the being and doing of the church. This notion of *pastoral de conjunto* is key in understanding this prophetic voice raised by the Latino/a people in the '70s and '80s. The Latin American Conference of Bishops gives us some clarity in translating *pastoral de conjunto*: "The term describes an action of the whole church, acting as an organic body" (CELAM 1971:31). *Pastoral de conjunto* should not be reduced to simply working as a team, but rather it is a lived expression of the essence of the church as communion. It is the interplay of doing and being and it is the doing that springs from the very being of the church (Zapata: 239). It is out of this understanding of being and doing of *pastoral de conjunto* that the Latino/a church identifies the following tenets:

---

[4]This illustration, and the ones following, were taken from a study guide/pamphlet, which credited the Midwest Catholic Commission for the Spanish Speaking. Their office was dissolved in 1996 by the Catholic Bishops of the region.

- To be a communitarian church would not be enough if it does not go out of itself and becomes also evangelizing and missionary.
- To be incarnate in its own reality is necessary for its own security and identity rendering it open to the universality of its being.
- To be an example of justice makes it credible when promoting it as a leaven in society.
- To develop leadership is not to limit to one dimension of its being. On the contrary, for its doing it needs an integral vision of all its members.
- And it is this total pastoral ministry that makes it possible for the Church to be leaven for the Kingdom of God in Society. (Ibid.: 269–70)

The slogan for *pastoral de conjunto* states "From Fragmentation to Coordination capturing the spirit, perhaps the soul, of the U.S. Latinos' reflection on church"(Ibid.:267) Sister Dominga Zapata of the Southwest Regional Office of Hispanic Affairs extends this slogan to say, "from fragmentation to communion" (Ibid.). A grass-root medium for reflecting on this notion of church is drawn from one of the many pamphlets that were used as a means of reflection and a guide among the faith communities during the *Encuentro* process. The brochure or "booklet" on evangelization begins with a question: "What should the Latino Church that Christ wants, look like?" The very first page identifies Christ as an example.

Jesus' example: As Jesus did, the community must denounce all errors and injustices perpetuated in society. Jesus denounced injustice in society; so should his followers.

The illustration above includes a picture of a family in poor living conditions, with a person covering their mouth. It reads, "When a Christian is silenced, it is God who we are covering the mouth of because it is God who wishes to speak." Drawing from "Evangelization in the

Modern World" (*EVANGELII NUNTIANDI*–an Apostolic Exhortation promulgated by Pope Paul VI on December 8, 1975), these communities further articulate their notion of church, as a church formed by the poor. They critique society in which the poor exist only to serve the rich: "En la sociedad el pobre sirve al rico, en la iglesia, el rico para ser cristiano debe servir al pobre. La Iglesia no es un supermercado." The church is not a supermarket, says these faith communities. In the discussions that occur among the people, they critique what they see as having been the communities' relationship with the church. During the *Encuentro* process, the participants critique how the Latino community has been in relationship with the church.

Todavía queda gente en la Iglesia que se siente como un cliente en el gran supermercado de la fe: va allí sólo a comprar bautismos, misa de enterro o de casamiento. Termina su compra y se va sin conocer a nadie.

The Latino community has been marginalized historically and engaged mostly as consumers who shop for sacraments as products to meet their needs. The communities, however, challenged one another in this manner: that, as church, they must raise their voices for those who have no voice. They desire, seek, and promote a church that knows how to pray and celebrate, a church that is a leaven church, a focus on the reign of God, a church that wants a world without misery, divisions, or hunger –a world where everyone is a brother and a sister.

A key component in the vision of the Latino/a church calls for *Una Iglesia Pobre*, a poor church:

1. *Una Iglesia pobre que: Si no tiene templo, se reune en las casas.*
   If there is no temple, they will meet in homes.

2. *Si no tiene altoparlante, se contenta con la guitarra de un joven.*
    If there is no speaker, they will content themselves with the guitar of a youth.
3. *Que si alguien necesita ayuda, la pide a todos.*
    If someone needs help, all will be asked. So that each home is a church, each voice is heard, and each hand offers 100 hands.

Foundational to this understanding of church is the significance of language as a source for theological insight. The models of church that surfaced from the *Encuentro* process reflect a social-centric and organic way of being a community. The very language indicates a different ethos in terms of the nature of relationships. For example, one of the liturgical eucharistic prayers serves as an example of a particular epistemology that lives in the Latino/a psyche. In the offering of the eucharistic prayer, the priest, in naming the Pope and the local bishop, prays that the people be connected to the local community and they to the institutional church. The offertory is a prayer/petition for unity. The English prayer asks that the people may be made one with the Pope, the bishops, etc. What is significant is that the Spanish version presumes this union, "Unidos al Papa" (United with the Pope), which shifts the institutional model to a more collegial tone because we assume we are already united with the Pope and bishops. If the people are already united with the hierarchy, then this relationship is directed toward God.

The eucharistic prayer is also a call to action as the assembly gathers and is commissioned to continue its action of service. Its call to action keeps hope alive. In the light of this hope the church is able to discern the sign of the times and to offer guidance and prophetic criticism. The Spanish version communicates an explicit hope that has no parallel to the English version. The last line of the offering is "que todas encuentren en ella un motivo para seguir esperando–may all find in them the motivation to continue hoping" (*Misal Romano* 2001:864). It captures the different experience and perspective of the Latino/a community. Amidst war; poverty; and political, economic, social, and religious persecution, the people place in the church their ultimate hope. From this hope, the church is moved to witness, to serve, to do justice.

The Spanish offering presents a vivid picture of how the church needs to go forth as a Servant. In the last verse, what in English is expressed as opening eyes to human misery, from the Spanish translates to God giving people the guts, the innards of mercy in the presence of all human misery. Service and justice require more than seeing. They require action that the heart of mercy calls people to do. In the English version what is asked is that eyes be opened; in the Spanish version what is asked for is the courage and the guts to do something. Our eyes are already open, and perhaps our eyes are already open because for many people our lives are lives of survival.

Each home a church, each voice a bell, and each hand 100 hands.

CHAPTER 6

Church

A Latino/a Protestant Perspective

■ JUAN FRANCISCO MARTÍNEZ

Introduction

Any attempt to write about *the* Latino/a Protestant understanding of the church is destined to fail because of the nature of Protestant ecclesiology. There are many views of the church within Protestantism. Latino/a Protestant churches reflect most of the ecclesiological traditions one sees in the United States, although most Latino/a Protestants practice a similar type of ecclesiology. Instead of attempting to describe every Protestant perspective, this chapter will focus on the believers' church perspective represented by Pentecostals, Baptists, Mennonites, Disciples of Christ, and others.[1] The majority of Latino/a Protestants are part of churches from these denominational traditions and they are the churches

---

[1]There are different ways to define a believers' church ecclesiology. It was born as a response to the concept of a state church and rejects the idea that the church should be linked to any state. Its basic understanding is that the church is a voluntary body, made up of people who make a conscious faith commitment, and therefore only people baptized as "adults" (usually including adolescents) can be members of the church. A believers' church perspective implies a common understanding of what the church is and how it functions, and not a historical or denominational link between the various movements that practice this ecclesiology. For more information see Durnbaugh, *The Believers' Church,* 1968, or Basden and Dockery, *The People of God,* 1991.

that are growing the fastest in the Latina/o Protestant community.[2] The focus here will be on how the major tenets of a believers' church ecclesiology are lived out in a Latino/a Protestant context and not on a detailed explanation of this theological perspective.

Believers' Church, Latino/a Style

Those within a believers' church see it as a church modeled in the book of Acts and would argue that other ecclesiological traditions developed later. Today's believers' church developed in response to the concept of the state church in medieval Europe. Personal Christian commitment was often lax because all those born in a "Christian" country were baptized as infants (which also made them citizens of the country) and made members of the church. Many Christians began to call for a return to a New Testament model of the church as a voluntary society of people who consciously chose to follow Jesus Christ. The first manifestations of this concept were seen among the Waldenses in the twelfth century. Some two hundred and fifty years later John Wycliffe made a similar call in England and Peter Chelcicky's preaching in Bohemia led to the formation of the *Unitas Fratrum* (Moravians). During the Protestant Reformation the "Radical Reformers" (Anabaptists and Baptists in particular) began to practice believers' baptism and to develop churches with a believers' church ecclesiology. Later revival movements that also adopted this understanding of the church include the Church of the Brethren, the Disciples of Christ, and the Pentecostals.[3]

Early nineteenth-century Protestant missionaries in Latin America, and Latinos in the United States, did not practice an ecclesiology from a believers' church perspective. It was not until the beginning of the twentieth century that churches like the Pentecostals and the Baptists began significant mission work in the Spanish-speaking world, bringing a believer's church viewpoint with them.[4] These types of churches began to grow rapidly in Latin America and among Latinas/os in the United States by the middle of the twentieth century, and today comprise the

---

[2]According to the initial report of the *Hispanic Churches in American Public Life* study presented in Washington, D.C., on May 3–4, 2002, the three largest Latino/a Protestant denominations are Pentecostal (Assemblies of God, *Iglesia de Dios Pentecostal*, and *Asamblea de Iglesias Cristianas,* in that order), and the next two are Baptist (American Baptist and Southern Baptist). These five denominations account for about half of all Latino Protestants. Overall, 77 percent of Latino Protestants are from churches that practice a believers' church ecclesiology. The complete results of the study are forthcoming.

[3]For a detailed history of this development see Driver, *La fe en la periferia de la historia,* 1997, or Durnbaugh, *The Believers' Church,* 1968.

[4]The modern Pentecostal movement began with the 1906 Azusa Street revival in Los Angeles.

overwhelming majority of Latino/a Protestants, and Protestants in Latin America.

The principal theological understanding in a believers' church perspective is that the church is a voluntary community of people who have made adult commitments of faith and have been baptized (mostly by immersion) as a testimony to that commitment. This means that membership and participation in Latino congregations is a voluntary commitment made by people old enough to take personal responsibility for their decisions. Children of believers can grow up in the church but do not become a part of it unless, and until, they make their own "adult" commitment and are baptized.

Mission and witness are an integral part of these churches and all members are expected to be involved in evangelism. Evangelism is understood as the task of calling people to a personal, adult commitment to Jesus Christ and to baptism as a sign of that commitment. That call is also an invitation to conversion, to experience God's transforming power in specific lifestyle changes. This aspect of the evangelistic call often has very practical implications, particularly for people in destructive lifestyles. It tends to have the greatest impact among Latinos/as (often nominal Catholics) who have not found a vibrant spiritual life in their current religious tradition and who are searching for meaning and power to address the frustrations and addictions with which they are struggling.[5] In practical terms this means that most Latinos/as who leave the Roman Catholic Church join these types of Protestant churches.

Conversion experiences are often very dramatic and life changing. Some people leave addictive lifestyles and experience emotional, psychological, physical, and spiritual healings of various types. The conversions often also have practical implications, such as better family relationships and an improved financial situation.[6] Sometimes conversions create tensions, especially when Latino/a converts become estranged from their extended families, often those with strong Roman Catholic commitments. This is usually interpreted as the price to be paid for following Jesus Christ.[7]

---

[5]Edwin Hernández, in his essay "Moving from the Cathedral to Storefront Churches," describes the attractiveness of this type of church to Latinas/os by stating: "Sectarian groups, therefore, are more likely to attract followers who are powerless and who have experienced a severe crisis in their lives, such as immigration. The benefits and rewards of belonging to such a religious group arise from the social experience of a living, vibrant, energizing, creative, empathizing, affirming and hoping community" (1999:235).

[6]The phenomenon, referred to as "redemption and lift" by evangelical missiologists, occurs when a person leaves a destructive lifestyle. A person who previously had difficulties holding down a steady job, or who spent a significant amount of his or her budget for cigarettes or alcohol, now has more income to spend on the family and a desire to see the family situation improve (McGavran 1970:295–313).

[7]A Latino/a Protestant traditional hymn still sung in many churches, *Hay una senda* (There is a path), is a description of the costs of becoming a Protestant convert. It includes a stanza that states that friends and relatives despised the convert when he turned to Christ (written by Tomás Estrada, © 1960 R.C. Savage).

The local church community is central in the lives of most Latino/a Protestants. The church services are where people experience God. Particularly in Pentecostal churches, going to church is an opportunity to experience God's touch through the singing, prayers, and spiritual ecstatic experiences, such as speaking in tongues. God is experienced as real, personal, and involved in the lives of the people. The community of believers also validates the experience of the convert and reaffirms the sense of having a new life in Jesus Christ. Many Latino/a Protestants have powerful testimonies (spiritual narratives) about the presence of God in their lives usually shared during their worship services. These in turn become part of the evangelistic strategy to draw new people. Many of the songs and hymns written by Latino/a Protestants and sung during church services also reaffirm these experiences.

The preaching of the Bible dominates in most Latino/a Protestant churches. Historically, most of the revivals that have given birth to believers' church movements and denominations have been based on the reading of the Word and have been defined as attempts to return to a biblical model. Most Latino/a Protestants see themselves as people of the Word. When a person begins to publicly carry a Bible to church (or even to work) it is usually a sign that that Latina/o has been converted. Regular Bible studies are a part of church life and worship services will often include long sermons, all of which are crucial to a sense of seeking God's will through the Word.

Latino congregations often have several prayer services during the week, including home Bible studies and prayer meetings. Prayer times become opportunities to share personal and concrete needs with a church community that believes strongly that God hears and answer prayers. Sharing prayer requests often becomes an opportunity for members of the community to respond concretely to each others' economic, physical, or emotional needs by becoming "God's means" to address the stated need.

For the most part, the liturgy in these churches tends to be very informal, with significant congregational participation, particularly in smaller churches. Church services can extend for more than two hours and might include multiple participation from church members, even those who have little or no training in leading worship.

Believers' churches usually have a congregational form of government and each local congregation has significant autonomy, even if it is a part of a denomination. Pastors may follow a *caudillo* model of leadership learned in Latin America, but they are ultimately responsible to the local congregation. Since membership is completely voluntary, people "vote" against an unpopular pastor by not giving their offerings or by leaving if they are unable to influence change in the pastor. This form of church governance results in many Latino/a Protestant churches missing a clear accountability and having weak organizational structures.

It is not uncommon to see congregations split when there are tensions between pastors and lay leaders.[8]

Most Latino/a Protestant churches are relatively small, with less than one hundred regular participants, including children and nonmembers. In urban areas Latino/a churches often rent storefronts or depend on using other congregations' facilities during "off" hours. Even so, these congregations provide believers with concrete support systems and a network that responds like an extended family. The church is a place of affirmation, where people can develop and grow. Though these congregations may have a marginal role in the larger society, they often play a very crucial part in the lives of their members and in local communities. And because so many Latino/a Protestants are converts, they tend to have strong ties and commitments to their churches.[9]

Leadership in the Latino Protestant Church

There are different models of pastoral leadership among Latino/a churches from a believers' church perspective, but also some common characteristics. Leadership is usually seen as a charismatic gift. Churches often have Latino, and a small though growing number of Latina, pastors who began as lay leaders in their congregations and later developed into pastors. Often people with dynamic conversion experiences become pastors. In many of the smaller churches, pastors will be bi-vocational, usually living and working in the same community as their church members. Many Latino/a pastors lack formal education, and in many denominations or independent churches formal ministerial training is not a requirement for ordination. Some would go as far as viewing too much formal training for ministry as suspect.[10]

A key component in these churches is that the vast majority of the pastors are Latinos/as. Those pastors who are not Latino/a usually have extensive experience and service in the community and are strongly committed to it. This makes Latino/a Protestant churches one of the few places where Latinos/as control their own local organizations. A believers' church ecclesiology enables Latino-led denominations to develop and thrive in the United States, giving Latinos and Latinas leadership roles they seldom hold in Roman Catholic or mainline Protestant denominations.

The concept of the "priesthood of all believers" means that most church members have a role and a responsibility in Latino/a Protestant

---

[8]Some say that Latino Protestant churches really grow by division, not multiplication.

[9]This means that, as a whole, Latina/o Protestants tend to be more active in the lives of their churches than their Roman Catholic counterparts.

[10]Some Latino congregations become suspect of seminary education after seeing leaders educated out of the community, or noting that those with a seminary education seem to have lost their "fervor" for ministry.

churches. Church members may be seen as marginal in the larger society because they are undocumented, have little formal education, or work in menial jobs. But in Latino/a Protestant churches they have the opportunity to find a space to serve, contribute, develop skills, and take leadership responsibilities.

Church and Latino Identity

Historically, Latino/a Protestant churches have played an ambivalent role in Latina/o identity issues. On one hand, Latino/a churches have played an important part in cultural identity maintenance. During the nineteenth century and throughout the twentieth century, Latino/a Protestant churches have often been one of the few places where formal Spanish was used, and a new generation of Latinos/as might learn to read and write in Spanish.[11] Since their churches have been in the hands of Latino/a leaders, worship styles and services are (usually) free to reflect the linguistic, cultural, national background complexities of the community. In these congregations there is the freedom to have services in Spanish, English, *Spanglish,* or in various bilingual formats.

On the other hand, Latino/a Protestant churches have struggled to find their place in larger society. It has not always been easy to maintain a Latino/a Protestant identity because of the pressure to acculturate. For many Latinos/as, one sign of cultural identity is popular Catholicism, and therefore Latino/a Protestants do not seem to be fully Latino/a. Thus to be or to become a Latino/a Protestant means to be a part of a minority within a minority in the United States. Historically, Protestant missionaries repeatedly have seen their evangelizing task as including making Latinos/as good Protestants and good Americans. This tendency continues among some evangelical churches that encourage Latinos/as to cut their ethnic and cultural ties and fit in the new community of believers.[12] Often younger acculturating Latino/a Protestants become part of larger churches where Latinos/as have few or no leadership roles.[13] A believers' church ecclesiology provides the space for Latinos/as to develop and lead their own congregations, but these churches are part

---

[11]As a U.S. born Latino, my first regular exposure to Spanish outside the home was in church. Like many other Latino/a Protestants, I was expected to read the Bible in Spanish, and regularly wrote in Spanish for various church activities.

[12]See Sánchez-Walsh, *Latino Pentecostal Identity,* 2003, for a description of how that tendency has played out in a specific Pentecostal denominations.

[13]Because missionaries from majority culture churches evangelized many Latino/a Protestants, it is not uncommon for some Latino/a Protestants to assume that "Anglos" by definition practice Protestantism better. This sense, mixed with acculturation pressures, can create situations in which some Latino/a Protestants prefer to worship where there is no Latino/a leadership. This tendency can be seen among Latino/a Protestants of most denominational traditions, even those without a believers' church ecclesiology.

of larger denominational and social structures in which they are often on the margins and under pressure to acculturate. So while Latino/a churches support a Latino/a Protestant identity, that identity is also often undermined by the mere fact of being a Protestant in the United States.

Latino Believers' Churches and Other Christians

From a believers' church perspective the church is most clearly manifested as a local visible community of believers. While there is theological affirmation of a sense of a universal church, there is also a feeling that unity among Christians is possible, even if there are denominational differences. The universality[14] of the church is manifested in concrete relations between local congregations, particularly between those from the same denomination. The presence of Christians around the world is felt in these churches and some reach beyond their local setting, particularly with churches in Latin America. Other times Latino/a churches struggle to work together. Even when churches are from the same denomination, they often maintain a sense of competition between churches and a vague suspicion of those who call for churches to work together across denominational lines.

The situation is exacerbated as churches look beyond their own cultural and theological framework. Linguistic and cultural differences often limit relations with non-Latino/a churches, but they often also seem to serve as a buffer to avoid relating with churches that are not Latino/a. More importantly, the theological framework of a believers' church in the Latino/a community does not provide clear tools for developing ties with churches, even Latino/a ones, from other theological traditions. Since any attempt to define the universal church structurally[15] is resisted, this leaves unanswered the question of how Latino/a Protestants can gain a sense of being part of, and relating to, a worldwide church. In other words, what does it mean to be part of a universal ("catholic") church and how does it manifest itself in practice?

Churches with a Growing Impact

It is clear that the believers' church model attracts Latinos/as and will most likely continue to do so in the foreseeable future. The call to radical conversion and experience of God's power in the midst of difficult life situations will continue to appeal to Latinos/as, particularly those in the midst of change and social dislocation. The *Hispanic Churches in American Public Life* (HCAPL) study (referred to in footnote 2 of this chapter)

---

[14]Many Latino/a Protestants feel uncomfortable with the word *catholic* because of its potential identification with the Roman Catholic Church.

[15]Some in the believers' church tradition question any attempt for structural unity to the church around the world, such as the World Council of Churches or formal ecumenical efforts of any sort.

indicates that these types of churches will thrive and impact the Latino/a community. It also seems to be the type of Protestant church that will continue to be most attractive to more acculturated Latinos/as. Nonetheless, it also seems clear that this model of church encourages more religious diversification in the Latino/a community. New Christian religious movements from Latin America and from among Latinos/as in the United States will continue to stretch the definitions of Protestantism and of the believers' church perspective.[16] Nonetheless, it is among these types of movements that new generations of Latinos and Latinas will find spiritual life and a vibrant relationship with God through Jesus Christ.

---

[16]Jean Pierre Bastian, in his book *Protestantismos y modernidad latinoamericana,* 1994, questions whether many of the new religious movements in Latin America can really be called Protestant.

CHAPTER 7

Sacraments

■ EDUARDO C. FERNÁNDEZ

A North African lawyer of the third century, Tertullian (d. ca. 220 C.E.) was the first to translate the Greek *mysterion* into the Latin *sacramentum*. *Mysterion*, a concept laden with a sense of hiddenness, means "mystery," that is, any manifestation of God's loving power in space and time. This association "stems from the use of the word *mysterion* in the Greek version of the scriptures to indicate the hidden plan of God manifested in human history and made accessible to those who have faith (see, e.g., Wis. 6:22; Mt. 13:11; Rom. 16:25–26; Eph. 1:9–10)."[1]

In the Roman Empire of the first century, when the church was born, *sacramentum* was the pledge a soldier made upon joining the army—often a visible sign of that pledge being a tattoo of his general's name borne on the soldier's body. Today the term "sacrament" often refers to a liturgical rite, but an earlier understanding of the word was much broader. A sacrament was any manifestation of God's power and love, or grace, in concrete time and space. "The life of Jesus Christ, culminating in his suffering, death and Resurrection (the 'Paschal Mystery') is the realization of God's loving intention to save humanity and the basis not only for the Church's sacramental worship, but also for its existence."[2] In the Roman Catholic Church, post-Vatican II sacramental theology has emphasized a

---

[1] McBrien, *HarperCollins Encyclopedia of Catholicism*, s.v. "Sacrament," by Mark R. Francis.
[2] Ibid.

return to this larger notion of sacramentality, a notion that some would argue has great affinity with Latino/a spirituality and practice.[3]

After sketching more of the historical development of the term "sacrament," this essay will explain how it is that sacraments function in general, and then specifically, in the Latino/a context. As the sacramental principle emphasizes, it is through the concrete, the tangible, the material in the here and now, perceived by the senses, that God becomes present. In the words of the great Spanish mystic, St. John of the Cross, "the moment is pregnant with God." And there is no better way to be present to the moment than through the senses.

Sacraments function, therefore, as gateways to the sacred.[4] Instead of posing a dichotomy between the human and the Divine, God the Creator of heaven and earth, through Jesus, becomes one of us and in the Incarnation assumes our vulnerable human condition. Sacraments as the special presence of God become not only the sign of this Incarnation, but, at key moments such as birth, maturation, commitment, service, healing, and forgiveness, transform our lives. We are no longer the same and we are no longer alone.

While this essay focuses on Christian sacramentality, it is not an idea unique to Christians. Bernard Cooke argues that sacramentality extends to all human experience. "Basically, sacramentality involves three elements: 1) the ultimate meaning of human experience, 2) divine saving presence, and 3) some transformation of humans individually and communally."[5] Of all the theologians who reflect upon sacramental theology, Cooke provides a starting point that is most marked by what is happening humanly. In other words, it is only through the human that we can know the Divine. We can only know the love of God, for example, if others have loved us. So the gift of human love and friendship assumes a primary sacramental function in his theology. Sacraments operate at the level of meaning. What does it mean that we are born or drawn into a believing community? that we mature? that we live our lives in service? that we are saved by God's grace when sin, loneliness, alienation, sickness, and the immanent fact of death threaten our true happiness? Such questions point to the ultimate meaning of human experience.

---

[3]In a forthcoming book by Empereur and Fernández, *La Vida Sacra: A Contemporary Hispanic Sacramental Theology,* they argue that the Latino/a experience of sacraments is rooted and nurtured by an authentic tradition–popular religion. It is also one that has maintained a sense of the larger, more cosmic or creation-centered reality.

[4]For a remarkable exposition of the history of the sacraments and how it is that they function as gateways to the sacred, see Martos, *Doors to the Sacred,* 2001. A commonly used sacramental theology text in Latin American seminaries is González Dorado, *Los Sacramentos del Evangelio,* 1993.

[5]See Fink, *New Dictionary of Sacramental Worship,* s.v. "Sacraments," by Bernard Cooke.

For Christians, an awareness of God's saving presence reveals this decisive meaning. It is God who first creates and invites us into relationship. It is God who "began a good work among [us, and] will bring it to completion by the day of Jesus Christ" (Phil. 1:6). Thus, this ultimate meaning is much more than an intellectual understanding; it is something we live through our bodies in community. That is one of the reasons that some Christian denominations practice infant baptism. For them, faith is not about an intellectual assent but has more to do with the gift of relationship one receives by being welcomed into a believing community. For Christians in general, the ultimate meaning of life thus comes from "the *presence* of God, a presence that is the result of divine communication with humans through God's word of revelation and the human response in faith to that word" (Fink 1990:1116). This openness to the divine presence in our lives, and its implications for life or death, alters our lives radically. This divine-human relationship colors the attitudes we have toward death, which becomes—not the end of life—but a new birth in Christ, for "If we have died with him, we will also live with him" (2 Tim. 2:11). Early Christian baptismal fonts were often built in the shape of a tomb to illustrate this dying and rising in Christ. Thus, because of Jesus' life, death, and resurrection, Christian sacraments, which flow out of the paschal mystery, have been described as "sacred signs, instituted by Christ, to give grace" (Ibid.).[6]

The Emergence of Christian Sacraments

The spirituality of Israel in the Old Testament is filled with examples of how God becomes present through physical means in creation and the cosmos. Ancient Israel celebrates a God who creates matter that is good and holy. The refrain, "And God saw that is was good," closes each of the days of the first creation account in Genesis (chapter 1). Psalm 19 opens with "The heavens are telling the glory of God; and the firmament proclaims his handiwork." The many *berakoth,* or blessing prayers, witness the goodness of creation as manifested in the material. This was the world of Jesus, one that was imbued with the symbolic realism of sacred meals, anointings, washings, blessings, and other symbolic gestures. The followers of Jesus draw on this symbolic character of Jewish faith, together with other metaphorical cultural realities around them to practice communal washings or immersions, blessings, meals, and anointings—sacraments that made Christ present in their midst. In recalling his life, death, and resurrection, these primitive Christians are changed.

In the early centuries of the church the notion of sacramentality was very broad. Because all of the cosmos was sacred, God's presence could

---

[6]I am particularly indebted to Cooke's article in Fink for this section on the wider meaning of sacramentality, together with its unique Christian manifestation.

be acknowledged and celebrated in a number of ways. Gradually, certain rites such as baptism and the Lord's supper, or eucharist (from the Greek *eucharistia,* meaning "thanksgiving"), became crucial for initiation into and sustenance of the Christian community. At the time of Paul, the followers of Jesus usually worshiped in house churches. These small group settings encouraged active participation by all present and are described as early as the mid-second century.[7] The manner of celebrating sacraments and their inherent theology was not uniform. In some places an anointing preceded the baptismal immersion; in others, it followed. At times, the emphasis on baptism as a washing away of sin took precedence over an understanding of the rite as a way of celebrating the arrival of new members, as when the children of believers were baptized.

With the increasing toleration and finally acceptance of Christianity as the official religion of the Roman Empire in 392 C.E., the celebration of these rites was radically altered. The number of converts to Christianity grew dramatically, as did their participation in the eucharist. Gradually, the house church was replaced by basilica-type structures, formerly large Roman auditoriums. Laypeople were gradually distanced from the eucharistic table and, in many cases, the rigorous initiation process known as the catechumenate was abandoned. As Christianity spread to different parts of Europe and the Middle East, climatic and cultural factors shaped how these rites were celebrated. The full anointing and immersion that were celebrated in warmer climates, which had the tradition of the thermal baths, became more difficult in colder ones. The banquet aspect of the Lord's supper, similarly, became less obvious when the laity was positioned so far away from the table and their reception of the body and blood of Christ became more sparse and stylized. Over the centuries, a certain type of minimalism, which concerned itself more about "bare essentials" than about the abundance experienced through the language of symbol and gesture, gradually took hold. In the case of baptism, the mere sprinkling or pouring of water replaced the rich symbolism of immersing the body fully into a pool.

This minimalism became even more acute when coupled with an instrumental approach to the sacraments. This view

> considered the liturgical acts as means used by God, acting through the mediation of the ordained minister, to give grace to people. In this perspective Christians came to liturgy to *receive* sacraments, to be freed from their sins, to be blessed. This receptive approach to the role of the faithful coincided with their increasing exclusion from active participation in sacramental liturgy. (Fink 1990:1117)

---

[7]See Justin Martyr's letter, written around 155 C.E., *The Catechism of the Catholic Church* 1994:1345.

This instrumental approach to the sacraments was substantiated during the "Scholastic" period (eleventh through thirteenth centuries C.E.) by a more systematic approach strongly influenced by the revival of the thought of Aristotle. During this period, in 1274, the Western Church delineated the official number of sacraments at seven. (Earlier there had been as many as 30.)

> The seven sacraments were thus distinguished from sacramentals in that the sacraments are "instrumental causes" of grace, the means by which God chooses to sanctify humanity and unify the Church. God unfailingly acts in these signs because they were instituted by Christ himself. (McBrien 1995:1147)

The designated sacraments include Baptism, Confirmation, Eucharist, Reconciliation (or Penance), Anointing of the Sick (which at times has been called Extreme Unction), Marriage (or Matrimony), and Holy Orders (Ibid.).

As the laity became more separated from the physical celebration of the sacraments and less informed about their meaning because they had not been through the catechumenate of the earlier ages, they found solace in other faith practices. Certain popular rituals of piety, which were often not clergy-centered, allowed them the opportunity to experience God through the material. Bruce Morrill describes some of the devotions that surfaced during the Middle Ages:

> Even when, for various reasons, the faithful have had little direct access to the symbols and actions of the sacramental rituals of the Church, other forms of "popular piety" have emerged and flourished. One has only to think of the pastoral effectiveness of St. Francis' creation of the Nativity scene (the "crèche") and promotion of the Stations of the Cross, let alone the myriad cultural renditions of the crucifix. All of these symbols have flourished since the Middle Ages, for they represent and foster faith in God's identification with and presence to people in their very bodily experiences of joy and wonder, struggle and suffering. For Christians, the most spiritual of realities can only be experienced or known in and through the materiality of our bodies. (Morrill 1999:3)

It is important to keep in mind that much of Latina/o spirituality, whether Roman Catholic or Protestant, has its roots culturally in these practices. Justo L. González, a Methodist, has commented on the necessity for Latino/a Protestants to reconcile themselves in some fashion with their Roman Catholic roots (1997:4). Latin America was not as involved in the theological controversies surrounding the Protestant

Reformation as was Europe,[8] and the issues that surfaced through the introduction of Christianity to large indigenous populations were entirely different. From the question of whether the native peoples had souls to the need to defend the rights of those so violently subjugated, certain prophetic voices spoke out in desperation.[9]

In some ways, the Reformation sought to restore the spirit and practices of the church that had become excessively formal, and in some cases conducive to mechanical, superstitious distortions. One such superstitious belief was that gazing on the sacred host (consecrated bread) during the celebration of the eucharist would bring good luck to the person: for example, the birth of a son. The reformers found it difficult to recognize the New Testament "Lord's supper" in the multiplicity of masses that priests frequently celebrated simultaneously in large cathedrals and monasteries for a required fee or stipend. In many ways, the Protestant Reformation ushered in several changes that only came about in the Roman Catholic Church after Vatican II (convened in the 1960s), such as the importance of the priesthood of the faithful. This is the belief that all Christians, by virtue of their baptism, participate in the priesthood of Christ (thus de-emphasizing somewhat the mediation of clergy). The use of the vernacular as opposed to Latin and the sharing of the cup at the eucharist are stark reminders that the priest is not "saying" mass for the people, who are merely present as spectators, but rather the priest is "presiding" or actively leading the Christian community in the church's great prayer of praise and thanksgiving.

Protestant and Catholic theologians have written extensively on the sacraments, especially since some Protestants, such as the Quakers, eventually chose to abandon them entirely, opting instead for a more spiritual, or nonmaterial emphasis on the "Inner Light of the Living Christ."[10] Others, such as those in the Anglican tradition–Methodists, Lutherans, and Presbyterians, for example–have retained some of the Roman Catholic practices regarding the sacraments of baptism and eucharist, which, as Martin Luther pointed out, are more explicitly found in scripture. The contemporary understanding of the origin of the sacraments in Roman Catholic theology focuses on the actions of Jesus in initiating, feeding, forgiving, attending to the sick, etc., rather than on actual rituals which he prescribed. The phrase "instituted by Christ" reveals how the primitive church as the body of Christ active in the world

---

[8] See Virgilio Elizondo's comments in González, *Mañana*, 1990:13.

[9] See Gutiérrez, *Las Casas*, 1993.

[10] See Fink, *New Dictionary of Sacramental Worship*, s.v. "Sacraments in the Reformation Churches," by Susan J. White. This, together with James F. White, *The Sacraments in Protestant Practice and Faith*, 1999, are excellent resources for a nuanced understanding of some of the relevant key issues.

carried on his mission through these rites (for a designation of the church as the body of Christ, see Eph. 4:12). Bernard Cooke sums up the effect of the Protestant reforms on the wider church's celebration of the sacraments:

> On the positive side, the Reformation drew attention to the role of personal faith and the active participation of the faithful in sacramental liturgy; on the negative side, many of the Reformation churches downgraded the role of ritual and tended to substitute reflection on the Bible for sacramental celebration. (1994:1118)[11]

Post-Vatican II theology seeks to expand the notion of sacramentality, at the same time emphasizing the Incarnation of Jesus Christ as the "first" sacrament. In a similar manner, the church, existing in time and space as a continuation of the work of Jesus—in fact, the body of Christ in this world—is also a sacrament. Better ecumenical relations between Christian denominations, as well as more accurate scholarship surrounding the evolution of the sacraments, are bringing about a greater consensus as to what more faithfully constitutes Christian worship. Protestants have helped Roman Catholics recover the importance of the Word in sacramental worship while Catholics have helped many Protestants in their understandings of sacraments.[12] Some liberation theologians view the sacraments as prophetic symbols of the Kingdom, that is, "...in the light of a theology of the cross and of the Crucified One, Christ is made present in the poor. And responding to the cry of the poor becomes an ineluctable condition for entrance to the Kingdom (Mt. 25:31–45)" (Codina, 1993a:665).[13]

Recent Latino/a Contributions to Sacramental Theology and Practice

Historically, "sacrament" has been intimately linked with worship incarnating the church's ancient dictum *lex orandi, lex credendi* ("as the church prays, so she believes"). This stresses how faith and worship existed before doctrine, perhaps an apt description of Hispanic worship or *culto*, as it is often referred to in Hispanic Protestant communities. While some Hispanic churches do not have "sacraments," many do

---

[11]Of course, not all Protestants see this downgrading of ritual and greater emphasis on the Bible as a negative development.

[12]Susan J. White notes: "Beginning in the late 1960s [after Vatican II], Episcopalians, Methodists, Lutherans and Presbyterians each underwent their own versions of a sacramental revival, resulting in a whole generation of revised rites and texts. Many of the ecclesiastical descendants of the reformers remain untouched by these changes. Revivalist, romanticist, and Enlightenment sacramental pieties are still strong among large numbers of Protestant Christians" (Fink 1990:1134).

[13]Victor Codina's little book in Spanish, *Sacramentos de la Vida*, 1993b, is an excellent popular work, which integrates current sacramental theology, popular religiosity, and the theology of liberation.

practice "ordinances," which, as in the cases of baptism and the Lord's supper, are their equivalent.

Approaches like Cooke's that begin with human experience are helpful in understanding Hispanic spirituality, described as diverse, popular and communal, festive, relational, and transcendent.[14] Latino spirituality proceeds from the concrete to the abstract, a very sacramental principle. Another way of describing this flow is to see it as a product of a "high-context" culture. High-context cultures, among them Italian, Spanish, Greek, Arab, and Latin American, place more emphasis on *how* the message is communicated rather than on *what* is communicated. Low-context cultures, on the other hand, which include northern European cultures such as German, Scandinavian, and English, stress word over gesture (Pérez Rodríguez 2002:165).[15] Arturo Pérez Rodríguez applies these categories to Hispanic worship or liturgy.

> Because of its Semitic origins and its variant cultural adaptations through the centuries, the liturgy is a high-context form of communication, dependent on the sensual nature of the body to communicate its message. As it is interpreted and celebrated through low-context communication cultures, it is transformed into a word service. Words take precedence over actions and gestures...Hispanic liturgy is grounded in a high-context cultural communication where the senses interplay with the word. (Ibid.:161)

The fiesta-like atmosphere of Hispanic worship embodies the importance of *ambiente* over pure reason. Music, decoration, food, dance, and gesture do more to create a healing, welcoming environment than a logical, meticulously researched sermon. Latino/a Protestants and Catholics writing on Hispanic Christian worship stress the importance of gathering, movement, and sensuality in calling attention to this spirit of the *fiesta*.[16]

---

[14]For an application of each of these terms, see Sheldrake, *The New Westminster Dictionary of Christian Spirituality*, s.v. "Hispanic Spirituality," by Eduardo Fernández; as well as Cooke's seminal work, *Sacraments and Sacramentality*, 1994.

[15]For an elaboration of how this principle of high/low context works in the Hispanic reality, Pérez Rodríguez recommends a work by the Archdiocese of Newark, *Presencia Nueva*, 1988:258, footnote 9.

[16]See González, *Alabadle!*, 1996a, especially his introduction. This collection of essays, which includes representative works by Pentecostal, Methodist, Baptist, Presbyterian, and Catholic scholars, together with an introduction to Hispanic hymnody, is a gem for its "grassroots feel." For the importance of singing among Hispanic Protestants, see Aponte's "Coritos as Active Symbols," 1995. For a pastoral perspective from the Catholic point of view, see Davis, *Misa, Mesa y Musa*, 1997, as well as the book he edited with Presmanes, *Preaching and Culture in Latino Congregations*, 2000. An indispensable pastoral tool, which takes the minister through the Latino/a Catholic life cycle, especially as it relates to the celebration of the sacraments and popular religiosity, is Pérez Rodríguez and Francis, *Primero Dios*, 1997.

The importance of relationality, or a person's ties to the community and to the cosmos or nature, cannot be underestimated. Like other traditional cultures, Latinas/os derive their identity more from communal than from individual accomplishments. Therefore, when gathering to worship sacramentally, relationships–to each other, to their God, and to the good earth, as manifested in powerful symbols–are celebrated and strengthened. As in the case of a family reunion, not only do members celebrate their being family; they, in fact, become closer as family. Hispanic sacramentality, facilitated through symbols and gestures that utilize all five senses, harkens back to the paschal mystery. By entering into Christ's life, death, and resurrection, Hispanics, who like other traditional cultures value rites of passage, find meaning in knowing that, in any given life's critical moment, they are not alone. Their suffering is not in vain and there is hope because of *la cruz*, a symbol not only of Christ's death but also of his triumph over death. Thus, seasonal dyings and risings are expected when one is a Christian. A greater sensitivity to tradition often marks the Latino experience of sacraments, expressed in the material objects used in worship that speak of the faith of ancestors who in Christ are still present.

Whether through music, language, art, or other cultural manifestations, Latinas/os know that Christ is encountered through others. This encounter involves more sharing than is apparent, such as in water, oil, bread, or wine, and marks a sharing of lives, in good times and in bad. Latinas and Latinos contribute to a church's bond to its own sacred history because of the importance they give to relationality. Studies today manifest the importance of material culture for the belief of peoples, and for many Christians sacramentality is the way this Christian culture is maintained and passed on through generations. Symbols and gestures have a history and facilitate one's entrance into that history.

The ecumenical dialogue on sacramentality that is currently taking place between Latino/a Protestants and Catholics, the fastest growing religious ethnic groups in the U.S., will undoubtedly continue to expand the horizons of their respective denominations. If as the church prays, so she believes, these holy experiences of finding God through the beauty of creation will enable her to be a sacrament in the world, a living, breathing reminder that the body of Christ is alive and well among us– and that, like Jesus, we too are called to be poured out in service to a hungry world.

CHAPTER 8

Theological Anthropology

■ MIGUEL H. DÍAZ

Theological anthropology is the discipline that relates human and divine life (Ladaria 1996:9–15) with a wide range of themes stemming from Judeo-Christian sources. These themes include: (a) the relationship between Creator and creation, (b) the relationship between anthropology and christology, (c) the relationship between human freedom (agency, liberation, and the building of just societies) and God's grace (gift, salvation, and the coming of the reign), and (d) the relationship between the communal human and the triune life of God. Recently, largely as a result of renewed efforts to underscore the contextual basis of all theological investigation, Christian theological anthropologies have increasingly and consciously embraced particular social, racial, cultural, and gender experiences. U.S. Hispanic theological anthropology has emerged among many U.S. voices (Asian American, African American, Black Catholic, Native American, feminist, etc.) that seek liberative answers to the age-old question: What does it mean to be human? Turning to the communal experiences of U.S. Hispanics, this anthropology seeks to correlate these experiences with the life of faith. This correlation "requires the examination of historical, social, community realities, as well as economic, ethnic, racial, gender realities within which faith is known and religious life experienced" (Maldonado, 1997:100). Thus, U.S. Hispanic theological anthropology offers a distinctive contribution to Christian theological explorations of human realities. This essay briefly maps the methodological and thematic landscape of U.S. Hispanic theological anthropology.[1]

Methodology in U.S. Hispanic Theological Anthropology

Reflecting the "turn to context" in contemporary faith-seeking efforts to understand what is human, U.S. Hispanic theological anthropology has as its methodological starting point U.S. Hispanic communal experiences. More specifically, the focus on commonly shared cultural (familial ethos, religious traditions, Spanish language) and sociopolitical experiences (oppression and marginalization) reflects this methodological preference. This preferential option for Latino/a communal experiences is not intended to deny distinct differences among Latinos/as or exclude the validity of other Latino/a communal experiences.[2] Nor does this anthropological starting point refute in any way the *theocentric* basis of theology. While avoiding anthropological reductionism, U.S. Hispanic anthropology offers the communal experiences of Latinos/as as loci for encountering and critically reflecting upon the theological realities professed in Christian faith (Christ, grace, kingdom, Trinity, etc.).

Among key U.S. Hispanic experiences that contribute to an ongoing qualification of traditional sources in Christian theological anthropology, the following should be highlighted: 1) popular faith experiences, 2) sociocultural experiences, and 3) historical experiences. These human experiences offer particular loci that qualify traditional sources that inform Christian understandings of the human, as well as providing a basis to construct a particular narrative that embodies "in concrete social, cultural, and religious ways the 'big' Christian story" (Díaz 2001:21).

Firstly, popular faith experiences provide for Catholic and Protestant theologians an indispensable locus for understanding how U.S. Hispanic communities perceive and understand what is *latinamente* human and how this human experience relates to the Divine. Whether in the word-based popular testimonials and *coritos* of Protestant U.S. Hispanic communities, or the iconic-based imagination of popular U.S. Hispanic Catholic devotions, these religious experiences serve as signposts for attending to sociopolitical realities in understanding the constitution of the communal self and mediation of the experience of grace (Aponte 1995; Maldonado 1997:105–06; Díaz 2001:60–78; Recinos 2001:116–28).

---

[1]For a more thorough analysis of U.S. Hispanic theological anthropology, particularly from the perspective of U.S. Hispanic Catholic theologians, see Díaz, *On Being Human*, 2001.

[2]I use the word *distinct* rather than *individual* because the former represents a fitting term for a U.S. Hispanic understanding of what is particular within the communally human. While the word *individual* suggests separation from others, the word *distinct* suggests uniqueness, not in opposition, but rather in relationship to others.

Second, U.S. Hispanic theological anthropology methodologically attends to the sociocultural experience of *mestizaje/mulatez.* This experience, rooted in intercultural, interreligious, interracial, and inter-gender relations lies at the foundation of and continues to constitute the identity of U.S. Hispanic communities. Set forth as a vision and a fundamental option to realize the inclusive relationships and communities proclaimed by Christ, this sociocultural experience lies at the heart of U.S. Hispanic efforts to revision the human reality in the image of the Divine.

Finally, U.S. Hispanic theological anthropology reflects the increased attentiveness to history and cultural context that characterizes much of contemporary theology. In particular, U.S. Hispanic explorations of what it means to be human have reflected upon the historical experiences of colonization shared by Latino/a communities. More recently, U.S. Hispanic theological anthropology has become mindful of the culture of globalization that threatens the very survival of particular human communities, including U.S. Hispanic communities. How these historical experiences shape approaches to the human and mediate or hinder relationship to God's life-giving presence continues to be part of U.S. Hispanic methodological concerns.

Themes in U.S. Hispanic Theological Anthropology

Theological reflections rooted in methodological concerns have yielded a number of U.S. Hispanic contributions to the ever-recurring question: What does it mean to be human? Similar to other theological anthropologies of the past, U.S. Hispanic theological anthropology embraces critical readings, qualifications, and appropriations of Christian sources. While the uniqueness of U.S. Hispanic theological anthropology lies in its ability to be nourished by the everyday and ordinary experiences (*lo cotidiano*) of Latinos/as and the specific critical and preferential approach given to these experiences, this anthropology implicitly and/or explicitly parallels traditional Christian ways of relating human and divine realties.

A. *Creator and Creation*

One of the most salient influences on Christian anthropologies comes from traditional approaches to the doctrine of creation. Few biblical texts in the history of Christian thought have informed Christian anthropologies more than Genesis 1–3. In recent times, various biblical scholars, especially feminist scholars, have provided reinterpretations of these biblical texts and in the process offered more gender inclusive and liberative visions of the creation of the human in the image and likeness of God (Gen. 1:27). Not only because of its Christian influences but also as a result of its indigenous and African roots, U.S. Hispanic theological anthropology draws significantly from the doctrine of creation. This thematic focus has been reflected in U.S. Hispanic efforts that analogously relate the intentional divine plan to create a diversity of creatures with the intentional U.S. Hispanic goal to affirm and promote sociocultural diversity (*mestizaje/mulatez*). This anthropological focus on creaturely differences sees the horizontal fellowship and asymmetric order of creation as something good and essential. In a similar way, this anthropology embraces creating and fostering diversity as something good and essential in community-building efforts (García-Rivera 1995:99).

Largely as a result of experiencing the denial of the distinct otherness of U.S. Hispanics within the U.S. landscape, U.S. Hispanic theologians have affirmed, in continuity with Christian traditions rooted in Genesis 1–3, recognition of and existence with others as the *sine qua non* of personhood. To be human in the image of God is to-be-for-the-other. Being-for-others is the alternative to being-alone, being without others (González 1990:125–38). In a society in which those in power often fail to recognize and empower others, especially marginalized others, the recovery and appropriation of this central teaching in the Judeo-Christian creation narratives offers a prophetic alternative way of realizing community. Analogously, but from the perspective of a U.S. Hispanic popular Catholic narrative, one can also highlight the overall anthropological significance of God's call of Juan Diego, as presented in the "creation" story of Guadalupe (Elizondo 1997:115–36). In this narrative, Juan Diego is challenged to become an agent in the construction of a new creation. This creation has to do with the emergence of an inclusive community of persons, a new way of relating in church and society that is ushered in by attending to the needs of the marginalized. Juan Diego's challenge is a signpost for the kind of prophetic human agency that U.S. Hispanics have embraced today with respect to the church and society. In rejecting the sin of exclusion, U.S. Hispanic theological anthropology embraces the biblical rejection of the idea that we were created to exist alone, without others (Gen. 2:18). In so doing, U.S. Hispanics discover in the Spanish word *nosotros* (the Spanish word for the English *we* that literally means "we-other") a most fitting and inclusive anthropological vision of what it means to be human (Goizueta 1992a:55–69).

B. Christology and Anthropology

In Christian theological anthropologies, the doctrine of creation is deeply tied to christology. Jesus Christ is seen as the beginning and end of all creation, and in a special way, essential to understanding the nature and agency of human persons. Who persons are in relation to Christ is a central theme in U.S. Hispanic theological anthropology. Among other things (i.e., Elizondo, Goizueta, Aquino, and Pedraja), anthropological implications have been drawn from Jesus' Galilean identity, from popular U.S. Hispanic practices of accompanying Jesus, from Jesus' egalitarian and integral personal praxis, and from the way he reveals God's agency in the world. In his Galilean identity, Jesus maps how we are to exist as human beings. To be human in the image of the Galilean Jesus is to walk in a preferential way with the poor and marginalized. To be human in the image of the Galilean Jesus is to embrace an interpersonal and intercultural way of existence (*mestizaje*) that involves crossing over into the human experiences of others. Perhaps even more prophetic and dangerous, being like the Galilean Jesus involves crossing over into the landscape of, and identifying with, the marginalized. Indeed, Jesus' identity as a Galilean and his geographical journey from Galilee to Jerusalem to confront the powerful of the land provides in U.S. Hispanic theological anthropology a symbolic geo-cultural-theological source that invites human solidarity with marginalized persons who abide in our lands, and peaceful confrontation with those who have the power to marginalize (Elizondo 2000a: 49–78).

In a sacramental and liturgical sense, the U.S. Hispanic popular celebrations of the Easter *Triduum*[3] exemplify this human solidarity with Jesus and provide a locus for exploring an U.S. Hispanic answer to the question: What does it mean to be human? The act of accompanying Jesus on the way of the cross suggests what is most significant about being human for U.S. Hispanics: To be human is to be *acompañado*—accompanied (Goizueta 1995:19–76). To be human is to exist in interrelationship and interactivity with respect to one's neighbor. This relational way of existing invites ongoing encounters with the "body" of Christ. Indeed, as the gospel reminds us, it is in one's neighbor, especially our marginalized neighbors, that we meet the face of Christ (Mt. 25:31–46).

The U.S. Hispanic anthropological focus on interactivity and agency echoes and qualifies central insights drawn from christology. For instance, the portrayal of Jesus as a "verb" (here, verb is understood as God's active personal presence in history) reflects and qualifies from a U.S. Hispanic perspective Christian anthropologies inspired by the doctrine of the Incarnation. The Spanish biblical translation of the Greek *Logos* as "*Verbo*" ("Verb"), rather than the more static and nominal translation in English of this notion as "Word" supports a U.S. Hispanic understanding of Jesus as God's life-giving praxis. In the image of Jesus as God's incarnate activity, U.S. Hispanic theological anthropology embraces an integral, egalitarian, and relational anthropology. As God's activity in Jesus Christ both reveals and constitutes Jesus' identity, so

---

[3]The liturgical celebrations during Holy Week begin with the memorial of the Last Supper on Holy Thursday and end with the celebration of vespers on Easter Sunday. The celebrations recall key events in Jesus' life—namely, his last meal with his disciples, his passion and crucifixion, and his resurrection from the dead.

should Christ's activity in his followers reveal and constitute them in the world. For U.S. Hispanic theologians, human activity in the world carried out in the image of Christ should reflect Christ's egalitarian (with respect to male and female relations) and integral praxis (with respect to personal, social, public, private, transcendental, and historical realities). More specifically, to be human as Christ is human is to act with and on behalf of the liberation of the poor and marginalized within the worldly realities they inhabit (Pedraja 1999b:107–24 and Aquino 1993:141–44).

C. Human Freedom and Grace

An anthropological focus on interactivity and human agency naturally evokes ancient Christian discussions on the relationship between human freedom and grace and human ways of responding to the coming of God's reign. In U.S. Hispanic anthropology, talk of human agency is generally associated with the ongoing struggle (*la lucha*) to overcome social injustices, especially the struggle for the physical and sociocultural survival of Latinas/os (Pineda-Madrid 2001:187–202; Isasi-Díaz 1993:16–22). In underscoring interrelated forms of communal oppressions (with respect to gender, race, class, and culture), U.S. Hispanic theological anthropology proposes an integral understanding of what it means to be human and an integral way of envisioning the life of grace. Thus, in U.S. Hispanic theology, grace is first and foremost God's gift to a community of persons within worldly realities. As such, U.S. Hispanic theology highlights the mediation of grace through various communal experiences that include, among others, cultural, sociopolitical, and religious experiences (Díaz 2001:23–78).

Ordinary life experience (*lo cotidiano*) offers a central locus for exploring the self-identity of Latinos/as, and understanding the interrelationship of their personal, communal, and social experiences with God's life. In this way, this anthropology witnesses the preferential option for *lo cotidiano*, which includes opting for marginalized domestic places, the subjects that abide therein, and their popular religious expressions. Although rooted in ordinary, domestic, and familial experiences, U.S. Hispanic anthropology underscores how daily life permeates public as well as private life, since daily relationships ground and foster social relations (Aquino 1993:30–41). This integral approach to ordinary life experiences provides the locus for explorations into the presence of sin and grace in Latino/a life experiences (Espín 1999:121–152). The proclamation and actualization of God's kin-dom is central to the U.S. Hispanic theological vision that underscores social relations as a context for understanding the mediation of grace and sin.[4] God's kin-dom offers a relational model for realizing inclusive

---

[4]I borrow this inclusive use of the word "kin-dom" from the writings of Ada María Isasi-Díaz.

communities. The kin-dom is a life-saving universal gift, but this gift often breaks through and is actualized in preferential ways. Thus, U.S. Hispanic theologies clearly evidence that God's gift of the kin-dom is universally offered and reaches greatest historical realization when God's saving grace empowers and liberates those who suffer from personal, institutional, structural, and systemic sin (Rodríguez and Martell-Otero:8–124). This preference is demanded by the very inclusive nature of God and by how God wills to structure human communities, namely, in conformity to the kin-dom made manifest in the life of Christ.

D. The Communally Human and the Triune Life of God

Finally, talk of the social experience of grace naturally conjures up the image of the triune God in whom the human has been created and challenged to exist in a community of persons. To exist as God exists is to embrace interdependence with respect to personal, communal, and social ways of existing. In doing so, U.S. Hispanic theological anthropology rejects individualism and individualistic-minded practices of realizing human life. Instead, U.S. Hispanic theological anthropology embraces divine *perichoresis* (personal interdependence that constitutes the triune life of God) as a model for the engendered, cultural, racial, social, and political constitution of the self (Sauceda 1997:22–32; García 1992:88–103). Beyond the latter, the life of God also serves as a signpost in a nation and world that is increasingly preoccupied with maintaining tight borders. In the image of God whose presence in Jesus Christ is defined by a "border crossing" (from the Divine to human) and actualized as "border-like" identity (Jesus Christ is *both* human and Divine), U.S. Hispanic theological anthropology invites human persons to cross over into the reality of others, and as a result of this experience embrace ongoing *mestizaje/mulatez*. This crossover is not intended to erase legitimate distinctions (with respect to gender, cultural, racial, and sociopolitical realities). Rather, in the image of God who relates to and welcomes the human without diminishing what is particular about the human, U.S. Hispanic theological anthropology presents a challenge: to practice the fundamental Judeo-Christian virtue of hospitality (Gen. 18), especially toward those in the U.S. who as a result of various sociopolitical processes have been gated within and without humanly constructed borders. In welcoming these others, what is particular about their humanity is to be received as gift rather than exiled as a threat to the communal-building process of reaching oneness *as* diversity.

Conclusion

This essay has briefly examined the contribution of emerging U.S. Hispanic theological anthropology. It has discussed central methodological foundations and theological themes that comprise this discipline. This discussion does not represent an exhaustive list of issues that delineate U.S. Hispanic theological anthropology. Moreover, these reflections are limited by the very fact that what is communally human does not exist as a static reality. Consequently, other complementary theological reflections on what is "Hispanically" human will follow. In the future, U.S. Hispanic theological anthropology is likely to take much more seriously than it has until now anthropological issues related to generational differences. Recent studies revealing the youthful nature of the U.S. Hispanic presence invite such considerations. This evolution, however, would be consistent with the central methodological vision of U.S. Hispanic theology. Indeed, given its attentiveness to particular human contexts, U.S. Hispanic theological anthropology finds itself poised to deepen and expand its understanding of what is Hispanically human, and how this particular humanity relates to the life of God.

CHAPTER 9

Scriptures

■ LETICIA A. GUARDIOLA-SÁENZ

As a collection of distinct books with contrasting theologies, the hybrid configuration of the Bible suggests the possibility of multiple and diverse readings. Likewise, as a cluster of distinct groups with idiosyncratic heritages and diverse experiences in the U.S., the Latina/o community suggests by its hybrid configuration the presence of numerous voices and diverse perspectives in multiple contexts. So when Latina/o communities read the Bible, the outcome is a polyphonic hermeneutic that speaks to both the intricacies of the text and the complexity of the multiple readers who approach it as individuals and in discrete communities. Increasingly the formal religion and popular spirituality of Roman Catholic and Protestant Latinos/as includes the study of the Bible (Espín 1997:142; González 1996b:27–30).

The readership of the Bible has generated numerous hermeneutical approaches throughout history, each of them bearing the marks of the sociohistorical contexts of their production. Using the ideological framework of cultural studies as my platform through my hybrid/border subjectivity assembled in the political grounds of neocolonialism, I read and appropriate the texts that surround me as hybrid texts (Guandiola-Sáenz 2002a:136). This hybridity is described by Homi Bhabha "as the sign of the ambivalent and shifting forces of colonial power which cannot be registered at a purely mimetic level within colonial discourse but exceed it, resisting containment and closure" (Rossington: 52). The complex, ambivalent, and hybrid biblical texts are the intersections of multiple cultures and perspectives that are in turn read and used by complex and ambivalent Latino/a communities that are also the intersections of multiple cultures. The following overview maps the main interpretive paradigms within biblical scholarship that lead to the emergence of Latina/o biblical hermeneutics.

Biblical Hermeneutics: A Synopsis

Biblical interpretation has been both the source and the product of historical change from its inception. Just as philosophical, political, scientific and artistic movements have influenced biblical hermeneutics, biblical interpretation has influenced other disciplines and often mirrors history. In church history through the Reformation, biblical hermeneutics operated between two interpretive approaches: the literal and the allegorical. Literal interpretations emphasized the internal elements of the texts as the key for interpretation, while allegorical interpretations sought external clues to uncover the symbolic sense of the text. Both approaches helped to construct the European medieval view of the perfect world, created and governed by God.

This perfect world image began to fade as the medieval world, stirred by the explorations of the "new world," scientific interest, and the growth of individualistic faith, eventually moved toward a "mechanistic" view of the world. Challenged by the new scientific worldview and empowered by the Enlightenment's motto that reason was the guide to all knowledge and human endeavors, biblical hermeneutics adopted a rationalist approach. With it, the foundation of the modern historical-critical method emerged and scholars began to study the Bible using the same conventions of analysis applied to other cultural texts of its time.

The throne of reason began to crumble almost two centuries later, just when reason seemed to be guiding the world toward unstoppable progress and, with it, guiding biblical hermeneutics into a logical, clear view of the Bible. The world empires began to collapse as the horror of two world wars, the cruelty of the Holocaust, uncountable wars of nationalism and liberation, a global cold war, and the use of science to accomplish acts of massive destruction brought worldwide disillusionment. Reason became irrational as existentialist philosophers questioned objectivity and wondered about the personal and subjective motives involved in all human actions. Likewise, biblical hermeneutics acknowledged its presuppositions, opening itself to new ways of reading. From its exclusive quasi-scientific interest in historical evidence, biblical hermeneutics moved into two interpretive paradigms by the late 1970s: literature and the social sciences. The literary approach aims at bringing clarity to the biblical text by studying its narrative, plot, and linguistic structure, while the social-scientific approach uncovers the possible meanings of the text by using contemporary sociological and anthropological models of Mediterranean societies that somehow resemble those from the biblical world.

In the meantime, the latent seeds of a new interpretive paradigm began to germinate. With the collapse of the world's empires and the decolonization of the Indian subcontinent and Africa after the Second World War, the hopes of those struggling for liberation and justice were strengthened. During the 1960s and 1970s the vast majority of colonized countries gained their freedom from the imperial powers. Groups around the world fought their oppression and Latin American liberation theology emerged as a prophetic voice in the world. Those once silenced found their voice in the civil rights movements. African Americans, Chicanos/as, women's coalitions, gays and lesbians, as well as other minority groups became visible to the world. By the decade of the 1980s, a radical shift emerged in the interpretive paradigm of ideological criticism/cultural studies in biblical scholarship. Interpreters of the Bible from decolonized countries and minority groups shifted their focus from the text itself to the reader of the text. Ideological criticism focused the attention of biblical scholars on the complexities of a postmodern world and the resulting interconnectivity of reading practices with culture.

Just as the biblical text is the product of its historical context, so too do the readers read from specific social locations. This paradigm has at its core the presence of a socially and culturally positioned reader, who acknowledges her/his subjectivity and reads with a well-identified agenda. It is within this paradigm that the methodologies of Latina/o biblical hermeneutics have their roots.

Latina/o Methodologies: Reading in a Postmodern World

Postmodern and postmodernism are terms that are sometimes used carelessly. A. K. M. Adam provides one definition in saying that "Postmodern thought is not one thing. Indeed, most postmodern thinkers would argue that it cannot and should not be just one thing: most varieties of postmodernism strike out against the very notions of identity and unity in one way or another" (1995:1). Although distinct from postmodernism, a related methodology that some Latina/o biblical scholars find helpful is postcolonialism. One definition of postcolonialism is given by Simon During, who states that it is "the need, in nations or groups which have been victims of imperialism, to achieve an identity uncontaminated by universalist or Eurocentric concepts and images" (1995:125). Fernando Segovia develops a "postcolonial optic" for reading the Bible by which he means that initially one needs to explore the attributes of colonial power and presence within the biblical texts themselves. Second, postcolonial reading of biblical texts involves an appraisal of colonial presence in the history of the interpretation of any given text. Third, using a postcolonial optic means a consideration of the perspective of, in Segovia's words, "the children of the colonized" in understanding biblical texts (2000:119–32).

Latina/o Readers and Social Location: Reading from Ourselves

Beside the common threads of language and ethnicity, one of the strongest bonds that the people of Mexican, Puerto Rican, Cuban, Central and South American heritages share in the U.S. is their experience of otherness. The experience of being an "alien" in a foreign land permeates the theological and exegetical work of most Latina/o scholars in the past twenty-five years. This otherness has been theorized, among other things, as a hermeneutical lens, a theological model, an entry point to the biblical text, a reading strategy, or a philosophical stance. What seems paradoxical about Latina/o otherness in the U.S., however, is the role reversal that occurred in the history of the community. The U.S. is a nation founded by "others," the European "aliens" or "outcasts" who, in turn, invaded and cast out the indigenous from their land. Like the Mexicans annexed to the U.S. with the seized territory from Mexico, some of those natives are now considered to be "others"–outsiders who come to conquer and dispossess the descendants of the conquerors.

Although we can trace the experience of otherness as a common thread, it is an experience of social location that each group (and individual) lives differently, and it is interconnected to the political relationship between their countries of origin and the U.S. The political and geographical nexus between Mexico, Puerto Rico, and Cuba in relation to the U.S. have directly influenced the way in which the three largest constituencies of the Latina/o community in the U.S. read the Bible. By and large, the hermeneutical lenses used to interpret the biblical text by scholars from these three groups are in direct correlation to the political and geographical history of their countries and the U.S. foreign policy. Among Mexicans, for example, the relationship of unequal neighbors has developed an otherness that speaks of hybridity and miscegenation. Mexicans crossing the frontier do not see themselves as invaders because they know that their national territory was stolen from them by their powerful northern neighbor. They cross the border with a confidence that somehow they are claiming some justice for their stolen territory, despite the fact that they are considered "other" (Guardiola-Sáenz 2002b:82-86). Similarly, Puerto Ricans live on an island caught in the geo-political convenience of the United States. The dominant U.S. wants to possess the island without giving Puerto Ricans the full privileges of citizenship. Thus, Puerto Ricans living on the island are kept on the sidelines in terms of political and economic marginalization, creating another sense of otherness.

Cubans are in a different situation because their island has resisted domination, although the U.S. occupies the best natural harbor, Guantánamo, and exercises its power through tightening the longstanding embargo. This show of force feeds the feeling of diaspora and marginality in those of Cuban descent living in the U.S. because of their inability to return to their homeland due to the political tension between the two countries. And Latinas/os from other parts of South America and the Caribbean experience similar feelings of being exiled. For this reason, Segovia, among other scholars, insist that to read the Bible from the perspective of Hispanics is to read the Scriptures with a profound sense of "otherness" (1995:57–73). This reading legitimizes alternative perspectives that cross traditional boundaries and social categories, as it radically challenges what the dominant culture has labeled normative truths.

Latina/o Hermeneutics: Metaphors and Reading Strategies

This study addresses metaphorical hermeneutics rather than a specific hermeneutic because justice cannot be done to all the developing models and options among Latinas and Latinos in this limited space. Indeed, it is important to emphasize that the community is more complex than the generic term "Latina/o" that we use. Our history includes incredible extremes: from those who live in ostentatious wealth to those who live in dehumanizing poverty; from the illiterate to the well-respected intellectuals; from atheists to famous spiritual leaders; from the *barrio* on the periphery of society to the penthouse in the center of economic power. Certainly this may add to a stereotype of Latinos; but, nevertheless, to escape exclusive generalizations it is necessary to recognize these elements. Those Latinas and Latinos who participate in academic discourse characterize all of this complex reality.

Moreover, reading strategies for the Bible are not limited to Latina/o academics. At the grassroots level of the everyday (*lo cotidiano*) the Bible is read, believed, and acted upon in tangible ways. As Loida Martell-Otero states, "[W]hen U.S. Hispanics/Latinas read Scripture, it is not with a fundamentalist agenda. We read Scripture believing in God's promises of salvation and hope. We believe in Emmanuel–that God is with us" (2001:32).

It is difficult to speak of a Latina/o perspective that does justice to the complexity and richness of our community and its distinct elements. In this article, I have sampled the spectrum of the community, beginning from the perspective of Latina/o academics that read the Bible as Latinas and Latinos. How we read the text as Latinas/os accompanies the experiences we have had as our diverse cultures come into contact with the reality of life in the United States. In fact, every reading of the Bible emerges from the particularity of the reader's experiences even though some are candid about it and others seem oblivious to the impact of identity and particularity. We construct our reading strategies from what we experience, from our environment, and through our understanding of reality. Our experiences become the filters of all the information we receive, including the information we glean from reading the Bible. Latina/o biblical interpretation is intrinsically related to the ways in which we experience our identity in this country.

It should not be surprising that when Hispanics read the Bible from the perspective of our *lucha* (struggle) in the everyday, since those who first heard the gospel message also lived on the margins. The early church read the Bible on the edges of the Roman Empire, while Latinas/os read on the edges of the U.S. empire. In *Galilean Journey* (1983), Virgilio Elizondo developed reading the Bible from the perspective of *mestizaje* as a Mexican American priest. Meanwhile, Justo González, a Cuban Methodist, emphasizes marginality and social location as he draws on the common strains between different groups who discussed Latino/a perceptions of the Bible (1996b). In another Cuban perspective, Ada María Isasi-Díaz constructs a *mujerista* approach that asserts that when we use Bible stories they become ours–our need of these stories for our survival takes precedence over the text itself. The starting point, according to Isasi-Diaz in *En la Lucha* (1993), is the situation at hand and not the text; we read biblical stories as stories of struggle and survival. A different hermeneutic is expressed in *Christ Outside the Gate* by the late Puerto Rican scholar, Orlando Costas (1982), in which he outlines a hermeneutic using viewpoints from the periphery and the underside of society. With a different twist, Puerto Rican scholar Efraín Agosto draws on postcolonial analysis in discerning the urban context of Pauline churches situated on the edge of the Roman Empire. He applies this reading to the postcolonial realities of Hispanic/Latino churches, especially in terms of leadership development (Agosto 1995:103–122). Martell-Otero explores the Latino/a hybrid cultural identity and location through the metaphor of *sato/sata* ("mixed breed" or "mongrel") because the word "catches well the spirit with which terms such as *mestizaje* and *mulatez* were first proposed. It represents well the experience of many U.S. Hispanics/Latinas who live in the United States. They are stereotyped, rejected, insulted. They are relegated to the periphery of society, to the bottom rung" (2001: 8–9).

Conclusion: Scripture Reading as Border Crossing

A test is never read in a vacuum. Every time that a reader encounters a text, a cultural process is set in motion. The Scriptures, as a hybrid product with different sides and positions, are also the site where multiple meanings converge. Latinas/os' identity is shaped not only by the limits of the borders that surround them but also by the political ramifications of crossing those borders. Although there is no single Latina/o biblical hermeneutic, it can be said that U.S. Latinas/os approach the Scriptures from their U.S. borderlands experience. The biblical text marks the encounter of multiple borders–the sociohistorical context of production, the context of consumption, and the social location of the reader–that constantly merge with the Bible to produce what I call a hybrid text, a crossroads-text (Guandiola-Sáenz 2002a:133). This crossroads-text has no fixed meaning, but infinite meanings. In the end, the experience of reading ths Bible and producing meaning for ourselves as Latinas/os is a process of border crossing, of negotiating territories where borders are crossed, not to invade or oppress, but to invite and create liberating spaces for all.

CHAPTER 10

Ethics

■ ISMAEL GARCÍA

Introductory Comments

For Hispanics, ethics and morality deal with serious matters, matters pertaining to improving the quality of human life, honoring the respect and recognition due to human dignity, and with matters pertaining to the creation and preservation of communities that are caring. Latino/a ethics is characterized both by its relational and communal nature. Ethics is understood as the art of unveiling how our actions and goals affect what we do and who we become, and how our doing and being affect the life possibilities of those with whom we share our lives. The moral and ethical task is more comprehensive than the mere formulation of rules and laws that guide and regulate our actions (Cortese, 1982:353–66).

Hispanic Americans who are members of the Christian community of faith underscore the seriousness of morality by claiming it as being intrinsically intertwined with theological claims and the spiritual formation of the faithful. Thus our feelings, the manner in which we organize our daily practice and institutionalize our habits, as well as the way we rationally understand and justify that which we uphold as good and right, are shaped by ultimate convictions about God's nature and purpose for humanity as revealed in Jesus the Christ. Hispanic Christians[1]

---

[1]From a marginalized perspective, see the study by De La Torre, *Doing Christian Ethics from the Margins,* 2004b.

recognize that, while related, the ethical and the theological are relatively autonomous from each other. Theology cannot be reduced to the ethical dimension of life, and ethics is not merely an appendage or a mere "application" of theological claims and postulates. Ethics and morality are seen as embodying a universal intent and, as such, they speak beyond the boundaries of the church and address the world at large, pinpointing those forms of actions, relations, and character traits that make up the core of human integrity and dignity.

One can identify a number of shared concerns in the moral constructs of Hispanic ethics: (1) The importance of being aware of the context out of which one reflects ethically. This has led many Hispanic ethicists to preface their work with brief biographical sketches and descriptions of their social locations. (2) The shared conviction that morality should be at the service of improving the human condition. Particular attention is given to matters pertaining to social justice and making right those relationships that have been distorted by the dynamics of colonialism, economic exploitation, and political and cultural domination. (3) An expressed commitment to the reconstitution of the human subject, especially with the liberation of those social groups that have been denied full participation in the cultural, religious, political, and economic decision-making centers that affect their lives in significant ways. (4) A shared anthropological vision that defines the human in his or her capacity to become subjects capable of responsible participation within all spheres of life. (5) Finally, the epistemological commitment of privileging the point of view of the powerless and oppressed. These shared traits provide the "for whom and the why" ethics and morality exist. They also define the core of Hispanic ethics as moving between a countercultural prophetic voice and a culturally affirming ethics.

The Loci of Hispanic American Moral Reasoning

In spite of the presence of common motifs, not all Latino/as engage the ethical task in the same way. Given the unique historical experience and the particular contextual character of Hispanic American ethics, it ought not come as a surprise that their ethics have an inevitable pluralistic character. For example, some Hispanics opted to come to the United States and felt welcomed and supported by the dominant society and its way of life. Others came as refugees and were less inclined to "melt" into the new cultural milieu. Some Hispanics, whether migrants or refugees, were welcomed and supported while others have had to endure painful and demeaning forms of racial and cultural discrimination and many other obstacles that have made it difficult for them to improve the quality of their lives. Furthermore, differences of social class, educational history, regional location, gender and life-style options also impact the manner in which Latino/as engage in moral analysis. Latino/as have tended to work their moral and ethical concerns out of three distinct loci: the cultural sphere, the social sphere and the political sphere.[2]

The Cultural Sphere

At present, the dominant concerns of Hispanic American ethics have been the questions of cultural identity, respect for differences, and the quest for recognition.[3] From this perspective, it is morally imperative that one seek to consolidate and forward the distinct history and cultural identity of one's group. The preservation and enrichment of one's language, a positive attitude toward one's racial makeup, and the valuing of one's customs and traditions become the first order of business. This results in an ethics of resistance and conservation before the perceived threats of the forces of cultural assimilation; the multiple stereotypes that devalue the sense of beauty, truth, and goodness that have for centuries sustained the Hispanic way of life; and the discriminatory racial practices so pervasive within the United States. It is also an ethics of creative newness and an affirmation of new possibilities. Beyond the struggle to preserve language and traditions is a recognition of the fluidity of all culture and the need to be open to new influences as well as the need to influence the dominant culture. It is recognized that the new generations of Latino/as will redefine their cultural makeup in light of their living experiences in a new land, redefining their identities. Still it is important that they do so in ways that, while being faithful to their new experiences, build on the past that sustains them as a people. The term *Hispanic* itself points to a creative merger of Spanish-speaking people from Latin America, the Spanish Caribbean, and Central America who, having lived in the United States, have found they have more things in common than what makes them different, and that they can recreate themselves culturally in ways that fit who they are as a people. They also have discovered that they are not just consumers of the dominant culture but that they too have something to offer for the dominant culture to emulate, such as a renewed value of community life, family, and the importance of Sabbath keeping and creative leisure as part of a strong work ethic.

Some of the shortcomings of this kind of ethics are embedded within its strengths. A strong sense of loyalty and commitment to one's cultural bearing group, as well as the group's quest to preserve its cultural

---

[2]The three loci described have to be understood as ideal types. As abstract constructions they aim to describe the main traits of the type at hand. In doing so they omit nuances and exceptions that are part of the actual options authors make. As such it is best to see how a given author fits a type or, better still, how an author appropriates and mixes the types.

[3]By far the most influential person dealing with the ethos of Hispanic cultural identity is Father Virgilio Elizondo; see his *Galilean Journey*, 1983 and 2000a, and *The Future Is Mestizo*, 1988.

identity, nurtures separatist attitudes that promote social division, which devalues the recognition and inclination that we, as members of society, must care for the common good and the quality of life of society as a whole. This leads to forms of isolationism and provincialism with negative moral consequences expressed in defensive attitudes limiting reception of creative and constructive critique other groups can offer. Refusal to listen to creative cultural critiques contribute to the perpetuation of the inequality, discrimination, and impoverished life possibilities of many within the Hispanic community. This culturally deft attitude has resulted in many Hispanics giving minimum consideration to the various ways elements of our culture devalue, discriminate, and injure the life possibilities of Hispanic homosexuals, women, and people of African and indigenous descent. Finally, in the zeal to advocate and give priority to the needs of one's group over the whole of society, this perspective is also in danger of practicing injustices similar to the ones it so eloquently denounces, that is, being insensitive to the legitimate claims and needs of those it identifies as "other."

Normatively speaking, this perspective uplifts equality as a basic moral value. Equality understood in terms of equality of worth and self-respect is seen as foundational for its understanding and commitment to justice, which it defines in terms of fairness. Justice demands that all character-forming groups have access to those goods and services required for people to take full advantage of the opportunities society provides and to be able to compete on an equal footing for those privileged social positions available within society. Justice requires that educational opportunities, support, and job-training programs that contribute to self-worth, communal stability, and participation in the marketplace be provided for the least advantaged. This perspective is egalitarian in the sense of keeping social inequalities within reasonable limits.

Freedom is understood as the capacity of establishing meaningful relationships with others for the sake of mutual self-advantage. In this perspective, justice is related to love and emphasizes mutuality more than self-sacrifice. It is suspicious of any notion of love that only stresses self-sacrifice, because it smacks of being overly patient with injustice. Power and empowerment are also central values that allow for each culture-bearing group to be able to negotiate life with others from a position of relative equal strength. This point of view sets a hierarchical order of values in the following way: First comes equality, which sustains justice as fairness, which in turn allow all citizens the more or less equal opportunity to engage in meaningful choices. Justice, as the proper balance between freedom and equality, empowers people to remain active citizens and define and live in light of their convictions, producing a sustainable social order that provides the conditions for human flourishing.

The Political Sphere

While matters of power have been a constant concern of Hispanic American ethics, power has received less attention than matters pertaining to cultural identity and social advancement. Hispanics have been less explicit about looking at the moral institution of life from within the political sphere.[4] The dominant consideration within this perspective is the production and distribution of power in all its forms. The moral imperative aims at the political empowerment of all members of the political community and not just of Latino/as. From this more inclusive point of view, if it is true that power corrupts and absolute power corrupts absolutely, it follows that lack of power also corrupts because it allows those who have power to oppress and dominate the weak. The focus is more on matters pertaining to the common good than on just the interest of a given social group, fitting the need of group identity in ways that improve the quality of life of the whole community. It privileges the concerns of the powerless but with the intention of freeing the whole. While the goal is to reconfigure the present structure of power so that the interest of different members of society can be fulfilled within a structure of relative harmony, it recognizes that moral suasion is not a substitute for countervailing power.

We can mention the following reasons that account for the peripheral attention given to the political sphere: (1) The dominant emphasis Latino/as have given to matters of cultural identity result, sometimes unintentionally, in devaluing the art of compromise and the practice of solidarity with those beyond one's history-bearing group. The emphasis has weakened the sense of our need to be contributors in shaping the ethos of the whole of society and not just of our group. (2) The Hispanic American church has always suspected political life, particularly its conflict-ridden nature, its dependence on coercion and force to motivate people to do the good they are capable of doing, its reliance on balance of power over moral suasion, and its grounding in justice talk rather than on love talk. Latino/as have tended to keep the political and the religious separate; at least, they have tried not to mix them within the same space and time. (3) There has been much resistance to admitting the inner racial and gender prejudices and homophobia that are part of our cultural heritage, and therefore less inclination to create coalitions with gays, lesbians, women, African Americans, and other people of color even when doing so would be to our mutual benefit.

Hispanic women, whose moral focus many times concentrates on matters pertaining to gender concerns, have been the most politically

---

[4]For one of the most creative articulations of this perspective see Valentín, *Mapping Public Theology*, 2002.

minded ethicists among Latino/as.[5] They have been quite intentional in emphasizing the centrality of economic analysis, racial dynamics, and how globalization delimits the life possibilities of most of humanity; they also have understood how the imagery of gender used in political language plays a significant role in determining who can and who cannot have an efficient public voice. They have realized how the language of gender defines the parameters of power relationships, establishing who is equal and who is subordinate. On this basis, they also have understood how changes in the organization of power affect the manner in which we understand and approach gender roles. These political insights are among the enduring methodological contributions to Latino/as ethics. Hispanic women have also stressed the importance of ethics being done from and for the sake of uplifting people in their everyday struggles.

Hispanics who have emphasized the centrality of the political sphere argue for overcoming all forms of provincialism and isolationism and stress the importance of developing a public language and a vision that proclaim justice for the whole of society. In their view, the main purpose of transforming the social structure and its configuration of power is precisely to create conditions that sustain participatory justice. In this vision, to be human is to be an active participant in all matters that affect one's life. Politics, as the capacity to speak unique words and engage in creative actions in the company and with the support of others, takes priority over mere economic well-being. The creation of public spaces to enhance the opportunity for more encounters among different social groups takes priority over the capacity of consumption. One of our main dangers today is the danger of nihilistic attitudes and apathy toward our shared public life generated by the current state of affairs. Ultimately, politics ought to be defined and structured in terms of practices that promote the possibility of creating a healthy public realm in which we find multiple occasions to listen to one another and serve one another's needs.

A hierarchy of values uplifts the centrality of power defined in terms of the capacity we have to make others act in light of self-interest and vision of what ought to be. The empowerment of citizens who understand themselves as active and vigilant agents of the common good is the necessary and sufficient condition for justice. Empowerment is not an end in itself, but rather has as its reason for being the enhancement of justice. Justice, in this perspective, entails more than formal or procedural fairness. Justice is goal-oriented, seeking to secure a shared social vision, a sense of the common good and, within this context, the realization of the relative well-being of all social groups. Justice entails equality defined not as the attempt merely to control inequalities, but in the more radical

---

[5]See the groundbreaking work of Isasi-Díaz, *En la Lucha/In the Struggle* 1993; Aquino, "Theological Method," 1999; and Alcoff, "Latina/o Identity Politics," 1999.

sense of bridging those inequalities that prevent us from recognizing each other as equal members of the community with the same access to those centers through which a community can define its shared life and determine its common destiny. Equality sustains freedom with both the capacity to self-initiate and the solidarity and commitment to serve others. Justice is also related to love so that both these values promote mutuality and enable recognition that humanly and politically we must be inclined to undertake some level of self-sacrifice for the well-being of the whole. Political concerns must include the interest of others with the intention of creating conditions for all to have a meaningful shared life. For example, when I vote, I should ask not only what is good for me but also what will be of benefit for the poor so that a social order that is just and also sustainable will emerge.

The Social Sphere

Within this sphere, the moral imperative is to work for the creation of a network of well-organized autochthonous institutions that advocate and serve the needs of the Hispanic American community while accelerating the process of social integration into mainline society.[6] Most of the problems Latino/as confront are precisely due to the fact that they lack that institutional base through which they can exercise power effectively and in an ordered manner. A strong institutional base will empower Hispanics to negotiate with other institutions from a position of strength and will forward the much-needed balance of power that will allow our voices to be heard and our interests attended. Most importantly, it encourages the virtue of self-reliance and the spirit of taking personal and social responsibility for the well-being of the community and of one's group. This perspective is suspicious of the political state and takes pains to denounce the various forms of dependency that result from relying on state-sponsored aid.

Social institutions play a significant role in structuring the practices and habits of a community and are central to the process of character formation. Therefore, this perspective encourages us to create a plethora of voluntary associations, such as churches, community organizations, social clubs, and private institutions, all of which provide a relative autonomous space. These voluntary associations allow individuals and groups to live in light of those self-given values that give meaning to their

---

[6]Justo L. Gonzalez presents one of the most creative and progressive expressions of this point of view. Dr. Gonzalez's prolific work makes him a clear example of how one author can encompass all spheres. We include him within the cultural sphere for his passion of creating a number of institutions, among them the following: The Association of Hispanic Theological Educators (AETH), The Hispanic Theological Institution (HTI), and the Hispanic Summer Program (HSP), all of which have made significant contributions in forwarding theological education among Hispanics. For his social and religious point of view see his *Mañana*, 1990.

lives and provide a context for intimacy, recognition, the internalization of values, and, thus, for character formation. This perspective proclaims that human emancipation takes place through a process of gradual reforms of the present system and that our democratic institutional base is what keeps our society open to change. Given the reality of discrimination that Hispanics confront in their day-to-day lives, it is important that Latino/as remain vigilant and make institutions responsive to and inclusive of their interests.

This perspective also gives priority to the moral renewal of persons over the transformation of social institutions. Change takes place by putting people of high moral character in positions of social responsibility. The formation and conversion of the moral agent are the necessary and sufficient requirement for social transformation. Hispanics need to assume greater power, but it is imperative that power be carefully structured and institutionalized. Power is suspect and dangerous, and the more concentrated the power, the more dangerous it becomes, because it can lead to domineering and oppressive behaviors. Power must be distributed widely so that it enhances the possibility for more social groups to forward their interests and live in light of their vision of the good life. This point of view also allows for greater reliance on moral suasion and rational persuasion as ways to enact change and negotiate a common life together and rejects the use of coercion and countervailing power to achieve goals.

The configuration of values in this perspective identifies social order as the primordial moral good because all other personal and social goods are dependent on the existence of a well-structured society. Order enables us to enjoy freedom, from chaos and insecurity, as well as freedom to realize our conceptions of the good life. Freedom defined as self-initiation means to enjoy the right of not having others intervene, especially not the political state. Justice is defined in pure procedural terms: as long as people act voluntarily and freely, the result of their mutual dealings is just. As long as we are free, we will find the best way to improve our well-being. The priority given to freedom and the commitment to self-reliance limit the commitment to social equality. Justice allows for inequality while it rejects forced equality.

Concluding Remarks

The main moral challenge that Hispanics confront today is precisely that of being able to work in concert for the well-being of their community in spite of their differences. Working for the promotion of our cultural identity, the political empowerment of our community, and moral autochthonous and autonomous social institutions are worthy goals. An even more promising possibility is to recognize that we can define limited projects that are part of our shared concern and that we are able to work for in common. In this sense, we need to develop the skill of coalition building called for by those who work within the political sphere and co-opt the assistance of groups within and outside the community to bring them about.

Such a task might provide the occasion for us to develop more fully and to be more intentional in sharing with the church and with the whole of society elements of the spirituality that is intrinsic to the Hispanic way of life—a spirituality that emphasizes the importance of respecting human dignity in our mutual dealings and undertakings, the sense of ritual and celebration as intrinsic to a healthy work ethic, the centrality of community and family life as intrinsic concerns of our choice making and goal setting, and the reverence due to that transcendent source of being that infuses our life with meaning and purpose and that calls us to enhance the good.

CHAPTER 11

Sin

■ DAVID CORTÉS-FUENTES

Introduction

When we try to talk about sin from a Hispanic perspective many questions come to mind. Questions such as, *what is sin?, what is a Hispanic?,* and *what are the distinctive perceptions about sin that distinguish a "Hispanic" perspective from any other?* Finding answers to these questions is a difficult enterprise. As it will be seen in this chapter, different Hispanic theologians approach the topic of sin from a variety of methodological and theological perspectives. Consistent in Hispanic reflection on sin is the continuous reference and reflection on the Bible as a fundamental and foundational source of theological reflection and understanding. In addition, Hispanic/Latino theological discussion about sin is informed by the daily experiences of the people in their struggle for freedom and justice. It will be shown that Hispanic discussion about sin is both a biblically oriented enterprise in which the Bible is read as a source of understanding, and a theologically informed reflection guided by liberationist perspectives grounded in the historical experience of the people.

No Hispanic/Latino scholar will claim that his or her understanding and perspective of sin are independent from the perspectives and understanding of other Christians from different faith traditions. Hispanic American theological reflection and understanding of sin is an ecumenical enterprise anchored in a collaborative dialogue between Roman Catholics and different expressions within the Protestant denominations. Furthermore, Hispanic theological understanding of sin is deeply rooted in the experience of a socially and economically disenfranchised people. Their historical experiences as an ethnic minority and their historical roots relate more to people in the other lands of the Americas. Hispanic theological reflection on sin is a socially engaged and informed enterprise. From these three fundamental observations we can try to propose and summarize a Hispanic perspective on sin that is biblically grounded, ecumenically engaged, and contextually informed by the Hispanic experience within the North American context.

Biblical Perspectives

Old Testament. In the Bible (both New and Old Testament) a number of terms in the original languages are translated as "sin." They have both religious and social connotations. In the Old Testament the most common word translated as "sin" is from the root *ht'* which occurs more than 590 times. The basic meaning of the word, in its common use, can be understood as "to be mistaken, to be found deficient or lacking, to be at fault, to miss a specified goal or mark."[1] For instance, Judges 20:16 tells of seven hundred left-handed men from the tribe of Benjamin who could sling a stone at a hair and not miss. Proverbs 19:2 talks about a person who misses the way, and Job 5:24 speaks of a person who misses nothing.

According to Robin C. Cover the root *ht'* also carries with it a social or ethical sense expressing the ethical failure of "one person to perform a duty or common courtesy for another, as in the failure of a vassal to pay tribute to his overlord (2 Kgs. 18:14; cf. Gen. 31:36; 43:9; 44:32; Ex. 5:16; Judg. 11:27)."[2] But the meaning of the root *h '* is not limited to the common idea of missing something or the ethical ideal of social responsibility. For instance, 1 Samuel 2:25 says that a person can sin against another and against the Lord. In both instances the word for "sin" is the same. In the Old Testament this word takes a theological sense when the offense is committed against God. In Genesis 13:13, for example, the people of Sodom are described as "sinners against the LORD." The understanding of the root *h '* as "sin" is clear when the offense is committed against God or in the context of religious responsibilities. The Old Testament contains many regulations whose violation are considered "sin." If a Nazirite enters in contact with a dead body (even accidentally) he was required to offer an expiatory offering for his "sin" (Num. 6:9–11).

Another term in the Old Testament that is translated as "sin" comes from the root *ps'*, which occurs about 135 times. The word describes the behavior of the person who willfully and knowledgeably violates a norm

---

[1]See Freedman, *Anchor Bible Dictionary,* vol. 6, s.v. "Sin," "Sinners," by Robin C. Cover.
[2]Ibid.

or regulation. In many instances the word refers to political rebellion or defiance of the political institution, as the translation "to revolt" is used in 1 Kings 12:19 and 2 Kings 1:1. In the Old Testament this political connotation of the word is applied to the religious sphere and interpreted as rebellion of the people or individuals against God (Ex. 23:21; 1 Kings 8:50; Job 7:21; Psalm 5:10; Isa. 1:2; Jer. 3:13; Hos. 7:13; 8:1; Ezek. 37:23).

The third important term for "sin" in the Old Testament is from the root *'wn,* generally translated as "iniquity," "guilt," and "punishment," among others. The word occurs about 229 times in the Old Testament. In contrast to the previous two root-words, according to Robin C. Cover, "the root *'wn* is a deeply religious term, almost always being used to indicate moral guilt or iniquity before God."[3] Many other words in the Old Testament are used to indicate the concept of sin. As we can see, many of these terms do not have an exclusive religious meaning. On the contrary, the religious and theological meaning of the concept of sin seems to be derived from the social and political sphere. "Sin," as the Old Testament understands it, is not limited only to the personal offense against the divine, but also includes a broad range of relationships and social transactions such as the political, the interpersonal, as well as the religious.

New Testament: As with the Old Testament, there are several words that can be translated as "sin" in the New Testament. These words reflect, in many instances, a continuation of the Old Testament's understanding of sin, as well as the particular emphasis Christian communities understanding of sin. The most common word for "sin" in the New Testament is *hamartia.* It carries almost the same range of meanings of the root *ht'* and many other words in the Old Testament. In Greek nonbiblical literature the word *hamartia* and its cognates designate any kind of error, such as missing the mark with the javelin, or doing something wrong against others, or committing a mistake. In general religious terms the word *hamartia* represents a life that is oriented in opposition or disregard to the will of God. The early Christian preaching understood sin as the rejection of the message about Jesus. Sin is also understood in a broader sense than the actions or lack of actions of individuals. In the New Testament "sin" is understood also as a power that enslaves people (Rom. 5–7).

A biblical perspective of sin, then, should do justice to both the personal and nonpersonal character of sin. Sin is the actions (or lack of them) of the people that miss the goal of the will of God as well as a cosmological power that overcomes the will of the people and enslaves humans against their will. Sin, as an action and as a condition, provides the Hispanic theologian a tool to understand social and religious realities. Several Hispanic theologians echo this double sense of sin as both the

---

[3]Ibid.

actions of the people and as the institutional power that not only is sinful but also enslaves the powerless in a situation needing of redemption.

Hispanic Theologians' Observations

Several Hispanic/Latino theologians have inquired into the topic of sin in recent publications. For instance, David Traverso Galarza in 1997 proposed a discussion of sin with a special focus on a *Latino radical evangelical tradition.* According to Traverso Galarza, a Latino perspective on sin emphasizes that "sin is a reality, a force that delivers death and destruction to countless numbers of persons and communities daily. The social, institutional, structural, systemic as well as personal dimensions of sin require our attention and priorities. If sin is integral, then the dimensions of individual *and* corporate, of social *and* religious, of academic *and* practical are all part of the mix. No one piece, emphasis, or dimension has a monopoly on our attention and response" (1997:119).

This perspective emphasizes the importance of paying attention to the social reality of the people when talking about sin. Social realities such as the "abhorrent conditions of millions or U.S. Latinos who experience morally and spiritually devastating economic impoverishment, political paralysis, appalling educational dropout rates, or inferior housing and employment situations...Sin as a radical ailment with deadly consequences requires a *radical* or fundamental solution" (Ibid.:120). Nevertheless, this perspective on sin as "a radical ailment with deadly consequences" is not the final word for David Traverso Galarza. The Hispanic/Latino perspective on sin also includes a vision of the hopeful mission of the church that proclaims a risen Christ who has "challenged and defeated sin, death, and oppression in the world (Col. 2:15)" (Ibid.:122).

Orlando Espín offers other insights into the discussion of Hispanic/Latino discussions on sin and grace. He believes that any theological reflection and discussion set claim to be Latino/a should take seriously "into account the impact of culture, gender, and social position," (1999:121), acknowledging and incorporating in its methodology the real, daily life situations of Latinos/as The social location of poverty and gender discrimination and second-class social status is the context in which Latinos/as "experience grace and sin, and elaborated their hope for salvation" (Ibid.:125). In their experience of *lo cotidiano*, Latinos/as also experience grace in the form of the conviction that "God is on their side, fighting their battles with them, suffering their pains and humiliations with them, in solidarity with them in their struggles for dignity and justice, and empowering them to overcome the sin that seeks to overwhelm them in society and family" (Ibid.:126).

Ismael García emphasizes the experiential character for the understanding of sin among Hispanic/Latinos. According to García "sin manifests itself within social practices, including the accepted laws and moral regulations that allow some to live and prosper at the expense of others. Laws that allow the powerful to accumulate land and to move their centers of production outside communities that depend on them to survive, are means of sin in spite of their legality and accepted morality" (1997:137). In other words, García's statement emphasizes the structural nature of sin as experienced by the Hispanic/Latino communities. This perception of sin transcends the legalistic traditional approach and challenges the dominant and controlling powers. Sin is also viewed from the perspective of the victims of the legalized sin in the structures and social institutions that perpetuate their power and oppression sanctioned by these laws.

Elsa Tamez offers a different, but complementary, perspective of sin from a Latin American perspective in her book *The Amnesty of Grace.* Tamez's perspective is summarized by her dual understanding of sin. First, sin is understood in a traditional way as an offense or transgression of God's law. Second, Tamez proposes an understanding of sin from the perspective of its victims. From this point of view, the understanding and experience of sin are to be defined not only as religious acts of those who commit sin, but also from the concrete, social and historical realities of the victims of sin. For instance, exploitation, abuse, and murder are examples of actions that clearly are considered sinful in the biblical and traditional Christian perspectives. But the discussion of the meaning of these sins lacks the consideration of the experience of the exploited, the abused, and the murdered. The perspective of these victims of sin is the daily experience of the poor, exploited, and the victims of a variety acts of violence in the Hispanic/Latino communities and in Latin American countries.

Elsa Tamez advances another important aspect of the Hispanic/Latino perspective of sin. Putting it in abstract terms, the sins of the victims are not equal to the sins of the perpetrators. Accordingly, "the poor, whose sins cannot be compared to those of the powerful, are those who more consistently recognize their faults. Injustice becomes more obvious when it is committed against those who, with great frequency, remember that they are sinners" (1993:21). From this perspective, the struggle against sin becomes a struggle for the vindication and liberation of the victims of sins.

Finally, Miguel A. De La Torre and Edwin David Aponte also offer some insights on the Hispanic/Latino understanding and experience of sin. Echoing traditional language, they understand sin as opposition to God's purpose for creation and the responsible cause of the enslavement of human race as well as God's created order. But this traditional language is complemented by the interpretation of the consequences of sin as "alienation from God, God's community, God's creation, and God's will for each person" (2001:80). This inclusive understanding of the consequences of sin echoes the shared understanding among

Hispanic/Latino theologians of sin as a phenomenon that, more than a mere individual act, also carries cosmological as well as social consequences. In other words, "regardless of how private we may wish to keep sin, it always affects others because we are communal creatures. Hence, Hispanics maintain that sin has both an individual and a communal dimension" (Ibid.). So both the individual and communal aspects of sin are recognized and emphasized.

Common Patterns

As anyone else, Hispanic/Latino theologians are aware of the reality of sin in their lives and in the lives of the communities in which they live and serve. This reality of sin is interpreted by the theological reflection on the teachings of the scripture, both the Old and New Testaments. This theological reading of the scripture provides foundational and constant reference and serves as a continuous reminder of the biblical traditions that coined the words and charged different terms with religious and social meaning. The theological study of the biblical text is aware that the meaning of the different words is contextual, and that a single translation cannot carry the multiplicity of meaning and the possibilities of interpreting the text. Hispanic/Latino theologians are in continuous dialogue with scripture in a dynamic interaction that reads the text aware of the social location of the readers as well as the social location of the writers.

The reading and interpretation of scripture are a kind of dialectic dialogue with the daily experiences of the people (*lo cotidiano*), especially the experiences of vulnerability and victimization. Sin, from the perspective of this experience, is seen both as the concrete actions of the perpetrators of the violation of God's good will, and as the consequences of those actions, especially the painful experiences of the victims of sins. Sin is not an abstract theological term that needs to be defined according to a classical theological dictionary, but a daily experience that requires radical transformation of both the individual and the institutional (sometimes legalized) forces that cause and perpetuate the fallen condition and the lamentably consequences of sin.

A Word about Grace and Forgiveness

Hispanic/Latino theologians share the hope of Christians everywhere of *mañana,* that is, the hope and expectation that sin and suffering are not the last words of history. On the contrary the daily experience of sin is lived (and survived) by a deep faith in the Kingdom of God as a reality that is both eschatological and transcendent. In waiting for a better tomorrow (*mañana*) the Hispanic/Latin community hopes for God's grace to forgive not only its sins but also the sins of others, especially the sins of the ones responsible for its suffering. That forgiving grace is both a gift and a challenge. Forgiveness, as a gift of

God's grace, is God's eschatological amnesty. It is God's invitation and Hispanic/Latino persons' expectation that they will go and sin no more.

Because of this grace and opportunities of forgiveness Hispanic/Latino theologians can echo Ada María Isasi-Díaz's proposal for *mujerista* theology and theologians to develop methods that provide opportunities and enable everyone to speak and work for the creation of opportunities to live the fullness of life God wants everyone to have (2002:5–17). Grace and forgiveness are not only the antithesis of sin but also the needed antidote to heal and prevent the many evil consequences of sin, especially for the victims.

CHAPTER 12

Aesthetics

■ ALEX GARCÍA-RIVERA

The Sense of Beauty and the Talk of God

The relationship between aesthetics and the talk of God is crucial because the past two centuries have seen systematic theologians struggling with two serious challenges. The first came from the study of the "True." The great cultural success of scientific knowledge placed theology on guard that accurate and precise knowledge of the world could not be assumed or deduced but must be discovered. How one understands the world also influences how one sees the Divine, and theology's response to this critical challenge has been to distance itself from the True, a kind of intellectual cowardice. The other great challenge has been the exceptional suffering and violence of the past two centuries. Auschwitz, Hiroshima, and Bosnia have raised the issue of the "Good" to a seemingly insuperable challenge for both theological and humanist thought. Theologians can no longer propose tired and vacuous sentiments or horrendous and dogmatic moralism against what Marylin McCord has called "horrendous evils" (1999).

Talk of God today faces an even greater challenge than the True and the Good, posed by the sense of "Beauty." When the True and the Good fail to attract us, it is the sense of Beauty that can carry them into the imagination of our society.[1] Hans Urs von Balthasar, the Swiss

---

[1]Postmodernism has been unkind to the notion of Beauty and the limits of artistic freedom. See García-Rivera, "The End of Art," in *A Wounded Innocence,* 2003.

theologian, sounds the alarm to a great spiritual truth: It is the sense of Beauty that teaches us how to love God and our neighbor.[2] Toward this end scientific knowledge is less a means to solve the world's problems than a powerless endeavor while horrendous evils fascinate us with their cruelty instead of shocking us into loving our neighbor. It is the loss of the sense of Beauty that has made the talk of God increasingly irrelevant and morally impotent in our day.

Theology and the Arts

There has been an absence in modern times of people asking why theology should be interested in art. In the late twentieth century, theologians began to ask the question in two different contexts. One context saw the theologian von Balthasar raise the question from within a thoroughly secularized Europe, seeing more clearly than other European theologians that the problem of secularization was one with the problem of the loss of the sense of Beauty. Balthasar (2002) restored an ancient theological insight when he asserted that the only way we have of knowing God is through our senses, invoking a long theological tradition that insists that one of the ways that God is known is through Beauty. Whatever participates in Beauty is beautiful and reveals something about God. The beautiful is a means for the soul to ascend to a blissful union with God.

If Beauty is divine, then the sense of Beauty is key to knowing and loving God, and then the sense of Beauty is also key to the talk of God. In other words, the sense of Beauty is both an aesthetic and a religious experience. Today, however, we have reduced this crucial relationship between the sense of Beauty and the talk of God. The beautiful for us today has become a highly specialized type of experience, which is a mere aesthetic experience, an experience dogmatically guarded by the merchants of art, the profiteers of the elite who buy and sell works of art for their investment value rather than their beauty, and the profiteers of the masses that offer up a pale shadow of beauty in order to sell a trinket, a name, or even our souls.

The sense of Beauty, however, as a fundamental ground for the talk of God is at once an aesthetic and a religious experience, not a given or self-evident experience. The sense of Beauty is not some immediate gratification, nor the manipulation of aesthetic design principles, nor forged at Sotheby's auction block. Indeed, the sense of Beauty is not an empty imputation of "beautiful" onto some object simply because it was made by an "artist." The sense of Beauty that grounds the talk of God is more like a profound religious insight than a valuable commodity. The

---

[2]Balthasar, *Seeing the Form*, vol. 1, *The Glory of the Lord,* 2002.

sense of Beauty is found not only on museum walls but also on our knees in the church's nave, and is, at its heart, the fruit of a spiritual journey.

That such statements sound strange to the contemporary ear is the result of having separated aesthetic experience from religious experience, traced to two influential traditions in the European context. The first tradition is ancient and is first seen in the writings of Plato. Iris Murdoch wrote *The Fire and the Sun: Why Plato Banished the Artists* (1977),with a simple but profound thesis that Plato banished the artists because he felt religious experience was fundamentally different than aesthetic experience. Though Beauty is divine, the beautiful is a mere appearance. Thus Plato rails against the works of artists but strongly encourages the spiritual seeker to follow the sense of Beauty, which will reward the spiritually hungry by taking them into the sunshine of the Good.

The second tradition is modern, influenced by Immanuel Kant (1724–1804) and various modern philosophers, and has provided a powerful aesthetic paradigm. Let me call this tradition "aesthete," which tells us that aesthetic experience is radically unlike any other. Thus a work of art cannot be judged by any other standards of experience except that peculiar to art itself. One expression of this paradigm is the phrase "art for art's sake." Artists create an aesthetic experience, not a work of art. By insisting on the uniqueness of the aesthetic experience, the "aesthete" tradition has the same effect as the Platonic in that it separates aesthetic experiences from religious ones, only this time it is the aesthetic experience that is valued over the religious.

These two traditions, the "aesthete" and the Platonic, function powerfully against the theological sense of Beauty in which aesthetic and religious experience meet and become one. While the Platonic tradition tells us that the sense of Beauty can only be a religious experience, the "aesthete" tradition tells us that it can only be an aesthetic one. These two traditions oppose seeing a viable relationship between religion and the arts and discourage religious institutions and the arts from engaging each other, with the tragic result that many talented artists have avoided exploring the intersection of aesthetic and religious experience or, at least, have only done so in secret.

The other context that generated the study of the relationship between the sense of Beauty and the talk of God is Latin America. Those of us in the context of Latin or Hispanic America also asked the question of the relationship between theology and the arts, but in a very different way than European theologians. In the Latin American context, the question was raised after Vatican II when Latin American theologian Enrique Dussel started an ambitious project to document an authentic Latin American theology. It was, at first, a practical issue of where the theologian could find the documents of an authentic Latin American theology. It soon became obvious that such documents were produced mostly by and for people in positions of power.

These power brokers, whether churchmen or secular, were rarely true Latin Americans. They were, for the most part, Europeans assigned to Latin America because Latin Americans were not trusted by Europe. For this reason, Pablo Richard quotes Dussel as saying, "Everywhere we were asked: A history of Latin American theology? Does such a theology exist? How do you make a history of the nonexistent?" (Richard 1980:7). Dussel's group responded with a striking affirmation, "Yes, an authentic Latin American theology exists but it will not be found in texts of theology. An authentic Latin American theology will be found in the symbols, rites, music, images, and stories of the living, Latin American Church" (1980:12).

There exists a type of theology that can be called "living," as opposed to "textual." Living theology has its home in symbols, images, and songs. There is a theology that lives in the music, imagery, and cultural symbols of those who must live out that which textbook theology attempts to understand. I am not disparaging textbook theology, but simply saying it is insufficient in the study of a living faith. Textbook theology dissects, while living theology appreciates and provides understanding of the static parts; living theology helps us appreciate the living whole.

As I began to explore the living theology of Hispanic America by studying the symbols, imagery, and stories of the Latino community of faith (alongside a healthy dose of textbook theology!), I also began to see that the Latin American question raised the issue of the adequacy of existing theological method. Traditional method emphasizes formality and rationality. What symbols, imagery, and music have in common, however, is an aesthetic dimension. If formality and rationality give substance to textbook theology, art and aesthetics animate a living theology. Aesthetics was the key to a living theology. Symbols, images, music, poems, drama, and dance articulate a living theology and give spirit and life to textbook theology. If formality and rationality are the flesh and bones of theology, then the arts are its very breath and life.

The Caves of Lascaux

Having come to this insight, I faced another question. Where would a theologian begin to rediscover this inseparable connection between textbook and living theology, between the talk of God and the sense of Beauty? I had no further to look than my own Latin American experience. Latin American theologians have raised the world's conscience to the horrendous existence of massive poverty. What liberation theologians such as Gustavo Gutierrez in his book *Las Casas* (1993) have pinpointed is that such suffering has, as a major spiritual cause, the lack of conviction that all human persons have a precious worth and dignity. If earlier theologians strived to defend God's goodness in the light of the existence of evil, then today's theologians must strive to defend the goodness of the human in the light of remarkable cruelty and violence.

It is this second insight of Latin American theology that convinced me that a viable theological aesthetics must also be a defense of the human person and start where the Renaissance started: with the rediscovery of the dignity, nobility, and worth of the human person–in other words, a new humanism. But where would one begin to discover such a new humanism given the grave misgivings society has today about the very worth of our humanity? The answer came to me in the form of a question. Why not begin at the very beginnings of our humanity?

The question took me to France, where such a question could be answered in the caves of Lascaux. Upon entering the primary cave, the heart stops and then races as it recognizes itself in a marvelous profusion of incredibly beautiful images. Bears, horses, and rhinoceroses prance, gallop, and stand in awesome majesty before our eyes. Whoever created this incredible Beauty was one of us, a human who lived 30,000 to 50,000 years ago! This fact makes us wonder which is more impressive: that the first humans were capable of such striking Beauty, or that someone should be moved so deeply by such ancient paintings fifty thousand years after their creation!

The paintings of Lascaux reveal a marvelous human dignity, a religious humanism that is manifested in the grace and Beauty of works of art. It also asks the question. Whatever happened to the relationship between humanism and the arts? If the modern era began with a celebration of the human person, the Renaissance, then it is ending with an almost cynical conviction in an insuperable violence and cruelty woven deep into the human fabric. Theology cannot respond to this profoundly cynical conviction by merely stating dogma about the worth of the human person. Rather, theology's task is helping the world to "see" again the worth and dignity of the human person. Such a task is not possible for textbook theology, but it is the very medium of a living theology, that is, the theology found in images, music, literature, and poetry.

Such living theology must address the vision of human nature that grounds the rationale of a profound cynicism over human worth. Such rationale takes the form of either a scientific reductionism that identifies our humanity as the symptom of more basic mechanical or biological causes, or a sociological reductionism that sees our humanity as essentially violent. On the contrary, what marks us as human is not some effect of biological and physical mechanisms, nor a penchant for violence, but rather a marvelous special innocence that is uniquely human.

Innocence and the Human Person

This unique human innocence cannot be understood from a purely secular point of view. Part of the problem in "seeing" the unique innocence of the human person is a reduction in the meaning of innocence. A great part of our understanding of innocence has been shaped by the legal system and a moral philosophy that can be traced back to Kant and the Enlightenment. A certain "conceit" of moral philosophers is that experience is permanently corrupting and that innocence is a mark of moral immaturity, a type of "pre-reflective, natural state." The philosopher, Alexander Eodice, puts it, "though experience corrupts, knowledge resolves the problem of ignorance" (2001:304). Thus, innocence is seen as a mark of moral immaturity because it is also seen as a kind of ignorance, thus, not only incompatible with experience but also incompatible with learning. Such a view puts innocence at odds with both aesthetic and religious experience and places a seemingly insuperable chasm between human innocence and a theological aesthetics.

Part of the problem lies in that such a view of innocence combines two very different senses of innocence that ought to be distinguished. There is innocence with respect to actions, but there is also innocence as describing a human condition. Innocence with respect to actions lends itself to legal language and concepts. A legal sense of innocence involves the notion of being absolved from guilt of some terrible deed. Innocence as describing a human condition, on the other hand, lends itself to theological language. Such innocence describes the nature or character of a person. Unfortunately, this type of innocence is very hard to describe.

Many describe this type of innocence in terms of "lacks"–the lack of self-critical ability, the lack of knowledge, and so on. Such innocence describes the innocence of a child. It is an innocence that describes a certain kind of moral purity. No wonder, then, that so many horror movies feature children. Evil in a child is horrific precisely because the child represents a kind of innocence that is synonymous with moral purity. What is more difficult to understand is the kind of innocence that would apply to an adult. Evil in an adult no longer seems to shock us. It is expected–indeed, prescribed by many. Yet how can the horror of evil be recognized, even judged, without the presence of some innocence in the human person? Yet our day has seen the loss of the conviction that such innocence is possible. It is, I believe, the consequence of equating innocence and moral purity. Innocence, if seen as moral purity, is impossible in an adult. But, as the theological tradition informs us, there is another kind of innocence possible.

This type of innocence is capable of exciting wonder and can be recognized as something beautiful and "particularly rare and wonderful." Indeed, it is the stuff of which the beautiful is made. It is innocence, Eodice tells us, seen as virtue and as something a person has fought to achieve, gained through experience and relying on knowledge to realize itself. Moreover, such innocence is not free of guilt but is, in Eodice's words, "the difference between a person who feels guilt and…one who chooses to redeem himself through internal suffering" (2001:304). This type of innocence is only possible through the requirement of love—and love, as Ludwig Wittgenstein puts it, is that which is needed by "my heart, my soul, [but] not my speculative intelligence" (1980:33). In other words, such innocence is the stuff of a living theology.

A Wounded Innocence

What Eodice and Wittgenstein are telling us is that there is a dynamic dimension to innocence that contrasts with the static view of innocence assumed in our attitudes about human dignity and worth. This innocence, a wounded innocence, can be found in Caravaggio's painting *The Incredulity of St. Thomas.* Caravaggio offers us a profound theology of innocence through the Beauty of his art. Known for his gritty realism, Caravaggio has Jesus grasping the hand of the apostle Thomas and thrusting it deep within the wound at his side, powerfully aligning Jesus' and St. Thomas' hands to form a lance. St. Thomas' face expresses profound surprise as his finger thrusts deep into Jesus' wound. Perhaps, the surprise has to do with his unbelief. It could also be surprise at the realization that he, too, is also pierced. Indeed, St. Thomas appears to clutch his side as if he becomes aware of a wound at his side as well. And we who wince at this gritty depiction feel a wound at our side as well.

Through the means of light Caravaggio alerts us that the risen body of Jesus is not ordinary, but what the theological tradition calls the "glorious" body, different from a mortal body in that it is a newly innocent body that has come through an awesome guilt into a marvelous, wondrous innocence. In Caravaggio's painting Thomas is invited into that innocence as well. This is the meaning, I think, of Jesus' sure and guiding hand on Thomas' physical seeking finger. Jesus takes Thomas into the woundedness of Thomas' own guilt of unbelief in order to transform it, as the light shows, into a profound insight. Thomas, in touching Jesus' wound, becomes innocent again and is given a taste of the possibilities of a full humanity.

Caravaggio's *Incredulity* illustrates that our age shall find again its sense of Beauty when it begins to see again a marvelous innocence in the woundedness of our humanity. Art shall find its religious power once again when it addresses and comes forth from such a dynamic innocence. Caravaggio's *Incredulity,* however, also suggests that the sense of Beauty is something that will always be a spiritual struggle in every generation. The sense of Beauty will always be one with the talk of God and possesses what theologians call an eschatological dimension. We may never, ever experience the fullness of the sense of Beauty, but there will come a day when that fullness shall be ours. Until that day, however, the arts can serve to give us a foretaste of that day, for the power of truly religious art is to enlighten and renew in us again the core and source of our human dignity: the human capacity to achieve and bear a wounded innocence.

CHAPTER 13

Popular Religion and Spirituality

■ ANITA DE LUNA

For the inhabitants of the *frontera,* where the U.S. and Mexico share the Rio Grande, life is lived bilingually and biculturally. This experience in the margins is rich with popular religiosity. I grew up with my Presbyterian father's love of scripture and my Roman Catholic mother's popular religiosity. I remember the worn Bible and the plaster statue of Our Lady of Guadalupe sitting side-by-side on a board nailed to a corner that served as a home altar. Two other images from my childhood are vivid as well: an old trunk where my mother pasted *estampitas* (holy cards) upon the inner lid, and a large canvas and wooden 2 x 4s that served to make a very small room for my father's spiritualist/healing activities wherever our migrant trails took us. In the barrio where I lived, I grew accustomed to hearing *los Hermanos,* as we called the revivalists, who set up the tents, filling the evenings with the sounds of tambourines and festive *Aleluyas.* I remember the *rosarios de aurora* (rosaries prayed at dawn) during the month of May and the Good Friday passion plays at San Martín de Porres Parish. There is some hope that indicates that the margins dividing Latino Protestants and Catholics may become more perforated, as culture and popular religiosity show potential for being dialogue partners. In this essay I briefly examine popular religion among Latinos in light of faith practice, witness, and mission.

Defining Spirituality

Because popular religion is an expressed spirituality, experience, practice, context, and subjectivity are core to the definition and understanding of it. I will use "spirituality" to refer to those religious experiences and practices that draw us outside of ourselves to the transcendent. Wakefield begins to describe this element of spirituality when he suggests, "Spirituality describes those attitudes, beliefs, practices which animate people's lives and help them to reach out."[1] Sandra Schneider's classic definition also speaks about spirituality as that which draws us to an ultimate reality but never in self-absorption (1986:268). Philip Sheldrake offers, "Spirituality concerns how people subjectively appropriate traditional beliefs about God, the human person, creation, and their interrelationship, and then express these in worship, basic values and lifestyle." That is why Sheldrake can say, "Spirituality operates on the frontier between religious experience and inherited tradition" (1999:34–35).

Spirituality is rooted and dependent in an experience that is culturally specific and thus we will find commonalities among Latino diverse denominations. Virgilio Elizondo argues that faith is based on cultural history, and the experience of God is always framed in that particular context. Sandra Schneiders affirms the contextualization of spirituality when she says: "[S]pirituality studies not principles to be applied nor general classes or typical cases but concrete individuals: persons, works, events" (1986:268–69). Context has been the locus for theology for recent decades, milieu has become an emphasis for faith formation; however, for spirituality context and particularity have always been a constant.

In support of spirituality as praxis, Schneiders writes, "Spirituality, as the term is used today, did not begin its career in the classroom but among practicing Christians" (Ibid.:254). She further adds that:

> There is no such thing as generic spirituality or spirituality in general. Every spirituality is necessarily historically concrete and therefore involves some thematically explicit commitments, some actual and distinct symbol system, some traditional language, in short a theoretical-linguistic framework which is integral to it and without which it cannot be meaningfully discussed at all. (Ibid.:267)

Spirituality is specific in its expression. It is subjectively appropriated and, as Elizondo offers throughout most of his works, it is historically and culturally contextualized. Spirituality is dynamic and active and emerges out of experiences and practices from our daily lives or, as Ada María Isasi-Díaz and others call it, spirituality is "*lo cotidiano*," the daily experience.

---

[1] Wakefield, *Westminster Dictionary of Christian Spirituality,* 1983, s.v. "spirituality" by Gordon Wakefield.

Catholic and Protestant scholars have identified similar elements for a Latino/a or Hispanic spirituality. Eldin Villafañe, Pentecostal theologian, understands Hispanic spirituality as the expression of a complex cultural phenomenon emerging from Spanish, Amerindian, and African roots. Villafañe identifies eight characteristics for Hispanic spirituality: (1) passion, (2) personalism, (3) paradox of soul, (4) community, (5) *romerias* (pilgrimages), (6) fiesta, (7) musical elán, and (8) family (1993:112–19). Other scholars reiterate several of the categories Villafañe suggests.

Orlando Espín and Virgilio Elizondo have articulated popular religion as an expressed *mestizo* spirituality that is contextualized in the Mesoamerican indigenous and Spanish roots. In their works the characteristics of this spirituality are: (1) the centrality of the suffering Jesus, and María de Guadalupe, (2) a belief in the God of Providence, (3) an attitude of hope amidst suffering, (4) and an emphasis on relationships (Espín 1995, Elizondo 1999). The *mestizo* roots of this spirituality are further affirmed in the *Tercer Encuentro* document: "Hispanic spirituality has as one of its sources the "seeds of the Word" in the pre-Hispanic cultures" (NCCB 1995:viii, 95). The relational dimension is further accented in the same document: "The spirituality or *mística* of the Hispanic people springs from their faith and relationship with God. Spirituality is understood to be the way of life of a people, a movement by the Spirit of God, the grounding of one's identity as a Christian in every circumstance of life" (Ibid.:iv, 16). Latinos/as see spirituality as expressive of the totality of life, going beyond the individual expressions of faith. This faith practice defines communal identity. Among the scholars who have written on popular religiosity there is similarity in the descriptors of relationality, family, fiesta, suffering, aesthetics, and its indigenous roots.

In looking at the commonalities in Latino/a spirituality, there is an understanding of a fundamental difference between Catholics and Protestants in their perception of the world within spirituality. Although the division between the secular and the spiritual is lessening, Protestant thought still speaks of the individual in and out of the world. Justo González reminds us of Protestant spirituality:

> The Hispanic Christian knows well that there is a dividing line between Christian and unbeliever, which means that, once crossed, one is in the world—in an alien land. In the present North American setting, the Hispanic believer finds a church that is fused with society and culture. At the beginning, the church spread within the culture and impacted it; however currently the dividing line has become vague and diffused. No longer is there a clearly defined demarcation: People come and go from the church to the world and back again. We as Hispanics

have clichés: "the world," he went back to the "world," the influence of the world. (1996a:84–85)

Along with the differences, there is a cultural similarity in its genesis because the traditions share the same century and European context. Protestant beginnings are marked in 1517 by Martin Luther's ninety-five theses, and Hispanic Roman Catholicism has its formal genesis in 1524 with the arrival of the Franciscan missionaries in the New World.

Popular Religion and Culture

To commemorate the fifth centenary anniversary of the evangelization of the Americas, a meeting of the Latin American Bishops in 1992 was held in Santo Domingo. Out of this conference came *Santo Domingo and Beyond,* which reaffirmed a cautious commitment to popular religiosity made during earlier Roman Catholic conferences in Medellín and Puebla. The text reads:

> Popular religiosity is a privileged expression of the inculturation of the faith. It involves not only religious expressions but also values, criteria, behaviors, and attitudes that spring from Catholic dogma and constitute the wisdom of our people, shaping their cultural matrix…We must reaffirm our intention to continue our efforts to understand better and to accompany pastorally our peoples' ways of feeling and living, and of understanding and expressing the mystery of God and Christ, in order that, purified of their possible limitations and distortions, they may come to find their proper place in our local churches and their pastoral activity. (Hennelly 1993:36–86)

Spirituality in its cultural context encompasses life and its experiences. Essentially, we learn to respond to life with the signs, symbols, and meanings of the culture that surrounds us and implicitly and explicitly transmit these. Through particular cultural expressions we particularize our faith. Using the image of an iceberg, the realm of beliefs falls on the waterline so that it is influenced by both conscious and unconscious aspects. This is especially true of spiritualities that are contingent on popular religiosity, with its expressed faith that is sensorial and visible yet deeply rooted in traditions and myths and values of the people. Popular religion in its colors, sounds, scents, and varied expressions mediates the message of salvation through culture. The ancient Nahua metaphor of *Flor y Canto* speaks of how the indigenous ancestors of Latinos/as have historically used beauty and song to communicate with the Divine.

Pentecostal spirituality finds its roots in the same cultural sources as popular Catholicism. Samuel Soliván explains, "This spirituality to a great extent manifests the pietistic and Reformed heritage of Europe as well as the Catholic roots of the Spanish ancestors. These are often coupled with the spiritualist practices of our indigenous foreparents" (1996b:140). Elizabeth Conde-Frazier, elaborating on the elements of Protestant spirituality, also alludes to its roots being in Spanish mysticism. As in popular Catholicism, Conde-Frazier adds, "A distinctive emphasis of Protestant Hispanic spirituality is that it belongs to the people or the laity, as opposed to the ordained or professional clergy" (1997:140).

Religiosidad popular is made concrete in rituals and relationships. Latino/a spirituality, born out of the *mestizaje* of the sixteenth century, is manifested in the festive and tangible expressions of the sacred that pervade Latino/a life. Popular religiosity surfaces from the people and as such joins the spiritual, historical, and cultural particularity of the expressions of faith.

Praxis

A person of faith in the scriptures is one who is a follower of Jesus and thus inherits the gifts that the Father gives the Son, such as a close relationship with the Father and the gifts of healing and protection. The episodes of Jesus and his apostles' gifts of healing are many. The account of the storm at sea and similar stories are dramatic representations of how the followers of Jesus were protected by remaining close to him.

Protestantism, especially Pentecostalism, and popular Catholicism display a closeness to the sacred that is often viewed as superstitious and, according to Solivána, characteristically premodern (1996a:139). However, basic to both faith practices is a confidence that the Divine is clearly accessible. The intimacy experienced with the Divine takes a number of forms, such as the gift of tongues, exuberant joy in song and movement, emotive prayer, and—among many others—the gift of healing.

In popular Catholicism there exists a whole tradition of *curanderas/os* (healers) who live in our *barrios* with names like Doña Juanita or Don Pedrito. We are familiar with their skill, their gift, and their prayer. Often times their houses are decorated with candles, holy water, holy images, and *hierbas* (herbs), and they recite prayers, psalms, and blessings upon request. These holy women and men can take care of ailments ranging from a sprained ankle to a spell cast on an unfaithful husband. True *curanderos/as* serve as counselors, confessors, faith healers, and so much more in the barrio. Shrines have been erected to these holy men and women, such as the one found in Falfurrias, Texas, to Don Pedrito Jaramillo. They live exemplary, faith-filled, and inspiring lives that serve to draw hearts and imaginations toward the power of God. That is not to say that inauthentic *curanderos* do not exist; these are fairly easy to detect because of their self-serving practices.

Within the Catholic tradition, another display of healing and restoration to wholeness is played out significantly through the saints. Traditionally, the request for a special healing includes the wearing of the saint's garb for a length of time once the healing has occurred. Today, amulets, medals, lighting of candles, and other less conspicuous ways are used to acknowledge the favor received. *Promesas* or vows to travel to the saint's shrine and deliver a *milagro* (a small figurine that represents the body part of the healing requested), remain very popular.

The Pentecostal story is also filled with healers such as Francisco Olazábal, born at the end of the nineteenth century in Mexico into a Catholic family that became evangelical. Olazábal became Methodist and later a Pentecostal preacher and embarked on an evangelistic healing crusade. Gastón Espinoza writes about Olazábal's healing ministry:

> In New York City outside of the church, inside the church they were claiming to find relief for their aching bodies and souls. The services were run the same way every night. Olazábal walked onto center stage, led the service in a time of rousing singing, preached an evangelistic sermon, and then lifted his arms in the air and shouted "Arriba, Arriba!" to those in the balcony. He commanded them to come down to the front of the church, repent of their sins, and receive Jesus Christ as their personal savior and Lord. Thousands answered his call. After the "altar call" Olazábal began what many, perhaps most, of the people came for–divine healing. While many turned to a *curandera* or a spiritualist for healing, others turn to *El Azteca*, as Olazábal was known by his followers. (1999:604–05)

Healing, without doubt, plays a major role in both popular Catholic and Pentecostal faith practice. The many healings brought about by faith healers and *curanderos/as* are evidence that Jesus channels his Spirit through the prayer, blessing, and faith pronouncements of many of these holy persons, all of whom rise up from the people, are popularly followed, and none of which are selected by the official church. The gift of healing within the community is a dramatic witness of faith, but is not the only one.

Witness

Popular Catholic and Pentecostal spirituality clearly demonstrate that religion belongs not only in private but also in public spaces. Roberto Goizueta affirms how popular religion is a religion not only of the home but also of the church, the plaza, and the streets. Because it is both public and private, popular religion also functions as a bridge between the public life and private life, so that the dramatic representations of Good Friday at San Fernando Cathedral in San Antonio, Texas, traditionally require–and indeed the people expect–that the main streets downtown be blocked for the 3:00 p.m. Good Friday processions. The businesses are closed because the merchants have no choice since the center of activity is the public procession. The private devotion to the suffering Christ becomes public and fills the streets and the plaza in downtown San Antonio.

Another basic characteristic that Goizueta assigns to popular religion is that of relationship, noting:

> By definition religion *is* relationship, or relationality. The end of religion is nothing other than the living out of this relationality. This is nowhere more evident than in U.S. Hispanic popular Catholicism wherein the community lives out and celebrates its relationships. Popular Catholicism is the liturgical celebration of life as an end in itself, life as *praxis*. (1995:105)

The intimacy between the Divine and the individual is part of the relationship dimension of popular religion. A profound belief that the Divine distributes its gifts to the individual and expects the individual to give witness through external means motivates Protestant spirituality. This is expressed in the popular *coritos* (little hymns). Edwin David Aponte explains, "[T]hese coritos are held in positive affection and esteem by the people in their everyday devotional piety, the accompanying tunes and rhythms are passed on informally. Sometimes a well-known *corito* is given a new verse that reflects the specific life-situation of a particular congregation" (1995:61). Beyond the singing, people are moved by the testimonials, perhaps baffled by the *glossolalia,* and disturbed by the very direct witness of these Christians who insist on sharing their faith unashamedly.

Villafañe writes: "The indigenous Pentecostal' *culto* is the strongest manifestation and witness to the cultural contextualization of its spirituality" (1993:126). Songs, coritos, *testimonios* (testimonies), prayers, offerings, liturgical expressions—open praise (i.e., "Amen," "Hallelujah," "*Gloria a Dios!*"), and the sermon all reflect an indigenous spirituality. The burst of faith in its varied forms is the expressed spirituality we know as popular religion. Comparable to the Protestant faith experience, Latino/a Catholics use festive music, *danzas* (sacred dances), colorful rituals, Marian dramas, and rhythmic instrumentation provided by nonprofessional—but very inspiring—music makers in the church.

The goal or purpose of the witness of the Christian faith is what we call mission or sometimes ministry. All Christians seek the imitation of Christ and the love of neighbor. However, the different traditions have developed particular charisms that are their gift to the individual or group for the good of others. That particular gift is derived from the reservoir of gifts they have received. "The great spiritualities in the life of the church continue to exist because they keep sending followers back to their sources" (Gutiérrez 1997:37). It is in the sources of these two traditions that we find their mission.

Mission

The mission of any tradition encompasses its hopes and aspirations for its followers and an articulation of their experience of faith. For both popular Catholicism and for Pentecostalism the agents for conversion and its advocates are the poor. Both traditions articulate clearly the option for the poor and the voice of the poor in the expression of the faith. Villafañe offers for Pentecostalism:

> The context of Hispanic indigenous Pentecostal is the inner-city "*barrios*" storefront churches that one encounters the dynamic and suggestive "*cultos*." There are the "barrios" marginal to the poor structures of downtown, inhibited by a disenfranchised and oppressed people. The storefront churches are, by and large, small, overcrowded, inadequate for classroom, office, etc., no stained glass windows, hardly any windows at all–by most estimation aesthetically unbecoming. (1993:126)

Justo González and Edwin Aponte also affirm in their works that popular religion is the expression of faith of the poor, *el pueblo sencillo, el creyente sencillo,* the grassroots people (González 1996a, Aponte 1995). It is the nontheologians, the uneducated, and those in need who are the practitioners. Orlando Espín writes along the same vein:

> Popular Catholicism was born from the marginalized poor. Its traditions and ministries, its memories and wisdom, are also preserved by the poor. The symbols, stories, and celebrations of popular Catholicism act jointly as bearers of its doctrinal and ethical contents, and as the preeminent evangelizing vehicle vis-à-vis the poor. (1995:127)

Virgilio Elizondo's work on Mexican American spirituality as popular religion has been marked by his emphasis and focus on giving for the poor, the rejected, and those whose lives parallel the suffering of the Galilean and vanquished Jesus.

The mission of the religious traditions is to evangelize. Soliván, as other Pentecostals, holds:

> It is this Pentecostal emphasis on the work and power of the Holy Spirit as the advocate, guide, and interpreter of the sources and norms that distinguishes the Pentecostal perspective...the Holy Spirit is seen as enlightening, directing teaching, discerning, and empowering the people in this hermeneutical process of becoming and announcing.

> The Holy Spirit is seen as given to the community of the disregarded and the dispossessed for the purpose of equipping them for the task of becoming signs of the reign of God in the world. (1996b: 138)

Latino/a popular Catholicism, as Goizueta examines it, emerges from the people and has as its function an ancient need of humanity to be close to the Divine:

> As long as human beings desire to make contact with the transcendent dimension of everyday life, as long as we seek to find meaning in life and death, as long as we strive to express the ineffable and to relate religious belief to everyday life—which is to say always—there will be popular religion. (1995: 25)

Conclusion

Both popular Catholicism and Protestantism's most significant contribution is a rich and vibrant spirituality. Popular Catholicism has brought a rich expression of faith to Christian spirituality and, in particular, a rich religious heritage for Hispanics. In *Ecclesia en America*, Pope John Paul II alluded to the fact that countries that have kept the external expressions of the faith have retained the faith. The expressed spirituality of these traditions responds to a profound need of humanity to express its longing to be near to the Transcendent and interrelate with the Divine in ways that confirm that humanity and Divinity can and do connect in palpable ways. As a postmodern society struggles with prayer in schools and public displays of faith, these two traditions shock the world in their very expressive popular religiosity. The use of the body, movement, senses, and sounds cannot be ignored. The murals, the *danzas*, the creative dramas, and the pilgrimages of popular Catholicism scream of a faith that is real and declares—in very real and concrete ways—that God is close to those who keep God close to them. The genius in popular religiosity is that these expressions of direct relationship to God are rooted in the interior renewal of the heart and lead to a quenching of the thirst for the sacred in our lives.

CHAPTER 14

Eschatology

■ LUIS G. PEDRAJA

As I stand at the supermarket checkout line, my eyes scan the tabloids, on which I see—among the headlines about two-headed extraterrestrial babies, the newest misadventure of a certain pop star, and the oldest living person on earth—an article about the latest predictions of the end of the world. They might vary a bit, but in essence they are always the same: A cosmic cataclysm is about to befall us, often coupled with the return of Christ or the unleashing of some evil force. At bookstores, the section on Christianity is filled with popular fiction about the "end times," often with very little basis in sound theology or biblical scholarship. In turbulent times, it should not surprise us that people are fascinated with such themes as the end of the world—and in that respect, Latinos/as are no different from the rest of the culture. The range of different beliefs about eschatology in Hispanic congregations probably mirrors that found in popular mainstream culture and among all the different Christian denominations. Beliefs are influenced by cultures and church affiliations. In writing about eschatology, my aim is not to describe beliefs that Latinos/as have about it, which are as vast as dispensationalist, millennialist, and spiritualized versions of an afterlife, but to describe the theological insights into eschatology from the perspectives of Latino/a theologians—insights grounded in their experience as Latinos/as.

Endings and Beginnings

Most Christians think of eschatology in terms of the end times, because, after all, it is the doctrine of the last things, the *eschaton*. What people fail to realize is that while eschatology is about the ending of something, it is also about the beginning of something new. Eschatology is not about the end of life or of the world, but actually about the end of death, evil, suffering, and sin in all its manifestations. In the final chapters of the book of Revelation, Satan, death, and Hades are all cast into the lake of fire (Rev. 20:10, 14). While people tend to focus on predictions of plagues, tribulations, death, and the destruction of the world when they read certain passages in the New Testament and the Hebrew Bible, eschatology does not end in hopelessness. According to biblical scholars, much of the apocalyptic writings associated with eschatology, such as the Revelation to John and several of the books of Daniel, were written to instill hope in times of crisis and oppression. Rather than approaching eschatology with dread and fear of the things to come, we should celebrate the hope it bears.

The forces that hold both the world and humanity captive to sin and suffering come to an end in Christian eschatology. Eschatology is about the restoration of creation's goodness, including the goodness of human life. God's creative activity continues throughout history (Isa. 43:19), and beyond history's culmination. In the end, God continues to create, making all things new again (Rev. 21:1–2). Ultimately, eschatology is about the culmination of restoration and salvation through God's continual creative work in history and the liberation of creation from the power of sin. For Latino/a theology this means that eschatology is about our hope for liberation from the structures of oppression, marginalization, and death.

Eschatology from a Latino/a Perspective

The eschatology of Latino/a theologians has been influenced by Latin American liberation theologies, our experiences as Latinos/as in the U.S., and our hopes for the future. Since most liberation theologies, including Latino/a theologies, have a strong teleological component—an end goal—it should come as no surprise that Latino/a theologies are in many respects eschatological. Just as Moltmann's theology of hope is driven by an eschatological hope, liberation theologies are also infused with a hope for liberation from oppressive and sinful structures and a prescriptive call for our active participation in making this hope a reality.

Because Latino/a theologies are infused with eschatological hope and a deliberative agenda for the future, it is often difficult to isolate Latino/a eschatologies from other doctrines. Eschatology pervades all of our theology as a subtext. Thus, Latino/a eschatologies are not simply relegated to a chapter at the end of the book. When we write about sin, there is an underlying eschatological subtext calling for our continual struggle against sinful structures, with an aim toward our liberation from their oppression. Similarly, we understand soteriology, christology, pneumatology, and other similar doctrines within the context of liberative action—with an aim toward the future hope of accomplishing such liberation. All of these doctrines, as well as others that we address, carry an inherent hope for liberation from structures of marginalization, oppression, and death. This hope implies an eschatological component that orients our theologies toward a common future for which we strive. Thus, it is difficult to isolate eschatology because it often permeates all aspects of Latino/a theology and is developed throughout the length of the different theological works.

Most Latino/a eschatologies share themes rooted in common experiences and similar hopes for our future, including a hope for liberation from all forms of oppression and oppressive systems, including economic oppression, racism, sexism, and cultural and political structures that enslave humanity. This is manifested in a radically different future that is discontinuous with the current course of history and human society. Some Latino/a theologians envision this future as impinging and placing a demand upon our present, calling us to act differently. Others associate this future with the establishment of God's kingdom, or with the resurrection.

For most Latino/a theologians, this future is not solely relegated to a supernatural realm located at the end of our lives or at the end of the world. Like their counterparts in Latin America, Latino/a theologians understand economic injustice and oppression to be structural manifestations of sin within the sociopolitical order. Hence, the eradication of sin would also require the eradication of oppressive structures and the establishment of a just and righteous social order. While we could say such a reality is only possible through divine intervention or in a different realm from the present, Latino/a theologians argue that it is not necessarily an otherworldly reality. After all, when we pray the Lord's Prayer, we do not say "let us go into your kingdom." Instead, we say, "Your kingdom come." (Mt. 6:10). The only difference between our present reality and God's reign is that on earth God's will is not done as it is in heaven, as the rest of the prayer indicates (Mt. 6:10). For many Hispanic theologians, it is in this future that eschatology is grounded, a future in which God's will is done on earth as it is in heaven.

Mañana People

Justo L. González derives the title of his book *Mañana: Christian Theology from a Hispanic Perspective,* from the word *mañana,* which in Spanish means "tomorrow." According to González, some people interpret the expression *mañana* used by many Latinos/as to be a sign of laziness or procrastination, leaving for tomorrow what can be done today. While this may be the case in some instances, González argues that for a people who live in bondage, suffering, and poverty, *mañana* can also be taken as a sign of hope (1990:164–65). Such a reading of *mañana* leads to two conclusions. First, *mañana* manifests the hope that the future can be radically different from the present, that tomorrow might be a better day than today. Second, it implies that this future places a demand on the present and upon us by asking why it is not so (Ibid.:166).

Theologically, this future is not simply a continuation of today. It is not just any future; it is God's future: a future in which God's will for humanity becomes a reality. Within this context, there is a radical shift away from the structures of oppression and injustice, which hold us in bondage, to new structures emerging in accordance to God's will. In this future the economic practices that rob people of life by preventing them from making a decent living are replaced with more egalitarian structures that eradicate hunger and poverty. Those who are culturally and racially different are included in society. Peace replaces violence and war. Instead of enslavement, degradation, and dehumanization, everyone is free to be what God intended them to be. Since such a future in accordance to God's will is not unimaginable or impossible, it seems reasonable for us to ask why this is not the case. Thus, God's future judges the present and demands change. Naturally, this requires more than divine intervention— it requires action from us. Instead of a passive eschatology that merely awaits the *parousia*—Jesus' return, or the end of history as we know it—we are asked to take action within history. Hence, Latino/a theology cannot be passive and solely future-oriented. It must be active, taking the present seriously and working to transform it. To paraphrase the often-quoted words of George Bernard Shaw, Latinos/as, as a *mañana* people, cannot merely look at how things are and ask why; they must also look at how things can be and ask themselves, why not?

Resurrection Power

Most Christians believe in a resurrection upon God's return at the end of time. Another belief today is that we have an immortal soul that leaves the body and enters a different realm, such as heaven or paradise, upon death. While these two beliefs are not necessarily mutually exclusive—there are biblical passages that can be interpreted as supporting both—their implications are not always compatible. An emphasis on immortality of the soul can easily create dualisms and hierarchies that minimize the value of our material and bodily existence. In contrast, the resurrection underlines the importance of our bodily reality and prevents us from ignoring the very real conditions of the world we inhabit. The resurrection binds us to the material aspects of creation as a whole, and to our own creation as incarnate beings. Rather than viewing our present existence as that of spirits trapped in the flesh, longing to escape the prison of the body, the resurrection reminds us that we are created as embodied beings.

While the Latinos and Latinas who attend our churches have a wide range of perspectives and beliefs in the afterlife, the resurrection of the dead is still central to the Christian faith. Belief in the resurrection does two things that are important for Latino/a theology. First, it destroys false dichotomies and hierarchies that subjugate our embodied reality to some sort of detached and disembodied spirituality. This forces us to contend with the material and physical aspects of both creation and humanity. To ignore either in favor of a spiritual or heavenly reality would minimize the significance of the resurrection. The resurrection reminds us that we are not solely spiritual beings; we are also embodied beings. Action cannot be deferred until the future, nor should it be solely concentrated on spiritual matters. We must act in the present in our struggle to liberate humanity and all of creation from the power of sin—including sinful structures of oppression, marginalization, and destruction.

Second, the Christian doctrine of resurrection also points toward a radical transformation. Resurrection is not the same as resuscitation. The life promised by the resurrection is not a continuation of our present life, often hellish for those who face alienation, suffering, death, and oppression on a daily basis. The apostle Paul contrasts the life we experience in our natural bodies with that of the resurrected body, which is a spiritual body (1 Cor. 15:44). The contrast here is not a contrast between our spirit and our bodies, but between states of bodily existence —one in accordance to our natural sinful nature and the other in accordance to God's spirit. The difference between our present existence and the resurrection is one of context. Our present existence is defined by violence, sin, and oppression; the resurrection is defined by peace, love, and life.[1] Regardless of how we interpret the resurrection and how we view Christian doctrines of life beyond death, the resurrection affirms a radical discontinuity, not between our bodies and souls, but between the structures of death that dominate this world and the affirmation of life that is inherent in God. It is a testament to those who live under the constant threat of death and violence that life will triumph in the end.

The resurrection also plays a significant role in the theology of Latino theologian Virgilio Elizondo. In his book, *Galilean Journey*, Elizondo offers three key principles: the Galilee Principle, the Jerusalem Principle, and the Resurrection Principle. The first speaks to the experience of marginalization and oppression experienced at the borders of society common to Latinos/as and one with which God identifies, according to Elizondo, through Jesus' Galilean roots and experience of marginalization. The Jerusalem Principle reflects the need to confront, as Jesus did in Jerusalem, the powers of domination and death. Confronting these powers carries a heavy toll—the possibility of violence and death, as Jesus' crucifixion demonstrates. In contrast, the Resurrection Principle attests to the triumph of love over evil, life over death, the promise of which empowers us to risk confronting the power of evil, knowing that in

---

[1]I develop this argument further in my book *Teología* (2004: 199–201).

the end, love and life will prevail (1983:115–17). The eschatological hope that the resurrection provides is what empowers us to act toward our goal of liberation in spite of the risks entailed. The resurrection is the eschatological *telos* that draws us into God's future—into the reign of God.

God's Kin-dom

The reign of God plays a prominent role in most liberation theologies and bears the promise of a radical transformation of the present. While God's reign is partly a present reality, it is also a hope to be fulfilled. The fulfillment of God's reign for liberation theologies is not simply limited to a future time at the end of history or to realm beyond our present life. The reign of God is a reality to be fulfilled within history with certain key characteristics. First, the reign of God subverts the current structures of power and dominance, because God rules through love. Second, the rule of peace, joy, and life become the rule that replaces violence, fear, and death.

Latina theologian Ada María Isasi-Díaz uses the term "kin-dom of God" in her work. Her choice of this nomenclature seeks to move us away from male images of God and patriarchal domination evoked by the term "kingdom." In its place, the term "kin-dom" offers an alternative image of inclusion and family, where we all are kin to one another, children of God to be treated with dignity and love. Rather than exclusion, marginalization, and suffering, God's kin-dom provides us with a place where we all belong. For Isasi-Díaz, God's kin-dom is bound with salvation, liberation, and Christian hope. Even though the kin-dom of God is never fully fulfilled within history, in history we find "'eschatological glimpses,' part of the unfolding of the kin-dom which do not make happen but which requires us to take responsibility for making justice a reality in our world" (2004:53). God's kin-dom serves as a source of eschatological hope and a guide to our actions in the present. It provides the paradigm of how things should be, which is held in contrast to our present conditions. While Latinos/as experience oppression, marginalization, exclusion, and death in the present, they maintain the hope of a radically different reality in which we all have a place at God's table, a reality in which love and life have eclipsed the hatred and death that often mar our lives today. In God's reign, those who have no place in society can finally find a place.[2]

Reversal of Fortune

Some literary works use the motif of a reversal of fortune to provide a setting. In many ways, this is the motif of the Bible and its eschatology.

---

[2]In my book *Jesus Is My Uncle,* I speak about how utopia literally means "no place." There I contrast the utopia of displacement, where those at the margins of society experience exclusion to the extent that they can have no place, with the *ouk*-topia, (good place) of God's reign, where all are included and find a place (1999:110–22).

Scripture is fraught with examples of a reversal or subversion of the things we value in life: status, power, privilege, and possessions. There is the story of the rich man who hoards his possessions, only to be told that he is about to die and be left with nothing (Lk. 12:13–21). The parable of Lazarus and the story of the widow's offering also attest to it. The power and wealth that we value so much are not what truly matters to God. While many biblical passages illustrate this theme, two would suffice to illustrate my point. One is Jesus' comment that the last will be first in God's reign (Mk. 10:21; Lk. 13:30). This passage is not about the order in which one enters God's realm, but about what we tend to value. Those who are considered the least and last in our society are those who God will lift up. Power and status might secure our position in this world, but these are not what matters to God. Service to others and love are what matter. Those who suffer at the hands of others and live under dismal conditions so that others might profit are valued by God. We might consider them the least, but God puts them first –because they have had to suffer at our hands. God honors those we dishonor and lifts up those we reject. God's reign subverts our sense of value, placing the last first. God's love is a reversal of fortune.

Second, the book of Revelation is filled with eschatological images such as the New Jerusalem descending from the heavens. In these description we are told that the foundations of its wall are made up of precious stones, and its streets are paved with gold (Rev. 21:18–21). For a casual reader, this might be seen as a display of God's power and wealth– an extravagant display of luxury and opulence. Our eyes might grow wide at such richness, and many have read these passages in terms of God's richness and power, or even of the plentiful bounty of our reward. Rather than seeing this as a display of wealth, it could be seen as a condemnation of our values. Precious stones and gold, which we value and crave to the extent of killing others to possess them, become mere building materials in God's Jerusalem, no more valuable than concrete and asphalt! The New Jerusalem, understood in this sense, serves to reveal to us the folly of our valuation of wealth.

If any one common theme encapsulates Latino/a eschatology, it would be this theme of reversal of fortunes. Those things we value actually serve as the backbone for the structures of sin in our world. They also are a paradigm for hell –the one area of eschatology that might not be addressed in Latino/a theology, for it is already a part of our experience in the here and now. Eschatology holds the promise that one day those things that God intended for us to value–love, life, and goodness–will replace the current structures of hatred, death, and oppression.

PART II

Contextual Essays

CHAPTER 15

The U.S. Hispanic/Latino Landscape

■ JOANNE RODRÍGUEZ-OLMEDO

Recently, I vacationed in sunny, beautiful Puerto Rico. While there I spent time with family, but I also stayed a couple of nights at three-to-four-star hotels, ate at least two to three meals in expensive restaurants, and did one or two excursions. This enabled me to relax and return to my home and job in New Jersey rejuvenated and ready to answer multifarious e-mails and huge bundles of mail. But as I thought long and hard about this time in Puerto Rico, I realized that what I experienced for a period of eleven days is not at all common for the majority of Hispanics/Latinos. At least two-thirds of the Hispanic/Latino population in the United States never have an opportunity to vacation like this in their lifetimes. Instead, many work two to three minimum-wage part-time jobs that have no fringe benefits. They work to make ends meet, to provide a better education to their children, and/or to send money back to their homelands where they have left their children, siblings, and parents. Even though some would love to attend college or a university if given the opportunity, they either do not have the time or the money. Even though most would love to live in decent housing, they cannot afford the rent or the down payment for new homes. Even though most would love to participate more in their local parish or congregation, they cannot because they are working every day of the week, with little time left over for family, friends, or even themselves.

With two-thirds of the Hispanic/Latino population in the above predicament, it is hard to image how the well-known and respected economist Samuel Huntington can argue in *Who Are We? The Challenges to America's National Identity* that Hispanic immigrants threaten America's identity, values, and way of life. Huntington stereotypes Hispanics as lazy welfare moochers who know nothing about the "American creed" of hard work. Despite the stereotype, at least two-thirds of the Hispanic population in the United States experience precarious economic and educational situations, no matter how hard they try, because they have been invisible and ignored for decades. Even when they are not ignored, claims such as these, written by widely respected scholars and political pundits, create unnecessary panic, resulting in the mistreatment of a faithful people, who—like other Americans—came to the United States looking for a better life for themselves and their families, fully in keeping with the historical identity of the United States.

To understand and obtain a more accurate point of view of the growing Hispanic minority group, we would have to first address the nomenclatures "Hispanic" and "Latino." Strictly speaking, there is no such type of person or group. The label "Hispanic" was coined in the mid-1970s by federal bureaucrats to ensure that those individuals with ancestral ties to the Spanish cultural diaspora were not being misidentified and could be grouped together. Hispanic is a name given and imposed upon us (indicating the power of the one doing the naming); it is not a name we gave ourselves. Although the term has been disputed for over three decades, it is still applied to people from Latin American countries with linguistic and cultural ties to Spain, and it is also used by the government to refer to Spaniards and even Brazilians, even though it is most inappropriate as a description for a community that speaks Portuguese, not Spanish. On the other hand, many in this grouping prefer the term "Latino" because it disassociates them from Spanish imperialism, and has as its focus Latin America rather than Spain. Nevertheless, many Latino or Hispanic persons in the United States would identify themselves by their country of origin or their parents. There are, of course, special cases that illustrate the complexity of the issues. For example, inhabitants of New Mexico who trace their ancestry to the Spanish colonial period and call themselves *hispanos* predate any designation by the U.S. federal government.

The Chronicle of Higher Education in its November 2004 issue showed a common and consistent breakdown of what the 2000 Census defines as the Hispanic population. It reported that Hispanics are already the largest minority group in the United States, representing over 13 percent of the total population. Furthermore, this population group was divided into six subgroups: Mexicans, Puerto Ricans, Cubans, Central Americans, South Americans, and Dominicans. Interestingly, in this typology the Central American subgroups only included Salvadorans, Guatemalans, Hondurans, and Nicaraguans—totally ignoring Costa Ricans and Panamanians. The South American census grouping is even more misleading because people from Brazil, Venezuela, Bolivia, Paraguay, Uruguay, Argentina, and Chile were not included, leaving out two-thirds of the South American continent. Not only is it problematic to group together all the diverse national groups of Latin America with umbrella terms such as Hispanic or Latino/a, it is not even clear that all people with roots in Latin America are being counted in the same way.

The largest subgroup, Mexicans, which in 2000 composed 34.3 million of the U.S. population, reside throughout the nation, with the highest concentration of Mexicans found in California, Texas, Illinois, and Arizona, although quite a number have also settled in Georgia, Florida, North Carolina, New York, and Nevada. The median age is twenty-four, making them the youngest Hispanic subgroup. However, they are struggling economically and educationally, with 26 percent under the poverty level, only 11 percent of U.S.-born having bachelor's degrees, and 60 percent of the foreign-born lacking high-school diplomas. In turn, 44 percent of foreign-born Mexicans between the ages of sixteen and nineteen work fulltime.

The second largest subgroup are Puerto Ricans, with 3.5 million on the U.S. mainland, and another 3.8 million in Puerto Rico. One distinction of this group is that whether born on the island or on the mainland, all are U.S. citizens. The largest concentrations can be found in New York, Florida, New Jersey, Pennsylvania, Massachusetts, and Connecticut. Linguistically, Puerto Ricans are the most assimilated, with 39 percent speaking primarily English, and just 21 percent relying solely on Spanish. However, like the Mexican population, they too are struggling economically and educationally, with 30 percent below the poverty line, only 37 percent attending college, and only 13 percent having bachelor's degrees.

Central Americans compose the third largest 2000 Census subgroup, with 2.3 million, mainly from El Salvador, Guatemala, Honduras, and Nicaragua. Many came to the United States escaping the bloody wars and the brutal U.S.-backed regimes of their homeland. This group mostly lives in California, Texas, Florida, and New York, with large concentrations in Illinois, New Jersey, and Washington, D.C. Unlike Mexicans, Puerto Ricans, and Cubans, 71 percent of Central Americans are foreign-born, and 34 percent immigrated since the early 1990s. But like Mexicans and Puerto Ricans, this subgroup also struggles economically and educationally, with 22 percent under the poverty line and those over twenty-four only having an average of 10.3 years of school.

The fourth largest Hispanic subgroup is composed of South Americans, totaling 1.7 million. This is another collective designation for diverse peoples who come mainly from Colombia, Ecuador, and Peru. A majority of this group lives in New York and Florida, and smaller groups can be found in California, New Jersey, Massachusetts, and Texas. Like

Central Americans, 74 percent are foreign-born, and 33 percent immigrated within the past ten years. But unlike Mexicans and Puerto Ricans, a large share of the foreign-born South Americans come from the middle-class and were well-educated back home. In 2000, their per capita income as a group surpassed that of Cuban-Americans. This group surpasses the overall U.S. population in educational achievement, with 35 percent having college degrees.

Cubans are the fifth largest subgroup, accounting for 1.2 million of the U.S. population. The highest concentration of Cubans is in Florida, with quite a number living in New Jersey, California, and New York. This group is the oldest, with a median age of forty-one. They average the highest household incomes, even though such averages are still substantially lower than the Euro-American average household income. It is the group with the highest levels when it comes to educational achievement, with at least 35 percent having a college education. According to the Cuban scholar Miguel De La Torre, these "accomplishments" can be attributed to the social location of Cuban immigrants when compared to other Hispanic groups. As a group, the first two waves of refugees (1959 through 1973, representing almost half a million people) were predominately white, middle-aged, educated, urban, familiar with the English language, and had business connections with North American corporations. Some from the first wave who left immediate after the Castro Revolution were able to transfer their wealth to the States (2003:33–34).

The final subgroup is comprised of Dominicans, totaling 912,000 with the majority living in New York City. Overall, they are the poorest Hispanic subgroup, with 36 percent falling below the 2003 poverty line of $14,100 for a family of three. Like South and Central Americans, the majority (68 percent) are foreign-born, and 28 percent have immigrated within the past ten years. In contrast to the other subgroups, although, only 9.5 percent of the foreign-born Dominican adults have earned college degrees, and nearly 22 percent of U.S.-born have done so.

These numbers clearly indicate that by removing the most educated and economically advanced groups (Cubans and South Americans, totaling 2.9 million), in the other Latino subgroups totaling 44.8 million, 27 percent are under the poverty level and 54 percent lack high school diplomas. Employed foreign-born Hispanics are also more likely to report being in blue-collar jobs (at 65 percent) than those who are native born (at 28 percent) (Slessarev-Jamir 2003:13). This does not mean that all Latinos are struggling financially, but it does mean that many are struggling financially and are not reaching the educational levels necessary to compete in some job market.

The struggles faced by Hispanics are not limited to economics. According to Miguel De La Torre and Edwin David Aponte:

Latinos/as are more likely to be victims of crime (39.6 per 1,000) than non-Hispanics (35.3 per 1,000). If convicted of a crime, they are more likely to serve longer sentences. According to statistics of the U.S. Department of Justice, Hispanics are likely to be released in only 26 percent of their cases. Non-Latinos/as are usually released before trial in 66 percent of their cases... Additionally, Latinas/os are more likely to live with pollution (19 percent) than Euroamericans (6 percent) or African Americans (9 percent) combined...Additional health concerns are many: Latinos/as are less likely to receive preventive medical examinations (15 percent for Hispanics vs. 9.7 percent for non-Hispanics); Latinas tend to receive prenatal care later than the general population, with only 61 percent receiving such care in the first trimester; Hispanics are also less likely than African Americans and Euroamericans to carry health insurance... When it comes to education...[t]he only group that has a higher dropout rate than Latina girls is Latino boys at 31 percent—compared to African American boys at 12.1 percent and white boys at 7.7 percent. (2001:22–24)

Over half (55 percent) of foreign-born Latinos have less than a high school education, compared to fewer than a quarter (23 percent) of native-born Latinos. Native-born Latinos are more likely than foreign-born Latinos to have completed high school (35 percent vs. 29 percent), have some college (29 percent vs. 9 percent), or have graduated from college or received a degree after college (13 percent vs. 7 percent). Foreign-born Hispanics generally live in households with lower incomes than those who are native-born. The majority (57 percent) of foreign-born Latinos report making less than $30,000 a year, while the majority (53 percent) of native-born Latinos report making more than $30,000 a year (Slessarev-Jamir 2003:13).

Some public policy analysts describe the various sectors of education as pieces of a pipeline. And from various studies performed, it is continuously reported that at every stage of the pipeline, Hispanic students are getting stuck or spilling out. For many Hispanic students who are below the poverty level and speak solely Spanish at home, the problems begin in the early years and continue to escalate throughout their education. For starters, many of the schools these students attend are in the most segregated and poorly financed parts of the nation, sometimes staffed with teachers with little experience in the field. The consequences of these discriminatory practices create a situation in which Latinos/as who are seventeen years of age, on the average, have the same reading and mathematics skills as thirteen-year-old Euro-Americans (Schmidt 2003:9). More than a third of the states recently surveyed by the

National Center for Education Statistics said that their Hispanic students are more likely to drop out of school than other students (Ibid.:9).

On the other hand, despite numerous obstacles and difficulties, Latino students are attending college at a record high, yet very few (in spite of the myth of Affirmative Action) are enrolled in highly selective, elite institutions. Over 50 percent attend community colleges, often the entry point into higher education for many marginal groups (Navarro 2003). Many never get the opportunity to transfer to a four-year institution because of nontransferable credits, and instead choose to join the work force because they are left without financial resources, energy, or motivation to persist through and obtain a baccalaureate degree. This has limited the progress of these students in terms of broader employment opportunities. Furthermore, Laura Rendon states that research by the National Center for Education Statistics shows that undergraduates are more likely to obtain a degree within six years if they begin their education at a four-year institution.[1]

Related to the educational challenges, overall, Latinos report a weaker financial situation than do whites. Research shows their having lower household incomes, that they are less likely to own the home they live in, and that they are more likely to report having experienced financial difficulties in the past year. This does not mean that all Latinos are struggling financially. Latinos who were born in the United States and those who speak English or are bilingual are much more likely to report having higher household incomes and are less likely to report experiencing financial hardship (Schmidt 2003:9).

When it comes to religious beliefs, about seven in ten Hispanics indicate that religion is an important component of their everyday life. They are likely to make religious services a regular part of their life, as 45 percent say they attend religious services once a week or more, and an additional 17 percent indicate they attend services at least once or twice a month. The large majority of Latinos identify as Roman Catholic, though foreign-born Latinos are more likely to report being Catholic than U.S.-born Latinos who are somewhat more likely to be Evangelicals. Mexicans, Dominicans, Columbians, and South Americans are somewhat more likely to report they are Catholics than are Puerto Ricans, Cubans, Central Americans, Salvadorans and Latinos from "other" countries. Conversely, Salvadorans, Central Americans, Puerto Ricans, and respondents from "other countries" are more likely than Mexicans and Dominicans to report they are Evangelical. Central Americans and Salvadorans are also more likely than Cubans to report they are Evangelical.[2]

---

[1]"Educating the Largest Minority Group: Views of 6 Experts," *The Chronicle Review,* November 28, 2003.

[2]Based on a social science contribution to a PARAL (Program for the Analysis of Religion Among Latinos) study by Ariela Keysar, Barry A. Kosmin, and Egon Mayer, The Graduate Center of the City University of New York and Brooklyn College.

As a whole, the diverse Hispanic population of the United States holds an array of attitudes, values, and beliefs that are distinct from those of non-Hispanic whites and African Americans. Even Latinos who trace their ancestry in the United States back for several generations express views that distinguish them from the non-Hispanic native-born population. For example, many still speak Spanish at home and continue to worship in Spanish congregations and remain connected to their native communities via family and friends.

One factor influencing Hispanic social identity is immigration. According to a recent survey, Latinos/as have a robust attachment to their countries of origin. While this attachment is naturally strongest among the foreign-born, it also extends to their U.S.-born children and even somewhat among Hispanics whose families are long-time U.S. residents. For example, many first and second generation Mexicans, Cubans, and Puerto Ricans are in constant contact with grandparents, parents, siblings, and close relatives who have never left the homeland. Many phone daily, weekly, or monthly, and forward money as well as other items back and forth. Regardless of nativity or country of origin, Hispanics who reside in the United States are engaging the English language and American ways to various degrees. Yet simultaneously, newly arrived immigrants are bringing new energy to how Spanish is spoken in the United States and to attitudes shaped in Latin America. In interpreting the survey results, it is important to keep in mind that these two processes—assimilation and immigration—are taking place side-by-side in Latino communities, often within a single family (Slessarev-Jamir 2003:18). Nevertheless, there is no homogeneous Latino opinion. A diversity of views exist among Latinos, and the differences between the foreign-born —regardless of their country of origin —and the native-born, and those between the English-dominant and the Spanish-dominant are most notable.

In conclusion, Hispanic/Latino faith communities reflect the racial/ethnic, national origin, class, as well as educational and generational diversity similar to the rest of the United States population. But unlike Huntington's Hispanic stereotype, most Hispanic/Latino understand and live out the "American creed" of hard work. We then need our respected and political pundits not to create panic and fear of one group in the population, but instead, to find ways to respect and honor these differences in order to address serious economic, educational, and religious obstacles of this large and growing population. This will not be an easy task, but it needs to begin with our respected scholars and political pundits. They are the ones who can bring impetus to this formidable, but not impossible, effort needed for development across the board, at the individual, familial, and communal levels.

CHAPTER 16

Identity and Social Location

■ ANA MARÍA DÍAZ-STEVENS

Social location has become an increasingly sophisticated tool for the understanding of religion. It entails the use of sociological categories in order to provide a multidimensional understanding of social context. The last quarter of the twentieth century saw an explosion of sociologically informed studies of the Hebrews conducted by biblical scholars. The appearance of Norman Gottwald's *The Tribes of Yahweh* (1979) made a considerable impact on the use of social location in biblical studies in the last two decades of the twentieth century among English-speaking scholars. According to Anthony J. Blasi, Gottwald filtered Marxist thought through the sociology of Emile Durkheim "to portray the emergence of Israel in Canaan as a heterogeneous, classless, decentralized association of tribes that came to conceive of themselves as an egalitarian brotherhood under the symbolism of the Israelite deity."[1] The description of the ancient Hebrew tribes in contemporary sociological terminology was considered an aid to understanding the scriptures.

The application of sociological theory to the Bible and religion did not begin with Gottwald, of course. Philosophers of the Enlightenment such as Hume, Locke, Voltaire, and Rousseau used biblical examples in exploring the theme of the social contract. Marx and Engels used the Acts of the Apostles in *The Holy Family* (1975) as a model for socialism. Emile Durkheim and Max Weber also expounded sociological principles with use of scriptural examples. For example, the sociological notion of

---

[1]See online entry by Blasi at http://hirr.hartsem.edu/ency/biblical.htm.

charismatic leadership was developed by Weber through a sociological analysis of the roles of Saul and David as described in the Bible. With such a powerful pedigree, matching sociology and religion has become commonplace today in both scripture studies and theology.

Social location seeks to place religion within the scope of people's life chances, and explore their religious experience in the context of socioeconomic circumstances. With such a tool, one can better interpret the subjective dispositions of the religious agent and be led to a more precise understanding of what they intended. Thus, for instance, the composition of the book of Deuteronomy (Dutcher-Walls 1991:77–94) or the concerns of the prophets (Carroll 1979:11–84) are clarified by including a sociological dimension to the society they addressed. Another study, such as the one by Anthony Saldarini, *Pharisees, Scribes and Sadducees in Palestinian Society* (1988), helps an understanding of the importance of Jesus' teaching by providing analysis of Pharisees, Scribes, and Sadducees in first-century Palestine. If we adopt Gerhard Lenski's (1966) sociological categories to consider the apostle Paul's writings, we capture a view of him as an urban person in the social milieu that had access to rich merchants, to members of the retainer stratum, and even the governing class. His concerns with ecclesiastical organization and authority, with the use of written communications as a teaching tool, his prominence in the early church, and even his status as apostle become clearer when these sociological circumstances are included.

Social location has successfully enabled a revisiting of early Christianity in order to examine themes with contemporary relevance such as gender roles (i.e., Funk 1981, Corley 1993), group dynamics (Schreiber 1977), social movements (Blasi 1989), sect and counter-hegemonic behavior (Watson 1986), and population analyses (Stark 1996). Commenting on the general field today, Blasi concludes, "Consequently, it has become difficult to take any discussion of biblical studies seriously that does not have a social scientific dimension."[2] Social location also enters into theologies that examine context (Schreiter 1985) and the specificity of location among racial and ethnic groups (Bevans 1992). The growing importance of diversity in religious experience has also entered the mainstream of the sociology of religion (Ebaugh and Chafetz 2000, Roof 1998, Warner 1997). Cultural historians such as Eric Hobsbawm and Terence Ranger (1983) have used social location to explore the emergence of cultural rituals in various societies, and Max Harris (2000) has connected the festival of Moors in Spain to a Mexican context by suggesting that social location opens opportunities for a transfer of religious rituals to new contexts. The same theme has been explored by David Carrasco (1995) in reference to Aztecs and Chicanos.

---

[2]See ibid.

Social location has become part of Latino/a theology. The classic work by Gustavo Gutiérrez, *A Theology of Liberation* (1971/1973), provided an outline of how social location might be used to better understand the political ramifications of liberation for Moses and Jesus from a Latin American perspective. This seminal reflection was elaborated on more systematically in some early works in the Spanish language that focused on scripture, such as José Porfirio Miranda, *Marx and the Bible* (1972/1974), and Alfredo Fierro, *The Militant Gospel* (1975/1977). It can be said, then, that the injection of social location into the theology of Latinos and Latinas in the United States has had a different trajectory than what has been described for a general English-speaking field of scholarship.

Virgilio Elizondo was the first to systematically compare the social location of Jesus and his early followers to the sociological status of Mexican Americans. Incorporating his many articles and presentations on this concept, his *Galilean Journey* (2000a) utilized social location as a basic premise. Elizondo explored the meaning of *mestizaje* as presented in cultural definition of Mexico by José Vasconcelos and turned it into a key for understanding Mexican Americans living in the United States. For Elizondo, the Mexican American's social location was largely influenced not only by sociological factors but also by subjective conditions that shaped cultural identity. Pointing out that Jesus as Galilean was looked down upon by the Hebrews in biblical times, Elizondo elaborated a theological meaning to racial and cultural mixture that could transfer to Mexican Americans today a social location similar to that of the Galileans in Jesus' day. Elizondo further developed *mestizaje* as a definition of Mexican identity by exploring the history of the devotion to Our Lady of Guadalupe, the national patroness of Mexico. Elizondo stressed the racial mixture that was a factor in the popularity of the devotion and applied it to pastoral ministry among all Latinos and Latinas.

Elizondo's contribution to a nascent Latino/a theology has been enormous and his inclusion of social location as part of his theologizing is a characteristic of most contemporary Latino/a theology today. It bears repeating, however, that social location is best developed by sociologists. It is not a biblical or religious studies' concept, but rather a contemporary tool adapted from sociological analysis. The use of social location by sociologists of the Latino/a situation to understand religion has proceeded independently from the field of theology (e.g., Peña 1997). The award-winning *Recognizing the Latino Resurgence in U.S. Religion* (Díaz-Stevens and Stevens-Arroyo 1998) uses social location to analyze many aspects of Latino/a religious experience since 1967. Sociological categories are employed to explain various social phenomena, such as the rapid rise of a cohort of Latino/a clergy to denominational prominence, the ecumenical character of church mobilization, and the rise of a specifically Latino/a theology in the United States. Many useful works on social location are cited and summarized in *Recognizing the Latino Resurgence,* including Deck (1989) and Hayes Bautista (1992), and a more recent work on social location is by Jones-Correa (2001).

The survey results of the Program for the Analysis of Religion Among Latinos/as (PARAL) Study, issued in three reports in 2002, are among recent sociological studies that supply a wealth of detail from which to construct social location for Latinos and Latinas. What emerges from these recent studies is the increasing segmentation of Hispanics in the United States in reference to residential patterns, regional distribution, socioeconomic status, and ethnic/nationality heritage. Summarized in the PARAL Study as "density, diversity and Diaspora" these traits provide evidence that no single social location is adequate to describe the increasingly complex Latino population in the United States. It is to be hoped that in the future, theological use of Latino social location will rely more on the pioneer work of Latino and Latina sociologists and less on establishment textbooks and generalized census data. This would be especially useful for Latino biblicists such as Fernando Segovia (e.g., *Reading from This Place,* 1995, coedited with Mary Ann Tolbert) who use Latino social location in reference to biblical examples of marginalization.

In many sectors of Latino scholarship, however, it is worth noting the use of the term "borderlands" as a surrogate for Latino social location. "Borderlands" can be understood in the physical sense of place, or the analogical sense of culture and society. These meanings are not divorced from each other, however. As a geographical term, "borderlands" refers to territories on the frontier of European (or Western) civilization. The most common application in U.S.-based scholarship is to the current states of Texas, Arizona, Colorado, New Mexico, and California. These were considered to be borderlands by the Aztecs, the Spaniards, the Mexicans, and the white settlers from the United States, each in turn. In the eighteenth century, Texas and California were developed as borderlands by the Spanish government working out of Mexico. The settlements were intended to serve as buffers against intrusion into Spanish-claimed territories by the French entering Texas from the Mississippi area and from the Russians entering California from the northern reaches of Canada. In the middle of the nineteenth century, these areas became borderlands for an expansive United States.

The term may also be applied to the Caribbean. Puerto Rico, Hispaniola, and Cuba were considered naval outposts to protect Spanish shipping lanes from pirates and privateers. These islands had colonial societies that were relatively underdeveloped because they lacked the resources of money and population to become more than a series of coastal forts and sheltered ports to take on water and fresh supplies for journeys to what were considered more important places. They were peripheries in Spain's far-flung empire.

"Borderlands" enriches the concept of social location by adding a psychological and historical dimension to the sociological categories. We not only consider the social factors that define the life chances and experiences of Latinos and Latinas, we also grasp how and why the social location came to be as it is. Taken in this wider socio-historical category, the concept of borderlands may be related to core/periphery studies. As developed in the works of Ferdinand Braudel and his colleague, Emmanuel Wallenstein, the core can only be a core when it exploits the periphery. These notions are masterfully applied to the U.S. Southwest and Florida in *The Spanish Frontier in North America,* a seminal historical work by David J. Weber (1992).

Weber's analysis traces the cultural and ideological application of "borderlands" to politics and literature. He shows the links to historian Frederick Turner's frontier thesis. According to Turner, the frontier is the cradle of an "American" character because it requires the acquiring of survival and adaptive skills that keep the national culture vital. Turner provided in the last decades of the nineteenth century a variation of James Fenimore Cooper's idea of the *Last of the Mohicans,* namely that the "noble savage" was doomed to disappear, and that the "Indian" legacy was to be inherited by white Americans.

This idea was convenient as a support for the idea of Manifest Destiny, painting people of Latin American Catholic heritage as inferior, superstitious, and so on, and not deserving of impeding the advance of the Euro-American Protestants. According to Weber, the inhabitants of Texas, the Southwest territories, and California fit into the category of "noble savage." However, the racist implications of Turner's frontier thesis were challenged by Henry Bolton, a historian of the early twentieth century. In Bolton's use of "borderlands," he stressed that the reality of the American Southwest contradicted the crude caricatures of politicians and pulp magazines about the "West." Bolton showed that the natives who pre-dated the white U.S. settlers had already made the transitions required for life in the area. Moreover, the adaptation to life in the American West had involved a true mixture of civilizations, entailing assimilation on both sides.

Bolton's approach gave new impetus to a revision of history in the Southwest and the notion of borderlands. His revisionist history did not completely escape a hint of racial prejudice. Bolton favored assimilation in which the Anglos maintained an inevitable power advantage. While he criticized newcomers from the East Coast who did not learn from the natives in the region, he also viewed Latino/a backwardness as the result of loyalty to traditional ways when assimilation was possible. In his view, Latinos and Latinas had not fully accepted their role as cooperators in changing the Southwest.

In the 1970s, the Chicano Movement revisited Bolton's use of borderlands and turned the equation on its head. As reflected in the work of scholars like Rodolfo Acuña (1972), injustice in the United States was the result of assimilation. The Euro-American newcomers had refused to learn really important lessons from the native Latinos/as. The premise upon which the notion of "backwardness" was constructed consisted of a blind trust in assimilation and opportunistic compromise that submerged the essential values and culture of the Southwest under the banner of "Americanization." Through Acuña's and other works in the spirit of Chicano militancy, "borderlands" acquired a strongly ideological characteristic.

Gloria Anzaldúa (1987) developed the politicized "borderlands" as a metaphor of the body, sexuality, and culture of the Latina. She identified the term coined by Bolton with the Nahuatl word *nepantla,* which means "in between land." Anzaldúa thus capped a decades-long process within Chicano/a scholarship to deny originality to much of non-Latino/a scholarship. For her and other scholars who adopted some of her premises, "*nepantla*" preceded "borderlands," and thus the definition of culture, society, and politics in Texas, the Southwest, and California belonged to Latinos and Latinas. In a theological context, Daisy Machado (2002) has been one among many who have connected the concept of *mestizaje* as developed by Elizondo with the introspective use of *nepantla.*

David J. Weber does not use the word *nepantla* in his analysis of the "Spanish" presence in the United States. He, however, reviews the emphasis that some scholars put upon the subjective and psychological meaning imparted to the experience of marginalization or borderland, especially when such marginalization occurs within a geographic setting considered for centuries a marginalized people's homeland. He analyzes their treatment with an eye toward certain ahistorical and counter-factual tendencies that distort rather than clarify the social location of the people. While all of Weber's observations reflect his standing as an academic historian and non-Latino, many of his observations serve to highlight a need to balance the factual with the subjective in describing social location. For example, the social location of Puerto Ricans and other Caribbean Hispanics is not clearly expressed by imposing the Nahuatl concept of "*nepantla*" upon their reality. "Borders" rather than "borderlands" would seem more appropriate (Flores 1993:203–04, 215–24). In sum, while social location has become an indispensable tool for describing the Latino/a religious experiences, analyzing and interpreting its importance demands a high level of competence in more than one field.

Mexicano/a Descent

■ Nora O. Lozano

A Historical Perspective

People of Mexican descent have a common root in their Mexican history and culture. Their original ancestors include the Olmecs, Mayas, Zapotecs, Tlaxcaltecs, Totonacs, Toltecs, and Aztecs. These groups developed complex societies that generated significant cultural, religious, and artistic achievements. For example, by 1519 when Hernan Cortés and his Spanish army arrived in Mexico, the Aztecs had built a strong and powerful empire ruled by the emperor Moctezuma, and had subdued many of the indigenous groups of the area (García 2002:2–3).

The arrival of the Spaniards produced a violent clash between the Spanish and indigenous cultures. Out of this clash, which included the physical and sexual violence of the conquistadores, a new race was formed: the *mestizo* (mixed) one. This *mestizaje* (mixture) comprised not only biological, but also cultural elements as the natives' worldview was destroyed and a new divinity, a different language, and foreign symbols and values were imposed by the Spaniards (León-Portilla 1966:129–36; Elizondo 2000a:9–11).

This mixture of people and cultures produced a stratified society in the new Spanish colony. The Spaniards rather crassly constructed the division of races as being Indigenous, Black, and Spanish. The combination among these three races determined the way in which a person was classified: as a subject or as a vassal, as someone who received tributes or gave them (Fuentes 1992:234). The Spaniards born in Spain and the ones born in Mexico were considered the most pure and had power in almost every area of life in the colony. The *mestizos* came after the Spaniards in ranking, while the indigenous groups and enslaved Africans were at the bottom of the social ladder (García 2002:6–7). The issue of race in the colony was further modified in some cases by the delineation of class according to richness or political power (Cosío Villegas 1981:Vol. 1, 348–49, 444–45, 451).

The nineteenth century witnessed the independence of Mexico from Spain, and the struggles of the new republic to keep its freedom and land. A challenge came in 1836 when Texas declared its independence from Mexico. This incident, followed by the annexation of Texas to the United States, plus other complicated political events in both Mexico and United States, led to the 1845–1848 war between these two countries. This war ended in 1848 with the signing of the Treaty of Guadalupe Hidalgo, in which Mexico ceded its northwest territory to the United States, and also accepted the annexation of Texas to its north neighbor. As a consequence, the border was moved and the people who had been living in the northern part of Mexico now lived in the southwestern part of the United States. Overnight these Mexicans became Mexican Americans living in a new country, culture, and society (1981: Vol. 3, 69–84). Virgilio Elizondo has called this new reality facing Mexicans "a second *mestizaje*" (Elizondo 2000a:13–16). Now these Mexicans of Indigenous, African, and Spanish descent were once again forced to encounter the process of mixing, but this time with the Anglo-Saxon culture of the United States.

Since the beginning of their encounters, the Anglo-Saxon people have perceived the Mexicans as "other," indeed as an inferior other (Machado 1999:89–90). This new pattern of relationships gave room to the racism and discrimination that has continued up to the present (Elizondo 2000a:13–18). Mexican Americans who live in the United States today are formed not only by all those Mexicans who were natives in this area and who were crossed by the borderline, but by all the Mexicans who later entered the United States legally or illegally. Today the people of Mexican descent are the largest Hispanic group in this country, followed by Puerto Ricans and Cubans (De La Torre and Aponte 2001:18).

Who Are They? Mexicans, Mexican Americans, or Chicanos/as?

Although people of Mexican descent live throughout the whole United States, they prefer the areas of the Southwest—Arizona, California, Colorado, New Mexico, and Texas—as their place of residence. They are a growing population because of the youthfulness of the group, a significant reproductive rate, and the flow of legal and illegal immigrants from Mexico (Sáenz and Greenlees 1996:9–10). Most of the people of Mexican descent are at least bicultural in the sense that they are familiar with Mexican and Anglo cultural traits.[1] This biculturalism does not represent a uniformity among them, but a diversity in terms of ethnic social orientation and loyalties, and use of language–Spanish, English, and/or Spanglish.[2] For instance, first generation people, those born in Mexico, usually feel more comfortable with Spanish and are more loyal to their Mexican culture, while second, third, and subsequent generations born in the United States feel more comfortable with English or *Spanglish*, and may be partially loyal to both Mexican and Anglo cultures.

This diversity is present also in terms of their preferred group name: Mexicans, Mexican Americans or *Chicanos/as*. The name "Mexican" is usually preferred by the Mexican-born people belonging to the first generation; however, there are many people of Mexican descent of the second and subsequent generations who also refer to themselves as Mexicans (Keefe and Padilla 1992:63, 79). According to Matt Meier and Feliciano Rivera, the term Mexican American is defined as "a citizen of the United States of America either by birth or naturalization who is of Mexican descent, usually of mixed European (largely Spanish) and Indian origins" (1981:220). If analyzed closely, one realizes that these two terms "Mexican" and "Mexican American" are not clearly defined, and thus are used interchangeably according to each person's preference.

The complexity of appropriately naming the people of Mexican descent is further intensified by the addition of the term "*Chicano/a.*" This complexity has led some people to also use the names "*Chicano/a*" and "Mexican American" interchangeably (Keefe and Padilla 1992:5). Yet others oppose it. According to Alfredo Mirandé, by deciding between these terms a person makes a political choice. For him, Mexican American is a term that is devoid of radical or militant meaning because it "connotes middle-class respectability and eschews ethnic consciousness and political awareness" (1985:3). On the other hand, *Chicano/a* "is a word self-consciously selected...as symbolic of positive identification with a unique culture heritage." For him "many have not realized that Mexican-American is analogous to Negro or colored, whereas Chicano is analogous to black" (Ibid.:2–3).

The term *Chicano/a* "signifies a proud, militant ethnicity with connotations of self-determination, rejecting accommodation and assimilation, and favoring confrontation strategies" (Meier and Rivera 1981:84). It derives from the word Mexicano (Xicano), and it was originally used as a pejorative to refer to the Mexicans of lower class. In the 1960s, it was adopted by the young people of Mexican descent to show pride in their heritage. Today it is seen as a controversial term

---

[1]As the United States becomes a place where many cultural groups coexist, people of Mexican descent are also becoming multicultural as they learn to live with all these different cultures.

[2]*Spanglish* is a combination of English and Spanish that involves a mixture of both languages, either in the same sentence or sometimes even in the same word.

because of its radical and militant connotations. It is probably most used in California (1981:83–84).

Among the many significant contributions that people of Mexican descent have made to the life of the United States is rich theological reflection. It is to the analysis of some of these theological contributions that we now turn.

Theological Contributions

The first theological concept to discuss is the notion of *Mestizaje*, which is central to the theological articulations of Virgilio Elizondo, a well-known Mexican-American priest and pioneer of Hispanic theology.[3] In its traditional use, the term *mestizaje* refers to the biological mixture between different races that gives birth to a new group of people. Most of the time it comes about through conquest, colonization, and physical violence. In this biological sense, Elizondo affirms that it is a natural, common process (Elizondo 1995: 9–10). But there is more to *mestizaje* than this biological mixture. For "mestizaje produced not only a new people but also a sense of peoplehood" (Maldonado 1997:103). This new peoplehood is "born out of two histories and in them begins a new history. The symbolic and mental structures of both histories begin to intermingle so that out of the new story…new meanings, myths, and symbols will equally emerge" (Elizondo 1995:12). In this sense, *mestizaje* is a powerful mixing process in which physical, cultural, social, and religious identities merge to form a new identity, usually dominated by the characteristics of the conquerors. It is painful, but inevitable, as the new group begins to forge a new identity and worldview that is both similar to and different than the parents' ones. The established parent groups fear this process of birth because it represents a threat to what has been already established as acceptable. Thus, *mestizos/as* encounter a life that was conceived through conquest and colonization, and that is marked by rejection and marginalization. Yet, in the midst of all the confusing and painful beginnings of a new group, there is a moment, sooner or later, in which the *mestizos/as* discover their rich and unique identity, worldview, and mission. These new discoveries may be unacceptable and incomprehensible for the parents' groups, but welcomed and understood by the new group (Ibid.:14–17).

As mentioned above, people of Mexican descent in the United States have gone through a double process of *mestizaje*: the first one in the sixteenth century involving the Spanish and indigenous cultures producing the Mexican culture, and the second one in the nineteenth century involving this Mexican culture and the Anglo-Saxon one. According to Elizondo, the cultural clash and pain that surrounded the first *mestizaje* was resolved and reconciled with the event of the Lady of

---

[3]See Elizondo, *Galilean Journey* (2000a), and *The Future Is Mestizo* (1988).

Guadalupe (the next theological contribution to be discussed). The defeat and conquest had been so traumatic for the indigenous people that during the first years of the Colony they wanted only to die. However, Elizondo affirms, this changed in 1531 because "the symbolism of *la Morenita* [the brown Lady] opened up a new possibility for racio-cultural dialogue and exchange" (2000a:12). As these dialogues and exchanges took place, a new identity was forged under the blessing of the one who came to be a mother for all: the Virgin of Guadalupe. In her, Elizondo continues, the early *mestizos/as,* and the later present-day Mexicans, Mexican Americans, and Latin Americans find their meaning, uniqueness, and unity (Ibid.:12–13).

The second *mestizaje* was also a traumatic experience for Mexicans. As the line of the border was moved, overnight these Mexicans became inhabitants of a different country with a new language and culture. As they once more tried to forge a new identity and worldview, they became the "other" for both the Anglos and the Mexicans. Since the *mestizos/as* no longer fit the standard categories for either group, they started to be seen as inferior. Due to these powerful dynamics, little by little, the Mexican Americans unfortunately began to believe that, indeed, they were inferior (Ibid.:13–16).

Elizondo argues that the way to deal with this problem is to help Mexican Americans find their unique identity and mission in life. Key for this discovery is their acceptance of themselves as *mestizos/as*–similar to both parents, but different and unique, a new creation. This new creation, this *mestizaje,* will reach its full potential and be actualized only by following Jesus, who brings new life out of death, says Elizondo. "It is in the Lord's way that the salvific and liberating role of our human mestizo way finds its ultimate identity, meaning, direction, and challenge" (1995:17).

In order to affirm the relevance of Jesus' life for the Mexican Americans, Elizondo introduces the idea of Jesus as a *mestizo.* Since Jesus was identified as a Galilean, and Galilee was a place of mixed people and languages, he experienced a cultural and linguistic *mestizaje.*

Yesterday, as today, mixed people are looked down upon. Jesus suffered the rejection and marginalization that are present in the lives of Mexican Americans. However, Jesus knew that he had a mission, so from out of this oppressive situation he proclaimed the new life that becomes concrete only through the reign of God. Because this proclamation challenged the powerful structures of his age, in time Jesus began to be persecuted and eventually was put to death by these negative forces. However, from Jesus' mission, vision, life, sacrifice, and resurrection, new life was created (Elizondo 1995:17–23).

With this in mind, Christian Mexican-American *mestizos/as* are called to follow Jesus' path and, from their concrete situation of suffering, to start challenging the powerful structures that are oppressive not only for them but for all humanity, with the goal of proclaiming new life to those who suffer. In light of this, the Mexican-American *mestizos/as* have many reasons to rejoice and celebrate because God has given them a unique identity and a special call (Ibid.:23–26).

A second theological contribution that I would like to discuss is the Mexican-American reflections on the "Virgin of Guadalupe." According to the Roman Catholic narrative, the Lady of Guadalupe appeared in 1531 to an indigenous man called Juan Diego. She referred to herself as "Tlecuauhtlacupeh," which the Spaniards heard as "Guadalupe." She addressed Juan Diego as her son and told him that she was his mother. She asked Juan Diego to build a temple for her and promised to comfort all who suffer (Franciscan Friars of the Immaculate, 1997:179–80, 193–204).

Once more, Hispanic Catholic theologian Virgilio Elizondo is a key pioneer in the contemporary religious reinterpretation of this event.[4] For him, this event is liberating and life-giving because it solved and reconciled the cultural clash and pain that surrounded the first *mestizaje*. By appearing to Juan Diego, an Indian man, the lowest of the low, the Lady of Guadalupe brought new hope and life to the indigenous people. She gave them back their dignity. Since the Spaniards had raped many indigenous women, the *mestizos/as* offspring of this violence were seen as a race of illegitimate children. Through her apparition to Juan Diego, the Virgin of Guadalupe radically changed this. She legitimized the *mestizos/as* race by becoming its mother. Through the Virgin, the indigenous people went from degradation to pride, from rape to purity, dignity, equality, and freedom. Elizondo suggests that this event affected not only the people of Mexican descent, but also all Latin Americans (2000a:11–13).

While Catholic people of Mexican descent usually interpret this event through the eyes of faith (Elizondo 1981:79, 86, Rodríguez 1994:6–17, 159), I contend that this is impossible for Protestants not only because of their lack of faith in the Virgin, but because they have actively been taught to ignore her. However, ignoring her is not easy because long ago the Virgin of Guadalupe became much more than a Catholic devotional figure; she became a part of the Mexican culture. Thus, I suggest that Protestant people, but especially Protestant women, deal with her as a cultural symbol that has affected what it is to be a woman in this patriarchal culture. By questioning, challenging, and providing feminist liberating reinterpretations of her, women of Mexican descent will find a path toward liberation (Lozano 2002:204–16).

Another theological contribution that is important to discuss is that of María Pilar Aquino, a feminist Catholic theologian who has written extensively about women's issues from a liberation perspective. Although Aquino's contributions to feminist theology can be seen as a

---

[4]See his books *La Morenita* (1981), and *Galilean Journey* (2000a).

unity, I would like to highlight two particular ideas. One is her emphasis on rediscovering the Latina feminist theology's connections with the *Chicana* and Latin American feminist movements. Aquino insists that as a feminist theologian, she, and many others, have found inspiration and empowerment in these secular movements that seek to transform society. Thus, there is a need to be in a learning dialogue with them (2002:133–36).

Another of Aquino's contributions is related to the importance of analyzing the real context of women's lives, and acknowledging in the theological task that many of their struggles and sufferings are related to the failure of the capitalist neoliberal global economy. "The dream of the capitalist neoliberal global economy to establish global integration through global markets, global technology, global ideas, and global well-being has truly become a nightmare for the majority of the world's population." Aquino continues by stressing that "in this global paradigm, it is the world's rich who benefit most at the expense of the poor, most of whom are women and children" (Ibid.:141). This connection is important because if theology seeks to provide a true answer to the suffering of the poor it needs to take seriously what is oppressive in their context.

Finally, there is a contribution that even though not predominant in theological circles, has the potential to impact in a significant way the theological discourse of the people of Mexican descent. I am referring to the concept of "*nepantla*" that Chicana artists have used to express their reality. According to Gloria Anzaldúa, "*Nepantla* is the Nahuatl word for an in-between state, that uncertain terrain one crosses when moving from one place to another, when changing from one class, race, or gender position to another, when traveling from the present identity into a new identity" (Anzaldúa 1998:165). *Nepantla* can mean a physical or emotional crossing of borders that sometimes can produce a sense of disorientation in a person. This disorientation is a reality for people who live in the borderlands. In the case of women artists, "The *Nepantla* state is the natural habitat for [them], most specifically for the *mestiza* border artists who partake of the traditions of two or more worlds and who can be binational" (Ibid.:166). By living in *nepantla*, these artists locate themselves in a space, but they question it, tear it apart, and then rebuild it. To live in this way brings a threat to the dominant culture that has the need of keeping clear identities and lines in their territories. Thus, in order to develop and maintain her identity, an ethnic artist needs "to scream loud enough and fight long enough to name herself" (Ibid.). María Pilar Aquino suggests that for Latina theologians "entering *Nepantla* means…that we are willing to engage in new explorations about God and ourselves from the creative 'border' locations" (2002:149). To do theology from this place, Latina/o theologians may have to also scream loud and fight enough to discover and/or redefine their own creative spaces and ways to articulate pertinent discourses based in the *nepantla* reality of their communities.

Conclusion

The story of people of Mexican descent in the United States has, from the beginning, been one of pain and suffering, but it is also a story of struggle, courage, empowerment, faith, and hope. The double experience of *mestizaje* forged a people with a unique identity. In the measure that they continue to claim and understand this identity, their self-esteem will be affirmed, and their contributions—such as the notions of *mestizaje*, *nepantla*, reinterpretations of the Virgin of Guadalupe, and Latina feminist theology—will continue to flourish and enrich the life of this country and of the entire world.

CHAPTER 18

Puertorriqueños/as[1]

■ LUIS N. RIVERA-PAGÁN

The creativity of Puerto Rican theology is a matter to which I have dedicated a good portion of my intellectual endeavors, and it is gratifying to note—and appropriate to celebrate—the tremendous and increasing output of great quality.[2] This impressive Puerto Rican theological creativity adds to the literary reflection on the Christian faith lived, believed, and pondered in our Caribbean and Latin-American cultural, social, and historic context. Without pretending to be exhaustive, here are some examples of this output:

- The recent work of Samuel Pagán, *El misterio revelado* (2001), is, as stated in its prologue, "a magnificent contribution to Iberian American biblical studies" and is, in my opinion, his major academic contribution up to the present.
- There is the reissued *Introducción a la teología* (2002) by José David Rodríguez Sr., with its added chapter, "Notes for a *Evangélica* Puerto Rican Theology," which brings up to date the contributions of *boricua*

---

[1]Translated from Spanish by the editors.
[2]See Rivera-Pagán, *Senderos teológicos* (1989), *Los sueños del ciervo* (1995), *Diálogos y polifonías* (1999), and "Pistas y sugerencias" (1998:27–75).

(i.e., Puerto Rican) religious thought and is a valuable addition to our theological literature.[3]

- In *Tú sobrepasas a todas* (1999), a significant group of women pastors and laywomen from the Christian Church (Disciples of Christ) reflected on the centennial celebration of the *evangélicas* churches of Puerto Rico with a book edited by Nohemí Colón-Pagán emphasizing the contributions of women to the life and mission of that denomination.

- Ediberto López has written an excellent book about hermeneutics and exegetical methods entitled *Para que comprendiesen las Escrituras* (2003). López's colleague Guillermo Ramírez has published in his own right *Introducción al Antiguo Testamento* (2003). Both works deserve a wide readership.

- Homiletics occupies a noteworthy role in our *evangélica* literature. Along these lines we have something novel in Pérez Álvarez, *We Be Jammin* (2002), and *The Gospel to the Calypsonians* (2004), a collection of sermons in English, edited in Puerto Rico at the Seminario Evangélico, and preached in the Virgin Islands by the Mexican/Puerto Rican Eliseo Pérez Álvarez. It presents a way to read Kierkegaard at the same time that one listens to calypso or reggae. In 2001, Pedro Sandín Fremaint and Pablo A. Jiménez published an excellent book of sermons, entitled *Palabras duras*, that makes a rich contribution to the Protestant pulpit.

- The participation of the Puerto Rican churches in the struggle of the people of the island of Vieques against the United States Navy has found literary expression and theological reflection in two recent books, the first by Lester McGrath-Andino, *Quo Vadis, Vieques?* and the second by Wilfredo Estrada Adorno, *¿Pastores o políticos con sotanas?* (2003).

- For my part, I continue to publish essays and articles in key anthologies on the theological debates concerning the Spanish conquest and evangelization of Latin America.

Moreover, the study of Puerto Rican ecclesiastical and theological traditions continues to multiply, notable examples of which are the following:

- *Evangélicos en Puerto Rico en la época española* (1997, 2001), by Ángel Luis Gutiérrez, and *Protestantism and Political Conflict in the Nineteenth-Century*

---

[3] *Editor's note:* Because of contemporary connotations of the English word *evangelical* in U.S. Protestantism, we have not translated the word *evangélica* in this essay because of the broader sense of the Spanish, signifying both "Protestant" and "evangelical" rather than one particular theological and cultural stream of Protestantism, as is the case in the North American English-speaking context. See the discussions elsewhere in this *Handbook* in chapters 23, 24, and 25.

Hispanic Caribbean (2002), by Luis Martínez Fernández, have both advanced considerably the investigation of Puerto Rican Protestantism prior to the United States invasion in 1898. Also, there is *Protestantismo y política en Puerto Rico, 1898–1930* (1997) by Samuel Silva Gotay, in which he systematically advances the academic analysis of the institutional and ideological development of missionary Puerto Rican Protestantism.

- An important anthology edited by Lester McGrath-Andino is *Un ministerio transformador: El Seminario Evangélico de Puerto Rico* (1998), about the history of this pivotal institution of theological education.

- *Impacto cultural de cien años de protestantismo misionero en Puerto Rico* (2000), edited by David Hernández Lozano and Héctor López Sierra, is a collection of papers delivered at the symposium "Cultural Impact of One Hundred Years of Missionary Protestantism in Puerto Rico," held in October 1998 at Inter-American University in Puerto Rico.

- *Cántico borincano de esperanza* (1999), written by Wilfredo Estrada Adorno, focuses on the history of the Bible Society of Puerto Rico.

These works on Puerto Rican ecclesiastical and theological traditions are the results of the opportune convergence of *evangélica* identity and intellectual curiosity. As was well written by the Brazilian theologian and poet Rubem Alves, they transform historical and theological writing into a communal sacrament:

> The historian thus is someone who recovers lost memories and distributes them, as if each one was a sacrament, to those who lost the memories. Truly, what better communal sacrament exists than the memories of a common past, marked by the existence of pain, sacrifice and hope? The historian harvests in order to disperse. He is not only an archaeologist of memory. He is a sower of visions and of hopes. (1981:364–65)

Puerto Rican theology has been the subject of study of two recent doctoral theses. The first of these is "The Social Thought of Protestant Christians in Puerto Rico in the 1960s" (1997) by Felipe Martínez, and the second is *"Praxis e Identidad*: Discourses and Practices of Puerto Rican Religious Education" (2001) by José R. Irizarry Mercado. Both dissertations, besides being excellent contributions to the study of our theology, beckon the attention of the U.S. academic environment for their relevance and value. I am especially gratified that they deal with four projects of theological creativity to which years ago I devoted my book *Senderos teológicos* (1989).

Mention of these doctoral dissertations brings to consideration a significant factor: the theological creativity of compatriots who live and work in the North American diaspora. From the other shore of the Puerto

Rican nation, often in English–the new global language–they teach, investigate, reflect, and write. And by so doing they preserve the tradition of Orlando Costas, who left us a legacy of impressive writings about ecclesiology and theology of missions.[4] Once more, without pretending to be exhaustive, permit me to point out some notable examples:

* *Dignidad* (1997) is a contribution by Ismael García to theological ethics from a Hispanic/Latino/a viewpoint.
* *Teología en Conjunto* (1997) is an excellent anthology edited by José David Rodríguez Jr. and Loida Martell-Otero that seeks to define the outlines of the new Hispanic/Latino theology in the United States.
* *The Spirit, Pathos and Liberation* (1998) is the published doctoral dissertation by Samuel Solivári in which the author coins the thought-provoking concept of *orthopathos*.
* *Mission: An Essential Guide* (2002), a recent publication, is a text written by Carlos Cardoza-Orlandi with the rhythm of Caribbean salsa, which enriches missiology, a discipline on the rise.
* *The Ties that Bind* (2001) is an anthology coedited by Benjamín Valentín and Anthony B. Pinn (an African American scholar of religion) breaking new ground in the dialogue between two minority and marginal theologies within the North American ecclesiastical spectrum: African American and Hispanic/Latino/a.
* *Justicia en nombre de Dios* (2002) by José David Rodríguez Jr. is a valuable collection of essays, sermons, and reviews that advance Puerto Rican reflection within the broader Hispanic context.

The works mentioned are distinguished illustrations that indicate the start of a possible dialogue and collaboration between theologians residing on the Island and those to whom destiny has allotted wandering in the diaspora. One should not forget the importance of the experience of diaspora and exile in the Sacred Scriptures. In the Old Testament, it constitutes a crucial painful dimension in the history of the people of Israel–from Egypt to Rome–traveling by way of the Babylonian and Persian exiles. In the New Testament, diaspora formed the first point of departure for the expansion of the Christian faith in the Mediterranean world. With respect to language, do we possess in our Holy Scriptures the genuine words of Jesus? On the contrary, do we not agree upon the popular Greek translation, the *koiné*? Also, this writer, from the diaspora of his academic and teaching location as professor at Princeton

---

[4]Among others, Costas wrote the following: *The Church and Its Mission* (1974), *The Integrity of Missions* (1979), *Christ Outside the Gates* (1982), and *Liberating News* (1989). The major study about Costas to date is the doctoral dissertation by Traverzo Galarza, "The Emergence of a Latino Radical Evangelical" (1992a). See also Martell-Otero's dissertation, "Liberating News: An Emerging U.S. Hispanic/Latina Soteriology of the Crossroads" (2005), in which she explores Latina/o ecumenical contextual soteriology, and specifically those of Orlando Costas and Virgilio Elizondo.

Theological Seminary, experiences continually what the Haitian historian Michel-Rolph Trouillot has described as "the pain and perverse pleasure of writing in a second language" (1995:xv).

Puertorriqueñidad in Puerto Rican Theology

What is *puertorriqueñidad* in Puerto Rican theology? Undeniably, it is not a new theme. Felipe Martínez and José Ramón Irizarry discussed it in their doctoral dissertations, mentioned previously. It is also a privileged object of reflection in recent essays by José David Rodríguez (2002a:89–100) and Luis G. Collazo (2001:95–106) as well as the subject of brief but significant debates between Luis Rivera Rodríguez (1990:5–7) and Moisés Rosa Ramos (1989:3–4) on the occasion of the publication in 1989 of my own book, *Senderos teológicos*. In a critical reference to said debate, Yamina Apolinaris and Sandra Mangual Rodríguez contributed a crucial feminist perspective through an important essay entitled, "Theologizing from a Puerto Rican Context" (1996). Nevertheless, the question of the *puertorriqueñidad* of Puerto Rican theology deserves to be renewed for two reasons–the perennial uncertainty about *puertorriqueñidad* and the incessant development of the cultural history of any human community.

As Umberto Eco said, "an Argentine is a person seated at a table in a bar asking what is it to be Argentine" (Scheines 1991:111). Uncertainty about Argentine national identity is shown in the enigmatic literary labyrinth that, in a diverse way, reigns in the stories by Jorge Luis Burgos, Julio Cortázar, and Ernesto Sabato. Something similar can be affirmed about what it means to be Puerto Rican: "A Puerto Rican is a person seated at a bar table asking, 'What is it to be Puerto Rican?'" The drink on the table that stirs up questioning about identity may be unique–a good Mendocino wine in the first case, excellent Barrilito™ rum in our case–yet the uncertainty is not very different, namely, what are the distinctive signs of nationality? Is it not perhaps the labyrinth, the crucial metaphor in the classic tale by Edgardo Rodríguez Juliá, *La renuncia del héroe Baltasar* (1974)? Is not the enigma of national identity, from the particular views of *puertorriqueñidad* (Puerto Rican-ness), a traditional theme in our literature, from Manuel Alonso to Rosario Ferré, from Manuel Zeno Gandía to José Luis González, passing through the anguish of René Marqués? "Our literature…constitutes a constant variation on the same obsessive theme: the symphony of national identity…," as rightly pronounced by Ana Lydia Vega (Gelpí 1993:185).

Argentine and Puerto Rican uncertainty about national identity is very different. The primary matrix of the former is the successive waves of European migration at the end of the nineteenth and early twentieth centuries; the source of the latter is that which Aníbal Quijano has characterized as colonialism: the political, economic, and cultural dominance successively exercised by the two imperial nations–Spain and the United States (1997:113–21). The Argentines endlessly debate, "What kind of nation is their society: Latin American, Indo-American, or Western?" Puerto Ricans passionately debate if their society is indeed a nation.

Puerto Rico possesses abundant creativity in many areas of social and cultural life. The recent retrospectives of the grand masters of Puerto Rican painting (Lorenzo Homar, Rafael Tufiño, Myrna Báez, and José Rosa), the intense and entertaining work of Antonio Martorell, together with the emerging extensive brood of younger painters, are authentic expressions in the fine arts of excellent creativity.[5] The same thing can be affirmed in other dimensions of the cultural existence. Nevertheless, a constant anguish impedes us to be or not to be. We seem to lack the knowledge and the necessary power to sketch our own path for our national community. The thread of Ariadne led us astray, which permits us to recognize our path in the confused labyrinth of the history. But, will not the anguish be the same confusion that nourishes our cultural creativity?

The present philosophical environment, primed by postmodernism, has cultivated a special sensibility for the paradoxes and ambiguities of *identity*. It is methodologically necessary to understand the role of Christian religiousness in the plural and paradoxical configuration of *puertorriqueñidad* to transcend the essentialist vision of our national identity. That vision, a return to a mythical past, *in illo tempore*, of the supposed definitive shaping of national identity, is found not only in sectors of Hispanofile Catholic Boricua, but curiously also in the famous essay by José Luis González, "*El país de cuatro pisos*" ("The Four Storied Country"), with its alleged fixation of past Island cultural personality shaped by the African slave trade (1980:9–44). The debate concerning Puerto Rican nationality suffers, now and then, from a metaphysical essentialism that obscures the historicity of all social order, and at other times from a fragmentation of thought and being that impedes the recognition of the formation of some distinctive characteristics of a particular plural and complex personality. Puerto Rican-ness (*puertorriqueñidad*) as a totally authentic national identity is not an unchanging essence that reaches its highest point by preserving itself without contamination, but rather it is a *process* being formed, polyphonic, subject to risk, and contingent on historical development.

In the context of that formative process of Puerto Rican identity, *evangélica* theology is able to come together incorporating the immense spiritual, existential, and intellectual resources of its religious traditions. The *evangélica* Christian faith is already a vital and crucial dimension of our national spiritual creativity. What is important is to avoid confusion

---

[5]See the excellent catalog published by the Museum of Art of Puerto Rico on the occasion of its opening: *Los tesoros de la pintura puertorriqueña* (2000).

by obsolete fixations on a supposed "Puerto Rican essence," and to recognize that we are able to contribute through a liberating pastoral ministry and theology to the decolonization of our society and to shape a deep and peaceful sense of liberty, sovereignty, and autonomy.[6]

However, so far we have just touched the threshold of the theme, that is, what is Puerto Rican theology? In what ways is it Puerto Rican? Setting out from the ground that we have covered so far, I believe that we can move forward on the following hermeneutical paths:

- I reiterate the thesis I expounded in my book *Senderos teológicos*: there does not exist *one* Puerto Rican theology. Serious and deep thought about the Christian faith and the human enigmas takes into account critical studies on the biblical scriptures, doctrinal traditions, contemporary theoretical currents, and the historical and cultural contexts of our people that produce a rich crop of a diversity of theologies. The plurality of Puerto Rican theological thought expressed in that book, through an analysis of four conceptual paths, undoubtedly has grown in the closing stages of the last century.

- The distinction that Luis Rivera Rodríguez makes between *teología puertorriqueña* and *teología puertorriqueñista* seems correct. The first asserts that "it is the critical reflection about God and fundamental matters of human existence and destiny in the direct or indirect historical record of the Puerto Rican experience." The second "is that reflection from Christian faith and praxis about God and the human condition and destiny in the Puerto Rican experience and context made…with an option for *puertorriqueñidad*" (1990:6–7). In the same way, it seems negative to me to consider both options as necessarily antagonistic.

- I consider accurate the critical observations of Yamina Apolinaris and Sandra Mangual concerning the dialogue/debate between Rosa Ramos, Rivera Rodríguez, and Rivera Pagán of limiting this discussion to the ideas of male theologians (1996:235). It is necessary to support current efforts to discover and highlight the feminist perspectives of Puerto Rican theology. The dominance of ecclesiastical patriarchy requires a feminist perspective for the reading of the scriptures and doctrinal traditions.

- The conceptual articulations of theology of liberation necessarily are modified and altered. Yet, there is no turning back from the correlation achieved between Christian faith, the kingdom of God, redemption, and human liberation. Even one very scholarly text, *The Oxford Illustrated History of the Bible*, ends with an extensive section

---

[6]The special edition of *Casabe: Revista puertorriqueña de teología*, 2d ed., 1998–1999, devoted to the theme "La pastoral descolonizadora: retos de hoy," contains various pertinent articles. Likewise see *Apuntes: Reflexiones teológicas desde el margen hispano* 21, no. 2 (Summer 2001).

dedicated to liberationist exegetical currents (Rogerson 2001:293–355). The premature predictions of the death of theology of liberation seem both erroneous and generally interesting. Rather than a demise, what is occurring is a diversification of themes and perspectives that do not abdicate the liberationist theological and biblical hermeneutics.

Puerto Rican theology is authentically worthy of that surname in as much as it contributes to the spiritual liberation and mental decolonization of those of us who work out our destiny in this Caribbean country. At the same time, Puerto Rican theological creativity is not limited to those who live, labor, and write on the Island. The diaspora is an important and vital dimension of the Puerto Rican nation, and a good part of the Puerto Rican theology is written in the United States, in English. Nevertheless, the intellectual interaction between Northern colleagues and Islanders leaves a lot to be desired. It is necessary to promote a dialogue between those who contribute to the formation of Puerto Rican theology on the Island and those who do it in the United States.

CHAPTER 19

Cubanas/os

■ MARGARITA M.W. SUÁREZ

At first glance one may view all Cuban Americans as similar to other Latin@s[1] in the United States. However, their particular history of exile, diaspora, and immigration distinguish them as a unique religio-ethnic group. One must also make the claim that while Cuban Americans make up a particular Latin@ group within the United States, they do not all believe the same way, either religiously or politically. This chapter will attempt to offer a lens into the various self-understandings among Cuban Americans regarding their social history, political inclinations, and religious practices.

History and Experience of the Cuban Diaspora

On January 1, 1959, after three years of guerrilla fighting in the Sierra Maestra and sabotage in the cities, Cuban "president" Fulgencio Batista gave up the fight and fled the country in the face of lackluster support by the United States and the continual pounding by the 26th of July insurgent army led by Fidel Castro. For the next ten days Castro's troops traveled west through the island to the cheers of thousands of Cubans who believed the time had finally come for their release from tyranny and oppression. With the exception of a few political cronies of Batista, the island believed that Fidel offered the most substantial hope for real social change. The middle class believed that with his victory they would

---

[1]The symbol "@" is often used in Spanish to create a written inclusive plural form of a noun. Since all nouns in Spanish are designated as either male or female nouns, using the "@" indicates that a word includes both male and female persons in that particular category.

be entering a time of economic freedom, without government corruption. The millions of Cuba's poor and illiterate hoped for a change that would bring them choices. Fidel's message of social change and concern for the most needy was threatening to the very wealthy, but many still believed that their economic fortunes would be better served by a populist than a repressive dictator. What the Cubans discovered shortly after the triumph was that Fidel Castro and his compatriots were going to institute a radical social revolution in which the poorest and most vulnerable would be the most favored within the society and all others would have to learn how to serve the majority poor, rather than their own desires. This radical transformation led to a mass exodus from the island within the initial years of the revolution and, for various reasons, a continued desire on the part of others to make a home elsewhere, particularly in the United States.

In order to recognize and discern the differences among Cubans in the United States it is important to understand the various reasons Cubans have left Cuba since the Revolution of 1959. More than a million Cubans have become exiles from their homeland since Fidel's 1959 revolution triumphed, and the varying reasons include economic and/or political differences, and religious persecution. People left for the vagaries of freedom and from fear of communist dictatorship. During the height of the Cold War (1960–1967), nearly a million Cubans left for the United States. The wealthiest Cubans made up the earliest wave of those who left for self-imposed exile. The new Cuban government appropriated their businesses and lands, as well as those belonging to professionals who either had no interest in working for a socialist vision of society or were easily discouraged by the difficulties encountered during the shortages and bureaucratic inadequacies of the new revolutionary government. This group was almost exclusively white, highly educated, and at least nominally Roman Catholic.[2] The U.S. government gave these exiles financial, social, and educational assistance that enabled them to make new homes relatively quickly.

The next wave to enter the United States was the group often referred to as the *Marielitos*. Starting in 1980, approximately 120,000 Cubans left Cuba when the government opened the port of Mariel, just west of Havana, to any who could find transportation to leave. Many left believing that the United States would afford them more freedom than

---

[2]While the majority of Cubans at that time had been baptized Catholic, relatively few were regular practitioners. In 1956 a study was conducted of the religious makeup of the island. According to this study, out of Cuba's population of approximately six million there were: "72.5% Catholic, 19% indifferent, 6% Protestant, 1% spiritist, .5% Masonic, .5% Jewish, .5% devoted to the saints." Of the 72.5% Catholics, 75% were not practicing and of the remaining 25% only 11% received the sacraments regularly. This amounts to 2% of the population, or roughly 120,000 people (Gómez Treto 1988:12).

they were experiencing in Cuba. Castro also sent about 20,000 people held in Cuban jails out of the country. The Marielitos faced a very different reception in the United States from the first wave of emigrants. Rather than preferential treatment, this group was first settled in a Tent City on Eglin Air Force Base in Orlando, Florida, and confined to this refugee camp until they were sponsored by a friend or relative in the United States who could vouch for them.[3]

The *Marielitos,* on the whole, were not mostly white, nor of the professional class. Some were artists and intellectuals whose ideas and creativity had been stifled by the restrictions imposed by the government. Some were gay and lesbian who had lived with repression by the society and the government. Others were those who had not found a responsible place within the new society and either practiced different forms of Afro-Cuban religion or had little or no religious affiliation because of twenty years of social pressure to conform to the atheist standards of Marxist-Leninist society. The *Marielitos* did not fit comfortably into the Cuban American society that had established itself in the early '60s in Miami. They came mostly from a different class and racial background, practiced a different form of religion, and had a difficult time fitting into their own society. Miami was not much friendlier to them than Cuba.

Many continue to leave Cuba, mostly because of the economic crisis instigated by the loss of favored economic status that had been afforded the island nation by the Soviet Union until its collapse in 1991. Many risk life and limb on the open sea in search of economic opportunities scarce in Cuba, because of Cuba's proximity to the United States. Cubans, similar to many Mexicans and Central Americans who risk crossing the Southwestern desert, attempt to go to a place where they can work and send money back home to their families left behind. The United States is seen as a temporary economic home until more opportunities exist in Cuba. Unlike the *Marielitos* and the original exiles, these Cubans come from varied educational backgrounds. Some are professionals, some misfits; some seek significant economic gain, free market alternatives, while others simply hope to survive better in the United States than in Cuba. Many of these exiles have experienced the newfound openness of the Cuban state to religious practice and belong to worshiping religious groups ranging from Catholic to Protestant to Afro-Caribbean traditions.

Religiosity of Cuban Americans

Approximately 65 percent of the Cuban exile community lives in Miami, creating an enclave of political and economic power unparalleled

---

[3]In 1984 the United States and Cuba finally discussed the situation of the *Marielitos,* some of whom were still in the Orlando refugee camp four years after arriving in the United States. Some 20,000 were returned to Cuba, and the balance eventually resettled in the United States.

by any other first generation exile/refugee community. The economic assistance offered by the United States to the initial exiles included "character loans" and resettlement grant aid. This initial infusion of capital by the U.S. government enabled those Cubans who were the most adept (because of their educational level and class status in Cuba) to build businesses and prosper. Though they left Cuba "with only the clothes on our backs," they were able, in a relatively short space of time, to become successful in their exile.[4]

Their economic success and eventual political hegemony in South Florida led to the Cuban exile community's religious self-understanding as the chosen of God. They, who were "*aquí*" (here) were successful, while the ones who remained "*allá*" (there) continued to struggle in poverty. It was obvious to them that God was rewarding them for their entrepreneurial spirit and their ability to overcome the difficulty of their exile. They had God on their side, whereas the Cubans who remained, who chose to follow the devil (Fidel), were being punished for their idolatry.

Although the practice of religiosity in Cuba had been rather low, this experience of exile, marked by the great loss they had suffered, combined with their successes here, caused religious observance and theologizing to increase dramatically. The idea of God and recognition of their salvation from the demonic powers "*allá*"—namely Fidel Castro, communism, and all those who followed him and his perverse power—gave the community a newfound religious fervor. As the chosen ones, they had a sacred responsibility to name the powers of evil and to fight against them with all their might. More complex even than just performing their sacred duty, the exiles created an idealized image of Cuba, which had never existed, nor would ever exist, except in their imagination:

> Cubans remember their dismembered past as a white people coming from a white nation, fleeing tyranny with only the clothes on their backs and leaving behind *la Cuba de ayer* (the Cuba of yesterday), which encompassed a seemingly idyllic way of life. The construction of this fictitious *Cuba de ayer* becomes a necessary strategy against oblivion, a tactic by which they can survive as a people. Its construction creates a common past symbolically linking them to the land they left behind while defining their new exilic identity. Exilic Cubans' attempt to avoid the pain of displacement leads them to construct a

---

[4]This mantra is heard over and over among first generation Cuban exiles. It accomplishes two goals. First, it demonizes Fidel Castro and his communist economic policies, which granted exit visas to those who chose to leave, especially in the early years, but would rob them of all their possessions, save those clothes they could wear. Second, it elevates their own initiative and capability of self-salvation, negating any help they had received by the U.S. government to give them a hand up/out.

mythical Cuba where every *guajiro/a* (country bumpkin) had class and wealth, where no racism existed, and where Eden was preserved until the serpent (Fidel) beguiled Eve (the weakest elements of society: the blacks, the poor, etc.) and brought an end to paradise. (De La Torre 2004a:78)

This newly imagined human "fall from grace" story fuels the vehemence Miami Cubans still feel and are so willing to manifest before millions of Americans on broadcast TV, as occurred during the Elián Gonzalez story.[5]

Cuban exiles, mirroring their counterparts in Cuba, participate in many different religious traditions throughout the United States, as well as in Miami and its surroundings. Catholic exiles, significant numbers of Protestant clergy and lay leaders, and those whose primary religious affiliations were with *Santería,* sought a haven outside of Cuba. *Santería* is a religious tradition that is West African Yoruba religion transplanted onto Cuban soil with overlays of Catholicism. Brought to Cuba with the African slaves from the seventeenth to the nineteenth centuries, the West African gods had to be worshiped covertly because of the harsh treatment by those found practicing *Santería* by the Catholic Church. The pantheon of African *orishas* (saints/gods) were overlaid with the names and dress of the Catholic saints. Hence, *Changó* became *Santa Barbara* and Lazarus became *Babalú Ayé.* It was not the Catholic saints who were being venerated, but their representative African spirits who had crossed the ocean accompanying their followers.

Followers of *Santería* became exiles in the United States and once again brought their deities with them across the Straits of Florida. *La Virgen de la Caridad de Cobre* (The Virgin of Charity from Cobre) the patroness of Cuba for the Catholics and the powerful *Oshun* has had a shrine built for her in Miami, overlooking Biscayne Bay. Here she can be worshiped while she watches over her people even as she did when she arrived in Cuba with the slaves. The shrine offers a sacred space to support the continued image of the idyllic Cuba left behind.

While the Cuban exile's religious life in Miami is circumspect, revolving around their privileged status, evident in their economic and political success, living outside Miami shifts one's perspective greatly. In the rest of the United States, Cuban exiles are often seen as just another group of Latin@s. In general, Cuban exiles have pursued higher education more than other Latin@s and have therefore gained more access to institutional success within the United States. The majority Anglo population, however, has not necessarily viewed Cuban exiles in

---

[5]For further information on the Elián Gonzalez story, see Kenneth D. MacHarg, "The War for Elian," *Christianity Today* 44, no. 3 (March 6, 2000):25. For a fuller analysis of the Elián saga and its relationship to the Miami Cuban community, see De La Torre, *La Lucha for Cuba* (2003).

any more privileged light than other Latin@s, as a group. For these Cubans who have not had the resources of Miami, or for those who left Miami, being just one among other Latin@s in the United States has meant feeling the sting of racism. While some of these Cubans still attempt to live in Cuban enclaves in which their religious self-perception is not challenged, many others have chosen to align themselves with other Latin@ groups. These Cuban exiles do not see their religious lives as reflections of God's elite, rather their solidarity with their Latin@ brethren attunes their eyes and ears to the problems of the powerless and the vulnerable in society. These exiles, most of whom were children when they left Cuba or are the first generation to have been born in exile, are more likely to see Fidel and the Cuban revolution as historical markers of an attempt to better the lives of the most vulnerable. While most would see the success of the Cuban revolution as minimal, they would not characterize Fidel as demonic, nor do they see those Cubans *aquí* as any holier than those *allá*.

These exiles are not the ones who make the 6 o'clock news, or the ones who staged demonstrations in front of the house of the family of Elián Gonzalez in Miami. These Cubans often work behind the scenes in not-for-profit agencies, doing social service work, assisting the newest Latin@ immigrants in countless quiet ways. These Cubans may see their religious lives as being the hands or feet of Christ in the world, making a difference a little bit at a time. These Cubans try to travel back to Cuba to learn. They have been members of the Antonio Maceo Brigade,[6] social workers, nurses, doctors, and just ordinary people, looking to make a difference. Religiously they are Christians and Jews, atheists and humanists, Buddhists and Unitarians. These Cuban exiles know themselves to be Latin@s, just as the Puerto Ricans, and the Mexicans, and the Central Americans. This recognition allows them to seek humility and solidarity rather than arrogance. These Cubans have contributed to the wider body of theological thought known as Hispanic/Latin@ theology in the United States.

Theological Contributions Made by Cuban Exiles within Hispanic/Latin@ Theology

Cuban American theologians straddle at least two worlds. They live and work in the United States, yet their history began in another place, an island nation, whose sun feels different on the skin, whose breezes blow carrying particular aromas, whose sounds and hues and

---

[6]Antonio Maceo Brigade is an organization believing in regularizing relations between the United States and Cuba. It is composed mainly of women and men in their 20s and 30s who were brought out of Cuba as children at the beginning of the revolution or are in the first generation of Cubans born in the United States. The Brigade supports many of the social goals of the Revolution, and an end to the economic blockade of Cuba by the United States government.

architecture reflect Spanish, African, and French sensibilities. These
women and men came to the United States at different times for a
multiplicity of reasons; however, very few have ever returned to their
homeland. Each of these theologians have also been shaped through
varying experiences as Latinos/as in the United States. As Christians,
they have been and continue to be in the forefront of the creation and
development of U.S. Hispanic liberation theologies.

Lourdes Casal, a celebrated Cuban poet, writes:

> But New York was not the city of my infancy,
> nor was it here that I grasped truth for the first time,
> not here the corner of my first fall,
> or where I heard the whistle that cuts the night.
> That is why I will always remain marginalized
> a stranger among the stones,
> even under the kingly sun of this summer day,
> just as I will always remain a foreigner,
> even when I return to the city of my infancy,
> I carry this marginality immune to all returns,
> too much a New Yorker to be
> – even to once again be –
> anything else.[7]

While this poem does not reflect the experience of all Cuban
American theologians, it expresses a universal sentiment of the
immigrant experience: living in exile/diaspora for many years and then
returning home.

Cuban Americans have been and continue to be significant voices
within U.S. Latin@ theology.[8] These Protestant and Catholic women and
men recognize their position as people who live and think "on the
margins." Often coming from middle-class backgrounds in Cuba with
advantages over their working class compatriots, they received
educations and had access to some systems of power, both in Cuba (pre-
1959 revolution) and in the United States (post-1959 revolution). Their
growing solidarity with other Latin@ groups is, however, evident in the
work that they have produced in the last quarter of the twentieth century.

Cuban Americans have a similar story of exile. All have left their
homeland and attempted to make a way in a new land while forever
looking across the Straits of Florida longingly toward home. Once on
U.S. shores many have chosen to see their exile in religious terms as the

---

[7]Lourdes Casal, "Para Ana Velford." The poem was originally published in the literary
magazine, *Areito* 3, no. 1 (Verano 1976).

[8]I use the term *theology* as an umbrella term that–for the purposes of this chapter–
includes many disciplines, including: church history, systematics, ethics, bible, religion, and
culture.

chosen of God. They consider themselves similar to the Israelite exiles in Babylon, waiting for the opportunity to return to their homeland, while creating a clear sense of their homogeneity and sense of chosenness. Others have left their privilege behind and chosen to understand their exile as part of the forced or chosen exilic status of other Latin@s in the United States: as one of many who have come to these shores with a story of struggle and hope.

CHAPTER 20

Central and South Americans, and "Other Latinos/as"

■ MANUEL A. VÁSQUEZ

Post-1965 changes in U.S. immigration law, together with economic, political, and cultural processes associated with the current globalization, have contributed to significant changes in the composition and patterns of settlement of Latino populations. Whether fleeing political repression and civil unrest, or dislocated by economic crises generated by the implementation of neo-liberal structural reforms, or in search of jobs in the expanding service and informal sectors of the U.S. economy, growing numbers of people from Central and South America have migrated North during the last three decades. As a result, while Mexican Americans, Puerto Ricans, and Cuban Americans are still the largest national origin groups among U.S. Latinos, the population of immigrants of Latin American descent in the United States has diversified considerably. According to the 2000 Census, between 1990 and 2000 Mexicans went from 60.4 percent to 58.5 percent of all Latinos, while Puerto Ricans went from 12.2 percent to 9.6 percent, and Cubans from 4.7 percent to 3.5 percent. In the meantime, the category of "other Hispanics" grew from 22.8 percent to 28.4 percent (Guzmán 2001:2).

The first sizeable wave of "other Latinos" to arrive were Dominicans, who began to settle in large numbers in Florida, and in Northeastern cities such as New York, Philadelphia, and Providence, in the early 1960s (Pessar 1995:1–18). In New York City–particularly in Upper Manhattan's

Washington Heights, locally known as *Quisqueya* Heights[1]–Dominicans have become key players in the cultural and political spheres. The ascendance of Dominicans in New York City is occurring simultaneously with the numerical decline of the traditionally strong Puerto Rican community, as many Puerto Ricans move to New Jersey, Pennsylvania, Florida, and back to the island. Beginning in the 1970s, Dominicans also began to settle in significant numbers in Boston, in and around the working-class neighborhood of Jamaica Plain (Levitt 2001:46–53).

Dominican migration flows have been conditioned by U.S. foreign policy. In an effort to release demographic and political pressure on the pro-American administration of Joaquín Balaguer, who was installed following a military occupation by U.S. Marines in 1965, the United States government made up to 20,000 visas available for Dominicans wishing to immigrate. Migration also served Balaguer and successive national administrations to mitigate the dislocation produced by the implementation of a capitalist model based on rapid industrialization and urbanization. By 1983, when the island experienced renewed economic and political turmoil, the number of Dominicans legally admitted to the United States each year surpassed the quota. What started as a Cold War attempt to counterbalance the influence of Cuba in the Caribbean gained a logic of its own, as immigrant social networks facilitated increased legal and illegal movement into expanding Dominican communities in the United States. The 2000 Census estimates 765,000 Dominicans living in the United States, about 2.2 percent of the total Latino population (Guzmán 2001:3).

Many Latin American countries were under military dictatorships during the 1970s, and political dissidents and asylum seekers from Chile, Argentina, and Uruguay arrived in the San Francisco Bay area, Chicago, New York, and Washington, D.C. In the early 1980s, years of economic polarization, military repression, and rising armed revolutionary movements led to open civil wars in Central America, generating widespread urban and rural dislocation. Thousands of Salvadorans, Guatemalans, Hondurans, and Nicaraguans fled to the United States, settling in Washington, D.C.; Houston; Los Angeles; New Orleans; Chicago; and Miami and Indiantown, Florida (Hamilton and Chinchilla 1991:75–110). Central Americans now constitute close to 5 percent of the U.S. Latino population. Since the United States was actively involved in bolstering the repressive regimes in Central America as part of a Cold War counterinsurgency policy, the federal government did not facilitate the process of settlement as it had done before for those fleeing communist countries (except for many Nicaraguans after the triumph of

---

[1] *Quisqueya* is the Dominican Republic's indigenous name.

the Sandinista revolution in 1979). Especially in the case of Salvadorans and Guatemalans, Catholic and Protestant churches filled the void, organizing a network of safe houses and legal support known as the Sanctuary movement. This movement drew its prophetic inspiration from biblical themes such as exodus, exile, the promised land, and the unfolding reign of God, all key in the development of post-Vatican II progressive Catholicism, particularly liberation theology, in Central America.

The 1980s, dubbed the "lost decade" of Latin America, also saw disorderly transitions to democracy and acute economic crises characterized by uncontrolled inflation, widespread unemployment, and drastic downsizing of the welfare state. These political and economic crises pressured urban middle classes throughout the hemisphere, providing a "migratory push" to the United States. The pace of migration from countries like Peru, Ecuador, Brazil, and Colombia quickened considerably, bringing many urban professionals to the United States. As the crises deepened, migration circuits were established between U.S. populations and South American rural communities, many of them indigenous. South Americans now represent close to 4 percent of the total U.S. Latino population.

Jointly, there are ten million U.S. Latinos of Dominican, Central, and South American origin, close to 30 percent of the country's Hispanic population. Table 1 shows the breakdown of U.S. Latino populations, particularly those labeled "other Hispanic" in the 2000 Census.

Table 1

NATIONAL ORIGIN/DESCENT	NUMBER	PERCENTAGE[2]
Total Hispanic/Latino Population	35,305,818	100.0[3]
Mexican	20,640,711	58.5
Puerto Rican	3,406,178	9.6
Cuban	1,241,685	3.5
Other Hispanic/Latino	10,017,244	28.4
Dominican	764,945	2.2
Central American	1,686,937	4.8
Costa Rican	68,588	0.2
Guatemalan	372,487	1.1
Honduran	217,569	0.6

[2]This table is adapted from Suárez-Orozco and Páez, *Latinos,* 2002.
[3]Latinos represent 12.5 percent of the total U.S. population. From 1990 to 2002 the Latino population grew by 73 percent (in comparison with the total U.S. population which grew only 16 percent in that period).

Nicaraguan	177,684	0.5
Panamanian	91,723	0.3
Salvadoran	655,165	1.9
South American	1,353,562	3.8[4]
Argentinean	100,864	0.3
Bolivian	42,068	0.1
Chilean	68,849	0.2
Colombian	470,684	1.3
Ecuadorian	260,559	0.7
Paraguayan	8,769	0.0
Peruvian	233,926	0.7
Uruguayan	18,804	0.1
Venezuelan	91,507	0.3
Other South American	57,532	0.2

Generally, scholars agree that the census has undercounted Latinos, especially those falling under the category of "other Hispanics."[5] Using an alternative counting methodology, Roberto Suro estimates the number of Dominicans at 938,000 (2002:2), representing an 80 percent increase from the Dominican population recorded in the 1990 Census. In contrast, the 2000 Census indicated only a 47 percent increase during the same decade. The case of Salvadorans is similar. Suro estimates that population stands at 932,000, representing a 65 percent growth from 1990 numbers, while the 2000 Census showed only a modest 16 percent increase. Other national origin groups that have shown substantial growth are Hondurans (at 315,000, for a 140.6 percent increase), Guatemalans (535,000, for a 99 percent increase), and Ecuadorians (at 347,000, for a 81.6 percent increase). Overall, Suro finds that in the decade of 1990–2000 the number of other Hispanics/Latinos has grown by 76.4 percent. This rate is higher that the 60 percent growth in the Mexican population in the United States during the same period.[6] This confirms the perception that recent migration flows from Latin America are highly active: 71 percent of Central Americans are foreign-born, and

---

[4]Brazilians are very ambivalent about using the term Hispanic or even Latino to characterize their individual and collective identities. On the one hand, they insist that they speak Portuguese, not Spanish, and seek to avoid the stigma attached to the terms Hispanic or Latino (which in the Euro-American public imagination are associated with poor, illiterate, and dark-skin migrants). On the other hand, they understand that in terms of receiving recognition and resources from local, state, and federal agencies it makes sense to associate with Hispanics/Latinos. On Brazilians immigrants, see Martes, *Brasileiros nos Estados Unidos,* 2000; and Margolis, *Little Brazil,* 1994.

[5]Janny Scott, "A Census Query Is Said to Skew Data on Latinos," *The New York Times,* 27 June 2001.

[6]Suro also argues that the 2000 Census undercounted Mexicans by almost 1.5 million.

34 percent have immigrated to the United States in the last ten years. For South Americans the figures are 74 percent and 33 percent, respectively (Schmidt 2003:8–12).

These numbers belie the socioeconomic, racial, and gender diversity within national categories. "Other Hispanics" include Honduran Garifunas; Dominicans and Colombians of African descent; indigenous groups like Guatemalan Maya K'iches, Ecuadorian Quechuas, and Bolivian Aymaras; as well as upper-middle-class, white, urban, and professional Peruvians, Argentinians, and Brazilians, many of whom have overstayed their tourist visas in the face of deteriorating economic situations in their countries.

Heterogeneity among populations of Latinos of Central and South American origin and descent is enhanced by the emergence of transnational social fields.[7] Using some of the same advances in communication and transportation technologies that have propelled the current episode of globalization (e.g., the Internet, inexpensive phone calls, and travel), many new Latino immigrants maintain close ties with their societies of origin, building dense networks of exchange and reciprocity, while, at the same time, establishing stable connections in the United States. This multiple "embeddedness" in fields of thought and practice that span national borders represents an attempt by Latino migrants to adapt and respond creatively to the dislocation generated by economic globalization, and to the effort of nation-states to control and police populations, even as they open their borders to an expanding neo-liberal capitalism.

Multiple embeddedness contributes to fragmented and hybrid identities among Latinos. On the one hand, by maintaining ties with the societies of origin, transnational linkages lend support to the affirmation of national, regional, and even local (village level) identities. In the religious field, this is illustrated by the proliferation throughout Latino communities of "fiestas" honoring local patron saints, which are often organized by hometown associations working in close connection with *cofradías* and *hermandades* in Latin America, as Larissa Ruiz Baia has shown in the case of Peruvians in Paterson, New Jersey (2001:97–102). On the other hand, multiple embeddedness may lead to transculturation, the mix of various ideas and practices across the transnational networks. Thus, some transnational youth gangs, like the Mara Salvatrucha, undergo a process of "*choloization,*" adopting some of the language and practices of long-established Mexican-American gangs in Los Angeles and blending them with elements of Salvadoran and Guatemalan culture (Vásquez and Marquardt 2003:125). Often affirmation of particularistic and hybrid identities occurs simultaneously, as when Latinos affirm

---

[7]See Portes, Guarnizo, and Landolt, "Pitfalls and Promise" (1999); and Levitt, DeWind, and Vertovec, "Transnational Migration" (2003).

national identities and in the same breadth declare themselves to be part of a pan-Latino culture standing at the margins of a world dominated by Euro-Americans.

In addition to the diversifying composition of U.S. Latino populations and their increasing embeddedness in transnational circuits, new patterns of settlement have emerged. Latinos continue to be a predominantly urban population, concentrating in large "gateway" cities in a few states, including California, Texas, New York, Florida, and Illinois. Because of the decline of the manufacturing sector (the traditional anchor of social and cultural life for immigrant groups in cities like New York and Chicago), and the expansion of the service sector, some of the fastest growing Latino populations are now in nontraditional states in the "New South," particularly in Georgia and North Carolina, and Arkansas (Ibid.:41, 146).[8] This shift is buttressed by the growth of transnational agricultural and food industries that require abundant and cheap labor. For example, many Central Americans have moved to the Carolinas to work in the poultry industry, or during the summer they might head to Nebraska and Wisconsin to work in the fields or in meat packing plants. Both the poultry and meat processing industries have a reputation for harsh labor conditions, with high turnover and accident rates. Social tensions emerge as Latinos move to places with relatively homogeneous (Euro-American) populations and without the infrastructure to receive the new arrivals.

Latinos often feel physically and psychologically isolated. Very often churches are the first social organizations that help reweave communities torn by the process of marginalization. Here transnationalism comes to the fore as churches often build associational life by reaching across national borders to stretch the boundaries of the community of origin. Rejection by the "host" society (even when Latinos are incorporated into the local economy, paying taxes, buying houses, establishing businesses, and sending their children to public schools) calls for the creative transposition of the village in Latin America, with all its geographical and moral landmarks, to the United States. For Christian churches, the challenge of this transnationalism is to reconcile Christ's universal message of salvation with institutional demands and the particularities of immigrant life in various contexts (Levitt 1998:83–84).

Demographic differentiation among U.S. Latinos has been accompanied by a religious diversification. This is not surprising, given

---

[8]According to Brewer and Suchan, six of the seven states with more than a 200 percent increase in Latino population between 1990 and 2000 are in the South. In Florida, Latinos are still heavily concentrated in the Miami-Dade County. However, they have progressively moved north, to cities like Orlando and Tampa, where they work in either in the tourist or construction industries. In addition, many Latinos have moved to places like Boca Raton and Fort Lauderdale to provide personal services to the growing population of retiring baby boomers and the seasonal "snow birds" (2001:92).

the growing religious pluralism in Central and South America.[9] One of the most important contributions brought by Central and South Americans to the United States is the rapid expansion of a "pneumatic" Christianity that centers around the notion of personal salvation through the blood of Jesus, as well as a direct and intense experience of the Divine through the gifts of the Holy Spirit (*charismas*). For example, in Guatemala some estimates place the percentage of Protestant population at between 19 percent to 30 percent, while in Chile it falls between 16 percent and 18 percent, and in Brazil between 12 percent and 15 percent. According to Paul Freston, 60 to 70 percent of Latin American Protestants are Pentecostals (2001:194). Originally emerging in the United States and carried to Latin America by missionaries, Pentecostalism has now returned to the United States with a distinctive Latino flavor.

A case in point is the Brazilian Universal Church of the Kingdom of God (*Igreja Universal do Reino de Deus*), a global neo-Pentecostal church that has temples in major urban centers in the United States, such as San Francisco, Boston, Los Angeles, New York, and Miami. With divine healing and exorcism sessions around the clock, the Universal has specifically targeted Latinos struggling to get a piece of the American Dream, offering a gospel of health and wealth that helps them negotiate the tribulations of daily life (such as domestic conflict, drug addiction, and sickness) and legitimizes the small socioeconomic gains they have made. Other transnational Pentecostal churches may help to affirm national identities abroad. This is the case of the Evangelical Church Prince of Peace (*Iglesia Príncipe de Paz*) among Guatemalans in Texas (Garrard-Burnett, 1998b:117–25). Alternatively, churches like *La Gran Comisión* in Paterson, New Jersey, contribute toward creating a pan-Latino identity by bringing together migrants from various countries in Latin America under a priesthood of all believers (Vásquez 1999:617–35).

In response to the rapid growth of Pentecostalism among U.S. Latinos, the Roman Catholic Church encouraged the Charismatic Renewal movement (CCR), a form of pneumatic Christianity that preserves Pentecostalism's intimacy and spontaneity while stressing loyalty to the hierarchy and the cult of Mary. Here the Catholic Church is building on the explosive growth of the CCR in Latin America, where there are an estimated twelve million Charismatic Catholics (Chesnut 2003).[10] With its emotive music and lively worship style, the Catholic Charismatic renewal has been popular among young Latinos. A large percentage of the movement's leadership is composed of Puerto Rican,

---

[9]See Smith and Prokopy, *Latin American Religion in Motion* (1999); and Chesnut, *Competitive Spirits* (2003).

[10]At the very high end, the International Catholic Charismatic Renewal Services based in Vatican City places that estimate at 74 million, representing 16 percent of the Catholic population in Latin America (http://www.iccrs.org).

Dominican, Colombian, and Costa Rican immigrants who have had contact with the movement in their sending countries. Like Pentecostalism, the CCR is a global movement involving a dense network of transnational events and connections, such as retreats, seminars, and exchanges of pastoral agents (Peterson and Vásquez 2001:208).

The diversity of nationalities in the growing U.S. Latino population has resulted in the revitalization of traditional popular Catholicism, particularly of the cult of the saints and Mary. It is now common in Latino parishes to celebrate the feast of the patron saints of the multiple nations represented. Processions, novenas, and special masses in honor of *El Señor de los Milagros* (from Peru), *Nuestra Señora de la Altagracia* (Dominican Republic), *El Divino Niño* (Colombia), *Nuestra Señora de Chiquinquirá* (Colombia), *Nuestra Señora de Suyapa* (Honduras) crowd the liturgical calendar alongside the traditional celebrations for St. John the Baptist (for Puerto Ricans) and *Nuestra Señora de la Caridad del Cobre* (Cuba). Within this diversity, the Virgin of Guadalupe, whom Pope John Paul II named "Queen of the Americas," continues to occupy a special place for Latinos, serving as the paramount symbol of pan-Latino Catholicism.

In multinational and multicultural parishes traditional popular Catholicism and the Catholic Charismatic Renewal movement have cross-fertilized and entered into tensile relations with the pre-Vatican II *cursillo* movement and with Christian Base Communities (Comunidades Eclesiales de Base or CEBs), which are connected to liberation theology and had a strong presence in Central America, Brazil, and Peru in the 1970s and 1980s. While CEBs experienced significant decline and reformulation, they played an important role in linking pastoral work and social action in places like Chicago, San Jose, and Los Angeles, and other parishes working closely with the Industrial Areas Foundation (IAF).

The contributions of Central and South Americans to U.S. Latino religion have not been limited to Christianity. The 1993 U.S. Supreme Court decision upholding the legality of animal sacrifice in *Santería* has opened the way for more visible expressions of other religions of the African diaspora. Particularly in cities like New York, Miami, Pompano Beach, and Orlando, where many Brazilians have settled, nascent *Umbanda* and *Candomblé centros* (houses or centers) anchor informal religio artistic networks that bring together religious practitioners with traveling *capoeira* (an Afro-Brazilian martial dance) troupes and drumming masters. Often these networks facilitate the circulation of leaders, beliefs, ritual practices, and money not only from cities such as Rio de Janeiro and Bahia, but also from Lagos, Nigeria, and Luanda, Angola. Thus far, there have not been any explicit or formal efforts to link Santería networks with other African-based religious-cultural organizations. However, in places like Miami and New York, one finds an increasing number of initiates trained in multiple traditions. Moreover, Santería *botánicas* often carry the sacred paraphernalia of Candomblé, Umbanda, and Vodou.

Also in New York City and Boston, Spiritist centers offer middle-class white Brazilians self-help networks and treatment for the psychosomatic stresses of life in the United States (Margolis 1994:167–94). Latin American Spiritism has underscored the rational aspects of the beliefs in reincarnation and afterlife, following the teachings of French pedagogue Allan Kardec. In the United States, Latin American Spiritism has interacted with folk healing systems like *curanderismo* brought by rural Mexican and Central American migrants.

Finally, chain migration has made possible the geographic concentration of Central and South American immigrants not only from the same country but also from the same province or town. This has had an important impact on the formation and maintenance of collective identity among migrants of indigenous descent. Guatemalan Mayas in Indiantown, Florida, or in Houston, Texas, for example, work closely with their sending villages in the Guatemalan highlands to organize cultural clubs and hometown associations dedicated to the preservation of their heritage, including their language and religion. Following the award of the Nobel Peace Prize to Rigoberta Menchú, exchanges between Native Americans in the United States and Mayan immigrants have grown as part of global efforts to develop a pan-Indian identity (Arias 2001: 16–19).[11]

In summary, Latinos of Central and South American origin and descent, as well as Dominicans, are contributing to fairly nascent and highly variegated Latino communities. This diversification is likely to continue into the twenty-first century, as families seek to reunify, transnational connections between home and host country are maintained, and as migration from countries in turmoil like Venezuela and Colombia grows. Such diversification has already enriched the U.S. religious field considerably. As migrants from different social classes and ethnic and racial origins throughout the hemisphere interact with each other and with African Americans and Native Americans in multinational and multicultural congregations, religious networks, and urban settings in the United States, new forms of religious "hybridity" and conflict are likely to emerge.

---

[11] An example of this is CornMaya. See http://www.geocities.com/cornmaya/home. html.

CHAPTER 21

Latino/a Catholic Theology

■ ANTHONY M. STEVENS-ARROYO

The Precursors of Latino Theology

Antonio José Martínez (1793–1867), the curate of Taos, New Mexico, at the time of annexation, merits recognition as the first person to produce written Latino Catholic theology. Ordained a priest in 1822 after the death of his wife, he was sent to Taos in 1826 and became pastor of the first church in the United States to be named after Our Lady of Guadalupe. Padre Martínez edited a newspaper *El Crepúsculo de la Libertad* that reflected his vision of a world in which religion and politics were reconciled on behalf of a better society. Because he was an elected deputy of the Mexican Territorial Assembly, these ideas developed in New Mexico Catholic principles for the republican form of government after independence from Spain.

Although few of his writings have survived the political and ecclesiastical tempests of his life, one of his sermons from 1832 (Stevens-Arroyo 1980:81–85) celebrated the achievements of Padre Miguel Hidalgo, who had begun the successful rebellion against Spanish power on the Feast of Our Lady of Sorrows, September 16, 1810. Martínez countered the objections of church support for armed rebellion by comparing Hidalgo to the Maccabees who had saved Judea from pagan Hellenists in the century before Christ. Although Hidalgo was excommunicated by the institutional church of colonial Mexico and later executed at the hands of the military, Martínez considered these sufferings comparable to the passion and death of Jesus. Martínez described Christ's death as an act bringing spiritual salvation as well as a moment of political liberation from Roman oppression. Martínez viewed Hidalgo's struggle to free Mexico as a continuation of Christ's salvific heroism, lending political persecution a theological meaning.

After the United States annexed New Mexico in 1848, Padre Martínez participated in the constitutional convention that organized the territory under rule from Washington. Subsequently, he was elected to three terms in the territorial assembly. More importantly, he represented the native Roman Catholic clergy to French-born Bishop Jean Baptiste Lamy, who arrived in 1850 with the expectations of being bishop in what was to become the Diocese of Santa Fe. Martínez argued against the bishop's decision to impose tithing and to set fixed sums on the donations expected for services such as baptisms, weddings, and funeral masses. New Mexico's first Catholics, wrote Martínez, would interpret such policies as simony. Without denying the bishop's canonical authority, he presented arguments against Lamy that articulated for the first time in Catholic theology the importance of Latino people's religiosity. Although Martínez was prophetic in his anticipation of the disaffection of New Mexican Catholics from the culturally insensitive policies of Lamy, he suffered excommunication by his bishop in 1857, similar to the fate of the Mexican liberator, Padre Hidalgo.

Padre Martínez's theological defense of cultural traditions was echoed in the struggle of the *Hermanos Pentitentes,* or *La Fraternidad Piadosa de Nuestro Padre Jesús,* to gain ecclesiastical approbation in New Mexico. The *Penitentes* grew in importance as the number of native New Mexican priests diminished under Bishop Lamy and his successors in the nineteenth century. Although there was little doctrinal opposition to their effort at preserving pious devotion to the passion and death of Jesus by prayer meetings at their priestless chapels or *moradas,* their preservation of New Mexican religious traditions challenged assimilationist views of Americanizers and the authoritarian vision of episcopal power. Thus, documents that argued for and against the acceptance of the *Penitentes* by ecclesiastical authorities present opposing theological visions of culture and contain the seeds of Latino Catholic theology.

The need to link popular religious movements to ecclesiastical authority are an important theme in Catholic theology. Catholic theology views the interaction of hierarchy and religious movements as essential. In Pauline theology, equality in the church does not imply that all believers exercise the same functions, but rather that specialization in ministerial roles is harmonized by a common faith. Thus, the magisterium of church authority reflects Catholic fidelity to the body of Christ. Early in its development, Latino Catholic theology denounced using the hierarchical nature of the church as an excuse to imitate social class divisions.

Theological concern with the institutional church is also found in the theology of the saintly Cuban-born priest Felix Varela (1788–1853), a contemporary of New Mexico's Padre Martínez. A seminary professor of philosophy and accomplished author, he represented Cuba in the Spanish *Cortés* in 1822, only to be exiled upon the fall of that government a year later. Unlike Martínez, however, who remained in his native New Mexico, the political arena for Varela was that of an exile in the United States seeking to attack injustice in his Caribbean homeland. Although Varela lived as a priest in Philadelphia and New York, where he wrote books and edited newspapers with rich theological reflection, his focus was not upon Latinos in the United States. This is not to deny Varela his place as a theologian of the Latino Catholic experience. His *Cartas a Elpidio sobre la Impiedad, la Superstición, y el Fanaticismo* (1835–1838), offer pastorally focused counsel to a patriot eager to reconcile his faith and spiritual life to a political cause, and is part of his legacy to Latino theology.

Annexation came to Puerto Rico in 1898, fifty years after the Stars and Stripes were hoisted over California and the Mexican territories. The first Latino Catholic theology on the island came not from a cleric, but from José de Diego (1866–1918), a lawyer and patriot who merged a sacramental theology focused on the eucharist and the right to self-determination. Affirming his faith in the eucharist as nourishment for the Christian soul, de Diego extended that faith in the body of Christ to the church of Puerto Rico. Anticipating a theological vision of the church itself as the "sacrament of the encounter with God," de Diego affirmed that a commitment to social justice was an essential expression of the faith and compared a denial of Puerto Rico's right to liberty in the civic sphere to a desecration of the consecrated host.

The writings of Catalán priest Jaime Balmes (1810–1848), especially *El Protestantismo,* resonate in the theology of de Diego. But the indebtedness to Balmes is most striking in the political philosophy of Pedro Albizu Campos (1891–1965), who was intellectually reconverted to the faith of his Puerto Rican childhood while a law student at Harvard University in 1916. He witnessed the mobilization of Irish Catholics in Boston for Irish independence by appeal to just war theory, the theology of Francisco Suárez about revolt against tyranny, and Balmes' idea that Catholicism and Protestantism had produced incompatible civilizations. Albizu articulated a Nationalist Catholicism that urged the church to assume a role in defense of Puerto Rican freedom such as had been the case in Ireland and Poland. More of an orator than a writer, and not a formal theologian, his views of race and religion were derived from life in the United States. Moreover, while many recognize the Mexican philosopher José Vasconcelos (1882–1959) as the author of *La raza cósmica,* which advances the concept of cultural *mestizaje* found in much of Latino Catholic theology, it is less well known that Vasconcelos claimed Albizu Campos as his teacher.

The Contexts for Latino Catholic Theology

By the 1930s, the outlines of a Latino Catholic theology had emerged. Careful interpretation of the sources discloses four traits that surface repeatedly.

1. Protestant Discourse: The United States is a nation with a Protestant majority. The conquest of Latino homelands often was viewed as Manifest Destiny for the United States to impose its values upon all peoples. As a result, early Latino Catholic theology is often focused in counter-arguments to Protestant prejudices. While today many of these denominational rivalries have been replaced by a shared theological and ecumenical perspective among Catholics and Protestants, it was not always so. In Puerto Rico, the brotherhood of lay catechists called *Los Hermanos Cheo* became a sort of local church militia against the armies of Protestant evangelizers, often supported materially by the U.S. regime.

Throughout the 1930s, defense of the faith figures prominently in theological production from Latinos in Puerto Rico, Texas, California, and the Southwestern Latino homelands. Often published in Spanish in local Catholic newspapers, this apologetic Latino Catholic theology focused on issues such as secularism in the public schools and birth control. It attacked governmental policies that promoted beliefs or practices contrary to Catholic teaching, considering them as contrary to natural law. Catholic theology argued that parents had principal responsibility for educating children—superseding political loyalties. This defense of Catholicism came as often from laity as from clerics.

In the first half of the twentieth century, two forms of Latino Catholic discourse engaged these issues. One, inspired by Balmes and a Hispanophile mentality, denied legitimacy to Protestantism and asserted Catholic superiority to the U.S. culture. The Cristero Wars in Mexico of the 1920s produced Mexican Catholic exiles to the United States, and the newspapers they published make secularism the target. The other discourse competed against Protestantism to exemplify American values, invoking political principles such as separation of church and state to present Roman Catholics as the victims of un-American prejudices. This approach in Latino Catholic theology emphasized that Latinos had made great contributions to the United States and its history. The Church Extension Society raised funds to restore and preserve buildings in the Southwest, preserving in stone its earliest Christian legacy. Such efforts revisited the traditions, culture, architecture, and foods of the original inhabitants in these parts of the country and placed Latino/as among the groups whose gradual assimilation as citizens did not diminish their unique contributions to the cultural diversity of the United States. The theological discourse of competition with Protestantism depended on these rereadings of history and culture.

2. Heritage: The writings of the New Mexican Franciscan, Fray Angélico Chávez (1910–1996), bridge the pre- and post-World War II periods. Poet, artist, novelist, translator, historian, and longtime archivist for the Archdiocese of Santa Fe, in 1937 he had become the first native New Mexican ordained a Franciscan priest. After retirement he published *Coronado's Friars* (1968), which rectified "400 years of erroneous history about New Mexico's Franciscans." The apologetic purpose in this text was eclipsed by *My Penitente Land* (1974) in which Fray Angélico demonstrated a mastery of archival documents and a contextualization of events that countered the assigned passive role to Latino Catholicism by many professional historians of the Southwest. With lay historian Carlos Eduardo Castañeda (1896–1958), the theological project was enlarged by a patient historical recovery of the Catholic heritage for Mexican Americans.

3. Pastoral Care: A neglected aspect of theological reflection in Latino Catholic history is the pastoral care brought by congregations of religious sisters who assumed missionary tasks in Puerto Rico, California, and parts of the Southwest. Usually at the invitation of Euro-American bishops who wished to provide schools and specialized ministries to the "Spanish-speaking," these sisters evolved a ministerial theology. Precisely because they were not male clerics under supervision of bishops, and because they often ministered to families, the sisters quickly perceived the need for pastoral sensitivity to Latino culture and tradition in ministries of education, hospital care, and outreach to migrant farm workers. Active work with the people produced a number of religious vocations among Latinas. In some instances, such as with the Dominican Sisters of Fatima in Puerto Rico and the Missionary Catechists of Divine Providence, new congregations were founded with a majority of Latina members by splitting off from the missionary orders that had begun ministering to the Latino/as. Native vocations are welcomed in Catholic theology because they show the faith taking root in diverse cultures and societies.

It was not always recognized by church leaders, however, that Latino/as represented a distinct new type of Roman Catholic in the United States. In the immigrant experience, each European group newly arrived in the United States was expected to bring its own clergy and build its own churches to provide services in the language of the homeland. It was anticipated that once English was learned, the need for such a national parish serving a specific language group would evaporate. Ironically, the Latino ancestors had been the first American Catholics, making the faith of Latinas in Texas or Puerto Rico older in the Americas than the immigrant Catholicism professed by the Euro-American missionaries. The model of immigrant Catholicism for Latino/as found in the policies of bishops often clashed with the experiences of missionaries. Not infrequently, we find complaints–from those actually doing pastoral work–in response to episcopal directives, and testimony that a different model for pastoral care was needed.

With the dispersal of large numbers of Mexican Americans to urban centers like Chicago and Puerto Ricans to New York after World War II, ecclesiastical leadership in metropolitan archdioceses tried to provide for their needs. With the churches in these areas in search of personnel with knowledge of Spanish, many of the priests and sisters who had been sent as missionaries to Latino/as in Texas and Puerto Rico returned to the Midwest and Northeast and were asked to continue among the urban migrants the culturally sensitive ministry that they had developed in the Latino homelands. Thus pastoral theology helped prepare in the 1950s a cohort of native Latino/as to assume leadership roles in the church in the wake of the changes produced after the Second Vatican Council.

4. Social Justice: The Catholic theology of social justice that developed out of papal encyclicals, and was given impetus by the New Deal after 1932, is another factor that shaped Latino Catholic theology. While Roman Catholicism always upheld the need to provide for the material needs of the poor, the church previously relied on Catholic institutions such as school, hospitals, and orphanages run by the church itself. Social change and advancement of the poor and working class under the New Deal produced a strain of Catholic theology that shifted moral obligation from private charitable efforts into the civic sphere. Progressive Catholic theologians argued that in a democracy the government represents the people and therefore believers could designate resources in the public square to supply for the corporal works of mercy demanded by faith, as well as impel the church to support labor unions to achieve economic justice.

Latino/as became the target of much of this activist Catholic theology that moved governmental resources to faith-based purposes. Latino/as became a target population for social justice apostolate focused on education and economic support for poor and working class people. Thus, 1945 brought the formation of the Bishops' Committee for the Spanish-Speaking to coordinate ministry for migrant farm workers in each of the several states in their seasonal route from Texas into the Midwest, financed by donations from each of the dioceses and designed with input from sociologists and social workers. These efforts made the church an ally of progressive government and permitted coordination. There was a strong anti-Communist flavor to this social justice activism that reflected the times. The church was "at war" for the souls of Latino/as who were being told that justice was possible only outside religion and the American system. Nonetheless, this cooperation eventually was to include direct funding of social welfare programs through agencies like Catholic Charities.

Francis Cardinal Spellman of New York followed the model for coordinated attention to social concerns for Mexican Americans in the Midwest for Puerto Ricans in the Northeast by establishing in 1953 an office to foster culturally sensitive ministries throughout the metropolis. Like Archbishop Robert Lucey of San Antonio, Cardinal Spellman established training programs in culture and language so that non-Latino priests and sisters would be more effective in the apostolate. These efforts represented a new phase in U.S. Catholicism because the "benign neglect" exemplified in nineteenth-century national parishes that were expected to relieve the bishop of obligations for ethnic ministry was replaced by an integrating approach that saw the spiritual and material welfare of Latino/as as an obligation for all church members. Some non-Latino church leaders came to see Latino/as not as "victims" needing to be Americanized, but as prophetic voices from "the margins" teaching the majority church in the United States about its obligations. Although he was not a Latino, as fruit of his service in the training institutes in Puerto Rico and Cuernavaca, Ivan Illich (1926–2002) developed in Roman Catholic theology a questioning of ethnocentric concepts about the role of the church and its relationship to social institutions.

The *Cursillos* of *Cristiandad* and the Theology of Being Hispanic

There has been theological consideration of the advantages that might have accrued to Latino Roman Catholics if more national parishes had been established for them in the 1950s instead of promoting integrated parishes. The argument for cultural segregation benefits from the success of the *Cursillos de Cristiandad* that were introduced to the United States as the decade of the 1950s ended. Devised by members of Catholic Action on the Spanish island of Mallorca as a method of educating potential pilgrims to Santiago de Campostella, the *Cursillos* rapidly evolved into an apostolic movement. The *cursillo* was, as its name suggests, a short course in Christianity and was organized around the idea of a retreat in Spartan conditions. Participants engaged in small work groups, supervised by trained instructors and guided through a series of tightly structured presentations of the elements of faith. Emerging in 1949 from Franco's Spain, the Cursillo was conservative, hierarchical, and sacramentally focused when, in 1957, it crossed the Atlantic in the person of two U.S. pilots who had been stationed in Spain and offered the first Cursillo in Waco, Texas, in Spanish under the direction of Father Gabriel Fernández. By 1965, when the movement was incorporated as a national organization in the United States, it had spread to virtually every part of the country where there were Spanish-speaking Catholics.

Although its theology had conservative content, the persons delivering most of the instructions on the faith were Spanish-speaking laymen (by 1965, Cursillos for women had been organized). The structure of the Cursillo came close to allowing lay preachers; it was structured around a fervent, renewed commitment to the faith, and encouraged the display of emotions as a legitimate effect of Catholic faith. It also relied upon laypersons for most of its organization, recruitment, and maintenance at the local level where parish *ultreyas* were held on a regular basis. It could be said that the Cursillo of the 1960s provided a "born again" experience for Roman Catholics and a weapon against Protestantism, especially Pentecostal proselytism, as well as a recruitment tool for engaging cultural Latino Catholics in a vital, sacramental life. Most importantly, it legitimized in pastoral theology the culturally expressive Catholicism that had endured despite the U.S. conquests and trained Latino/as themselves as teachers of these values.

The year 1960 also held special meaning to U.S. Catholicism because the election brought a Roman Catholic to the presidency for the first time. On his route to the White House, John F. Kennedy was obliged to articulate an explanation of his Catholic belief within the context of elected office in a largely Protestant nation. Ironically, Catholic bishops repudiated the impartial stance outlined by candidate Kennedy during the 1960 election for Puerto Rico's governor. Condemning Luis Muñoz Marin's policies of birth control and sterilizations, the bishops identified a vote for the governor as sinful. Although the subsequent election discredited the bishops' approach, these contrary political experiences of 1960 illustrated differences between Latino/as living in the United States as a minority and Puerto Ricans living on their island as a majority. It was in this setting, while sessions of the Second Vatican Council were still being held, that the Puerto Rican Jesuit, Antulio Parrilla Bonilla (1917–1994), developed a theology that simultaneously defined Puerto Rican Catholicism and the larger context for being a Latino Catholic in the United States.

Parrilla's theology transcended existing discourses of both de-legitimation and competition with Protestantism by introducing an anti-imperialist and international context of the Third World as the basis for Catholic liberation. A follower of Albizu Campos and an advocate for Puerto Rican independence, Parrilla entered the Society of Jesus, where he was ordained a priest in 1962. Shortly afterward he was named Titular Bishop of Ucres and Auxiliary Bishop of Caguas. Bishop Parrilla advocated for Puerto Rico a cooperativism consisting of small agricultural producers. His economic vision was linked to a social, cultural, and religious conviction that secularism and consumerism threatened Puerto Ricans not only economically and politically, but also spiritually. He opposed militarism, although not a pacifist, and viewed Puerto Rican participation in the armed forces of the United States as a fundamental contradiction of the Catholic teaching of the just war. Parrilla applied the teachings of the papal encyclicals, particularly *Mater et Magistra* of Blessed Pope John XXIII, to the Puerto Rican situation and protested with other religious and political leaders U.S. Navy maneuvers on the islands of Vieques and Culebra. Arrested and imprisoned on various occasions beginning in the 1960s, he protested the Vietnam War, traveling to various parts of the United States supporting and counseling conscientious objectors. Lastly, in accord with Church teachings, Parrilla bitterly opposed the sterilization and birth control policies of the island government.

Parrilla's theology is both radical and conservative: radical in confronting the political contradictions of the U.S. rule over Puerto Rico, but conservative in the adherence to the magisterium, particularly in his pro-life stance against what he called "Neo-Malthusianism" in Puerto Rico. Although centered on Puerto Rico and Puerto Ricans, the theology of Parrilla is truly "catholic" for its breadth, its ecumenism, and its relevancy. His legacy to Latino Catholic theology is an internationalist perspective that relates various Latino groups to each other.

The Latino Resurgence and the *Encuentros*

The reforms of the Second Vatican Council had two important effects on theology among Latino/as. First, the obligation to celebrate the liturgy "in the language of the people" effectively made the United States a bilingual-bicultural jurisdiction. The official body of bishops approved the Spanish language for every parish where that was a preferred language. Second, the Council demanded a reformulation of most of the Catholic theology then taught in seminaries and universities. Established theologians lost importance and new voices speaking to conciliar reforms became prominent. Moreover, suggestions for a Latino flavor to Spanish-language liturgical expression were eagerly sought, as pastors at the grassroots level learned that simply importing rites and translations from Latin America was not sufficient. Thus, Latino theology was welcomed because it was needed.

The ecclesiastical reforms of the Council by themselves, however, would not likely have produced a Latino religious resurgence of the magnitude of what took place. It required a series of important social and political events to magnify the religious changes. In this sense, one can describe the period from 1968 to 1980 by comparing it with the Great Awakening of colonial United States, or the Italian *risorgimento* of the nineteenth century. A unification of disparate groups and the "invention" of tradition similar to the Italian experience also took place for Latinos in the United States. After 1967, one can see Mexican Americans, Puerto Ricans, Cuban Americans, and others proclaiming solidarity with one another under a single cultural identity of Latino/a. Moreover, as in the Great Awakening, religious organizations help prepare Latino/as for participation in political changes.

The fast-moving political events included the radical rethinking of the "War on Poverty." This created neighborhood associations capable of receiving funds for social services, but with the obligation to include a majority of a "minority" leadership. Second was a change in the immigration law that permitted a greater proportion of Latin Americans to enter the United States. Third was the fruition of the civil rights movement led by African Americans such as the Rev. Martin Luther King Jr. Acceptance of the goals of this movement opened political opportunities for all people of color because it had fostered a sense of guilt among elements of the Euro-American population. Fourth, the War in Vietnam encountered radical protest within U.S. society. This radicalness engendered militant groups such as the Brown Berets among Mexican Americans and the Young Lords among Puerto Ricans in the United States. They protested both the Vietnam War and previous wars that had annexed their homelands. Finally, there was the emergence from the church of Latin America a theology of liberation that resonated with the radicalness of many of the Latino movements.

What ignited the Latino resurgence was the grape boycott proclaimed by César Chávez (1927–1993) in defense of the rights of strikers in Delano, California. Although Chávez always was grateful for support from Protestant churches and had learned a few lessons from Hispanic Pentecostals, he personally identified himself as a Roman Catholic, a union organizer, and a *cursillista.* The banner of Our Lady of Guadalupe was one of the symbols used to rally support for *la causa,* and the writings and speeches of Chávez may be considered a type of theology. In the first year of the struggle in 1969, Chicano/a students on Southern California campuses not only organized support for the farm workers, but questioned the stance of the Cardinal Archbishop of Los Angeles. But the organization *Católicos Por La Raza* (CPLR), found itself the target of arrests on Christmas Eve 1969 in the Los Angeles Basilica of St. Basil when some members tried to attend Midnight Mass after distributing leaflets to worshipers entering the church.

In reaction, many Catholic priests considered it important to organize national support for Chávez and the farm workers by promoting the boycott through the churches. The Puerto Rican Bishop Parrilla was in California to foster resistance to the Vietnam War and said mass in Los Angeles for CPLR, symbolically enlisting Puerto Ricans and anti-war Catholics into *la causa.* The effort to organize support for the farm workers led to the formation of PADRES (Priests' Association for Religious, Social, and Educational Rights) in February of 1970, which undertook a campaign for greater rights within the church using the networks that had been set up for the boycott and issuing a call for continuing reform of the church. An organization of religious women, *Las Hermanas,* was formed in 1971 with the same agenda. This cohort of young clerics and religious women carried a desire for a Latino religious resurgence into various apostolates, operating much like a Latino caucus within national associations of catechists, liturgists, etc.

The vision of gathering all these forces together in a congress or *Encuentro* was suggested by Father Edgar Beltán, a Colombian priest with extensive experience in preparing for the historic meeting of Latin American bishops that had taken place in Medellín, Colombia. Supported by various dioceses and the office for Hispanics at the United States Catholic Conference in Washington, D.C., the first *Encuentro* was held in June of 1972 at Trinity College in the nation's capitol. Together with the diocesan and regional *encuentros* that followed, and the Second *Encuentro* in 1976, they constituted a defining moment for Latino/a Catholic theology.

The theology espoused at the *Encuentro* was voted on and approved by the delegates, with the *Encuentro* process requiring each bishop to designate official representatives. The resolutions decided upon were then submitted to the NCCB for approval. In this way, the theology of the *Encuentro* process culminated in a pastoral application in the best tradition of the inchoate Latino/a theological expressions for more than a hundred years. Moreover, in the Second *Encuentro*, the Holy See sent a congratulatory audiotape of a message from His Holiness Pope Paul VI, thus linking the proceedings to the maximum authority in the Roman Catholic hierarchy. Second, Latino/as developed the content of the *Encuentro* theology, faithfully reflecting the concerns of the people. Third, the theological style of these documents was cast in the same mold as conciliar documents—providing biblical bases; citations from previous statements of the magisterium; and rational argumentation from philosophy, history, and sociology. Thus, if the *Encuentro* content was completely Latino, the form was completely Catholic. Fourth, the approval of the resolutions by a committee of the NCCB created a need for more regional *encuentros* that would continue the process of dialogue at all levels of church leadership, leading up to another *Encuentro*. Lastly, by stressing education as a primary concern, the *Encuentro* stipulated more centers for training, thus increasing the number of leaders, which in turn created the possibility of more posts for Latino/as in church agencies and institutions, which were capable of enlarging the opportunities still more. The *Encuentro* process had become an engine for growth in ministries, training, and theology, as well as for articulating in U.S. theology a new meaning for ethnicity and assimilation. Whereas in 1891 the nineteenth-century bishops had rejected in the Lucerne Memorial requests for pastoral reorganization around ethnic differences, when presented by the *Encuentro* with similar recommendations in 1973, the U.S. bishops acquiesced.

Theological themes found in the *Encuentro* documents summarize coherently the major themes of emerging Latino Catholic theology through social justice as expressed in the Catholic tradition of the papal encyclicals: support for the labor movement and Catholic Action; a church interest in developing community organizations using the impetus from the War on Poverty; cultural maintenance and linguistic preservation exemplified in liturgical reform, pastoral training, and religious education; and, finally, a restructuring of church administration and management so that more Latinos would be bishops, pastors, directors of policy-making institutions.

These trends in Latino Catholic theology can be grouped under two headings: a trend seeking change within the church, or the *pastoralist* vision on culture and restructuring of the church; and the *liberationist* focus on the secular world that sprung from social justice and community organizing. Pastoralists view the church as the arena for their apostolate: as long as the people acquire an education about social justice and a deeper commitment to faith, success can be declared. Liberationists, on the other hand, seek to erect better housing, to bring jobs into the community, and to keep crime out. Their ministry is incomplete until those material benefits are delivered. In real life, the pastoralists and the liberationists are not always so clearly divided: those interested in changing the church also are interested in changing the world, and vice versa.

The *Encuentro* process clearly benefited the pastoralist theology for Latino/as more than it helped liberationists. The national effort and the treasure of the bishops were easily focused on internal church needs for educators, liturgists, and leaders for the movements. The professional and political skills for the secular world were of less national importance. Moreover, the liberationist themes for both Puerto Ricans and Cuban Americans were highly politicized: the first with leftist tendencies against the United States, and the other with right-wing resonance from exile groups. Carried on by favorable political and ecclesiastical winds, the Mexican American Cultural Center (MACC) in San Antonio, Texas, became the pace setter for continued development of Latino Catholic theology, especially for the Latino theology required for religious education and the liturgy. The bishops' approval of the *Encuentro* conclusions specifically mentioned MACC as the model for new diocesan and regional training centers in Latino Catholic theology.

The founder and director of MACC was Father Virgilio Elizondo, a San Antonio native who had been trained abroad in missionary theology. He was a featured speaker at the *Encuentro,* along with one of the founders of PADRES, Patricio Flores, who was the first Mexican American ordained a bishop in the United States, and was to become the Auxiliary Bishop and then Archbishop of San Antonio. Elizondo's graduate degree, however, gave his message a resonance in the theology taught in seminaries and at MACC. In *Galilean Journey* (2000a), Elizondo interprets scripture so as to present Jesus, the Galilean, as the member of an regional subgroup despised in the society of his day in ways that mirrored the social status of Latino/as in the United States. Having drunk deeply from the wells of Mexican national culture, Elizondo gave a theological dimension to José Vasconelos' (1882–1959) notion of *mestizaje*. Our Lady of Guadalupe became the symbol of fusion between Catholicism and popular Mexican culture. Retracing the evolution of the painted *tilma* of the sixteenth century into a national symbol raised on the banners of both Father Hidalgo in 1810 and Emiliano Zapata in 1910, Elizondo argued that Our Lady of Guadalupe was not only a Mexican icon but also represented the aspirations of Mexican Americans. With the dramatic demographic increase of Hispanics in U.S. society and within the U.S. Catholic Church, Elizondo's vision is summarized in the title of one of his key books: *The Future Is Mestizo* (1988). While Latino Catholicism had always contained a strong Marian component, Elizondo deserves recognition for elaborating a rich theological theme of *mestizaje* around the ubiquitous image of *la virgen morena*. Moreover, since Marian devotion is not characteristic of Hispanic Protestantism, Elizondo also underscored a unique Catholic dimension to his theology.

The success of the *Encuentro* process in creating a Latino Catholic theology is hard to exaggerate, but in the 1980s there were a series of changes that penalized the resurgence. The ascension of John Paul II to the papacy, his criticism of liberation theology beginning at Puebla in 1979, the election of Ronald Reagan as President in 1980, and the discrediting of governmental activism on behalf of the poor changed the climate of both church and state. When the Third *Encuentro* was held in 1985, the bishops no longer viewed the Hispanic presence as something "new" or as one demanding a dramatic expansion of existing resources. Later the 1987 National Hispanic Pastoral Plan issued by the NCCB focused upon continuity with existing programs.

The Emergence of a Professional Latino Catholic Theology

Thus, in 1988 the organization of a group to promote the development and publications of a Latino Roman Catholic theology represents a new period. Previous theology had been written to argue or explain pastoral policies, represent better history and culture, or argue for Catholic and Latino rights; and the authors or practitioners of this theology saw their apostolic roles as primary. Persons who are professional theologians created The Academy of Catholic Hispanic Theologians of the United States (ACHTUS) and produced its *Journal of Hispanic/Latino Theology*. The role of ACHTUS has been to foster the analysis of key themes that characterized Latino Catholic theology and make them part of academic discourse. These efforts coincided with a loss of the coherence of the resurgence that had linked theology directly to pastoral care and its movements for social justice. Ironically, this brand of coherence passed to the theologies in Puerto Rico against militarism in Vieques, and to the Cuban-American communities seeking to explore their "exile." Moreover, not all Latino Catholic theology is published through ACTHUS, nor does ACHTUS only publish Latino Roman Catholic theology.

Latino Catholic theology fits into many universities and seminaries as one of many "local theologies." With impetus from theoretical trends of postcolonialism and postmodernism, Latino Catholic theology has been placed by the academy into a mix with various other ethnic, class, and specialized groups. While Latino Catholic theology has acquired a permanent place within the academy, the concept of local theologies had presented some new challenges. Is it possible to have one "Latino" local theology? Or does local theology limit expression to separate ones—one each for Mexican Americans in Texas, Chicanos in California, Puerto Ricans in New York, Puerto Ricans on the island, etc.? The atomizing of theologies extends to debates as to whether Latina women's theology is "feminist" or "*mujerista*/womanist."

There also has been an eclipse of liberation theology. It no longer has a favorable platform within Catholic theology because of various critical pronouncements from the Vatican. Also, liberation theology has been so widely accepted among progressive Protestants that it carries little if any specificity as a "Catholic" theology. The role of professional Latino Catholic theology has also been reduced. Liturgists developed independently of the professional theology and community organizers are more likely to turn to social science in search of strategies. Pastoral planning by offices such as the Secretariat for Hispanic Affairs increasingly lean on surveys and census data for assessing the needs of people at the grass roots.

Accelerating after the collapse of Marxism in Europe and the rethinking of the 500th anniversary of Columbus' exploration to Latin America, there is a resurrection of indigenous and African religions as emblematic of Latino/a identities. No longer accepting syncretism with Catholicism as normative, some advocate a return to paganism for an authentic religious experience. Although relatively small and limited to elites, this movement is doing to Latino Catholicism what Latino Catholics had done to Latino Protestants a half century ago: question their legitimacy as Latino/as. Finally, there has been a general softening of Catholic-Protestant differences because of ecumenism. Many Latino Catholic theologians teach in Protestant or interfaith seminaries, belong to religious studies departments rather than to theological faculties, or hold posts in secular and public universities. The sum effect of these factors is to relativize the definition of "Latino Catholic theology."

Latino Catholic Theology in Search of Definition

This chapter developed the historical emergence of certain traits that have defined Latino Catholic theology over a century and a half. Characteristics such as reference to scripture, incorporation of philosophical or theological trends, and reliance on social science findings are essential to current theology, but are not restricted to either Latino/as or Roman Catholics. The "Latinoness" described for our people's theology often carried a political dimension, an emphasis upon social justice and a linkage to pastoral care that is manifested in the cultivation of cultural symbols and historical awareness of the richness of Latino Catholicism. The distinctive Catholic identity of this theology can be found in an acceptance of a hierarchy within the functioning of the body of Christ; a liturgical and sacramental eucharistic dimension to ecclesiology; and a Marian component, such as with elaboration of the meaning of Our Lady of Guadalupe. It is not required that a theology exemplifies all of these characteristics simultaneously to qualify as both Latino and Catholic; however, it is difficult to imagine that most of these elements would not be present in some way.

The papal instruction *Ex Corde Ecclesiae* (1990) addressed the definition of Catholic theology. After a decade of, at times, heated discussions, the Catholic bishops of the United States issued a decree effective in June 2001 directed at those seeking to teach or write Catholic theology. It is important to recognize that it applies only to those holding posts in seminaries and universities with a Catholic identity. Hence, not every Latino/a theologian who professes Catholicism is required to adopt the "Mandatum":

> I hereby declare my role and responsibility as a professor of a Catholic theological discipline within the full communion of the Church. As a professor of a Catholic theological discipline, therefore, I am committed to teach authentic Catholic doctrine and to refrain from putting forth as Catholic teaching anything contrary to the Church's magisterium.[1]

For some, the Mandatum definitively answers all issues of Catholic identity in theology; for others, the decree itself requires continuing theological debate. Certainly, in an American culture in which individual conscience and academic freedom are interpreted as primary, limitations set by authority are unwelcome. Nonetheless, the hierarchical nature of Roman Catholicism has always required acceptance of the magisterium as one of the specialized gifts to serve the body of Christ. Rather than a threat, the Mandatum becomes a challenge as Latino theology contributes to the American Catholic experience.

---

[1]See http://www.boston-catholic-philosophical-forum.com/Ex_Corde_Ecclesiae__The_Mandatum_Contract.htm for an explanation of the Mandatum.

CHAPTER 22

Historic Mainline Protestants

■ ALBERTO HERNÁNDEZ

On the Margins of Liberty

Although most Latinos/as in the United States identify themselves as Roman Catholic, the number of Hispanics among U.S. mainline Protestant denominations is steadily increasing. The contemporary landscape reveals a denominationally diverse and growing Latino/a presence across mainline U.S. Protestantism, necessitating both pastoral and scholarly attention to what it means to be both Hispanic and Protestant at the dawn of the twenty-first century. David Maldonado offers some insight for examining the historical circumstances of Hispanic mainline Protestants: "To be Hispanic and Protestant means to exist in the margins of two realities, a Hispanic world in which being Protestant means being at the margins of a Catholic context, and a Protestant world in which being Hispanic means being at the margins of a non-Hispanic context" (1999:16). These "realities" and "contexts" are layered with the different trajectories by which Hispanics and Latinos/as encounter mainline Protestantism, such as those of the U.S.-Mexico border region; or the categories of legal immigrant, undocumented immigrant, and exile.

The Legacy of Spanish Colonialism and Roman Catholicism

The hyphenated identities and labels that U.S. Hispanics are forced to assume, such as "Mexican-American" or "Cuban-American," obscure the fact that Hispanic Christians, whether Catholic or Protestant, are the products of an extremely mixed and culturally rich Latino/a heritage known as *mestizaje*. We find persons whose national origins are as distinct from each other as El Salvador is from the Philippines, or as different as rural Nicaragua is from the Peruvian highlands. Cultural origin and ethnicity are equally significant in this milieu because Hispanics and Latinos/as may also be as distinct from each other as Mayan or Navajo culture was from that of the Spanish conquistadors, and as different as the Afro-Cuban flavor of the Caribbean is from the European styles of the Argentine capital in Buenos Aires. Yet the common thread of the Castilian Spanish and Roman Catholicism learned from their colonial overlords links all of these peoples and the various subcultures they represent. For those converting to versions of Protestantism inflected through Anglo-Saxon or Anglo-Celtic North American missionaries, there are yet other cultural layerings that define their identities.

Any attempt to sketch the historical outlines of the Hispanic theological presence in North America must begin with a clear understanding of the impact of Spain's sixteenth-century imperialistic project in the Americas, with its lasting social, linguistic, and religious legacy on the territories and inhabitants that became Latin America. The events of 1492 contributed to its particular epithet as "the miraculous year" in Spanish history. When Christopher Columbus sailed into the uncharted waters of the Atlantic, Spain's two most powerful feudal kingdoms, led by the recently united Roman Catholic Monarchs, defeated the last Moorish kingdom of Granada, and followed that with their subsequent Order of Expulsion against all Spanish Jews. Thus, the Iberian "*Convivencia*" (coexistence) of Muslims, Christians, and Jews came to an end when Ferdinand of Aragon and Isabella of Castile found themselves as the masters of the most culturally and religiously diverse nation in Europe. Spain's inability to affirm and nurture this diversity at such a decisive moment in world history had devastating consequences for its colonial subjects and for the future of Protestant movements throughout the Latin American world.

In 1492, Antonio Nebrija dedicated the first-ever book of Castilian grammar to Queen Isabella, patiently explaining: "Language, Your Majesty, is the ideal weapon of empire." Thus, the use of the Spanish language as an instrument of acculturation and assimilation into the dominant culture of the empire became an integral feature of both pedagogical and ecclesiastical endeavors with the native peoples of the Americas. Moreover, other Spanish administrative policies and practices designed to maintain the separation of the colonists from the indigenous population with whom they were intermarrying laid the groundwork for patterns of racism and discrimination that persist in present-day Latin American countries. Among these were the racial purity laws and the tight control exercised over colonial subjects' religious identities, both of which had already been tried and tested back in Iberia to keep Jews and Muslims out of administrative and social positions. Lastly, the rigid colonial class structures, aimed at securing the power and influence of the Iberians among their indigenous, *mestizo,* and mulatto subjects, led to racial prejudices favoring those who most closely embodied the Euro-Caucasian features of Spanish noble families. There is no better example illustrating the ambivalence of Latinos/as toward their colonial motherland of Spain than the ill-fated celebrations of the "Quincentennial of the Discovery of the New World." In the fall of 1992 news reports from Latin America showed crowds of angry protesters toppling statues of Christopher Columbus and police clashes with protestors hurling Molotov cocktails at statues of the famous explorer. For Hispanic mainline Protestants, whether born and raised in the United States or arriving in North America as immigrants, the collective ambivalence toward the Spanish colonial and Roman Catholic past is often a factor in their attraction to both the "American dream" and the Bible-based, heartfelt piety they perceive among Methodist, Baptist, Presbyterian, Pentecostal, and other churches.

Hispanics are not newcomers to Protestantism. The history of the first Hispanic Protestants actually begins in Spain at the time of the Lutheran Reformation. For Juan de Valdés and Casiodoro de Reina, the emphasis on individual reading and reflection of the Holy Scriptures was a key feature of their reformist dreams.[1] Although Valdés did not produce an entire vernacular edition of the Bible, he emerged as one of its first modern translators. His *Dialogue on Christian Doctrine* (1529) was condemned by the Inquisition as a heretical Lutheran and Erasmian work, and Valdés fled Spain for Italy, where he wrote and taught as a lay minister whose "followers in Naples numbered over three thousand" (González 1967:6). Casiodoro de Reina also fled into exile and later pastored a small congregation of Spanish Protestant emigrants and exiles in Antwerp. By 1569 he translated the entire Bible into Castilian and published it at Basel. Reina deserves a place in Spanish heritage alongside Cervantes for producing a text whose popularity and usefulness still serves Hispanic Protestants throughout Latin America.

Historic Hispanic Mainline Protestants in the United States

The history of Hispanic mainline Protestants in the United States may be divided into two distinct phases of contextual emergence and growth, each period with its own characteristic sociocultural dynamics of marginalization and assimilation. The first phase dates back to the 1820s and lasted through the early 1900s. This was the period of the territorial

---

[1]For an in-depth study of Valdés's theological works, see Nieto, *Valdés' Two Catechisms* (1993); and for a detailed study of Reina's life and work, see Kinder, *Casiodoro de Reina* (1975).

disputes concerning Texas independence from Mexico and the military conflicts along the U.S.-Mexico border, which culminated in the Mexican-American War of 1846–48. Historians are divided as to when this first phase ended, but it is clear that by the 1920s the role of emigration from Latin America and the Caribbean, and subsequent education and evangelization efforts by U.S. Protestant missionaries in these regions, signaled the start of a new phase that has continued to the present. Edwin Sylvest suggested that the Spanish-American War of 1898 increased contact among U.S. Protestant missionaries with the people of Cuba, Puerto Rico, the Philippines, and Central America. The excesses of Spanish colonial autocracy and Roman Catholic support of the status quo both attracted them to mainline American Protestantism and stimulated emigration from these nations in later years (1990:121–22). Thus, this still-unfolding second phase in the history of Hispanic mainline Protestantism should be dated from the early 1900s to the present.

Protestantism and the Mexican-American Experience: 1830–Present

The first phase of the encounter between Hispanics and American Protestants was characterized by a gradual increase in Protestant evangelization efforts aimed at Mexicans living in the newly conquered territories of the American Southwest. Over a period of three centuries, the region's American-born Spanish colonists (*criollos*) and indigenous subcultures had intermarried to produce a syncretistic blending of persons of Spanish, Native American, and mixed (*mestizo*) ancestry who made up the rank and file of the Republic of Mexico. Sylvest advanced the intriguing thesis of "borderer religion," which argues that Hispanic Protestantism developed in the cultural matrix of the Anglo-Celtic-Hispanic frontier of North America analogous to the late-medieval encounter among the Irish, British, Scottish, and Welsh peoples along the borderlands of North Britain (1999:21–37). After the U.S. war with Mexico and the 1848 Treaty of Guadalupe-Hidalgo, by which the United States annexed more than half of Mexico's territory, Mexican *criollos* and *mestizos,* along with Native Americans, found themselves living as foreigners and second-class citizens in what, to them, were the already familiar Mexican frontier provinces of California, Arizona, New Mexico, Nevada, Colorado, and Texas. It was here that Anglo-American Protestants began their missionary endeavors among Roman Catholic *mestizos.*

Presbyterians first initiated ministerial efforts among Mexicans in the Southwest during the 1830s as Sumner Bacon arrived from the Cumberland Valley to distribute Bibles in Texas. Methodist and Baptist ministers with experience in Mexico followed their Presbyterian counterparts just a few years later, as attempts were made to distribute Bibles and develop educational materials in Spanish, organize camp meetings and revivals, and train Spanish-speaking clergy. David Ayers and William Headen led early efforts for the Methodist cause, while Sumner Bacon and Melinda Rankin followed suit for the Presbyterians. In 1851, Rankin went to Mexico to bring the gospel to the "defeated Mexicans" of the "papal frontier," and in 1854 she opened a school for girls in Brownsville, Texas. On November 20, 1853, Benigno Cárdenas became the first Hispanic ordained in the Methodist Episcopal Church, South, and preached his first sermon in Santa Fe, New Mexico. The Civil War interrupted activities for all denominations, so that it was not until the 1870s that we find a Mexican congregation led by Spanish-speaking Methodist pastors in San Antonio. The first Mexican ordained in Methodism in Mexico City was Alejo Hernández, in 1874. It was not until the 1880s that Southern Baptists established a permanent mission among Mexicans in Texas, and that the Presbyterians appointed Walter Scott as "evangelist to the Mexicans." Similar patterns of Presbyterian, Methodist, and Baptist missionary activity were repeated between 1870 and 1910 in New Mexico, California, Arizona, and Colorado.

Nineteenth-century primary sources detailing motives for Hispanic conversions to Protestantism are extremely scarce. We can with reasonable certainty assert that social mobility, grievances over both Roman Catholic doctrine and Spanish colonial oppression, and the perceived social and economic benefits of assimilation all played as much a role for people living in this period as they do among today's Latin American and Caribbean immigrants. Unfortunately, much of the documentary evidence available represents the voices of the dominant culture and their rationale for initiating missionary work among Mexicans, a rationale with undeniable racist overtones and self-serving echoes of Manifest Destiny and anti-Catholic prejudices (Rankin 1875:58, 36).

The missionary period of the mainline Anglo-Protestant encounter with Mexican Americans eventually gave way to a segregated phase in the early 1900s in which Presbyterians, Methodists, and Baptists allowed the formation of a separate presbytery, conference, or convention to serve the pastoral needs of Mexican Americans throughout Texas and the Southwest. The challenges posed by decades of poverty, lack of education, and systemic North American racism plagued each denomination's efforts to train bilingual Latino/a clergy in California, Arizona, Colorado, Nevada, New Mexico, and Texas. Hispanic Methodist ministers of the Western Jurisdiction between 1940 and 1954 fared much better than their Presbyterian and Baptist counterparts, as their community experienced what Félix Gutiérrez and José Fernández referred to as the "Golden Era of Hispanic Methodism" (Gutiérrez 1991:65–83). However, by the mid-1950s it also became clear that the segregated Spanish-speaking churches faced serious financial challenges while remaining isolated from major trends in American Protestantism, and that these small ethnic churches were not serving the needs of both American-born Mexicans and the increasing numbers of new immigrants from Latin America moving into neighborhoods and cities. By the 1970s, each of the three denominations shifted emphasis to a more integrated model. On both sides of the Hispanic-Anglo divide some lamented, while others welcomed, this change, but it stands as an indication of the degree of assimilation or "Americanization" that Mexican-American Protestant leaders and their congregations felt had occurred in the twentieth century.

Latinos/as among U.S. Protestants: 1900–Present

The second phase in the history of Hispanic mainline Protestantism begins in the aftermath of the 1898 Spanish-American War, which opened a new era of relations between the United States and its Central American and Caribbean neighbors. Here again the specter of conquest, followed by occupation and then economic exploitation, cannot be ignored. U.S. economic policy and corporate interests, in addition to the legacies of Spanish colonialism, played a significant role in the turmoil that gripped this region during the twentieth century. Such socioeconomic instability, along with positive contacts with U.S. Protestant missionaries, has been attracting emigrants from these and many other Latin American nations since the early 1900s. Between 1950 and 1970, Puerto Ricans became the second-most numerous Hispanic subgroup, followed by Cuban-Americans. The Cuban Revolution of 1959 was the decisive event leading to their arrival as exiles and refugees to the United States. Since 1975, however, there has been a dramatic increase in the number of immigrants coming to the United States from El Salvador, Nicaragua, Guatemala, Honduras, the Dominican Republic, and Venezuela, as well as from other South American nations such as Colombia, Ecuador, Chile, and Peru.

Many new immigrants settled in the large urban areas of the United States where Mexican Americans, Puerto Ricans, and Cuban Americans already fostered Spanish-speaking communities. As a result, United Methodists, Presbyterians, and Southern Baptists situated in urban areas such as Miami, New York, Northern New Jersey, Philadelphia, Chicago, New Orleans, Houston, Denver, and Los Angeles all saw some of their congregations swell with new members. Reasons for conversions to Protestantism among the newcomers contain a mixture of anti-Catholic sentiment along with an attraction to the Bible-based piety of American Protestantism. However, many of these new immigrants are not practicing Roman Catholics, but rather Christians with roots and interests in the globally expanding Pentecostal movement.

In urban areas the desire for an evangelical outreach that would bridge the language barrier led some denominations to allow small neighborhood and storefront churches and urban ministry initiatives catering to mixed Latino/a populations similar to the segregated model followed in the Southwest during the early 1900s. The challenges of poverty, racial discrimination, and limited access to higher education are the most significant threats to future generations of Hispanic mainline Protestants, as their congregations tend to be poor and working class. Despite some resistance and limited resources at the national level, Methodists, Presbyterians, and Southern Baptists exhibit a growing awareness that—as the U.S. Hispanic population dramatically grows— there will be a need for mainline seminaries to train the professional clergy and religious leaders who will minister to this ever-expanding Hispanic presence. At the local level, mainline American Protestantism has responded with an increased awareness of the need to raise more funds for urban ministry, church-based ESL programs, and the training of Spanish-speaking clergy. For example, in Colorado by 2001 the Rocky Mountain Conference of the United Methodist Church, the Denver Presbytery, and local Baptist churches were all working hard at determining ways to meet the needs of Colorado's rapidly expanding Latino/a population, which now includes many more Hispanic subgroups than the previous patterns of Mexican-American mainline Protestants.

The Future of Hispanic Mainline Protestantism in the United States

Projections released in 2004 by the United States Census Bureau indicate that by 2050 the Hispanic population will increase to one fourth of the projected total national population of 420 million. In this rapidly changing milieu, the story of Hispanic mainline Protestantism across the United States is still very much a story in the making. Lack of resources and a scarcity of Latino/a clergy has led small Hispanic churches in many urban areas to pool their resources in an ecumenical sharing of pastors and facilities to provide worship services for all across denominational lines. The *alianzas*, or alliances, forged by this recent trend have stimulated the growth of the Pentecostal movement at the grassroots level and demonstrated that Latinos/as desire a much more emotive, experientially based encounter with American Protestantism than some mainline denominations have historically demonstrated. Given the steady pace of new immigrants from Latin America, Mexico, and the Caribbean, and the persistent socioeconomic and denominational challenges faced by some Latino/a subgroups, we remain a diverse group of peoples united by the common bond of our ancestral language. We are also empowered by the liberating word of the gospels to become a people moving steadfastly from the margins of liberty to the very heart and centers of mainline American Protestantism.

CHAPTER 23

Evangélicos/as

■ DAVID TRAVERZO GALARZA

The church is characterized by its theological integrity...We have to acknowledge that the confessing church is not homogeneous. It is a complex community of multiple structures, cultural backgrounds, and theological expressions. Its confession of faith is equally complex...The story of the faith reflects not only the complex reality of the churches but also their intellectual and spiritual resources. (Costas 1989:147)

Defining Center or Marginality?

I am a third generation Hispanic *evangélico*.[1] My grandparents and parents from Puerto Rico were Protestant evangélicos. We stem from American Baptist, Presbyterian, and indigenous Pentecostal roots. I really do not remember anyone who was Roman Catholic in my family, except my father's stepbrother or a distant cousin who we rarely saw. I never attended a Roman Catholic misa. This was simply taboo for us. Instead, I was raised in La Iglesia Unida (the United Church) in the Bronx, an independent Latin American parish with a Czechoslovakian pastor in a former Jewish synagogue. The pastor told us that God was

---

[1]Segovia says, "no term currently in use to designate the ethnic group is ultimately satisfactory" (1996:31–42). Escobar explains that *evangélico* "is a synonym of Protestant" (2002:190). Gill admits that Latino Protestants use *evangélico* to classify many groups into one category (1999:17). Armet notes that *evangélico* "reaches across a diverse field of ecclesiastical distinctions" (2002:380).

revealed to him in a Russian prison when he was a youth. Rev. Miloslav Baloun learned Spanish in Argentina and spoke with a Puerto Rican accent. He loved rice and beans and preferred strong Boricua coffee. On Sunday mornings, Rev. Baloun always preached from the Bible with Latino passion. His focus was loud and clear: "a personal experience with Christ." We were invited and warned: "Accept the Lord Jesus Christ into your heart and you will be saved. Reject Him and you will be forever lost!" The message was pressed as Pastor Baloun synchronized hands in the air, pounded the pulpit, stomped the ground, and placed his pale fat finger on the scripture text; as the altar shook, his face turned red and his thunderous voice blasted the microphone: "This world is totally lost to sin. Only Christ can save it. What we need today is a spiritual revolution! If you are in Christ, you are a new creation. Everything has changed. This changes human history. This changes the world!" I remember an overwhelming presence of God there.

At the end of his ministry, Pastor Baloun founded the New Order Corporation, a community-based agency with a global Christian vision. He died with this vision, along with the New Order Corporation. As I reflect on this faith tradition from the Bronx, I wonder if *fe evangélica* is at a crossroads? Hispanic *evangélicos* may play a crucial role in the unfolding drama of God's new order in Jesus the Christ. I ask: Can anything good come from the Bronx or from among Hispanic *evangélicos*? Did this Czechoslovakian Boricua pastor and *La Iglesia Unida* represent a prophetic and transforming faith that still awaits new hope for a new day?

This chapter will offer an introduction to Hispanic *evangélico* identity, focusing on the questions: (1) Who are Hispanic *evangélicos*? What is their sociohistorical significance in the nation? (2) What are the particular socioreligious and historical roots of this heterogeneous phenomenon? (3) Where might we locate a heuristic model to better understand the nature, role, and impact of Hispanic *evangélicos* in the present and future of Christian *evangélico* faith and praxis?

Clarification of Identification

Nearly three decades ago, C. Rene Padilla edited *The New Face of Evangelicalism: An International Symposium on the Lausanne Covenant* (1976),[2] and in the center of this global Christian movement was one of the most preeminent Hispanic *evangélicos* of the twentieth century, the late Rev. Dr. Orlando E. Costas.[3] Ten years ago, Guillermo Cook edited *New Face of the Church in Latin America: Between Tradition and Change* (1994), with a chapter "Voices of Compassion Yesterday and Today" by one of the

---

[2] Nearly 25 percent of the contributors were Latin American. A Latino contingent and U.S. Puerto Rican *evangélicos* spearheaded The *Radical Discipleship Group.*

[3] For a review of Costas' life and work in theology, missions, ethics, pastoral ministry, and holistic liberation praxis, see Traverzo Galarza, "The Emergence of a Latino Radical Evangelical Social Ethic" (1992a), and *Orlando E. Costas* (1995).

premier Hispanic *evangélicos* in the twenty-first century: the Rev. Dr. Justo L. González.[4] Today, the *new face* of U.S. Hispanic *evangélicos* and their *new voices* is erupting within the matrix of church and community.[5]

Despite conflicting reports, it is apparent that *evangélicos* are increasing in numbers.[6] When factoring in sampling and nonsampling error, the countless masses not interviewed, and the U.S. Federal Government's chaotic procedures, the number of U.S. Hispanic Americans might be closer to double the official statistics (Traverso Galarza 1998:234–35). The total Latino/a Protestant population in the U.S., combining the 9.2 million U.S. Hispanic Pentecostals or charismatics with the "nonaligned" and "mainline" Protestants, might be closer to double or more census estimates. It is possible that projections of Roman Catholics making up 70 percent of the U.S. Hispanic population may be far too high, especially when external analysis and the phenomenon of "cultural Christianity" or "nominalism" are factored in.[7]

Over the past few decades, U.S. Hispanic *evangélico* growth has become unrelenting news. In numbers, it has outpaced both the Jewish and Muslim communities in the nation (Espinosa, Elizondo, and Miranda 2003:16). From coast to coast the exponential and persistent increase is astounding. In the West, some Pentecostal churches reported numerical explosions from 20,000 to 40,000 in a few years (Day 1982:19).[8] In three decades, the number of Hispanic evangelical churches in Cleveland, Ohio, mushroomed from ten to forty, with some 4,000

---

[4]On August 6, 2004, at Fuller Theological Seminary a *Festschrift* was dedicated by AETH (Asociación para la Educación Teológica Hispana) to González, its founder and first president. As a charter member, I dedicate this essay to Dr. González in light of my unsolicited absence from this well-deserved national publication effort.

[5]See González on the "dissonance" and the "clipped rhythm of urgency" of these new voices (1992:vii-viii).

[6]Hunt states that "Protestantism is increasing among Hispanics" and that "the greatest transformations in Hispanic identity will be linked to leaving conventional patterns of organized religion…part of a more basic break with both Catholicism and traditional forms of Protestantism" (1988:843); and later, he adds that there is "little indication that conversion to fundamentalist Protestantism is winning over Hispanics to any appreciable degree. Both mainline Protestant affiliations and the nonaligned, while not as large in membership as the fundamentalist segment of Protestantism, have increased in the decade of the 1990s"(1999:1616). However, the research done by the Pew Charitable Trusts project on Hispanic Churches in American Public Life states that "the numbers of Latino Protestants and other Christians were growing" and that the majority of these Protestants are Pentecostal and Evangelicals (2003).

[7]Escobar, referring to a 1953 Roman Catholic study, affirms that in Latin America "the vast majority of Catholics are *solo de nombre;* that is, nominal Catholics" and that "most Latin Americans generally describe themselves as 'Roman Catholic, and Apostolic,' even though their ecclesial adhesion is often based more on a custom-based attachment to the church than on deep faith convictions" (2002:93).

[8]About 50 percent of the growth is from persons whom already were Protestant from Latin America. See Steve Sailer, "Latino Worship in Bomber Plant," *United Press International,* 14 July 2003.

persons.[9] In one year, a Hispanic Adventist church in Hillsboro, Oregon, received 125 new members, with over 400 persons attending in one Sunday morning service.[10] The U.S. Hispanic *evangélico* impact is apparent in national associations, Hispanic theological training, and booming scholarly production that offers dynamic leadership and prophetic vision. The AMEN (*Alianza de Ministerios Evangélicos*) claims some 10 million members; AETH (Asociación para la Educación Teológica Hispana) cites over 800 members and some 60 institutional affiliates; and scholar prophets release monographs and other works in the fields of Pentecostal theology, social ethics, missiology, ecumenics, pedagogy, biblical studies, diaspora studies, liberative pastoralia, popular religion, and postcolonial discourse.[11]

The quantitative impact of U.S. Hispanic *evangélicos* has left a qualitative mark in both church and society. The "Pentecostalization" of Christian faith in Latin America, the Caribbean, and the United States, for instance, has impacted both Roman Catholic and Protestant Hispanics.[12] Yet, there is a benign neglect of U.S. Hispanic *evangélicos* from U.S. religious history as seen in a survey of major works: Hackett (ed.), *Religion and American Culture*; Williams, *America's Religions: From Their Origins to the Twenty-First Century*; Tweed, *Retelling U.S. Religious History*; and Marty and Appleby, *Fundamentalisms Observed* have ignored the existence and contributions of U.S. Hispanic *evangélico* Christians. Justo L. González' notation over a decade ago rings clear: "We are speaking in the midst of a people that has often been ignored and has long been oppressed, not only by society at large, but also by the church and by theology…" (1992:viii). Such a patent and systematic omission might lead some to think that U.S. Hispanic *evangélicos* are hiding in basements or arrived last night into the Christian family. U.S. Hispanic *evangélicos* have a deep, rich, and multifarious religious legacy that extends to before the U.S. invasion of our lands.

Roots

Miguel De La Torre and Edwin Aponte assert that three major streams flow through the cultural, historical, and religious veins of U.S. Hispanics. The indigenous, European, and African influences have converged into a complex panorama of linguistic, biological, regional,

[9]David Briggs, "Evangelical pastors form group to help Hispanics," *Plain Dealer,* 30 January 2004.

[10]Sara Linn, "Find your religion; Pacific N. West Hispanics move to Protestantism," *Marketing News,* 13 October 2003.

[11]William Lobdell, "Building Respect for Latino Protestantism," *Los Angeles Times,* 16 June 2001; and telephone interview with Rev. Daniel Davila, AETH Executive Director, May 28, 2003.

[12]Over 25 percent of Hispanic Roman Catholics surveyed as "born-again" Christians. Of all Latino/a Protestants, some 88 percent were evangelical or "born-again" and 64 percent Pentecostal or charismatic (Espinosa, Elizondo, and Miranda 2003:14–16).

and spiritual textures. Diversity and particularity are governing patterns in the fusion of such "a crossroads of peoples, civilizations, and cultures" (2001:28–29). I would also include religions and spiritual traditions. With invasion and domination, the clashing of distinct worlds gave birth to something completely new and strange. Out of this product of a violent evangelism awoke *Boricuas, Quisqueyanos, Cubanos, Mexicanos,* and all the other births of *La Raza* throughout the Americas and now in the United States. The religious heritage of U.S. Hispanic *evangélicos* is therefore rooted within these converging rivers of life and death. What exist is an insistent plurality and hybridity, a combination of traditions and visions that moves dynamically within diverse and ever-changing religious systems and histories. Popular religion reflects indigenous practices and beliefs that arise in both Roman Catholic and Protestant faiths. Some expressions of African religion are also alive, as James Cone reminded us that "the Spirit will not come down until the music starts" (1972:1–7).

While some limit Hispanic *evangélico* roots exclusively to a nineteenth-century U.S. Manifest Destiny emphasis, others suggest that the U.S. foreign missionary impulse was both a culturally conditioned and a religiously motivated movement. Both Silva Gotay (1997: 271–72) and Luis Martínez Fernández (2002) documented how native Protestantism in the Caribbean (Puerto Rico and Cuba) has roots before the U.S. military invasion and subsequent colonial occupation of these lands. In Puerto Rico, in the late 1860s and 1870s, Protestant work had begun in Aguadilla, Ponce, Fajardo, and Vieques. On July 23, 1874, the first Protestant Temple was inaugurated in Ponce with some 400 persons attending (Silva Gotay, 1997:7). In Cuba during the late-nineteenth-century war for independence, a group of exiles who occupied the Key West and Tampa areas in Florida became Protestant and self-governing, with a Cuban nationalist pastoral consciousness. Protestant missions in Cuba had an autochthonous and progressive legacy before the U.S. military occupation of Cuba and the foreign missionary movement that followed (González 1990:68).

These roots have a progressive and revolutionary praxis, contrary to the notion that Hispanic Protestantism represents a monolithic conservative cultural capitulation to U.S. imperialism. Mexican Protestants fought in the Mexican revolution and promoted radical social change (Baldwin 1990). From the start, *"los evangélicos nunca fueron políticamente conservadores, ni por extraccion social ni por conviccion teologica. Tampoco es parte de su tradiccion la abstinencia politica total"* (Escobar 1986:168).[13] Revolutionary and progressive Protestants such as Gonzalo Báez

---

[13]"The evangelicals *never* [my emphasis] were politically conservatives, neither by social background nor theological conviction. Total political abstinence is also not part of their tradition" (my translation).

Camargo, Erasmo Braga, and Alberto Rembao stand out as paradigmatic figures of Christianity and radical social change.

A brief mention should be made of both the progressive and ecumenical roots of U.S. Hispanic *evangélicos*. The Hispanic American Congress at Havana in 1929 is a vital illustration of how a pastoral and prophetic matrix was imbedded in the early *evangélico* ethos where there was a call for international justice, Christian social legislation, self-support and nationalism, a global Christianity consciousness, Christian social responsibility, and a vision for a Latin American federation of Protestantism. A distinction was made between "our spiritual friends in the North" and U.S. economic and political hegemony. While a Christendom vision is at times apparent, the critical, collective, contextual, and public spirit of the congress is manifest:

> Social questions, relations between capital and labor, industrial problems, the place of women in the modern world, the civilization and christianization of the Indian population, the position of university students and the questions revolving around international peace, are some of the many world perplexing questions that we must face. (Inman 1929:9–10)

Hence, the new reformation of which Justo L. González writes may also ground its roots in this early Hispanic *evangélico* praxis. A national church with a cooperative spirit, for instance, is at the heart of early Puerto Rican *evangélico* history. *Boricua* missionaries were dispersed throughout the Americas with this missionary zeal. These are the marks of "an Evangelical ecumenism in which zeal for evangelism combined with contextual efforts and a strategic vision to penetrate all sectors of Latin American life with the Gospel" (Escobar 1994:28). The first generation transmitted this heritage to the next that took ownership of more indigenous models of belief and a more critical praxis. A third generation of *evangélicos* is now emerging with a more systematic and intentionally holistic paradigm of Christian faith and practice (Ibid.:167ff).

A Latino/a Radical Evangelical Tradition

As the third and fourth generation of U.S. Hispanic *evangélicos* emerge, the question of identity (being) and mission (doing) is crucial. As more youth and other "unchurched" are disconnected from these roots and this praxis, the qualitative gains might result in a Pyrrhic victory. We may have had numbers, but at what cost? The question of gospel integrity does matter. What kind of *evangélico* model might help to offer hopeful guidelines for this coming generation? In the battle of Christ and culture, where might we look for some clues to integrity?

Some three decades ago, Orlando Costas published a controversial text entitled *The Church and Its Mission: A Shattering Critique from the Third*

World, which was a clarion call to a holistic model proclaiming the whole gospel for the whole world. Costas advocated a total mission for all humankind, with the whole gospel to transform the entire world. The U.S. Hispanic *evangélico* communities today might receive clarity and impulse for their mission in light of Costas' emphasis on the integrity of mission grounded in liberating news on account of a Christ who died outside the gate, outside the comfortable, sacred, and idolatrous ecclesial compounds of temple life and religious doctrine. Costas' legacy might also reflect that of Pastor Baloun, both who walked the streets of the Bronx and proclaimed the power of the gospel from its pulpits and from their personal lives. Both died with a consuming vision for transformation grounded in Jesus the Christ, the son of the living God. Costas was quite convinced that the church was called and empowered for a mission, a holistic enterprise to be understood in terms of worship and service, presence and proclamation, Christian nurture and fellowship, personal conversion and social transformation, standing in solidarity with the poor and the oppressed in their struggle for liberation, and calling men and women to repentance and faith in Christ Jesus– building up the body of Christ and mobilizing it for witness in the world (1974:10–16; 306–10).

Such a liberating model speaks to the three audiences of church, academy and community. The question of integrity is the life or death of our life and mission. While issues of family values, abortion, immigration and amnesty, mainline church death and decline, postcolonial discourse, *mujerista* theology, postmodernity, and international terrorism might catch our attention and even drive our agendas, a truly liberating and integral gospel transforms, unites, and gives public witness to the God of our ancestors. This is the one who called a people who were no people to be a new and strange people–perhaps a people who would shock the world into belief, as their living witness went beyond *sana doctrina* and became a *doctrina que sana.*[14]

As we witness a growing disconnect between U.S. Hispanic youth (second and third generations, Gen X) and traditional/institutional forms of Christian faith, the question of integrity and complexity stares us in the face. Will we lose these generations as we have lost the last of the Baby Boomer public, clinging to impotent or idolatrous models? While the numbers might appear large for U.S. Hispanic *evangélicos,* an outstanding portion is probably among Anglo-American circles.[15] If such is the case, a central concern is the nature, extent, and cost of cultural accommodation and dislocation from one's roots. As more third generation Latinos/as become English dominant and assimilate into

---

[14] *Sana doctrina* represents *orthodox* beliefs in the Pentecostal experience. A *doctrina que sana* is an *orthopraxis* that heals instead of dividing or alienating.

[15] Luis Madrigal questioned the actual number of Hispanics in U.S. Hispanic churches. See Tapia, "Growing Pains" (1995:40, 42).

mainstream values and institutions, how might this affect the new face and new voice of *evangélicos?* Is ultimate cultural capitulation and identity devastation what lies ahead for this generation and others in the millennium ahead?

I would hope that as new generations of U.S. Hispanic *evangélico* theologians, ethicists, pastors, prophets, and practitioners emerge, they might embrace the locus that Costas identified as the Galilean periphery, the popular orientation for our evangelical praxis, which Costas called a *Latino Radical Evangelical* approach (Traverzo Galarza 1994:108–31). We continue as before:

> with an immersion in the pains and agonies of the people in the fringes and bottom of society, and the disturbing effect which such an involvement has upon one's conscience. In such an experience, one encounters the risen Lord, enlarging and deepening one's limited vision of human reality, challenging one's presuppositions, renewing one's mind, liberating and empowering one's life for service as a channel of grace in the "Galilees of the nations"—the shanties and ghettoes, the marginal provinces and forgotten nuclei of the world. (Costas 1992:23)

I close, and ask again, *Can anything good come from the Bronx or from among U.S. Hispanic* evangélicos? Justo L. González might answer with something like this: "Yes, something very good indeed is expected from the Bronx and U.S. Hispanic *evangélicos.* This is the place among the people, where Christ is born, lives, and has died. It is the place where the Spirit of the living God is very much alive. If we expect anything, it is good news from the Bronx, from God's *Mañana* people who announce and dare to believe in and live out God's reign on earth!" I then ask, but when will this come to pass? I can hear Justo almost whisper up close with a smile on his face and a wink in his eye: *Mañana!*—for it is already here!

CHAPTER 24

Pentecostals

■ ARLENE M. SÁNCHEZ WALSH

This chapter provides a historic overview for Latino/a Pentecostal theology, and discusses some intriguing future trends. Latino/a Pentecostal theology is rooted in an experiential, oral, and lived tradition. Theology that is sung, felt, and experienced through the person of the Holy Spirit. This chapter also seeks to place Latino/a Pentecostal theology in historical context. As a grassroots theology, how did it develop? What were the prominent trends? And what is its relevance in the lives of other Latino/a Christians? To begin the study, it is critical to define Pentecostalism and give proper emphasis to Spirit baptism and divine healing—two spiritual manifestations that were prominent in the early years of Pentecostalism's growth in Latino/a communities.

Pentecostalism is a movement within evangelical Christianity that stresses the manifestations of the gifts of the Holy Spirit as outlined in the book of Acts and chapters 12–16 of the first letter to the Corinthians. Indeed, what has separated classical Pentecostals (those who claim some lineage from the Azusa Street revival in 1906, and even before) from others who emphasize spiritual gifts, like charismatics, is the insistence that Pentecostals place on Spirit baptism, followed by speaking in tongues. Other spiritual manifestations regularly observed in Pentecostal churches are: prophecy, healing, words of knowledge, and other "signs and wonders." What Pentecostal churches try to do is recapture the significance of the day of Pentecost (Acts 2:4), when tradition holds that the Christian church was born and equipped for missions by the reception of the Holy Spirit. To focus on two spiritual gifts in particular will allow us to examine the historical development of how Pentecostal theology was received by Latinos/as as a lived faith that promised extraordinary things and captured two particularly needy areas of Latino/a life in the early twentieth century: the need for accessible health care, and the desire to retain Spanish as the primary language of the home and the church. As an orally transmitted faith, the way that much theology has been learned is through the process of *testimonios.*

Pentecostal worship forms the crucial ritualizing event of faith life. Therein lie the stages that lead Pentecostals to their desired goal of being in the presence of God and experiencing God's power. *Testimonios* operate on various levels: to allow a person to communicate to the congregation the reality of the Holy Spirit's power; to allow the congregation to be a part of that reality by assenting to the truth that this story brings, be it healing, be it deliverance from a life-controlling problem, or be it thanking God for something as mundane as fixing someone's car so that they would not have to buy a new one. *Testimonios* bring God's reality and presence into the everyday communications of congregants, who see that God cares about one's health, one's financial situation, and can deal with the most minuscule of concerns. *Testimonios* in some denominations served as the opening volley in the service as people seek the Holy Spirit. In a worship service of the Oneness Pentecostal denomination, the *Asambleas Apostolicas* (Apostolic Assemblies), for example, *testimonios* were used right at the beginning to usher the church into a reverence for God and a hungering for God's presence within their own situations. *Testimonios* led to prayer at the altar, where someone, moved by what they had just heard, asked for a similar need to be met. The altar time led to people asking for and often receiving Spirit baptism, and the laying on of hands for healing would occur.[1] Learning about Pentecostal doctrine for Latinos/as, and for most Pentecostals, comes from the orality of the faith and its experiential nature. When searching for what makes Latino/a Pentecostal theology distinct among other Christian traditions, we turn to the experiential. Pentecostalism's unique claim is to be transmitted by an active agent who is operating as described in the New Testament.

Pentecostalism, since its inception as a spiritual movement, has sought to break away from the reliance on *sola scriptura* (only scripture) to include *pneuma* (spirit). Latinos/as, faced with over a century of the supremacy of English as an indicator of their supposed inferiority, saw in Pentecostalism a freedom from language that made all "believers" equal. If you could not speak English, you could speak in tongues, and early Pentecostal periodicals record several instances of Mexican converts being used by God to serve the church, by speaking in Spanish, and by

---

[1]I am grateful to Daniel Rámirez for sharing his insights on the role of the *testimonio* in Oneness Pentecostalism.

speaking in tongues. There is a interesting account of a migrant worker in Amarillo, Texas, coming to the altar at a Pentecostal church, where he could only communicate his desire for conversion when another person at the altar received the gift of speaking in tongues, specifically, a unique manifestation appropriately called *xenoglossia* (the ability to speak a different language), and was able to communicate with the man in Spanish, thus facilitating the conversion (Casey 1914:3). Pentecostal theologian Samuel Sol1ván believes that the retention of language is part of what makes Latino/a Pentecostal theology different from other Pentecostal experiences.[2] Sol+ván calls this "cultural glossolalia." Latinos/as seek to empower themselves by retaining their language, which strengthens their faith. Sol1ván, like other contemporary theologians inside and outside the Pentecostal tradition, desires that Latinos/as not succumb to the pressures of assimilation as they convert, and as they seek to become part of the larger evangelical subculture.

Liberation from the dominant language would play a significant role in the theological development of Pentecostalism in the Latino/a communities of the United States, as well as being the reason that Latino/a Pentecostals converted to denominations that either ministered to them in Spanish (Assemblies of God), or were run by Spanish-speaking Latinos/as (Apostolic Assembly and Latin American Council of Christian Churches). Very early Latinos demonstrated a desire to retain their language and culture, and often desired autonomy for their churches.

Another significant spiritual gift with a special place for Latino/a Pentecostals is divine healing, which not only fit into already prescribed notions that supernatural forces could secure health for an individual but served as a palliative for the spiritual and social ills of being part of a marginalized community. From Azusa Street to the healing crusades of pioneer evangelist Francisco Olazábal, healing encompassed more than one's physical ailments, as accounts often mentioned being "delivered" from a variety of ills, such as drug addiction and alcoholism.

A crucial aspect of Olazábal's ministry was his healing campaigns from California to New York to Puerto Rico. They hearken back to Azusa Street testimonials of converts like Abundio Lopez and his wife Rosa, who both experienced Spirit baptism and claimed to have been healed—Abundio at Azusa Street, Rosa some years later at another Los Angeles healing campaign. Healing, a fixture of Pentecostal theology, was key in convincing Latinos/as that the breakaway from Catholicism was worth it, because healing as a component of a faith experience was already a part of the larger Latino/a religious matrix (Sánchez-Walsh 2003:20–21). As Sol1ván notes, healing the body, healing community, and commiserating

---

[2]Sol+ván is one of few Latino Pentecostal theologians who has attempted to systematize and synthesize what Latino/a Pentecostal theology is and what it means to the community. See Solíván, *Spirit, Pathos and Liberation* (1998).

with the suffering of the community all emanate from the same Holy Spirit (1998:5–6).

Soliván notes that suffering incorporates all of who we are. The Holy Spirit as Comforter is the one responsible for helping us to overcome sin and evil:

> [f]or many suffering people, miracles are not only believed, they are expected. The experiences of promises fulfilled today serve as first fruits of what is yet in store…It is this conversion experience on various levels (spiritual–the turning away from the rule of sin; physical–in the healing power of the Holy Spirit; and social–in the restoration of community and family) that fundamentally informs the authority of the Scriptures" (Ibid.:91, 105).

It is a fact that Latino/a Pentecostals cannot or do not see the work of the Holy Spirit as multidimensional, as Soliván does, that leads to the varied ways they live out their faith. Sometimes, those expressions of faith contain explicit work toward the restoration of the community in overt political ways that demonstrate some attachment to theologies of liberation. More often than not, Latino/a Pentecostals are very much like many of the their Euro-American evangelical brethren in their approach to piety, holiness, and an internalized faith that focuses on the eradication of personal sin. By focusing on a few examples throughout Latino/a Pentecostal history, we can see how this theological bifurcation operates in the community, and conclude with some thoughts on the future of Latino/a Pentecostal theology. "For Pentecostals, reaching out to the unwed mother, the homeless, the poor and the alcoholic is as politically important as electing a local official. From a Pentecostal perspective, the preaching of the gospel in the most politically and socially radical activity the world has known" (Ibid.:145). Out of the social realities of many Latino/a communities, a shift occurred among classical Pentecostals in the 1960s. A case in point would be how Pentecostal theology was transmitted to ministers in training at the Latin American Bible Institute (LABI), in Los Angeles.

LABI, up till the 1960s, was inwardly focused on training Latinos/as to be ministers, and focused heavily on preaching, teaching, Spirit baptism, and other spiritual gifts. Socially, the focus was piety and holiness of the individuals. In the mid-1960s, the social realities of the life of many young Latinos/as could no longer be hidden (Sánchez-Walsh, 2003:64). The social ills of gangs, crime, economic depravation, drug abuse, and alcoholism were brought to the LABI campus by zealous men and women who had had that radical healing experience with God and sought to spread this message back in their old neighborhoods. Some of those young men and women like Cruz "Sonny" Arguinzoni, Nicky Cruz, Julie Arguinzoni Rivera, among others, received their ministerial training at LABI from 1964–65. The Arguinzonis founded "Victory

Outreach," a Pentecostal social mission that since 1967 has operated hundreds of rehabilitation homes and churches in inner cities around the world, with the overarching message that only a radical experience with Jesus, and supernatural deliverance from drug addiction, will "deliver" a person from their own personal demons. Cruz also founded a ministry to drug addicts and gang members that taught many of the same spiritual principles. This was spiritual, classical Pentecostalism wedded to social concerns. Not explicit in any teaching of the Arguinzonis or Cruz, but implied, was the idea that faith, in order to be activated in a person, especially a person bound by life-controlling problems, needed to be socially reconnected to family and community. Pentecostalism became a gateway for reconciliation and liberation. The Arguinzonis and Cruz are only three of a much larger network of Latino/a Pentecostals who utilized the faith to form churches and parachurch movements to marginalized Latinos/as in prison, in gangs, and on drugs. Another notable Pentecostal who founded a church and was instrumental in very significant movement was Leoncia Rosario (Mama Leo), founder of the Damascus Youth Crusade, who since the 1950s had actively sought to reach Puerto Rican youth in New York.

Academics, many who have only recently begun to study Pentecostalism as a liberation movement, are finding that preconceived notions of liberation, particularly from North American feminists, will require refinement to explain how Pentecostalism is viewed as a faith that offers opportunity, hope, and liberation to Latin American and U.S. Latinas. As Anna Adams has found in her study of Latina Pentecostals in Allentown, Pennsylvania, in order to examine Latinas in the Pentecostal church, the loci of liberation come from the family and the home. Adams found that her informants experienced many avenues of agency through gaining a theological education, being missionaries, transmitting the faith, teaching, counseling, and even have more availability to reproductive strategies by opting for birth control and also being more in control of family issues by being able to divorce their husband under certain circumstances (2002:98–113). Adams's work supports scholarship on Pentecostal women in general, and particularly, the view that Latina Pentecostals, in the Northern and Southern hemispheres, Latinas experience freedom and liberation as they convert to Pentecostalism. This liberation should be viewed as equally legitimate even though it is emanating from a wholly conservative religious tradition.[3]

Such movements and a growing awareness among Latinos/as throughout the United States gave rise to a new type of Pentecostal.

---

[3]The literature in this respect is growing. Of note are Brusco, *Reforming Machismo* (1995); Garrard-Burnett, *Protestantism in Guatemala* (1998a); Drogus, *Women, Religion and Social Change in Brazil's Popular Church* (1997); Burdick, *Looking for God in Brazil* (1993); and Chesnut, *Competitive Spirits* (2003).

Forged by years as ministers and as academically trained theologians, Puerto Ricans Eldin Villafañe and Samuel Soliván brought practical experience and their seminary training to the task of trying to capture an often unwieldy Pentecostal theology and recast it to explain how Latinos/as carved out their own space in this environment.

Academic theologians like Soliván and Villafañe, and nearly all other academically oriented Latino/a Pentecostals who self-identify with the faith, situate Latino/a Pentecostalism in a way that suggests that the faith can and should be liberative not only in a faith context, but in the context of liberating Latinos/as from systemic social ills. Villafañe's work on social ethics clearly calls Latino/a Pentecostals to become active in seeking liberation from social marginalization. Soliván's work mirrors this idea. Soliván, like Villafañe, writes for both academic as well as pastoral audiences: "This new hermeneutic approach must bring together the best insights of liberation hermeneutics; that is, it needs a starting point and praxis, and the best of an evangelical understanding of the authority of scripture..." (1998:43). The problem is that the evangelical understanding of scripture has often led Pentecostals to assume that the focal point of any good Christian life begins with piety and holiness. That is the starting point, with little emphasis on anything else. This constitutes a "piety trap". Getting away from the individual nature of sin, is not possible for a movement focused on the Word as the sole authority and rooted in the efficacy of grace for salvation without benefit of works. This "piety trap" also keeps evangelicalism focused on the need for personal conversion, which at its core is about individual repentance and acceptance of Jesus Christ, not collective repentance for the sin of racism. This negotiation of faith has no enduring answer, aside from pockets of Pentecostals socially engaged in various drug and alcohol rehabilitation ministries, urban ministries, and other ministries to the disadvantaged. Pentecostalism tends to be inwardly focused, and, of late, focused on the theology of prosperity, rather than the theology of liberation.

What can be said about the failure of liberation theology in the Roman Catholic churches of Latin America to catch on with the masses can also be said to have been a portent to Pentecostalism's growth in Latino/a communities in the United States, Latin America and the Caribbean. The Pentecostal movement seeks new streams of religious competition to revitalize itself. As Pentecostalism in the Latino/a communities continues to grow at a steady pace, generations continue to be nurtured in Pentecostal churches and the traditional Pentecostal church becomes routinized.[4] One such stream has been the movement

---

[4]Margaret Poloma's work with Pentecostals, especially the Assemblies of God, has been instrumental in uncovering the routinization of charisma in this classical Pentecostal denomination. Typical charismatic expressions, once a key part of the denomination's worship and practice, have become quite routinized, to the point where only a small percentage of AG members responded positively to the question of whether they spoke in tongues. (See Poloma 1997:104–11.)

among Latino/a Pentecostals to embrace the "prosperity" gospel. The prosperity gospel is a movement within Pentecostal/charismatic circles that has its beginnings with American charismatic figures such as Kenneth Hagin, Oral Roberts, Kenneth Copeland, and Pat Robertson, among others. Their success, particularly in harnessing media outlets (television, satellites, Internet, and a variety of print media), has made tremendous inroads into a loose network of nondenominational charismatic churches. Their leadership, along with preaching about the gifts of the Spirit, preaches a unique gospel of health and wealth to congregations that are asked to believe that God's plan for them includes deliverance from debt, and to abundance of financial and spiritual wealth. Critics of this theology, especially from a Latino/a perspective, point to its lack of concern for the impoverished on a systemic level, and the extreme individualistic nature of this theology that tends to see financial and physical well-being as tied to spiritual maturity. This leap to the prosperity gospel in terms of the historical trajectory of Latino/a Pentecostal theology is revolutionary.

Classical Pentecostal theology, with its roots in the Holiness movement of the late nineteenth century, promoted the rigorous piety of evangelicalism, and the experiential necessity of the work of the Holy Spirit. Spirit baptism, with the evidence of speaking in tongues, is still the standard doctrine of classical Pentecostal denominations like the Assemblies of God, but is not what commands the attention of most AG congregations. Latinos/as, in their third generation of being Pentecostals, have seen that for some of them, the traditional, often legalistic, often ethnically specific churches of previous generations do not offer them the tools that they require to operate in contemporary American society. Seeking a way to inculcate individual efforts at spirituality, while also providing practical solutions to the systemic problems of poverty and the perpetuation of a permanent underclass, many Latino/a Pentecostals have left their classical roots for the postdenominational road of the charismatic mega-church, the prosperity gospel, and the therapeutically oriented comfort of churches like Calvary Chapel and the Vineyard. In doing so, theologies, like faith identities, have changed. For, if there is anything certain in examining the postmodern proclivity of uncertainly and flux, it is that Latino/a Pentecostals, like other people of faith, will create and recreate their theologies to suit their needs as their social, cultural, and political lives change.

CHAPTER 25

Alternative Traditions[1]

■ MIGUEL A. DE LA TORRE
■ EDWIN DAVID APONTE

Contrary to common assumptions, all U.S. Latino/as are not Roman Catholics. That does not mean, however, that all the non-Catholic Hispanics are Protestant. In fact, not all U.S. Hispanics are even Christian. Some Hispanics view themselves as a comfortable combination of several traditions. For a number of Latinas and Latinos, their religious worldview and day-to-day spiritual activity draws heavily and directly upon indigenous Amerindian traditions, African sources, or even, in some specific contexts, Asian sources. These religious alternatives reflect diverse ways Latino/as connect their concrete realities with visions of the Ultimate and particular beliefs, disciplines, practices, and personal actions as they negotiate *lo cotidiano*, the everyday.

Some of the better-known alternative expressions and practices include *curanderismo*, a Mexican American and Central American path of folk healing and medicine; different types of *espiritismo*, or spiritism; and Cuban *Santería*. Yet belonging to one of these alternative traditions does not necessarily mean that the practitioner does not see himself or herself as Christian. In fact, these multiple avenues may be viewed as complementary and acceptable combinations for faith and life.

---

[1]This chapter is a revision of chapter 5 of our book *Introducing Latino/a Theologies* (2001).

Curanderismo

Mexican *Curanderismo* predates the Spanish conquest of Mexico and today can be understood as a combination of indigenous Mesoamerican and Spanish popular religious outlooks and orientations to the physical world and spiritual realms. For many Mexicans, *Curanderismo* attempts to find an expression of health practices and healing, hence the name that finds its roots in the Spanish verb *curar*, "to heal, cure." This tradition has developed into an extensive health care system that assumes sickness may have a natural *or* supernatural cause. It is holistic in its approach. Therefore, any given circumstance may require a natural or supernatural cure, or even a combination of both. *Curanderismo* contains an extensive collection of rituals and customs, explanatory stories and myths, and a complex symbolic system that seeks to understand life on its own terms.

Curandero/as (both men and women) are specialized healers who are from the people but also are recognized as having received a special gift or *el dón* for healing. Their knowledge is rooted in the ancient ways, and includes remedies for a variety of sicknesses, physical complaints, and injuries. Although to the casual outside observer this health system appears to be composed of independent agents, each healer is really part of a sophisticated alternative worldview with a hierarchy of healers. Reflecting different approaches to healing within *curanderismo*, the major categories of healers include first the *señora/abuela* (a woman, a grandmother), then the *yerbero* or herbalist, the *sobador* (a type of massage therapist), and the midwife or *partera*. The final referral is made to a *curandera* or *curandero*. As the ultimate specialist who addresses both spiritual as well as physical concerns, a *curandero/a* is the healer who can treat *mal puesto*, illnesses caused by an evil spell or hex. Spiritual interpretation is important to the people who come to *curanderos/as*, thus it is not uncommon that the local Roman Catholic priest or Protestant minister may be the second choice of a person for consultation.

A complex interplay between the material and immaterial worlds is evidenced in the way illness and healing are treated in *curanderismo*. Illness, *mal de ojo* (the evil eye), and *susto* (loss of spirit and deep profound discouragement and hopelessness) are considered afflictions on material, spiritual, and mental levels for spiritual as well as physical healings. The *curandero/a* may prescribe an herbal remedy or conduct a religious ritual. The cure may employ a type of counter-magic, herbal remedies, potions, or rituals–depending on the illness–and may use common religious symbols such as the crucifix, rosary, or holy pictures (Trotter and Chavira 1997).

Espiritismo

Founded by an engineer named Hippolyte Rivail, who wrote under the pseudonym Allan Kardec, *espiritismo* originated in France and spread to the Western Hemisphere in the mid-1800s. As this movement took root in different nation states, cultures, and/or regional groups, it developed a variety of unique manifestations. *Espiritismo* practiced in Puerto Rico differed considerably from that practiced in Mexico or Argentina or Brazil. In fact, even within the same country, different social classes or races practiced *espiritismo* differently.

Also known as Kardecism or spiritism, it was considered by its adherents as a scientific movement, not a religious movement. It was a combination of scientism, progressivist ideology, Christian morality, and mysticism. Rivail hoped to subject the spiritual world to human observation and then, from these observations, develop a positive science. As the movement spread, it took the form of small groups of mediums assisting their clients in communicating with the spirits of the dead. A group of believers would gather at someone's home, then sit around a table, make specific invocations, fall into a trance, and allow a medium to become a bridge to the spirit world. They insisted their practice was not ritualistic; rather, it was pure experimental science in which the practitioner verified the experience by speaking with the dead—through the medium—who provided immediate solutions to what ailed them.

Among the first to be attracted to this movement were the middle and upper classes, but it quickly spread to other urban groups of less power and privilege, eventually reaching the rural countryside. Poorer segments of society turned to *espiritismo* for help and guidance with the struggles of daily life, specifically in areas of material need and health problems. In many cases, *espiritismo* absorbed into its practice elements of Spanish folk religion, specifically herbalism, African religious practices, and Amerindian healing practices (Brandon 1997:85–87).

Santería

Santería, from the Spanish word *santo* (saint), literally means "the way of saints." The religion was legally recognized as a legitimate religion on June 11, 1992, when the United States Supreme Court ruled that practitioners of *Santería* had a constitutional right to sacrifice animals in connection with their rituals. It originated when the Yoruba were brought from Africa to colonial Cuba as slaves and were exposed to Catholicism. They immediately recognized the parallels existing between their traditional religious beliefs and this new religion of their masters, which they were forced to observe. Both religions had a high god who conceived, created, and sustains all that exists. Additionally, both religions consisted of a host of intermediaries operating between the supreme God and the believers. Catholics called these intermediaries saints, while Africans called them *orishas.* In order to continue honoring their African spirits under the constraints of slavery, they connected their *orishas* with images of Catholic saints, identifying specific *orishas* as specific saints. Eventually, the religion made its way to the United States, in part due to the 1959 Castro revolution that sent about a million Cubans north seeking refuge.

These quasi-gods, manifested as Catholic saints, are recognized as powerbrokers between the most high God and humanity. They personify the forces of nature, and manifest themselves as amoral powers, which can have either positive or negative implications for humans. Like humans, they can be virtuous or exhibit vices as they express emotions, desires, needs, and wants. Basically, the believer of *Santería* worships the African gods, masked as Catholic saints, by observing their feast days, "feeding" and caring for them, carefully following their commands, and faithfully obeying their mandates. Attempting to affect natural forces is done when it contributes to a believer achieving his or her full potential. Rain can be summoned, seas calmed, death implored, fate changed, illnesses healed, and the future known if it will help the follower come closer to his or her assigned destiny.

Santería's components consist of an Iberian Christianity shaped by the counter-Reformation and Spanish "folk" Catholicism blended together with African *orisha* worship as practiced by the Yoruba of Nigeria and as modified by nineteenth-century Kardecan spiritualism. While the roots of *Santería* can be found in Africa's earth-centered religion, medieval Roman Catholic Spain, and European spiritism, it is neither African nor European. Christianity, when embraced under the context of colonialism and/or slavery, can create a space where the indigenous beliefs of the marginalized group can resist annihilation. And, while many elements of *Santería* can be found in the religious expression of Europe and Africa, still, it formed and developed along its own trajectory (De La Torre 2004d:xi–xiii).

Christianity vs. *Curanderismo, Espiritismo,* and *Santería?*

Due to persecution, many practitioners of *curanderismo, espiritismo,* and *Santería* maintained an outward appearance of belief in the dominant religion in a particular social context. Over time, the official faith traditions began to share quite similar sacred spaces with these unorthodox religious expressions. Still, for some, these expressions are an authentic search on the part of believers to grasp the reality of the Divine where, nonetheless, the priest's role is to gently correct practitioners of their errors and lead them to the official faith of the church. Others voice harsher criticism, claiming that *curanderismo, espiritismo,* and *Santería* adulterate the purity of Christianity and therefore need to be denounced as evil and taboo. For Protestants, specifically Pentecostals and some non-Pentecostal *evangélicos,* these religious expressions represent satanic cults and are therefore not only denounced but actively opposed. For others attempting to assimilate to the Euroamerican culture, these alternative traditions are not a theological problem, but rather a source of embarrassment, appearing both backward and primitive.

Christians usually portray *curanderismo, espiritismo,* and *Santería* as the dialectical product of an indigenous belief system and Iberian Roman Catholicism, in which a "confused" and idiosyncratic merging of the traditions occurred. Throughout the Americas, the phenomenon of cultural groups simultaneously participating in two diverse, if not contradictory, religious systems is widespread. Nevertheless, quite often the official Catholic or Protestant church places itself above the "unofficial" popular religion of the people and seeks to reduce *curanderismo, espiritismo,* and *Santería* to the spheres of ignorance, heresy, heterodoxy, and impurity. Power is exercised in the way the official religion "sees" the religion from the margins. "We" (read "official religion") operate from doctrinal knowledge, "they" (read "object") are confused. "Our" beliefs are pure, "theirs" impure. "Our" task is to correct their confusion. Seeing the Other as "confused" relegates them to an inferior social position while elevating the establishment religion, whether Catholicism or Protestantism, to an authoritative location from which paternal correcting can originate. Yet followers of these unconventional religious expressions do not consider themselves "confused" in their beliefs, nor do they necessarily comply with parental injunctions to behave and believe in a certain way. Resolutions to these issues usually occur within the context of a particular faith system.

Judaism and Latino/a Jews

The impact of medieval and early modern Iberia upon the Americas is undisputed. Therefore any discussion of Hispanic Jews in the United States should acknowledge the significance of the Jewish *conversos* (converts). Throughout much of the Middle Ages, Iberia, the region now consisting of Spain and Portugal, was the home to a large and culturally thriving Jewish community. As the Christian kingdoms of Iberia embarked on a campaign of *reconquista* (reconquest) of lands under Moorish (Muslim) control, Jews within those lands often faced the choice of conversion, expulsion, or worse. Many tried to escape persecution in Spain by going to the "Indies" (the Americas). Some changed their names to circumvent the royal decree that Jews could not immigrate to the new lands. Several fled to the north into a wide area that now are the states of California, Texas, New Mexico, and Arizona, where many of their descendants still live. For descendants of these exiles from Latin America, Judaism has been an uninterrupted faith, while for many others it has been a well-kept but persistent secret in family histories. More recently, some Latinas and Latinos are discovering their Jewish roots and are converting to the Jewish faith of their ancestors. Additionally, in the nineteenth and twentieth centuries European Jews emigrated to various parts of Latin America, notably Mexico and Cuba, and in turn some of their descendants have migrated to the United States, bringing a different Jewish experience to the reality of Latino/a life in the United States.

Islam

An additional manifestation of the diversity of faiths of Latino/a peoples is Islam. This includes both historical echoes in the sense of the cultural influence of Islam on Spain and Latin America, as well as the more recent embracing of Islam by Hispanics in the United States. The formal presence of Islam in Iberia, lasting more than seven hundred years, left a profound and sometimes forgotten influence on Spanish and Portuguese culture. This imprint was transferred to the Americas with emigration and is an element in the *mestizaje* of Latin America and in the United States. Islam affected Spanish language, literature, music, and thought. In fact, it is believed by some that a Moorish influence persists in Mexican American *curanderismo.* Just as some Hispanics are exploring the possibility of Jewish roots, others are finding a connection with their Muslim heritage from Spain. In recent years a small but growing number of Latino/as are converting to Islam, with Hispanic Muslim communities in places such as New York, Chicago, and Los Angeles. This continues despite the increased prejudice some U.S. Muslims experience in the wake of the September 11, 2001, terrorist attacks on the United States.

Conclusion

While the majority of Latinas and Latinos may identify themselves as Christians, this does not give license to ignore those who say they are not. Moreover, impermeable religious barriers do not always neatly define the Latino/a religious experiences in the United States. Oftentimes Latino/a religiosity may be a mixture of Christianity and other religious traditions, traditions usually opposed by the "official" religious institutions. Yet, for both the disenfranchised and those with social power and means (and there are Latinos/as in both categories, and in social places in-between), these alternative religious expressions attempt to provide an immediate remedy for the struggle of daily life. A common feature of all is the perception of a world that experiences a vibrant interaction between what has been called the natural and supernatural. Although at times at odds with various understandings of what constitutes official orthodox faith of Christian institutions, these expressions become a sacred space by which to understand the movement of the Divine or the supernatural or spirit in their lives. If this is the case, then the examination of these, as well as other alternative religious and spiritual traditions and practices, has a place in the study of Latino/a religion and theology. As such, any exploration of Hispanic theological perspectives requires a wide-ranging understanding of the interaction between "official" and "unofficial" religions, as well as assorted alternative traditions that combine elements from multiple sources.

CHAPTER 26

Health and Healing

■ KENNETH G. DAVIS

Introduction[1]

A catechetical exam from an aspiring communicant included a lad's reference to the sacrament of "Annoying the Sick." Ministers to ill Christians may in fact annoy when they mean to anoint if they do not appreciate the congregant's culture. Because a growing number of U.S. Christians are Hispanic, and the vast majority of our ministers are not, attention by non-Hispanic ministers to a Hispanic understanding of sickness and health is all the more important. Bridging that cultural gap is the intent of this essay, which will explore a traditional Hispanic approach to health, the power of ritual, and the role of the healer, concluding with reflections on how the anointing of the sick might be celebrated with the Hispanic community.

One Traditional Hispanic Approach to Health

Curanderismo may be the best bridge between the non-Hispanic minister and an ill Hispanic (or at least Mexican-descent) parishioner.[2] *Curanderismo*, however, is complicated and constantly changing. A more specific (and for some more palatable) term for the most basic and widespread conceptual underpinnings of this particular traditional

---

[1]This is a revision of "Annoying the Sick?" which first appeared in *Worship* 78, no. 1 (January 2004): 25–50.
[2]In fact, many people effortlessly negotiate popular religious traditions and Christianity, including folk healers.

Hispanic approach to health could be the neologism *naturalismo*. That is because even though *curanderismo* is usually associated with those of Mexican descent (the majority of U.S. Hispanics), it is found among other Hispanics who share its unifying, conceptual elements that are here termed *naturalismo*.[3]

Furthermore, this specifically Hispanic approach to alternative medicine is resurging even among the more acculturated. Hence, although *naturalismo* literally means "naturalism," it points to the traditional, often premodern views about health and illness common to most Hispanic Christians as described below. Note, however, that just as the specific practices of Hispanic popular religion differ by ethnicity, geography, and acculturation yet still share certain beliefs about the divine, so the particular practices of traditional Hispanic health ways are often distinct, although they also share certain unifying religio-cultural elements here termed *naturalismo*.

One unifying, religio-cultural conviction is that the goal of life and death is communion with God through community. Health is conceived as not just the absence of injury or biological contagion, but also as having personal, sociological, and spiritual concord. Health includes at least the following consequent prescriptions and proscriptions: (1) personal integrity, (2) harmonious interpersonal relationships, and (3) trust in God. Health requires harmonious relationships among oneself and others, as well as between oneself and God. For relationships to be harmonious, one must be honorable and responsible, interdependent, mutually forgiving, and devoted to God.

As with health, illness is biological, personal, sociological, and spiritual. It is personal because it may challenge one's sense of self-worth, and self-understanding. It is sociological because it affects one's role in the family and community or even compromises one's accepted gender role. It is spiritual because it may test how one understands and relates to God. God provides the means of any healing, which include people (family members and "folk" healers as well as medical doctors, nurses, etc.), home remedies, medicines, instruments, symbols, rituals, and therapies. Because all healing arts and apparatuses are gifts of God, they should be equally available to all. In *naturalismo* this means addressing the biological, personal, sociological, and spiritual ramifications of illness. Sickness may endanger a person biologically, and a Christian personally

---

[3]Although *curanderismo* (a *mestizaje*–a mixture of Native American and Spanish/Catholic healing practices) is relevant to a large proportion of the Latino population, mostly Mexican, it does not appear to be prevalent on the U.S. East Coast. *Espiritismo*, more popular among the Puerto Rican population, is strongly influenced by the writings of Alan Kardec and the practices of Catholicism. *Santería* is a syncretic belief system, based on the beliefs of the Yoruba people (present day Nigeria) and Catholicism, mostly developed by Cuba's African slaves (Espín 1996:7).

because it can make one feel abandoned by God and dislocated from the healthier community. A consequence of illness is the struggle for integrity amid suffering, which may require personal conversion, meaning that a Hispanic retrieves and reinterprets her or his own religio-cultural values in such a way that personal integrity is reinforced in that crisis.

Because of the communal aspects to illness, family is essential to both maintain and restore health. The sick or elderly should never be abandoned or unnecessarily burdened, because expressions and actions of sincere sympathy and solidarity are healing. Thus, for the family to fulfill its healing function, it must be included in the health decisions of the ill member. Harmonious interpersonal relationships are essential to maintain health and to heal illness.

Power of Ritual

Traditional healing rituals among some Mexican-Americans frequently begin with a nurturing person (often a female family member) who evaluates the severity of the illness and whether or not it is within her competency to alleviate it. This extra attention and expression of familial connection is itself healing and usually sufficient, especially when combined with home or over-the-counter remedies.[4] If the sick person does not improve, informal healers outside the family may be consulted (with or without the medical establishment being consulted as well). Language and cultural barriers, financial or insurance difficulties, improper documents, or even transportation problems or childcare needs can hinder a family from seeking formal medical assistance.[5] All these difficulties can actually exacerbate the sick person's situation. However, none of these impede traditional healers, who share the same language and culture as their barrio clients, charge small fees (and often only accept free-will offerings), require no documents, and usually live in the same neighborhood.

The treatment setting is conducive to healing, with no inflexible institution, stringent appointments, or cold professionalism. The healer usually operates from her home with perhaps one room set aside and filled with religious symbolism, herbs, incense, and candles. The patient is received warmly and interviewed at length with a culturally congruent

---

[4]Along with time in the United States, English acquisition, out-group marriage, and other factors, higher income and greater education are associated with greater acculturation by Latino groups. This is positively associated with greater use of professional medical services, since the acculturated are more likely to have medical insurance, speak the cultural idiom, and afford co-payments, transportation, etc. However, just as one may speak English without losing Spanish, so one can also use the medical establishment without disinterest in the general health principles enculturated in childhood. As a believer may have faith both in an accomplished but atheistic physician and his or her own religion, so Latinos may negotiate both modern medicine and the traditional health ways of *naturalismo*.

[5]For a discussion concerning why families may or may not choose formal health care see Roeder, *Chicano Folk Medicine,* 1988.

"combination of verbal suggestion with physical contact," relieving anomie and restoring hope (Kiev 1968:138). Healing is holistic: massage, oils, incense, tea, counsel, proverbs, parables, and prayer may all be dispensed.

Ritual functions through public acceptance of the sick person's condition of (at least temporary) impairment, which invokes socially acceptable responses from both the sick person and her or his family. The importance of interpersonal relationships is reinforced, and difficult circumstances are reinterpreted in ways meaningful to all. Because illness in this culture is not just about biological dysfunction but also social and spiritual imbalance, healing rituals must use "culture-specific methods" that address the effect of the illness on the sick person, her or his relationships, and faith. *Naturalismo* rituals have adapted the universal script of Christian healing to the actual circumstances of the sick person. Culturally congruent rituals bring coherence to a frightening situation, assuage fears of isolation, and help the sick person regain the organic harmony so important to a *naturalismo* approach to health. For these rituals to be effective, they must also be practical and proportionate and include a competent ritualistic leader. This last component touches on the importance of the role of the healer.

The Role of the Healer

Traditional healers manifest behaviors similar to that of traditional saints. First, they normally have had a calling or vocation to heal. The power of this belief in divine calling gives self-confidence despite a lack of professional credentials and also makes it socially acceptable to break from gender roles without censure. Second, vocation means that the healer is perceived to be an instrument of the Divine, who is loving and wishes to cure. As an instrument, he or she is excused from usual social and gender roles, but is also expected to act with sympathy, self-sacrifice, and dedication. For instance, many people claim that the mark of a good traditional healer is that she or he only accepts free-will offerings.

Third, it is precisely the qualities of sympathy, self-sacrifice, and dedication that give the traditional healer an entrée into the confidence of the sick person. With this confidence the healer acts as a "cultural interpreter" of the illness and its consequences, has the power to deal with the illness, and is trusted to do so in a way congruent with the patient's cultural expectations. Healers are not empowered simply by their credentials and certainly not through impersonal professionalism, but rather through vocation, experience, and the entrée necessary to gain patient confidence so that the entire person (physical, spiritual, moral, relational) can be treated.

Thus the healer depends more on community validation than some distant graduation. This publicly validated authority channels the "social forces of the group" contained in symbols and expressed through rituals to address the biological, sociological, and spiritual dimensions of illness. Patient confidence that the healer is the holder of "culturally sanctioned defenses" against illness is essential to the healing process. A healer, therefore, can challenge culture in order to promote health. For example, under normal circumstances a man is respected for "*aguante*," that is, the strength needed to endure pain. This is valuable for hard work and resiliency, but for a dangerously ill patient it can be life-threatening. The healer as cultural interpreter can intervene in such a case and find a way to broker the impasse. Indeed, there are times when a person or family must break old rituals and create new ones; the healer has the authority to sanction this.

Anointing Celebrated with the U.S Hispanic Community

What can non-Hispanic ministers learn from traditional healers? First, a minister should emphasize a theology of holistic healing consonant with *naturalismo*. Second, the minister should attend to the psychosomatic quality of the rite so that it harmonizes with Hispanic popular religion. Finally, the minister should help ill Hispanics deal with the personal, sociological, and spiritual consequences of diminished physical capacities.

Recall that for *naturalismo* the goal of life and death is communion with God through community. And health is not perceived as solely the absence of injury or contagion, but personal, sociological, and spiritual concord. The prescriptions and proscriptions that result from that religio-cultural understanding strive to help the person and the community cooperate with the original harmony intended by the Creator. Moreover the various treatments and therapies are also ways of restoring that same wholeness to individuals and communities. That is why both the role of the healer and her healing rituals are important: they help the sick person reintegrate the experience of suffering into a culturally congruent self-understanding, aid the family and community in reinforcing interpersonal relationships, and remind all that ultimately God will embrace us in love when we cooperate with the grace that helps us both flow in gratefulness and ebb with gracefulness.

How might one attend to the psychosomatic quality of the ritual so that it is more obviously and explicitly congruent with Hispanic popular religiosity? Rosa María Icaza has made two helpful suggestions, summarized in two events virtually always included in "folk" healing: *tocar y ensalmar.*[6] *Tocar* means "to touch," but in Spanish, it is more likely

---

[6]Rosa Maria Icaza is a member of the Congregation of the Sisters of Charity of the Incarnate Word of San Antonio. Involved in Hispanic ministry since 1978, she is a faculty member at the Mexican American Cultural Center, a member of the Subcommittee on the Liturgy in Spanish of the Bishops' Committee on Liturgy. She is also a consultant for the Hispanic National Institute of Liturgy and was its president for six years. Interviewed by the author at the Mexican American Cultural Center in San Antonio, Texas on January 22, 2002.

to connote a concrete effect. For instance, in Spanish one does not "play" a musical instrument, one "touches" it. But the effect is music. Thus "touch" in Spanish is much more an action with a presumed effect. Popular Hispanic religiosity is tactile. Throngs turn out to feel the grit of ashes, grasp the sleekness of palms, sense the warmth of candles, and heft the weight of statues. Images are caressed, kissed, and left love notes. Beads are counted, crosses carried, breasts beaten, water sprinkled. People want to touch God and to be touched by God.

The laying on of hands and the anointing with oil are tactile symbols that recall the somatic quality of Hispanic popular religion. The words of blessing and anointing also speak of comfort, consolation, fortitude, and protection. These are at the heart of the popular spirituality of this community, who Miguel Díaz has reminded us finds God in the concrete, historic, ordinary experience of relationships both human and divine (2001:80–86). For this community, health and disease are not just physical or even only social realities.

Just as touch in the context of the sacrament should attend to the psychosomatic quality of Hispanic popular religion, so too the operative theology should be consistent with the holistic anthropology of *naturalismo*. Finally, the minister should be able to evoke the best of both in order to help ill Hispanics deal with the personal, sociological, and spiritual consequences of diminished physical capacities. This may be done explicitly through the folk healing approach to prayer, or *ensalmar*.

Like the touch of oil, *ensalmar* is mutual as well as biblical. *Ensalmar* literally means to pray the psalms together, and like the liturgy of the hours, is a communal act of praise, thanksgiving, and petition. Like the liturgy of the church, the folk healer also has a ritual to prayer that is instructive. Usually the healer uses an environment that can be summarized by the symbol of the *altarcito* or little altar. Kay Turner notes the elements of this prayer ritual: (1) a respectful approach that may include a bow, closed eyes, the sign of the cross, and finally raised or clasped hands; (2) the use of fire to burn incense and light candles; (3) visual meditation that culminates in an action such as adding or manipulating a symbol or sprinkling holy water (Turner 1999). All this precedes the auricular prayer, which may include formal orations or spontaneous praise and petitions.

The altar represents both the divine and (e.g., through religious images) the community (through photographs and memorabilia). It is sacred space that, when used in folk healing, consecrates a moment in time. The *altarcito* focuses attention on healing of the whole body (personal, sociological, spiritual) because the body is our way of being in the world personally as well as the vehicle for communicating with God and others.

There are both historical and cultural reasons to continue to use an *altarcito* in domestic celebrations of the rite of anointing in order to evoke

Hispanic popular religion. But the minister must take care to incorporate both the ritual presence and symbolic significance of the *altarcito* into the celebration of the sacrament. It would not be inappropriate to include in the sacramental celebration some of the gestures Turner describes.

Again the minister can help choose scriptures, focus brief preaching, and elicit full participation by making appropriately explicit what is implicit in a celebration that is sensitive to the rituals and symbols of *naturalismo*. An operative theology consonant with *naturalismo* and attentive to the psychosomatic quality of the Hispanic popular religion (e.g., *tocar* and *ensalmar*) can help the non-Hispanic minister evoke the personal, sociological, and spiritual healing promised by the sacrament through the culturally congruent use of symbol and ritual (e.g., *el altarcito*).

It is important to note that healing also plays a role within the established church structure. Pentecostal (and by extension Catholic charismatic) healing can be defined by the following characteristics: (1) explicit and exclusive references to Christian scripture's citations for healing; (2) sole and unambiguous reference to God as the only and direct healer, though employing mediating symbols such as oil, altars, and the laying on of hands; (3) healing proclaimed as and often accompanied by gifts of the Spirit, especially glossolalia; (4) healing as declamatory and therefore usually public and emotional; and (5) consequent emphasis more on healing as a manifestation of grace than as the cessation of symptoms (Davis 1994:68–79).

Conclusion

Hispanics are a large and growing part of the U.S. Christian landscape. However, they still make up a small percentage of those in ministry positions. Therefore many non-Hispanic ministers are called to the hospitals and homes of people who are culturally distinct from themselves and asked to extend the healing mission of the church. Helping to bridge that cultural gap is the intent of this chapter. An appreciation of the operative theology in *naturalismo* and some understanding of its symbols and rituals deeply rooted in popular religion will help the non-Hispanic minister anoint rather than annoy a Hispanic member of the congregation, and help the whole community experience the healing of the Anointed One.

CHAPTER 27

Pastoral Anthropology in Latino/a Cultural Settings

■ Harold J. Recinos

This chapter discusses what the culture concept and methodological contributions of the discipline of anthropology bring to understanding Latino/a cultural settings. As a Latino theologian trained in cultural anthropology, my work has centered theological reflection on the historical experience of crucified people in the barrio, those whom the anthropologist Eric Wolf named "the people without history" (1982). For me the anthropological perspective raises theologians' awareness of Latino/a cultural voices that critique established ideologies, promote a hermeneutics of justice and diversity, and seek a more just life in a less crucifying world.

For the most part, academic theologians have not been particularly concerned to examine how religious ideas are produced and enacted in Latino/a cultural settings, paying more attention to texts and the theological discourse of religious elites. The anthropological perspective enhances the value of theology by showing how an experientially grounded and dialogically focused methodology leads to counting as knowledge the ideas, symbols, and actions of social groups that have been mostly absent within conventional theological discourse. Latino/a cultural settings make plain that there are no ready-made answers to matters theological in a culturally plural world. The variety of Latino/a theologies affirms that belief never stands alone, since religious viewpoints are always culturally patterned.[1] Theological difference suggests understanding the confessional pluralism of the present, studying the role of religion in society, its impact on identity and behavior, and the cultural forces shaping it. An anthropological perspective contributes to an understanding of religious diversity by exploring what religion tells us about cultural identity and the moral and intellectual organization of social life.

The Latino/a context requires serious attention be given to the theological ideas and practical ethics expressed by Latino/a cultural groups who center theological identity on the God who exists in the struggle and hope of oppressed and suffering humanity. The Latino/a theological identity now capturing the imagination of theologians and social scientists is the Christian witness that enacts belief in a God of life who is not indifferent to the poor who struggle against life-denying systems. I think ethnographic research in the barrio promises to uncover the various ways theological discourse and symbols are used in Latino/a cultural settings to both image and challenge the sinful structures in the social order.

What Is Culture?

In modern society, scientific rationality was supposed to replace the superstitious worldview of religion.[2] Yet religious beliefs and practices have not been driven from modern life; instead, they have increased and established new and various realignments between religion and culture. The wider American culture evidences people yearning for direct contact with something greater than themselves, and is reflected in the fascination with angels; consumption of religious books; and the proliferation of religious themes in talk shows, film, MTV, and musical forms such as country music, hip-hop, reggae, rap, and *salsa*.[3] In the U.S., spiritual longing suggests that theological self-awareness must continually change and transform to be meaningful. In this regard, a working definition of culture helps in understanding theological identity shifts and provides insight into a culture group's reinterpretation of the sacred.

---

[1]See Segovia, "Hispanic American Theology and the Bible," (1992); Fernández, *La Cosecha* (2000); and De La Torre and Aponte, *Introducing Latino/a Theologies* (2001).

[2]Early social scientists–Tylor, Durkheim, Weber, James, Freud, Marx–examined religion and its relationship to society. The study of religious experiences, identity, belief, and practices in the social science tradition declined once interest in the sociology of knowledge, postmodernism, feminism, and ethnic violence came into vogue. In the post-September 11 world, the study of religion, religious politics and violence, and religious discourses are of renewed interest. See Rappaport, *Ritual and Religion* (1998); Taylor, *Varieties of Religion Today* (2003); Eck, *A New Religious America* (2001); and Juergensmeyer, *Terror in the Mind of God* (2000).

[3]See especially Dyson, *Between God and Gangsta Rap* (1996); Sample, *White Soul* (1996); Ehrlich, *Inside the Music* (1997); Flores, *From Bomba to Hip-Hop* (2000).

Anthropologist Clifford Geertz defines culture as a "historically transmitted pattern of meanings embodied in symbols...by means of which men [*sic*] can communicate, perpetuate and develop their own knowledge about and attitudes towards life" (1973:89). Geertz's definition suggests culture is learned behavior common to a social group that offers individuals a comprehensive way of thinking, feeling, and acting. Hence, the thousands of things that seem "natural" to us are in fact patterns of learned meaning and behavior. The specific material, ideational, and behavioral patterns that people take for granted in their daily lives are acquired through the process of learning and interacting with others in a cultural environment.

For me culture is: (1) a socially conditioned meaning system through which people interpret their experience and act in the world; (2) a context in which belief, behavior, values, social events, institutions, and worldviews are intelligibly expressed; and (3) the product of specific social groups to be grasped in terms of a global, material social process of interconnection and change. Cultural research within the U.S. Latino/a context means one will work with a single group or any combination of seventeen national groups constitutive of the Latino/a national population. Also, each social group expresses a unique cultural identity that informs others to whom a person belongs and to what cultural group they are related. Attention must also be given to cultural variation within group life. In other words, not all Puerto Ricans, Cubans, Mexicans, Salvadorans, Peruvians, Dominicans, or Guatemalans reflect their cultural system of meaning and behavior in the same way. There are differences in cultural identity within each national group such as ethnicity, race, gender, class, educational level, place of residence, and exceptional historical events (LeCompte and Schensul 1999:24). Understanding Latino/a cultural settings requires both a working definition of culture and an understanding of internal variations in cultural identity within social group life.

Church leaders who inspire growth in cultural understanding can be counted on to advocate a commitment to explore with greater depth what makes human beings different and what constitutes our common humanity. The study of Latino/a cultural groups guided by the culture concept produces a rich understanding of cultural realities and contributes a theological perspective that affirms all people experience God in the time and space of different cultures. In the process of conducting ethnographic field work in local Latino/a contexts, I have discovered that if you are a "Hispanic-American" or an undocumented Mexican, a Roman Catholic Guatemalan or a Jewish Argentinean, a Cuban *Santero* or a Puerto Rican Buddhist, or are from Texas or El Salvador, culture is the basis of your interpretation of experience and generation of behavior.[4]

---

[4]See especially Griswold, *Cultures and Societies* (1994).

The diversity of Latino/a cultures suggests religious institutions need to take cultural identity seriously in order to more fruitfully formulate new understandings of the sacred and new ways to see religious life in the world. From an anthropological perspective, what must be kept in mind is that faith communities may not generalize about beliefs and behavior by drawing on standard religious categories of understanding produced within the particularity of mostly Western middle-class culture histories. The analytical capabilities of anthropology provide the church with a way to increase understanding of the religious beliefs and practices issuing forth from the community-based theologies of Latinos/as. For example, De La Torre and Aponte in *Introducing Latino/a Theologies* note how differences in Latino/a historical experiences in the United States have issued forth in three types of otherness with hermeneutical implications for the construction of theological identity: (1) exiles–a category linked to the Cuban community and Latinos/as who were involuntarily displaced from their homeland; (2) aliens–the classification associated with the Mexican experience of otherness, which includes a unique cultural history of land dispossession; and (3) outsiders–a typology aiming to reflect the experience of otherness and marginalization typified by the Puerto Rican experience and the experience of other Latinos/as who live in ambiguity in their only known home, the United States.

Anthropological tools provided me with insight in Salvadoran contexts in which theological identity makes claims on the collective consciousness of America with a message that condemns economic exploitation, poverty, and death-dealing structures. In the 1970s and 1980s, political violence in El Salvador pushed 1.5 million Salvadorans into refugee life. Faced with enormous human rights violations and state-sponsored terror, Salvadoran citizens and refugees searched for a way to understand and respond to the structures of death and their experience of suffering. Because the fundamental categories of thought in Salvadoran society are religious, the story of Christ's passion and the experience of Salvadoran political killings were situated in the context of martyrdom and God's coming reign of justice. A new popular theological worldview unfolded that reflected a conviction that God favors persons who are despised, tortured, and killed by the wealthy. In the words of one Salvadoran living in a D.C. barrio:

> When reading the gospel one feels that it was written directly for people like me who have suffered. Suffering happens to us, but God does not will human suffering. Those who suffer persecution, torture, murder, massacre, displacement, hunger, and refugee life are the Christ of our time. You see Christ in suffering people. I must try to do what Christ did, struggle for

what Christ struggled for, and live as Christ lived. Jesus lived and died for the poor. We must do the same thing.[5]

In short, anthropology's study of human diversity is relevant to our everyday lives in a multicultural world.

Discovery Strategies for Working in Latino/a Cultural Settings

Some of the wider cultural issues congregations face when working in the Latino/a cultural setting include a strong anti-immigrant context characterized by four racist nationalist themes. First, there is a strong feeling among a growing number of Americans of European descent that certain "peoples" from Latin America are racially and culturally inferior. Second, "inferior" Latinos/as are unable to assimilate into the controlling Anglo-American culture. Third, "inferior" Latino/as take jobs away from native-born Americans and cause national economic decline. Lastly, undesirable Latino groups stress the welfare and school system and may someday become a threat to White political dominance (Feagin 1997:13–14).

In addition, congregations working with Latino/a populations on the edge of society will need to bear in mind the following social dynamics: (1) limited social and immigration services to the Latino/a community; (2) the experience of economically marginal youth living in crime-ridden neighborhoods; (3) lack of political representation and general isolation from social institutions; (4) high levels of unemployment and under-employment; (5) lack of adequate housing, educational opportunities, and health care; and (6) inter-ethnic tensions and gang violence in local settings. I suggest the use of *pastoral anthropology* for congregations working within Latino/a populations.

Pastoral anthropology is useful for cross-cultural ministry in Latino/a settings because it provides methods for crossing boundaries of difference to experience other worlds and identities (Recinos 1992) and encourages members of congregations to undertake the task of cross-cultural immersion by engaging cultural diversity through studying belief and behavior as they maintain, amend, and give shape to specific narratives of identity and behavior.[6] Pastoral anthropology is designed to enable theological communities to ethnographically understand, for instance, why *La Virgen de Guadalupe* emerges as a central figure in

---

[5]Author interview of Salvadoran refugee, Washington, D.C., September 2003.

[6]Pastoral anthropology assumes face-to-face interaction and the use of specific tools of data collection. It does not require that one have specialized training in ethnographic research methods. For basic guidelines for ethnographic research such as: see (1) Schensul and LeCompte, *The Ethnographer's Tool Kit* (1999); and (2) Spradley, *The Ethnographic Interview* (1979).

Mexican popular piety in the setting of conquest society or the reason why Archbishop Oscar Romero surfaced in the context of El Salvador's military regime as a symbol of the poor's aspirations for justice, freedom, and dignity.

Pastoral anthropology engages human diversity and the various ways social groups construct their beliefs and practices by recognizing the epistemological privilege of the poor and people discounted by those better off in society. Because preferential attention is given to the theological and ethical perspectives socially constructed by cultural groups experiencing unequal development, insight is gained about how marginal groups negotiate and seek change for their place in society and how God draws the world into community by self-disclosing through the vehicle of human culture. As congregations implement pastoral anthropology, they should form a cultural listening group (six to eight persons from the congregation) to prepare to enter the Latino/a cultural setting. The task of the group will be to discover the cultural frame of meaning responsible for the organization of thought and behavior in a local setting.[7]

Listening groups seeking sustained relationship with other ethnic communities increase congregational cross-cultural competence, which consists of "the ability to think, feel, and act in ways that acknowledge, respect, and build upon ethnic, [socio]cultural, and linguistic diversity" (Hanson and Lynch 1993:50). Initial cross-cultural learning can take place through examination of literature, film, and art; contact with local individuals; and participant observation in the daily life of a contact community. Listening group members immersed in the Latino/a cultural setting should pay special attention to cultural themes that critique the established order of society, because this local talk increases understanding of the community cultural worldview and the issues and concerns organizing thought and behavior.

Informal conversations with persons from the selected local context will identify themes in people's thinking and culture and focus attention on how the specific contact community views its life and problems in light of established structures of meaning and feeling. This process facilitates a broadened experience of others, which is altogether important in multicultural societies where there is a strong desire for a community exclusive of separation determined by race, ethnicity, class, and gender (Gal. 3:28). Below is a list of questions focused on four areas to guide a listening group in immersion in local Latino/a contexts:

---

[7]Membership in the listening group is open to persons willing to understand another cultural way of life. I suggest primarily the laity constitute the listening group and that it reflect the diversity of their community and be persons who have the time to consult data collection guidelines for ethnographers and willingly place themselves in other cultural communities that permit them to see other ways of being in the world.

- *Economic Life:* What are the key economic issues faced by your community? How does your community view the relationship between the local and global economy? What cultural factors guide the economic decisions you make each day?
- *Cultural Life:* What cultural themes reflect the consistent pattern of values, thought, and behavior in your social group? Can you describe the beliefs and behavior that include or exclude persons and groups relative to your cultural community? What cultural knowledge are people using to generate behavior in their environment and to organize a meaningful self-identity?
- *Political Life:* What is the relationship between political life and the system of beliefs constitutive of the local culture? What are the political priorities of churches, grassroots organizations, and institutions in your community? What is the nature of political leadership? Who has a voice and decision-making power? What inter-ethnic relationships need to be nurtured?
- *Religious Life:* What is the religious climate of the local group? Does the church maintain a religious presence in the local neighborhood? Are categories of thought religious or secular? Does religion give expression to the cultural group's ultimate concern? What changes need to be brought to local religious institutions and what difference would they make for you?

As the listening group engages in firsthand observation and conversations in other cultural communities, it then can present information that helps local congregations understand that entering the Latino/a cultural setting begins by unfolding a process of crossing the boundaries of difference to examine the unique historical experiences that explain Latino/a concepts of self-identity, faith interpretation, and perceptions of their place within the wider social context. Certainly, pastoral anthropology guided by the concept of culture and the commitment to sustained relationship in other cultural settings makes plain that Christianity acquires its truest form by finding God in the territory of difference and otherness.

Conclusion

Local congregations whose members seriously engage issues of faith and culture can embrace the Latino/a cultural context to transcend the barriers preventing relationship with others and to deeply open up to the gospel. In intentionally engaging Latino/a cultural settings by organizing a listening group and doing pastoral anthropology to develop cross-cultural competence, local congregations will learn to understand and respect others who live out of different worldviews, value systems, beliefs, and behaviors. Pastoral anthropology suggests that by embracing diversity in the Latino/a cultural setting, church members learn through other cultural communities that their own faithful views are incomplete.

From the perspective of pastoral anthropology, listening groups gain knowledge about a local culture by asking questions, observing the behavior of people, and participating in and recording daily experiences. What are the practical benefits of pastoral anthropology for a local community? Presently, there is a great deal of anti-immigrant sentiment in the wider American culture that holds that new Latino/a immigrants are a threat to the controlling culture.[8] A listening group working with Latino/a immigrants is in the position to report views that challenge the anti-immigrant climate of the wider culture. For instance, it can report that new Latino/a immigrants who cross territorial, psychological, and cultural borders when entering the United States revitalize the national work ethic, the meaning of religious life, and family values.

Working with a listening group in the nation's capital, I discovered that for Salvadorans religion is a focal point of ethnic identity and that they have an expectation that religious institutions provide a space for ethnic gatherings, celebrations, the articulation of social justice concerns, and cultural expression. Thus, listening groups formed in non-Latino contexts that engage in cross-cultural interaction on matters of religion can revitalize their communities' theological identities. This is what happened in one congregation I worked with that had a largely African American and European American membership when Salvadorans became part of the community. Salvadorans revitalized theological identity by demanding religious life be centered on the concern to defend human rights, allegiance to economic justice for the poor, lobbying for the demilitarization of society, and a politics of decision-making that includes marginal people.

Diversity in creation manifests difference as part of the internal structure of the God who calls us to the task of reconciling unity. From a theological viewpoint, engaging diversity within and outside of the barrio issues forth from the assumption that God saves human beings created to express a multiplicity of languages, lifestyles, and ways of thinking and acting in the world. Cross-cultural competence increases awareness that the God of our differences, who poured love in all peoples and cultures, gives individuals the capacity to achieve unity through difference. Pastoral anthropology helps local congregations become contexts of cross-cultural empowerment and intercultural exchange, thus making them embody the gospel in the spirit of bearing witness to the greatest love.

---

[8]For example, see Perea, *Immigrants Out!* (1997).

CHAPTER 28

Latina Feminist Theologies

■ GLORIA INÉS LOYA

Introduction

In this essay of *pensamientos* (thoughts), I will explore the roots and location of an emerging and unique Latina spirituality from within several current feminist theological anthropological views, which are interrelated, yet very much distinct. In reviewing many Latina authors, and from my experience of ministry with Latinas, I have increasingly become aware that, from various feminist theological voices, a spirituality, which is central to our identity and leadership, also continues to emerge.[1] By navigating through various feminist theologies, I will describe the uniqueness and richness of a Latina spirituality that is a font of life and beauty, expressing a new humanity, as well as God's grace present in the very struggle, chaos, and discrimination experienced by Latinas in North America.

In reviewing five distinct theological anthropologies, I will emphasize and clarify a Christian feminist perspective. They do not necessarily indicate that Latina theological and spiritual growth must proceed according to each chronological stage or category, but describe key theological and anthropological markers that contain the distinctions and similarities between various views and realities of a Latina feminist theology as a *locus* for spirituality.

---

[1]To examine this theme in more depth, see my work "The Mexican American Woman" (1996).

Clearly, Latina feminist theologians are providing the basis for our spirituality by the way in which they write about the Latina experience of life in the struggle, religious and moral symbols, the community and family, and eschatological hope. Numerous excellent works of my Latina *compañeras* contain not only a Latina feminist theology, but also the roots of this spirituality. For example, my students readily approached *Mujerista Theology: A Theology for the Twenty-First Century* (1996), by Ada María Isasi-Díaz, as a personal reflection of not only the author, but also of readers from all cultures who can identify with her expression of *being in the struggle*. In *Our Cry for Life: Feminist Theology from Latin America* (1993), by María Pilar Aquino, students of Latina feminist theology discover a much-needed systematic discourse by which they learn the importance of integrating the gospel story of Jesus with their own call to discipleship, liberation, and the recognition of their personal story as part of what Aquino names *the logic of life*. In *A Reader in Latina Feminist Theology: Religion and Justice* (2002), edited by Aquino, Daisy L. Machado, and Jeanette Rodríguez, there is a scholarly and well-documented body of Latina feminist thought that is powerfully spiritual.

Stage One: Passive-Acceptance[2]

Women in this stage represent a more fundamentalist vision of life. In a fundamentalist interpretation of the faith sources—for example, of the scriptures—the meaning of the passages and accounts are taken quite literally (Wilson-Kastner, 1983:2). The role of woman is defined and even limited to an exclusive responsibility within the family. This stage should not be confused with the "traditional" view, because in Latino/a culture, the traditional also includes a living heritage of spiritual values, symbols, and respect for the leadership and authority of the woman in the family, as well as in the larger society. In contrast, in the "passive acceptance" stage, the status of women is based on the identity of the father, and in adult life her identity is transferred to the husband. In such a romanticized view, women are held to a higher moral standard than that of males. Rather than mutual responsibility for the family and the education of children, she is expected to carry these obligations almost totally alone.

Stage Two: The Post-Christian

Both Euro-American and Latina women take this position. For example, Mary Daly critically reminds us how patriarchy must be confronted and changed. She states:

> All so-called religions legitimating patriarchy are mere sects subsumed under its vast umbrella. Women who are willing to

---

[2]The term "passive acceptance" is used by Derald Wing Sue and David Sue, not to stereotype, but rather to clarify (1999:318).

make the journey of becoming must recognize the fact of possession by the structures of evil, and by the controllers and legitimators of those structures. (1990:39)

Daly analyzes the crushing reality that patriarchy has been for all cultures and faiths. Her work is foundational for a new feminist psychology or for a fresh feminist theological anthropology that is crucial for spirituality. Daly speaks of a post-Christian feminism that calls for "re-membering our selves" by recalling our "original integrity" (Ibid.). She names the challenge to develop an authentic and creative psychology based on a true humanity for women, or a "be-friending," on the reweaving and reestablishing of genuine friendships and reconciliation with past fragmented relationships, especially those involving our mothers, living and dead (1989:200).[3]

From a Latina perspective there are several authors writing in this line of feminist critical thought. Gloria Anzaldúa is prominent among these who are in search of the goddess as the central figure for an understanding of the divine. She centered her work on the unearthing of the divine in the image of the goddess, based upon the pre-Columbian world. Yet if the divine or the God figure is now only portrayed in the feminine, doesn't that continue to limit our image of God? The Christian faith tradition from the Hebrew Scriptures presents a God who has the characteristics of both a loving father *and* of a nurturing mother, or of a God that is multivalent. Even in the ancient indigenous "cosmo-vision" as described in the creation story within the *Popol Vuh,* the divine is named mother and father of the universe.

Anzaldúa sees the ancient figures of the indigenous goddess Tonantzín and of Guadalupe as one. This stance is impossible as the historical accounts give credence to the Guadalupe event as witnessed by Juan Diego, revealing the woman as the Mother of God, in the tradition of the *Theotokos* (Virgin Mary*).* However, apart from these questions, Anzaldúa does offer new insights about Guadalupe, also named *La Morenita,* which are unifying and reconciling for all peoples of the Americas:

> Today, La Virgin of Guadalupe is the single most potent religious, political and cultural image of the *Chicano-mexicano.* She, like my race, is a synthesis of the old world and the new...she is a symbol of hope and faith, she sustains and insures our survival...Guadalupe unites people of different races, religion, languages: *chicano,* Protestants, American Indians, and whites. (1989:79)

---

[3]I believe Daly makes an important contribution to the discussion of spirituality from a theological anthropology. As Latina-*Mestizas,* there is much to learn from this aspect of Daly's work.

Stage Three: The Liberal Reformist

A strong characteristic, from the perspective of a feminist theological anthropological dimension, in this stage or vision of the liberal reformist, is the contribution to the dialogue and debate around the concept of gender and equality for women:

> To question gender, rather than women, provides a comparative framework of analysis that allows for understanding the relational experience of women and men in different situations. The implications of gender stretch from the personal and familiar worlds to the social, political, and public realms and to the meaning of the whole, which is the province of religion. (Carr 1990:83–84)

In North America several expressions of the liberal reformist feminist stage emphasize the need for the equality of women, especially in the political, economic, and social forums. They are the women who in North America fought for equality and freedom for women at all levels, and from all races, including the Latina. The focus on protecting the individual rights of each person has been a benefit to women, as well as to men. Women have won significant ground in gaining rights and having equal access to institutions that were traditionally totally patriarchal, such as in the political area, in business and economics, in medicine, in law, and in theology.

However, there is a problematic side to extreme dependence on liberal philosophies, especially in this age of postmodernity. As Christians and peoples of various religious faith traditions, there is a new urgent challenge by which questions are asked regarding a liberalism that places strong emphasis on a radical individualism that excludes and that dominates other worldviews. Liberal philosophies and theologies, particularly in the U.S., devalue those cultures that do not exalt the importance of the individual as the central principle of society and of religion.

From a Latina view, I do acknowledge that there are wonderful values in North American liberalism that have been beneficial for all women, such as the respect for the individual person, and the opportunity to make economic gains because of a strong work ethic. However, the Latina emerges from a reality that is far more socio-centric. This reality places great dignity on the person, while valuing the community from which the person was born and formed. The Latina finds her humanity and spiritual growth in the integration of, and in dialectic between, personhood and community, taking responsibility for herself and for the community.

The extreme emphasis placed on the importance of the individual rather than seeing the person in relationship to the community is questioned by a number of thinkers in the U.S. Roberto Goizueta challenges the liberal individualism that has supported and legitimated extreme consumerism and capitalism: "Such distortions legitimate a social order that undermines the very values which these traditions themselves uphold–namely, the priority of the individual vis-à-vis religious, political, and economic systems" (1992b:5)

This is a call to discover and search for a new social order and worldview that engages in a socio-centric world and society rooted in the community, rather than exclusively on the individual. As Goizueta points out, Latino/a cultures are not simply liberal and individualistic, but rather they are organic in character and in historical tradition (Ibid.). Therefore, a Latina feminist theology and spirituality evolves from this ongoing dialectic between the person and the community. For the Latina, the spiritual journey includes the human quest in search of personal identity and dignity. Her unique personhood emerges within the light and life of her cultural and religious community.

While the liberal reformist view offers new insights, especially in the reconstruction of anthropologies regarding gender and in a focus on the importance of equality, nevertheless, this anthropological view remains incomplete. "The single anthropology is more adequate, but fails if it capitulates to an individualistic, or single male or female model; all the virtues of the gospel are needed by all persons and must inform public, ecclesial, and societal structures as well" (Carr 1990:133).

Therefore, a feminist theological and spiritual vision constructed from liberal individualism can easily become lost in a heightened religious privatization closed to the guidance of universal values and teachings, which flow from a body of common beliefs of a given faith or spiritual tradition. Radical individualism leads to a religious privatization and institutional religious voices lose their impact, respect, and moral strength in public discourse. Latina theological anthropology and spirituality are challenged by these perplexing and terrifying realities, as they take hold in the U.S., and in the world. This communal dimension allows us to bring about transformational change in oppressive structures because we are united as one body, guided by God's grace within the public debate.

Stage Four: The Liberation View

According to Anne E. Carr, who also names this feminist theological anthropology as a transformational view, there is a need to examine societal structures and the root causes of oppression, not only of women, but also of men, and of families. This entails going beyond equality to a commitment to the marginalized–to the poor and the oppressed in society. For Christians, this means liberation not only for women but for the whole society. Therefore, the gospel must be lived out in the liberating service of compassion, mercy, and justice. The barriers of race, of class, and of gender must be transformed (Carr 1990:127).

Feminists describing liberating theological anthropologies include scripture scholars and women theologians who represent Euro-Americans and Latinas who have researched, reconstructed, and reinterpreted sacred texts and documents from a feminist view, giving form and voice to the presence of women who seek a liberating praxis and finding new meanings in the symbols and narrations of the faith history (Weaver 1988:156–57). According to Weaver, Elizabeth Schüssler Fiorenza, states that the work of feminist theology is to integrate and to connect the theory with a transforming praxis. Rosemary Radford Ruether notes that past feminist anthropologies limited women, and she emphasizes the quest for a new sense of wholeness, based on relationality. Mary Jo Weaver observes this of Radford Ruether:

> In rejecting earlier attempts at equalitarian anthropologies—
> eschatological, liberal feminist, and romantic—she formulates the
> question under her liberationist and prophetic argument for an
> integrated social order. As [in] her earlier work, she advances
> feminist issues within the framework of ecology, ecumenism,
> socialism, and a liberated world order. (Ibid.:169)

In reviewing these stages and the unique aspects of each of these theological anthropologies, I have shown the depth and new insight of each. The limitations of each stage have also been presented. I believe that the Latina is present in each of these perspectives. Latinas who are active in fundamentalist churches hold a "passive acceptance" theological anthropology in which women are rewarded for their absolute silence and obedience. Many young Latinas adopt the post-Christian feminist view as they search for an adequate feminist image of the divine. Many professional Latinas strive to bring equality, as well as competency, to the workplace. In the liberationist dimension, Latinas throughout the Americas struggle with their Euro-American counterparts in the liberation and transformation of oppressive institutions and structures.

Stage Five: A Latina Christian Feminist View

In a Christian feminist theological view, spirituality is recognizing the movement and inspiration of the Spirit in one's life, in a manner through which women and men practice their faith (*en la vida cotidiana*). The sources of such a theological and spiritual journey include the Christian faith tradition, the Latino/a cultural context, and one's personal life experience in which our God is present in suffering, in death, in the commitment to justice, and in the family and community.

A Theology of Beauty

Sor Juana Inés de la Cruz is a major historical and cultural figure who stands alone because her religious writings and poetry are pivotal in creating a theology that contains critical aspects of a spirituality. Her insights were unique for seventeenth-century colonial Mexico, especially as they came from a *mestiza*. Sor Juana based her theology of beauty on the Augustinian understanding that through the Word, the beauty of Christ—or *grace*—is manifested in creation. This theology of beauty, found in her poetry, makes it possible for readers to savor and delight in her understanding of the relationship between beauty and grace, beauty and spirituality, and beauty and the human body. Her theological thought communicated beauty through Spanish poetry, which explodes in bright, colorful descriptions (Loya 1998:496).

Through the voice of Sor Juana, we can capture how a theology of beauty is foundational for discovering the spiritual. While the authorities of her time placed enormous barriers and obstacles in her way in an effort to silence her, she continued to study, and to write poetry and theology. She understood that women's experience is sacred. It is more than a chronology of events. It holds as central to the spiritual life the potential for God's transforming grace and recognizes the place of human relationships and intuition, as well as our intellectual and emotional life. Feminists today also find in women's experience the ground for interpreting and discerning the movement of God's spirit in our lives.

Ora-praxis

For the Latina the spiritual pathway is nurtured and sustained by a life of ongoing prayer, not only in the church, but more so in everyday life. This rich and abiding life of prayer is intimately integrated as part of the *logic of life,* an expression used by María Pilar Aquino (1993). Therefore, I would characterize this type of prayer within a Latina feminist theology and spirituality as one of "ora-praxis" (*oración* and praxis). Prayer and emancipatory action in the name of mercy, peace, and justice becomes ora-praxis. This is much more than social activism and private piety. Women demonstrate such prayer in their families and in their communities through rituals, blessings, anointing the sick, preparing the dead for burial, preparing for the communal celebrations of family feasts, and for the feasts of our beloved saints such as Our Lady of Guadalupe and San Juan Diego, the Talking Eagle. An expression of such prayer can be found in the following conversation/prayer between the grandmother, Doña Margarita, and Guadalupe. Doña Margarita is the head of her household. Her family has struggled beyond human understanding to immigrate from Mexico to California. In her prayer we recognize our own experience of the spiritual in the longing for unity within our families:

> She continued laughing, looking at the statue of the Virgin Mary [within the church]. Her eyes overflowed and her sides began to hurt, but still, she couldn't stop laughing. Laughter was the

greatest healing power of all. But then she wiped her eyes, stopped her laughter, and looked up at the statue of the Virgin Mary and said, "All right, My Lady, enough of this. Now let's You and me get down to business!" And saying this, she stood up. "What I came to ask You for today—I do not ask! I demand as one mother to another! Do you hear me, Maria? I demand that You send my son home to me before the end of the next full moon, and I don't care if Domingo has been killed or drowned or fell off the end of the world and gone to hell!...After all, we're good friends, You and I. You lost one son and so You know how I feel. I lost seven! Seven!" she repeated, tears streaming down her face, "that came here from my loins and I had baptized in Your Most Holy Family's name." (Villaseñor 1991:426)

Shared Wisdom

Within the rituals and stories of the community, and shared among Latinas, there is a constant flow and organic play of the Spirit. I believe that at the heart of such beautiful and powerful expressions of God's grace, women exchange their shared wisdom. Latina feminists, such as Jeanette Rodríguez (1994:146–58), remind us about the story of Jesus, with the stories of our families as sources of revelation and wisdom. While such *cuentos* tell of our identity, wounds, and ancestors, they also grasp and contain a living faith and a thriving spiritual courage that has given substance and meaning to our lives.

One of my cousins told me such a story. It is about my 90-year-old mother, who carries the value of shared wisdom. Her family came from Jalisco, Mexico, during the time of the revolution in Mexico. My cousin's husband died a few months ago after a long illness. She said that as he died, she left a cross about three inches long in his hands, and that this cross brought them peace during their ordeal. As she spoke to me, she went on to recount that it was the same cross that her mother held as her own mother passed on to her death in 1943. At that point, my cousin continued, saying that this cross that meant so much to her was a cross that was given to her by my mother in 1943. I stood in awe, thinking about how my mother had handed on this symbol that became a sign of strength and of blessing for my cousin and her family over the years. Even more powerful was when I was told by my cousin that it was the cross that my own grandmother held at her death, as my mother placed it in her hands during her last hours on this earth in 1941. I retell this *cuento* because it is not about the words, but rather the loving communication and spiritual wisdom from one woman to another, both finding meaning, support, community, and God's abiding grace within the experience of death and life.

Reconciliation

Latinas, as all Christians, find the courage to welcome and embrace reconciliation in one's life. For example, Mary Daly reminds women (1989, 1990) of the need for befriending one another and for healing our brokenness and reestablishing our connections within ourselves and our relationships with family and friends. Some years ago I had the opportunity to interview Dolores Huerta, the vice president of the Farmworkers Union. She spoke of the work of seeking justice for the farmworkers, but she also spoke of her spirituality, and how important it was to respect and become reconciled with the *patrones,* or the bosses, who were blocking the farmworkers from developing the union. Those of us who believe in the gospels as a source of faith must consider reconciliation as a pathway of ethical courage, as well as of spiritual insight, because our world needs women and men of moral virtue and character. Latina feminists know the difference between a superficial "reconciliation" that is imposed or artificial, and one that calls for the depths of Christian love for the other. Latinas are in a unique position to use our collective wisdom in the spirit of reconciliation. God's grace present in our history has taught us how to reconcile the seemingly opposite aspects of our own lives. Our integration of our Latina race, culture, and faith with the best of our North American education and heritage creates rich underpinnings from which to be able to respect and to transform the racial and economic barriers, hatreds, and violence existing in this age of fear and terrorism. Our spiritual and theological maturity will guide us in crossing the cultural barriers, leading us to an authentic and deep reconciliation that is much needed in our world today. In exploring some aspects of feminist theological anthropology, it is possible to capture the voices of Latinas as they are committed to mercy, peace, and justice flowing from their spiritual depths. By these initial ideas, I have simply shared my own *pensamientos,* with a hopeful concern that in the new millennium, the Latina will continue to express her theological voice, and her spiritual wisdom and insight, which already has been a guiding force for the Latino/a community throughout its history.

CHAPTER 29

History and Theology

■ PAUL T. BARTON

The Influence of Liberation Theology on the Historiography of Latino/a Christianity

There is currently an effort by a number of Latino/a historians to deconstruct and reconstruct U.S. history in such a way that illuminates the ideologies undergirding the oppression of marginalized peoples in the United States and that offers alternative concepts for engaging in discourse about U.S. history. This movement has two constituencies in mind—those in positions of power who produce the dominant narrative, and the marginalized persons whose histories are often distorted or omitted within the dominant narrative of our nation.

Moreover, this is an exploration of the relationship between the methods of theology and those of the history of Hispanic Christianity. In Latin America in the 1960s and early 1970s, the emergence of liberation theology encouraged the dispossessed to strive for the reign of God by asserting their power in history. One of the outcomes of liberation theology was a method of doing theology in community, known as *teología de conjunto*. Theology done in community corresponded to a *pastoral de conjunto*. In this chapter, I examine some of the approaches to the history of Latino/a Christianity and suggest that there has been, and indeed needs to be, a *historia de conjunto*, a way of undertaking the history of Hispanic Christianity that is informed by a theological basis rooted in the Latin American and U.S. Hispanic experience. This illumines a method of undertaking a history of Hispanic Christianity. In doing so, I will also undertake a historiography of Hispanic or Latino/a Christianity in relation to Hispanic theology. A brief overview of the phases of historical writing on Latino/a Christianity reveals the characteristics of major shifts in this historiography, allowing examination of a *historia de conjunto.*

First Phase—Missionary Models of History

In the earliest phase of historical writing on Hispanic Christianity, most works were produced by or about Anglo-American missionaries, often by persons who had spent considerable time in the mission field. These works took the form of autobiographical accounts, such as Melinda Rankin's *Twenty Years among the Mexicans: A Narrative of Missionary Labor* (1875). Sometimes a person was so inspired by a particular missionary that he or she produced a biographical history of a missionary, such as Harriet Kellogg's *Life of Mrs. Emily J. Harwood.* Generally, these histories placed the missionaries and their labors in the spotlight. The objects of their missionary work, the Spanish-speaking, served as a backdrop for the missionaries' exploits and adventures. From a historical distance one can see clearly the relationship between the missionaries in the Spanish-speaking mission field and the larger U.S. colonial expansion.

These works promoted the dominant narratives in U.S. history, which invoked the favor of God upon Protestants originating from northern Europe and the British Isles. Works that praised the missionary and condemned the unconverted Spanish-speaking perpetuated this narrative. This was even more the case because the Spanish-speaking in the Southwestern borderlands produced few written histories in the nineteenth century. The works by and about missionaries also provided an ideological and, indeed, theological basis for the Anglo-Americans' dominance over and oppression of the Spanish-speaking people in the U.S. Southwest.

Second Phase—Latin American Models of History
CEHILA

A second phase of the historical writing on Latino/a Christianity began with the emergence of the liberation theology movement in Latin America in the late 1960s. As the objects of mission, Latin Americans began to demand their own historical agency and recognized the need to write their own histories. Latin American theologians realized that the history of Christianity in Latin America actually contributed to the oppression of the people because it failed to take into account the experiences of Latin Americans at the grassroots level. Enrique Dussel states:

It is because Latin America was not taken into account by European ecclesiastical historians from the sixteenth century until the later half of the twentieth century that Latin Americans felt cut off from themselves. They felt they were alienated, non-authentic beings, for they had been annihilated by the process of Europeanization. In order to recover their being, therefore, it is essential that the Christian history of Latin America be interpreted—this moment in salvation history that proceeds toward completion on our continent, this indivisible moment of our unique theology—if we are to think of ourselves as being a part of Christian history. (1981:18)

In an effort to promote a Latin American perspective of history, the *Consejo Episcopal Latinoamericano* (CELAM), the Latin American Bishops' Conference of the Catholic Church, through the *Instituto Pastoral Latinoamericana* (IPLA), authorized the establishment of the *Comisión de Estudios de La Historia de la Iglesia en América Latina* (Commission for the Study of Church History in Latin America, also known as CEHILA). The commission was established as an independent academic and research organization in 1973 and expanded to include the United States as part of its organization in 1975.

Born out of social, economic, and political unrest, CEHILA represented a major shift in the historical study of Latin American Christianity. A new cadre of scholars began to examine their religious history from their Latin American contexts and perspective. That perspective took into account the violence that was endemic in Latin America's history, including its religious history. Following the principles of liberation theology, historical studies under CEHILA focused on the history of the poor in Latin America. In doing so, these scholars sought to provide a critical rereading of traditional histories on Latin America while also uncovering many of its hidden stories about the prophetic struggle of individuals and groups for justice in Latin America. Thus, this was a religious history that focused upon the popular religion of the people while also taking into account institutional religious history.

CEHILA was also ecumenical in its work. This too was a radical shift, since the history of religion in Latin America was one of conflict between different religious groups. CEHILA formed a Protestant group in Latin America to answer the needs of Protestants on the continent.

Enrique Dussel

Enrique Dussel helped found the *Comisión Ecuménica para el Estudio de la iglesia Latinoamericana* in the 1970s. Dussel is to Latin American church history what Gustavo Gutiérrez is to Latin American theology. He helped bring about a new era of historians in Latin America, bringing together the disparate efforts of church history into a hemispheric organization and a systematic and coordinated effort at writing the history of Christianity in Latin America.

Dussel brought together a number of influences to lay the theoretical foundation of this new movement in the Latin American history of Christianity. He argued for a history of Latin American Christianity from the perspective of "*los de abajo*," those from below. This new reading of the history of Latin American Christianity took into account the lived cultural, political, and faith experiences of the common people of Latin America. Indeed, Dussel argued that the history of Latin America needed to be undertaken by Latin Americans so that they could gain their own recognition as "authentic beings" and subjects in Christian history.

U.S. Latino/a Models of History

The U.S. branch of CEHILA, established in 1975 at the Mexican American Cultural Center in San Antonio, undertook a history of Latino/a Christianity. At the organizing meeting, Dussel urged the CEHILA U.S. members to write a history of Hispanic Christianity in the United States. Moises Sandoval, the president of CEHILA at the time, served as the editor of the volume, *Fronteras: A History of the Latin American Church in the USA since 1513* (1983).

Fronteras provides a clear example of the merger of theological commitments within historical approaches. The writers of the volume had strong ties to the church, yet were also able to criticize the church for its neglect of Latinos/as and the injustices perpetrated against them by the church. The theology implied in much of the contributions to *Fronteras* was based on the *imago dei,* incarnated in the Latino/a cultural values of dignity and respect. *Fronteras* represents an effort by Latinos/as to call the church to account for its unjust treatment of their people, while also highlighting the efforts of Latinos/as to gain respect from church leaders. Even the single chapter on the history of Latino/a Protestantism, written by Edwin Sylvest, gives considerable attention to the ideologies that fostered injustice within Hispanic Protestantism (1983:279–338).

Fronteras was the first work in which we see evidence of a *historia de conjunto* in the United States. It was a compilation of essays by various persons who had deep theological commitments rooted in the love for particular Latino/a communities and the church. The authors of these essays had experienced the turbulence of the Latin American theology movement and the Chicano/a and farmworkers movements. They had experienced discrimination within their own church, and they brought these lived experiences and resulting theology to their historical writing. While chapters were written by individual authors, the common threads of their experiences of injustice and discrimination are clearly evident.

The editor of *Fronteras,* Moisés Sandoval, published a condensed version of *Fronteras* called *On the Move: A History of the Hispanic Church in the United States* in 1990. Sandoval integrated the many voices of *Fronteras* to produce a more focused narrative history. Significantly, the title indicates a common image of the church among Latinos/as. The church is not a static entity, but a community on a pilgrimage, always moving onward toward the reign of God. The church as a pilgrim people resonates with the experience of many Latinos/as who have also immigrated and migrated to the United States. The Latino/a people have been a people on the move, moving into new lands and new parts of the United States.

As CEHILA continued its work, Latino/a Protestants felt the need to organize themselves for the purpose of recovering and documenting *their* particular religious and cultural traditions. With the support of the Pew Charitable Trusts and McCormick Theological Seminary in Chicago, Illinois, Dr. Daniel Rodríguez-Díaz convened several dozen scholars and church leaders at a national conference at the seminary in May 1993. The purpose of the conference was "to create a network of persons working on Latino Protestant Church History, to exchange information, to assess needs, and to begin planning future steps" (Rodríguez-Díaz and Cortés-Fuentes 1994:xi). Several papers were presented and workshops held on ways of recovering their Latino/a Protestant tradition. A number of the papers at the conference were published in the book titled *Hidden Stories: Unveiling the History of the Latino Church.* The participants of the conference also formed the Latino Church History Academy (APHILA). The organization was short-lived because its work was merged with the newly formed Association for Hispanic Theological Education (*Asociación para la Educación Teológica Hispana*, also know as AETH).

The thematic emphasis of the conference paralleled that of CEHILA. Just as the members of CEHILA sought to uncover the history of Latin American Christianity from the perspective of the poor and the oppressed, participants at the "Hidden Stories" conference sought to uncover the undocumented histories of their people. Daniel Rodríguez-Díaz states:

> At issue is not only the question of historical inclusion or exclusion, but *how the history of both oppressed and oppressors reveals the underlying contradictions of American society.* What we need is a critical socio-historical analysis with insights into multiple religious histories. To discover the true genius of a nation it is important to uncover the hidden identities of all the social, ethnic and cultural groups that make that nation. (Ibid.:5)

Also like CEHILA, the participants at the "Hidden Stories" conference emphasized the prophetic nature of their historical work. Recognizing the relationship between a people's history and their identity, the participants noted that the recovery of their history would affirm the historical existence of the many groups comprising Latinos/as.

Daisy Machado states:

> For many Latinos in the United States simply being able to acknowledge their presence in the nation's history, being able to say "we too were there," is a necessary liberating and affirming act. Surely the Latino historian wants to write a well researched and carefully analyzed history, but even more than that the issue is to document and validate the historical presence of a people who for centuries have been invisible in this society and culture. (1994:49–51)

Machado's observation above about the need for Latinos/as to validate their historical presence correlates to Dussel's comment earlier that persons need to engage their own particular histories as a step toward becoming authentic human beings.

Anticipating the quincentennial anniversary of Columbus's arrival in the Western Hemisphere, the Mexican American Program at Perkins School of Theology sponsored three symposia titled "Redescubrimiento: Five Centuries of Hispanic American Christianity, 1492–1992." These symposia were held at Perkins School of Theology January 16–18, 1987, October 6–8, 1989, and November 12–14, 1992. According to Justo L. González, the initial symposium "was organized around three themes: a re-reading of our history, a rediscovery of our mission, and the development of a pastoral ministry appropriate for our situation" (1987:23). The subsequent two were organized in much the same way. The reconsideration of the history of Hispanic American Christianity was the focus of the first symposium; and the third symposium, while still considering historical questions, included presentations on Latina and Latin American women, and considerations for pastoral ministry in the new millennium.

What was accomplished through these three symposia? First, the symposia provided a space for presenters of papers and attendees to question the dominant historical narrative of the conquest of the Americas and its aftermath. There was a community of discourse created that represented the concerns and interests of the Hispanic or Latino/a community in the United States, the Caribbean, and Latin America. The concerns and interests included a rereading of our history that examined the injustices that have occurred in our history in order to understand the present situation and condition of Hispanics/Latinos/as today (González 1987) Second, the symposia demonstrated the methodology of *historia de conjunto*. The gatherings were not simply a place for academicians to present their ideas on the history of Hispanic American Christianity; rather, a genuine discourse among all attendees occurred as participants met in small groups to discuss participants' papers and then returned to respond to the presenters in plenary session. Third, the pastoral concerns enumerated in the symposia led to the document *Hispanic Ministries:*

Challenges and Opportunity in 1992. This document formed the basis of a proposed National Plan for Hispanic Ministry to the General Conference of The United Methodist Church in 1992.

Conclusion

These are just a few examples in which Latin Americans and Latinos/as within the United States have engaged in historical projects critical of the dominant narratives of U.S. society and offered alternative concepts for producing autochthonous narratives. Born in the turmoil of the late 1960s and early 1970s, the projects endured and manifested themselves intermittently in conferences, collaborative works, and in the exchange among Latino/a historians and church leaders.

Hjamil A. Martínez Vázquez, in his "Shifting the Discursive Space," insists that the trajectory for the project maintains some of the commitments established early on–a concern for popular and lived religion, a perspective from the poor, an uncovering of hidden stories–while gaining sophistication using new theories such as postcolonialism, borderlands theory, and postmodernism (2003). These new theories highlight the roles of class, race, gender, and power both in the process of doing history and in the focus of study. It is expected that newer works will continue to benefit from these theories while continuing to engage both constituencies–colleagues in U.S. American history and *el pueblo* with whom we maintain firm theological and faith commitments.

CHAPTER 30

Mary

■ KRISTY NABHAN-WARREN

When examining U.S. Latino/a Roman Catholic cultures, amid the rich historical and cultural diversity exists continuity in devotion to the Virgin Mary. Roman Catholic Latinos/as have nurtured an enduring Marian piety since the colonial period in the Americas, and have made the Catholic faith and the Virgin Mary *their own*. They have constructed a dynamic Catholicism and trust in the Virgin Mary through culturally specific and personal devotions to Mary, also known as the Mother of Jesus, the *Madre de Díos*, and the Blessed Mother. From an anthropological perspective, it is clear that she is a powerful symbol of Latinos'/as' "moods and motivations," in that she is a prism that reflects their deepest dreams, desires, and hopes (Geertz 1973:90). In other words, the Virgin is multi-faceted, a malleable symbol whose meaning is open to change. As a powerful symbol for U.S. Latinos/as, the Virgin Mary is a tangible manifestation of the divine. Like other symbols— "abstractions from experience fixed in perceptible forms, concrete embodiments of ideas, attitudes, judgments, longings, or beliefs"–she represents what matters most to the men and women who revere her (Ibid.:91.) The Virgin is a powerful, living symbol of motherhood, hope, love, ethnic pride, and endurance for U.S. Latinos/as.

Each Latino/a group has its own designated, patron Virgin. She is their mother and is believed to have appeared for them; there is an apparitional story behind each Virgin Mary, and the consensus is that when she appears to a group, she takes on the local, as well as national, ethnic, economic, and political identities of those to whom she appears.

Latinos'/as' devotion to the Virgin Mary is rarely, if ever, without political overtones, as the Virgin is believed to represent them in their struggles against oppression. Whether Mexicans' *la Virgen de Guadalupe*/The Virgin of Guadalupe, or Cubans' *Nuestra Señora de la Caridad del Cobre*/Our Lady of Charity, or Puerto Ricans' *La Virgen de la Providencia*/The Virgin of Divine Providence, or Dominicans' *Nuestra Señora de la Altagracia*/Our Lady of Highest Grace, or Ecuadoreans' Virgin of Cisne–to name several Latino/a Virgin Marys–the Virgin is believed to be the same, the one Virgin Mary, who nevertheless takes on cultural specificity.

Although the various Marys are said to be the one Virgin Mary, we are also able to see competition between cultures and their Virgins and the importance of Marian cultural specificity. In East Harlem, New York, for example, "Puerto Rican and Ecuadorian devotees are lobbying for space for their own patronesses–the Virgin of Providence for Puerto Ricans, the Virgin of Cisne for Ecuadorians."[1] She looks like those to whom she appears, speaks their language, and understands their particular needs. Just as there is a diversity of Latinos/as in the United States, so too there is a Marian pluralism–not all Marys are the same, nor do they have the same exact meanings. Still, while it is important to recognize the diversity of Latino/a cultures and experiences, U.S. Latinos/as have more in common than they do differences. The concept of solidarity is an important one for all U.S. Latinos/as, as the Virgin is one with them and takes on their specific pain and suffering. For Mexican American pilgrims in South Phoenix, Arizona, for example, the Mexican Virgin of Guadalupe and the Mexican American Virgin of the Americas listens to their prayers, comforts them in times of trial, and offers them her "candy kisses" and "slices of heaven."[2] These two *mestiza* Virgins understand their children in ways that no one else can.

What sets Latino/a Catholics apart from other Roman Catholics is the way in which Mary has taken on a central role in their culture and society and the intensity with which she permeates their beliefs and practices. The Virgin *is* Latino/a as she both assumes and represents their identities. For U.S. Latino/a Catholics, mainstream "official" Catholic beliefs and popular piety merge to form a distinctive and vibrant form of ethnic Marian devotions and beliefs. For Latinos/as, the Virgin is an important symbol of liberation, transnationalism, motherhood, Catholic piety, and ethnic identity. She is believed to deliver her *mestizo* children from oppression and marginalization, and she provides them with love, hope, and redemption. The experiences of Latinos/as in the United

---

[1]Mireya Navarro, "In Many Churches, Icons Compete for Space; Multiple Shrines to Patron Saints Testify to a Rivalry of the Devout," *The New York Times,* 29 May 2002.

[2]In my own ethnographic work, which has spanned ten years at a Mexican American Marian shrine in South Phoenix, Latino/a pilgrims who claimed to feel the Virgin's presence at the shrine commonly invoked these phrases. See Nabhan-Warren, *The Virgin of El Barrio* (2005).

States largely have been one of struggle, oppressed and discriminated against in multiple spheres: economic, political, social, and religious.

As a result of their multiple oppressions, U.S. Catholic Latinos/as have invoked the Virgin Mary's help and have rallied around her image in times of distress. Latino/a immigrants who are exploited in their jobs, but do not complain or go to the authorities for fear of deportation, pray to *la Virgen.* Salvadorans, Mexicans, Guatemalans, and Hondurans who currently labor in the Long Island city of Glen Cove, for instance, are underpaid, overworked, and victims of racism. Many of these men and women see their only recourse in prayers and petitions to the Virgin, seeing her as their mother who will help them survive in the United States.

Belief in the Virgin's intercessory abilities is a pervasive one for Latinos/as. Her image has been invoked in numerous social and political causes. The Virgin of Guadalupe's image, for example, was displayed and carried on banners during the Mexican War of Independence by figures such as Father Miguel Hidalgo, and later, during the Revolution by luminaries such as Emiliano Zapata. Years later, during the 1960s and 1970s, Latino/a farmworkers rallied around banners of the Virgin of Guadalupe as Chicano activist César Chavez appointed Guadalupe as the patronness of farmworkers and exploited migrant workers.[3] Connecting the Virgin to political causes is a historically constant theme and when we look at Mexican history, Guadalupe's image was invoked as supporting the workers' cause. We then turn to the Cuban wars for independence from Spain—the battles of Cuban insurgents in 1898—and, by the time the Cuban republic was established in 1902, "the Virgin of Cobre had become '*la Virgen Mambisa.*' She had become the rebel Virgin, the patriot Virgin, the national Virgin" (Tweed 1997:23). As with the Virgin of Guadalupe, she was believed to have stood by her creole, *mestizo/a* children.

With more recent Latino/a migrants to the United States— Dominicans, for example, the Virgin Mary remains a rallying point and cultural conservator. She is a constant reminder of their homeland and reinforces ethnic identity and pride in the American diaspora—primarily in New York, and northern New Jersey (Castro and Boswell 2002:3). Dominicans, one of the fastest-growing Latino/a groups in the United States, and currently fourth in size behind Mexicans, Cubans, and Puerto Ricans, are overwhelmingly Roman Catholic. They reflect a nationwide trend of Catholic immigration, in which forty percent of "recent legal immigrants" self-identify as Roman Catholics, compared with twenty-four percent of native-born Americans.[4]

---

[3]For the definitive historical work on the Virgin of Guadalupe, see Brading, *Mexican Phoenix* (2001).

[4]Monica Rhor, "Parishes Replenish From Other Shores," *The Boston Globe,* 29 July 2003.

A reality that distinguishes Catholic Latinos/as such as Dominicans from other Catholic immigrant groups is that they are transnationals— men and women who travel back and forth from the United States to their homeland, and who live in both worlds as a result. The image of the Virgin Mary and devotion to her is a link between the two worlds that these transnationals experience and live, enabling them to cope with the trials they experience in the United States, and gives them strength to endure. Veneration of the Virgin Mary is, as a result, a diasporic devotion, one born out of the particular struggles, hopes, and dreams of transnational peoples.[5] Whether Dominicans, Puerto Ricans, Mexicans, or Cubans, all U.S. Latinos/as are transnationals; men and women who live in two worlds: in the United States and in their home countries, literally and figuratively. As mid-twentieth–century and twenty-first–century migrants, U.S. Latinos/as–whether we are talking about Puerto Ricans, Dominicans, or Mexicans–do not have to leave "home" behind as did their nineteenth- through early twentieth-century European immigrant counterparts who left the "Old World" behind for the "New World." For Latinos/as in the United States, the Virgin Mary is herself transnational; for Cuban exiles living in Miami, for example, the *Virgin del Cobre* reminds them of their homeland and legitimates their identity as Catholics and as Cubans. She is believed to protect Cubans on their journey from Cuba to America; she is the Patroness of and for exiles.

For Latino/a Catholics, veneration of the Virgin is inextricably tied to their homeland. The *Virgen de la Caridad,* for Cubans in the United States, *is* Cuba and represents pre-Communist, pre-exile Cuba and is allied with their particular struggles. As theologian Miguel H. Díaz has written, "it is precisely the association of Our Lady of Charity with exiles that makes this Marian devotion capable of speaking to the reality of other U.S. Hispanics. U.S. Hispanic 'exiles' come to this land not only on rafts that cross the Florida Straits but also on rafts that cross the Rio Grande...Exile is our most basic shared U.S. Hispanic experience" (1999:163).

For U.S. Latinos/as, devotion to the Virgin Mary is a point of continuity between their Latin American roots and the United States, and eases the pain of being away from home and in an oftentimes unwelcoming United States. She symbolizes ethnic identity and is a continual reminder of home. For Mexican Americans, the Virgin of Guadalupe *is* Mexico and represents *mestizos/as* who are betwixt and

---

[5]Another shared experience for U.S. Latino/a Catholics is that the Roman Catholic Church, which has oftentimes failed to appreciate or understand Latino/a devotions to the Virgin and specific cultural ways of worshiping, historically has discriminated against them. See Stevens-Arroyo, *Prophets Denied Honor* (1980); Dolan and Deck, *Hispanic Catholic Culture in the U.S.* (1997); and Sandoval, *On the Move* (1990).

between Mexican and U.S. American cultures.[6] The Virgin of Guadalupe is the patron Virgin of Mexican Americans, for whom the mythic story of the Virgin appearing to Juan Diego carries important theological and political messages.[7] The significance of the Virgin, according to Latino/a theologians, is that she gives hope to Mexicans and Mexican Americans, who find deep meaning in the story that she appeared to a peasant ten years after the Spanish Conquest of Mexico's capital Tenochtitlan, and spoke in his native Nahuatl language. As Eric Wolf has written,

> On another level, the myth of the apparition served as a symbolic testimony that the Indian, as much as the Spaniard, was capable of being saved, capable of receiving Christianity...The myth of Guadalupe thus validates the Indian's right to legal defense, orderly government, to citizenship, to supernatural salvation, but also to salvation from random oppression. But if Guadalupe guaranteed a rightful place to the Indians in the new social system of New Spain, the myth also held appeal to the large group of disinherited who arose in New Spain as illegitimate offspring of Spanish fathers and Indian mothers, or through impoverishment, acculturation, or loss of status within the Indian or Spanish group. For such people, there was for a long time no proper place in the social order. (1958: 38)

Like other Latina Virgin Marys, her Latino/a devotees interpret Guadalupe as an intercessor on behalf of the poor who gives them "a stake in the colonial system" (Taylor 1987: 20). Guadalupe is interpreted as delivering her *mestizo/a* children from oppression and providing them with hope–from Mexico's colonial period to the present. Theologian Virgilio Elizondo has promoted the *mestizaje* thesis that Guadalupe has become a cultural symbol for Mexicans and Mexican Americans, both *mestizos/as* who were conquered by colonial forces and who crafted, through the Guadalupe apparitions, a new cultural and religious identity. Indigenous cosmology (the goddess Tonantzín) combined with Spanish Catholicism (the Virgin Mary) to create a new *mestizo* religion of liberation (2000c:118–25).

---

[6]See Rodríguez, *Hunger of Memory* (1982); Rodríguez, *Our Lady of Guadalupe* (1994); Léon, "Born Again in East L.A.," (1998); and Elizondo, *The Future Is Mestizo* (1988), *Galilean Journey* (2000a), and "Popular Religion and Support of Identity," (1986).

[7]The standardized story of Guadalupe is that she appeared to Indian peasant Juan Diego in 1531 a total of four times, and that each time she requested a shrine built in her honor. Juan Diego made two unsuccessful attempts to convince Bishop Juan de Zumárraga that he was indeed receiving apparitions and that he needed to have a shrine built. The Virgin, the story goes, was patient and told Diego to pick fresh roses to give to the bishop. Finally, on his third visit to the basilica, Diego opened up his cactus fiber *tilma,* cape, and the fresh Castilian roses he had picked earlier had become embedded in the cape, along with a glorious image of Guadalupe.

Liberation theologians also promote the theory that the Virgin Mary is a symbol of the poor and oppressed and that as a mother figure she empowers her children. As a symbol of the feminine and of motherhood, the Virgin is revered; motherhood is accorded power and prestige and as the divine *Madre*, the Virgin—whether she be Guadalupe, del Cobre, la Providencia, or Altagracia—is a symbol of divine female strength. Latinos'/as' revisionist works have posited the Virgin Mary as a powerful symbol of sexuality, women's strength, and cultural pride.[8]

Devotion to the Virgin Mary is culturally rooted and is deeply informed by the importance of women in Latino/a cultures. The Virgin is the ultimate mother/*madre* and she is believed to care for and to nurture her children. Within Latino/a cultures, Marian shrines are prominent; whether in Phoenix, Miami, New York City, Chicago, or Los Angeles, Marian yard shrines dot the landscape. Many of these shrines have become places of pilgrimage, especially those places where the Virgin is said to appear. Outdoor shrines attest to deep, enduring devotion to the Virgin, and pilgrims honor her with their prayers and petitions. When we look at Latinos'/as' pilgrimage experiences, whether they are to the Basilica in Mexico City, or to the shrine to the Virgin of the Americas in South Phoenix, Arizona, the belief in reciprocity is powerful. Prayers to the Virgin, invoking her aid, are coupled with *promesas* to honor her after the request is granted.[9]

Within Latinos/as homes, home shrines and altars, *altarcitos,* are ubiquitous and signal the high regard with which the Virgin is accorded.[10] Outdoor shrines devoted to her allude to—as Thomas A. Tweed has argued—a return to the womb, and exiting the shrine space is like being reborn (1997:115). Within Latino/a cultures, there is a deep respect and reverence for mothers as givers of life and as nurturers. The symbolism of the Virgin as mother figure is part of mainstream Catholic theology as well, but for Latino/a Catholics, cultural construction and the importance of mothers takes the veneration of Mary to a new level, as she is seen as a liberator from racism, oppression, and discrimination on a daily basis.

Another important layer to Latino/a Marian devotion is the lay-driven expressions that are manifested. Historically, U.S. Latinos/as have both challenged and expanded the Roman Catholic Church's definition of Catholicism by adding ethnic devotions and praxis, what many scholars of U.S. Catholicism have referred to as "popular" piety. Latinos/as have grafted their strong and enduring beliefs in the Virgin Mary onto "official" and traditional Catholic piety, such as attending

---

[8]See Castillo, *La Diosa de las Américas* (2000), which examines the Virgin of Guadalupe from revisionist, feminist, and liberation theological perspectives.

[9]For a good overview of the relationship between Latinos/as and saints in the Southwest, see Oktavek, *Answered Prayers* (1995).

[10]See Turner, "Mexican American Home Altars," (1982); and Turner and Seriff, "Giving an Altar," (1987).

church and praying the rosary. Men and women parade the Virgin Mary through the streets on her feast days, they hold street parties and picnics—*fiestas* for Mexicans, *romerías* for Cubans—and they hold candlelight vigils, as Dominicans do for the Virgin of Altagracia on January 21, her national holiday. For Mexican Catholics, December 12 is the *día de Guadalupe*, a day full of festivities, candlelighting, singing, dancing, and other modes of celebration.

U.S. Latinos/as are creating a third space of American Catholicism. By fusing popular religious expressions such as *fiestas* and *romerías* with official acts of piety, these men and women are forging a dynamic Catholicism for the twenty-first century, one that is defined by both the laity and the church hierarchy. The Virgin Mary is continually being reimagined by Latinos/as, and the common denominator is that she has always been seen as a symbol of strength, hope, and cultural endurance. The diversity of Latina Virgin Marys reflects the diversity within Latino/a cultures, yet the shared experiences of migration, oppression, and hope continue to bind Catholic Latinos/as together.

CHAPTER 31

Sacred Space/Public Identity

■ TERESA CHÁVEZ SAUCEDA

In a large Roman Catholic Church in Miami, Florida, there is an alcove to the side of the central worship space where worshipers from all over Latin America and the Caribbean can find figures representing the manifestation of *La Virgen* honored in their home country. In the Mission District in San Francisco, California, a bilingual Protestant congregation, the majority of whose members are newcomer immigrants from Mexico and Central America, opens its doors for a community celebration of *Las Posadas,* a centuries-old traditional Christmas season reenactment of Mary and Joseph's search for a place to stay, which is a common practice among Roman Catholic communities in Latin America. In San Antonio, Texas, a Roman Catholic church in the Mexican barrio of the city's West Side sponsors a troupe of performers for *Las Pastores,* a Mexican traditional drama that tells the story of the nativity through the eyes of the shepherds. The troupe performs in a variety of settings—in their local parish, the homes of neighbors around the barrio, and one of the city's historic Mexican missions for tourists and the city's social elite. In Los Angeles, California, English-dominant Latino/a evangelicals, struggling to find a faith community that fits culturally and theologically, form a network to promote bilingual and bicultural ministries targeting young, urban, middle-class and college-educated Latina/os.

The local congregation is both a place of worship and a social organization that provides public space in the life of a community. As a public space where people come together around common interests and commitments, the local congregation is one place where public identity is created and articulated. As part of the life of that congregation, worship is one area in which that common sense of identity is most clearly defined. In the life of any congregation, worship is the focal point and foundational experience that shapes community life. It is where the community gathers to nurture and sustain the faithful as they offer praise and prayer to God and share beliefs and commitments; the things that unite a particular community of faith are celebrated.

Worship also represents the public face of a congregation—it is where visitors and potential new members usually make their first contact with a congregation. Worship reveals what a community believes about God, and what it believes, values, and celebrates about itself. Thus, worship also nurtures, sustains, and reproduces the character and identity of the community gathered. For communities marginalized socially, politically, and economically from the centers of power in society, the local congregation gathered in worship is an autonomous public space where the community can name its own identity, and its own vision of society in light of its own faith claims and theological commitments.

Liturgy—quite literally, *the work of the people*—is a cultural product. Worship employs the tools of culture—language, art, music, symbol, and experience. As scripture is read and interpreted through proclamation, prayer, and music, the contemporary cultural context provides the backdrop for interpreting the meaning of faith—the lens through which truth is communicated, even where that interpretation of truth serves to critique the culture. In the United States, where Latinas/os are a racially marginalized community, the patterns and practices of worship in Latina/o congregations reflect the realities of the cultural hegemony of the dominant Eurocentric culture and the struggles of the Latina/o community to carve out a self-defined identity and voice in the larger society. As a worshiping community gathers to praise God and proclaim their faith, they "narrate in word, act and song the community's memories and hope." As the community names and praises God, they also "renew their vision, to hear and to speak the grand metaphors about how life and the world should be, and [to] do so with such trust in God that past tenses will be used as though these things were already true" (Craddock 1985:41). In the sacred space of worship, the Latina/o community claims a public space—articulating an identity for itself and a vision of society over against the silencing and marginalizing power of the dominant culture.

The Latina/o community in the United States is a unique confluence of people who bring a wide diversity of cultural and historical experience, incorporating the migrant worker seeking economic opportunity and the exiles of civil conflict; the second and third generation of new immigrant families who struggle to make their way into the middle class; and the descendants of centuries-old colonial settlers in the Southwest who still confront the legacy of systemic racism that has marginalized their communities for generations. Latinas/os in the United States typically identify themselves first in terms of their particular heritage—*mexicana/o, cubana/o, puertoriqueña/o, dominicana/o, salvadoreña/o,* and perceive the terms Hispanic or Latina/o as assigned and artificial and homogenizing labels.[1] For Latinas/os, their distinctive cultural heritage and identity is fundamental to the language and core values that connect them. In many ways, what brings these disparate ethnic groups together and contributes to a sense of community is a common struggle to participate fully in the socioeconomic and political life of the United States, and a shared commitment to not do so at the expense of their cultural heritage and identity.

The term "Latina/o" refers to a broad and highly diverse cross section of people. It is important to reflect briefly on who is encompassed within the rubric of the term "Latina/o." Latinas/os are the descendants of sixteenth-century colonial settlers from Spain and Mexico in Florida and in the Southwest from Texas to California. Latinas/os are also new immigrants from cities and rural villages throughout Latin America who have come seeking sanctuary from violence, poverty, and/or political repression. They come seeking an opportunity to create a better life for themselves and their families. Latina/os are a fusion of peoples and cultures—a rich *mestizaje* of the indigenous peoples of the Americas, European conquerors, African slaves, and Asian laborers. Historically, Latinas/os have been incorporated into the United States through conquest, political expansion, and continuing migration. From the first encounters in the westward expansion of white settlers to the West and Southwest, Latinas/os were racialized as "other" and marginalized in the social, political, and economic life of the United States.

Increasingly, as the Latina/o population in the United States grows, the experience of the community involves more interaction between diverse Latina/o ethnic groups. It is no longer possible to speak of Mexican, Puerto Rican, Cuban, Salvadoran, Guatemalan, or Chilean communities as isolated groups in distinct regions of the United States. Especially in urban areas, there is a lively mix of Latina/o ethnic groups creating opportunity for dialogue and impacting what it means to be Latina/o in new ways.

Latino/a worship is as varied as the community. The Latina/o Christian community divides along the same denominational lines as the larger society—Roman Catholic, mainline Protestant and Evangelical. Within each of these three categories there are congregations

---

[1]See the Zogby Poll national survey results, which found that the majority of Latinas/os surveyed had no strong feelings about either term, suggesting that they may be terms of convenience, http://www.nclr.org/files/25235_file_ NCLR_Poll_2004_Report_2_ Revise_7_16_04.pdf.

intentionally and creatively reinterpreting the Eurocentric traditions of their respective denominations through the lens of Latina/o culture and experience. And there are congregations whose worship looks no different from their Anglo counterparts. In the Roman Catholic tradition there has been a burgeoning of scholarly study and institutional acceptance of the spiritual practices of the people, described as "popular religion." Among Protestants there is a similar recognition that practices characterized as "Catholic" have meaning and significance in Protestant worship and spirituality. Protestant pastors have developed liturgies for *La Quinceañera*–a coming of age ritual for girls on their fifteenth birthday–and routinely incorporate godparents in their services of baptism, recognizing the pastoral importance of this practice of *compadrazgo* in Latina/o families. All of these efforts indicate a community marginalized by race asserting a culturally distinctive identity that represents a movement of resistance to the systemic patterns of racism and sociopolitical invisibility.

There is significant variety in the demographic makeup of Latina/o congregations. Some congregations are made up almost completely of new immigrants, and others are made up largely of families who have worshiped in the same congregation for a century. In some congregations, the members may come from one region in Mexico, or they may come from several nations and ethnic groups from throughout Latin America and the Caribbean. They may be undocumented laborers or middle-class professionals. Most congregations struggle with questions of what language to use in worship–how to be responsive to those who speak only Spanish, those who speak only English, and those who are fully bilingual. In the context of worship, this means that Latinas/os struggle to give voice to their own identity in and through the forms and practices of religious traditions defined by a Eurocentric culture.

The struggle to find a way to be authentically Catholic, Protestant, or Pentecostal *and* authentically Latina/o is an inherent part of a larger struggle in the Latina/o community to define itself in a way that is self-determining and empowers participation in the dominant culture, without surrendering the connections to a culture and an identity that is life-giving. Renato Rosaldo has defined this dynamic as "cultural citizenship," describing the way in which Latinas/os create a distinct social space for themselves within the larger culture and society (1997:27–38). As a racialized group in North American society, the Latina/o experience is shaped by the highly interactive complexities of ethnicity, language, and culture, as well as race, class, and gender. Despite a lengthy history north of the Rio Grande that predates the formation of the United States as a nation, Latinas/os are increasingly seen as foreigners and outsiders even where their citizenship has come through conquest and colonial expansion. This outsider identification works to render Latinas/os invisible politically and socially.

Cultural citizenship looks at the ways in which Latinas/os "are incorporating themselves into the larger society in the United States, while simultaneously developing specifically Latina/o cultural forms of expression that not only keep identity and heritage alive but significantly enrich the cultural whole of the country." Cultural citizenship describes the ways "cultural phenomena–from practices that organize the daily life of individuals, families, and the community, to linguistic and artistic expression–cross the political realm and contribute to the process of affirming and building an emerging Latino identity and political and social consciousness" (Flores and Benmayor 1997:2–6). Cultural citizenship is a mechanism to gain access to major institutions–voting power, visibility in public policy, education, healthcare–which challenges the assumptions of the dominant culture that those who are "different" must surrender their difference in order to benefit from the goods of society.

Latina/o identity in the United States is deeply influenced by the dynamics of systemic racism. Racial politics in the United States are on a trajectory moving from a society historically rooted–culturally, economically, and politically–in social institutions highly structured by race and the power to define the significance of race controlled almost exclusively by a white Eurocentric power structure, and heading toward a more open society in which those groups who have been historically defined as "other" are claiming public space and voice to contest the way they have been defined by the dominant culture and assert their own self-understanding, claim political voice, and redefine their social reality through their own cultural and historical experience.

Marginalizing Latina/o culture (including the devaluation, by the church, of the contributions that Latinas/os make to U.S. society) renders Latinas/os invisible and silent in decision-making processes of our social institutions. It obliterates their long history within the borders of what is defined as the United States and obscures the long and complex economic and political relationships between the United States and Latin America that contribute to the continuing migration northward. The articulation of a distinctive cultural identity and sense of community represents a movement of resistance to racism. The church in the Latina/o community is an important arena in which Latinas/os are defining their identity on their own terms–a new cultural *mestizaje*. This identity is cognizant of the influence of the dominant culture of the United States, and participates in the culture of the larger society on its own terms and in its own voice. In claiming a distinctive cultural citizenship, Latinas/os are challenging the cultural hegemony of the larger society that equates unity with homogeneity. In an increasingly multicultural society, Latinas/os assert that difference is a resource enriching and strengthening society. The same is true for the church. The institutional church in the United States has perpetuated the Eurocentric cultural norms of its own historical roots, norms that reinforce the values and social norms of the dominant culture and its social institutions. In the sacred space of worship, there is deep resistance to change.

In my own Presbyterian tradition, I have heard the question raised: If the look and feel of Latina/o worship is so radically different from the normative practices of traditional (white) congregations, is it still Presbyterian? Latinas/os have responded by asking, Exactly what does it mean to be Presbyterian? They insist that the core beliefs we hold, the distinctive tenets of our Reformed theology make us Presbyterian, not the style of music in our worship service. This same debate is taking place throughout the church. By redefining what it is that unites us, Latinas/os exercise great freedom in choosing their own styles and forms to express their common faith. By asserting their own cultural norms (using the language, music, and symbols of their own culture), they exercise true liturgy (giving the work of the people to God), and affirm the goodness of their own humanity in the eyes of God–by not having to adopt the language and cultural forms of another in order to glorify God.

In worship the Latina/o faith community makes intentional collective choices about their own emerging cultural *mestizaje* and identity as a community, navigating the interplay between their distinctive ethnic identities in relation to each other and the dominant Eurocentric culture. Worship is religious drama–remembering the historical narrative of a community, creating collective memory, interpreting their shared experience today. This collective identity resists the social fragmentation and loss of identity that is symptomatic of systemic racism. In the process, there are some core values and theological themes emerging that reflect the shared experience of the Latina/o community.

Perhaps the most fundamental of these is the understanding of community as a core value in the Latina/o faith community. It is articulated as a foundational theological theme as Latinas/os reflect on their own experience in contrast to the highly individualistic cultural norms of the dominant Eurocentric culture. It is found as a central paradigm in the work of Latina/o theologians who come from diverse religious traditions and yet share an understanding of community as central to their theology as a source of their theology, as a lens through which God is understood and as the method through which faith is articulated. It is also reflected in a commitment to do theology in community–*teologia en conjunto*–that has generated a lively theological dialogue between Roman Catholic, Protestant, and Pentecostal scholars (Chávez Sauceda 1997).

The understanding of community for Latinas/os is rich and complex. As a lived experience it usually encompasses an intricate network of family, church, and work that is not limited or defined by geographic boundaries. It is recognized in the context of common language, food, rituals, and cultural celebrations, through relationships built on shared values and shared social and political commitments. Those shared commitments reflect the shared experience of marginalization that defines Latinas/os as "other," as much as they reflect a shared vision of a better world. The church is a critical institution in the life of the community as it works to create social and political space—cultural citizenship—in the larger society. Worship articulated in the language and symbols of Latina/o cultures affirms the rich humanity of this community as they share who they are in the service of God, and equips a marginalized community with an articulated vision and shared vocabulary to confront the systems of oppression that have disenfranchised it.

CHAPTER 32

Sexuality

■ CARLA E. ROLAND GUZMÁN

Sexuality, "the quality or state of being sexual,"[1] is a complex topic involving subjects such as sex and relationships. Who has intimacy with whom (male/female, female/female, male/male), in what context (in or out of a monogamous relationship), and for what purpose (pleasure, procreation, prostitution), are all questions people pay keen attention to, perhaps even judging what configurations are acceptable/normative for each individual or community. Moreover, other topics are related to a person's understanding of sexuality, such as abortion, gender, sexism, misogyny, *machismo*, heterosexism, homophobia, and marriage.

In the early years of the twenty-first century, talking about sexuality has become "code" for talking about homosexuality (as if gay and lesbian people are the only ones who have sexuality).[2] This implies a religious, moral, and political stance regarding homosexuality. In this chapter, while the primary focus will be on the topic of homosexuality, the reader must understand and be prepared to recognize that any question regarding sex, sexual orientation, and marriage equally applies to heterosexual persons. Moreover, the fact that the subject of homosexuality seems to be a topic in the mainstream cultural currents of

---

[1]Mish, *Merriam-Webster's Collegiate Dictionary*, s.v. "Sexuality."

[2]Because of the complexities of sexual orientation and gender identity, I do not address here bisexual and transgendered persons. Similarly, I am limiting my chapter to a Christian religious background.

the United States does not give Latinos/as license to say that it is not an issue in our communities. In *Introducing Latino/a Theologies*, De La Torre and Aponte refer to a "conspiracy of silence" regarding gay and lesbian issues among Latino/a theologians (2001:158–59). This chapter aims to add a voice to the emerging conversation within the Latino/a theological community.

As a Latina woman living in the United States, I can both understand (and relate to) the secular and religious discourse regarding homosexuality in mainstream U.S. society, and the sentiment of Latinos/as in the United States who feel that the mainstream hegemonic discourse (regarding sexuality and other issues) is being imposed on a different set of cultural values, continuing the legacy of oppression and colonialism.

In the Beginning

Any Latino/a stance on homosexuality must begin with the biblical principles of *Imago Dei* and the great commandment. Furthermore, any Latino/a stance on homosexuality must have the ethical values of reconciliation, justice, and love as foundational. Our sexuality is a gift from God since our creation: "Then God said, 'Let us make humankind in our image, according to our likeness'" (Gen. 1:26a). It is in our creation, in history, that we enter into our covenant with God, and therefore our responsibility to live up to the image of God. Our image of God has a direct impact on who we call ourselves to be. Believing in a God of reconciliation, justice, and love entails living a life of reconciliation, justice, and love. We are called to continually evaluate our covenant with God, to assess the places in our lives where there are contradictions. That we are all made in the image of God serves as a foundation to any discussion of sexuality inside and outside our Latino/a communities.

The renewed covenant, in which we entered with the coming of Jesus, reemphasizes our covenant with God by focusing on the great commandment: "'You shall love the Lord your God with all your heart, and with all your soul, and with all your mind.' This is the greatest and first commandment. And a second is like it: 'You shall love your neighbor as yourself.' On these two commandments hang all the law and the prophets" (Mt. 22:37–40). As Latinos/as, we have worked for the liberation of our communities. We have done this through the interpretation and study of scripture through Latino/a eyes. We have fought for our dignity in this world. Therefore, we have the tools and the foundation to understand the justice and liberation sought by gay and lesbian persons. We have fought to not be judged: "Do not judge, so that you may not be judged" (Mt. 7:1). We seek the kingdom of God: "But strive first for the kingdom of God and his righteousness, and all these things will be given to you as well" (Mt. 6:33).

Time

Sexuality, in general, has been a subject of reflection throughout history. Homosexuality, in particular, has publicly been a part of U. S. dialogue for at least thirty-five years, especially following the Stonewall riots in New York City in 1969. Sexuality, in general, has been a subject of reflection throughout the history of monotheistic religion. Moreover, the subject of homosexuality has been an important topic of theological reflection for churches in the United States and around the world for over thirty years. At the beginning of the twenty-first century, social, political, and religious dialogue about homosexuality has burst into a national and international forum of conversation.

In Puerto Rico, in October 2003, I was interviewed by several news organizations regarding my upcoming ordination to the priesthood. The fact that two out of three ordinands to the Episcopal priesthood, that day, were women was noteworthy for all newspapers on the island, and for other publications, but so was the election of a priest in a committed same-sex relationship to be a bishop-coadjutor in the Episcopal Church.[3] Inevitably, we were all asked about the ordination of gay and lesbian persons in the Episcopal Church. The religious (national and international) conversation has brought to the fore scriptural exegesis, moral arguments, and intense debate about the place of gay and lesbian persons within the body of Christ and within particular congregations or denominations. The debate revolves around several issues: homosexual acts,[4] sexual orientation, same-sex unions (or blessings), and the ordination of noncelibate gay or lesbian persons.[5]

Of the four issues mentioned above, scripture only refers to homosexual acts. Scripture refers to homosexual acts on seven occasions: Genesis 19:1–11, Leviticus 18:22 and 20:13, Deuteronomy 23:17–18, Romans 1:26–27, 1 Corinthians 6:9–10, and 1 Timothy 1:9–10. In approaching these passages we must keep in mind that a literal reading of the passages, especially in translation, does not take into account the historical context from which each passage emerges, and therefore is misleading regarding the relevance of these passages for our contemporary society. For example, in Genesis, the verses regarding the sudden destruction of Sodom and Gomorrah refer to issues of hospitality, violence, and rape. The verses found in Deuteronomy ought to be

---

[3]Rev. Gene Robinson was elected in the Diocese of New Hampshire of the Episcopal Church of the U.S.A. He was consecrated in November 2003.

[4]I refer to homosexual acts as those referred to in scripture. No church condones any act, homosexual or heterosexual, done for violence, exploitation, idolatry, and prostitution. The difficulty here is that scripture does not speak to what we understand today as sexual orientation, and the terms homosexual and heterosexual were first used at the end of the nineteenth century.

[5]Some believe that only celibate gay and lesbian persons should be ordained.

understood in the context of temple prostitution and the condemnation of idolatry. Likewise, the verses found in Leviticus, as part of the extensive holiness code, which in itself is concerned with cultic practices, can be understood in relation to the condemnation of idolatry. In both Deuteronomy and Leviticus, idolatry is understood in the term "abhorrent" or *abominación*.[6] The term refers specifically to the rebellion in our relationship with God.

In the New Testament, the passage from 1 Corinthians can be understood similarly to Leviticus. This is the context of prostitution between a male and an effeminate male prostitute, therefore a form of pederasty. The list of vices found in 1 Timothy aim to explain the proper place of the law. The reference to sodomites, and perhaps also the reference to slave traders, is in the context once again of prostitution and pederasty. Finally, the passage of Romans appears in the context of our rebellion in our relationship with God. From these passages it is clear that scripture condemns homosexual acts as understood in the historical contexts (idolatry, unequal power dynamics) addressed in the passages, and does not condemn homosexual orientation.

Literal biblical interpretations have led to the mantra, "Hate the sin, not the sinner." This begins from a place of judgment that does not address the issue of homosexuality. The underlying statement is that heterosexual is not sinful and homosexual is. It does not start from the place of our common fallen human nature. The analogous secular mantra is, "Don't ask, don't tell."

Increasingly in the United States there is a growing consensus that sexual orientation is not a choice, but is determined by biology. What is predicated by society is the choice of a person to live out their sexuality openly in one or more spheres of a person's life (family, friends, colleagues, work, and/or church). It is significantly easier for a heterosexual person to make this choice (especially since the choice is most likely made unconsciously) than for a homosexual person, whom society has vilified and closeted.

The third topic of national and international conversation is that of same-sex unions or blessings, and domestic partnerships. There are legal and religious issues at play. Scripture makes reference to marriage between a man and a woman, yet it does not explicitly exclude any other affectionate/sexual consensual relationships among persons of the same sex. We need to interpret scripture in a way that speaks to the needs and

---

[6]This is a case in which translations are misleading. For example, the Deuteronomy passage in the *NRSV* reads, "None of the daughters of Israel shall be a temple prostitute; none of the sons of Israel shall be a temple prostitute. You shall not bring the fee of a prostitute or the wages of a male prostitute into the house of the LORD your God in payment for any vow, for both of these are abhorrent to the LORD your God." The version Reina-Valera reads, "*No haya ramera de entre las hijas de Israel, ni haya sodomita de entre los hijos de Israel. No traerás la paga de una ramera ni el precio de un perro a la casas de Jehová tu Dios por ningún voto; porque abominación es a Jehová tu Dios tanto lo uno como lo otro.*"

concerns of our contemporary society, otherwise scripture may become irrelevant. Furthermore, if we take scripture literally, we cannot pick and choose which aspects to uphold in our world today.[7]

The issue of marriage is one in which the church and the state are intricately entangled. It is the only instance in which clergy act as agents of the state. Marriage in the church is not about licenses, tax brackets (benefits and responsibilities). Marriage in the church is a sacrament, an outward and visible sign of grace, in which two people make a public profession of love and commitment in front of a congregation and God. Marriage in the church is when the church, through its representative, blesses a relationship in front of a congregation and both the church and the congregation profess their commitment and responsibility in helping that marriage endure and succeed. The church should be in the business of blessing relationships rather than acting as an arm of the state. The church, whether or not it eventually supports the blessing of same-sex unions, should have no objection on the basis of justice for the legality of civil unions or civil marriage, whether among persons of the opposite or same sex.

The final issue is that of ordination of gay and lesbian persons who are in monogamous relationships. Candidates for ordination should have the psychological and educational preparation to perform their duties in ordained ministry. Moreover, ordained ministry is a call from God. The recognition of a call to ordained ministry is seeing the grace of God working among us, and the grace of God cannot be boxed, categorized, or limited to certain people. This discernment of a call to ordination is done within the context of a church community. For example, the church has increasingly recognized the call of women to ordained ministry, and many denominations have assented to this call and seen the value of it in our contemporary society. This is similar to the ordination of gay and lesbian persons. Historically, many churches have accepted that it is God who acts in the sacraments *(ex opera operato)*; therefore, the condition of the person mediating in the sacraments has no bearing on the efficacy or legality of the sacraments.

Reality: Pastoral Concerns

There is a pastoral reality in our communities and congregations that gay and lesbian persons, as children of God, deserve the ministrations of the church. This in many ways is no different that the recognition by mainline churches for the need of Latino/a ministry. Most churches, regardless of their stance on homosexuality, have come to the understanding that gay and lesbian people have pastoral concerns. Some

---

[7]For examples of some of the contradictions that arise from the literal reading of scripture, see Álvarez, *Exposición del Obispo* (2003), e.g., slavery, polyester, circumcision, pork. See also Wink, *Homosexuality and the Bible* (1996).

churches only have been able to understand this in the case of AIDS, and in their attempts to show gay and lesbian people the "true way" to Christ. The Anglican Communion has recognized the pastoral concern by stating, "We commit ourselves to listen to the experience of homosexual persons and we wish to assure them that they are loved by God and that all baptized, believing and faithful persons, regardless of sexual orientation, are full members of the Body of Christ." Yet it rejects "homosexual practice as incompatible with scripture."[8] While this statement has no binding authority throughout the Anglican Communion, it is indicative of the place of many churches on the issue, and is indicative of the split between churches in the Northern and Southern Hemispheres.

De La Torre and Aponte state, "even though several Hispanic theologians are gay or lesbian, the adage '*Se dice nada, se hace todo*' (Say nothing, do everything) remains an accepted norm of the Hispanic theological community" (2001:158). As Latino/a theologians are confronted by fellow theologians who happen to be gay or lesbian, they are confronted with several outside forces dictating their reactions: the Latino/a perceptions of gays and lesbians, and the denominational stance on homosexuality. Those theologians who have been willing to forge friendships have had to do some heartfelt reflection between their understanding of sin and the gospel imperative of reconciliation, justice, and love. These relationships have led to a deeper conversation regarding homosexuality and the Latino/a community. They are a necessary step for Latino/a theologians to be able to develop an autochthonous stance on homosexuality.

The Legacy of Colonialism: In search of a Latino/a Stance on Sexuality

As mentioned before, churches have been dealing with the issue of homosexuality for decades. In the Anglican Communion, at the Lambeth Conference of Anglican Bishops in 1978, section three from the statement on "Human Relationships and Sexuality" states:

> While we reaffirm heterosexuality as the scriptural norm, we recognize the need for deep and dispassionate study of the question of homosexuality, which would take seriously both the teaching of Scripture and the results of scientific and medical research. The Church, recognizing the need for pastoral concern for those who are homosexual, encourages dialogue with them.[9]

---

[8]Both of these quotes come from the end of paragraph C and beginning of paragraph D of Resolution I.10 on Human Sexuality, passed at the 1998 Lambeth Conference of the bishops of the Anglican Communion. See www.anglicancommunion.org/lambeth/1/sect1rpt.html

[9]From http://www.anglicancommunion.org/acns/archive/1978/1978–10.htm.

In 1998, the Anglican bishops approved resolution I.10 on Human Sexuality. The resolution defines marriage as between a man and a woman and also recognizes the pastoral needs of gay and lesbian persons. Important in this resolution is the reference made to the Kuala Lumpur Statement from February 1997, in which one of the major concerns of the Anglican bishops of the Southern Hemisphere is the imposition of values from bishops in the Northern Hemisphere. The concern of an imposition of a hegemonic cultural norm on the greater church has become the dominant issue springing from the actions of some churches in the North. The issue of imposition of cultural norms has been elevated to such an extent that the topic of sexuality is no longer central to the discussion.

Anglican bishops in the North have had to recognize the "cultural differences right across our Communion."[10] And this recognition is a good thing. But, it also means that the churches in the South are tabling their discussions on sexuality until the constitutional and canonical questions regarding how the different churches remain in communion are resolved, when in actuality churches in the South should look to develop their stance regarding homosexuality.

In 2003, after the consent to the election of an openly gay partnered priest as bishop in the Episcopal Church, some in Puerto Rico felt that the church in the United States was imposing on them a different set of cultural norms. The media attention did not help to minimize the situation, since it gave the perception that the Episcopal Church as a whole was in agreement about the ordination of gay and lesbian persons. What has become clear for churches in the "two-thirds" world is the resentment regarding further imposition from the North's dynamics of colonialism and oppression. This is an issue of globalization, where the bishops of the Southern Hemisphere shout that "each province needs to be aware of the possible effect of its interpretation of scripture on the life of other provinces in the Communion."[11]

In this chapter I have tried to present in very brief terms some of the major issues regarding homosexuality and the church. These issues are the scriptural understanding of homosexual acts; homosexual orientation; same-sex unions (secular and religious); and the ordination of gay and lesbian persons. These concerns are affected by the desire of the churches of the "two-thirds" world to not have a stance on homosexuality imposed on them by the North. What is also clear is the need for Latinos/as to develop a stance on homosexuality. I contend it must be rooted in the scriptural principles of *Imago Dei* and the great

---

[10]Statement by Robin Eames, Primate of all Ireland, during the meeting of the Anglican Primates, October 15–16, 2003. *Anglican Communion News Service,* 15 October 2003.

[11]*Episcopal News Service*–see Statement from the Primates of the Anglican Communion, 16 October 2003. www.anglicancommunion.org/acns/articles/36/25/acns 3633.html.

commandment, as well as the ethical values of reconciliation, justice, and love. Moreover, the Latino/a stance on homosexuality must be autochthonous and free from the perception that it has been imposed by the dominant culture (similar to the process of defining/developing *mujerista* theology in continuity and contrast to the dominant feminist theology). I suggest four avenues for further conversation.

First, any Latino/a stance on homosexuality, in particular, and sexuality, in general, must address the issues of *machismo* in our culture (therefore addressing issues of sexism and heterosexism). Second, we must follow the principles of *teología en conjunto*. If there is a community of theologians that could work toward a level of consensus, it is the Latino/a theological community. Third, Latino/a liberation theologies must voice the concerns of all segments of its communities, including gays and lesbians. Fourth, as Latinos/as we have the tools to develop a liberative stance on homosexuality. Straight Latinos/as can be allies with gay and lesbian people in their communities because, as Latinos/as, they understand the dynamics of oppression and injustice that work to exclude persons from full participation in society based on one aspect of their identity (gender, sexual orientation, ethnicity, race, bodily or mental impairment, religion). The same applies for alliances that can be built with gay and lesbian persons outside of our community. Moreover, Latinos/as understand not only the overt dynamics of oppression but also how society forces persons to erase part of their identity to succeed and fit in. Latinos/as who can pass and become part of the dominant society understand the pain of hiding a part of their identity. Therefore, Latinos/as have an understanding of feelings gay and lesbian people have about being closeted. Developing an autochthonous Latino/a liberative stance on sexuality is ultimately an issue of justice.

CHAPTER 33

Language, Community, and Identity

■ CARMEN M. NANKO-FERNÁNDEZ

Handing on Faith en Su Propia Lengua[1]

In the February 2003 issue of *Vanity Fair* magazine, satirical advice in a column by humorist Dame Edna struck a raw nerve. In a flippant response to an alleged reader's question about the value of learning a foreign language, Dame Edna advised: "Forget Spanish. There's nothing in that language worth reading...Who speaks it that you are really desperate to talk to? The help? Your leaf blower? Study German or

---

[1]Here I engage in a theological analysis of diversity and fluidity in language, which has a direct and visible impact on my own use of language(s). First, words and expressions in Spanish are not italicized to indicate the dynamic interaction between Spanish and English in the daily lived experience of U.S. Latinos/as. Second, I deliberately use "Hispanic" and "Latino/a" interchangeably, and I use the grammatically gendered endings (Latin*os/as*) so as not to suggest false correspondences between grammatical and natural gender. Third, in keeping with the accepted practice among Deaf scholars, "deaf" refers to an audiological condition and "Deaf" connotes membership in a community that shares a common language, American Sign Language, as well as other cultural values, activities, etc. In referring to Deaf Latinos/as, I use "Deaf" in recognition that communities are created among deaf people who share signed languages other than ASL. In direct quotations, I have respected the usage of others. One of the characteristics of theology done latinamente is that it is done en conjunto. I am grateful to the following for their insights and input: Min Seo Park, a Deaf graduate student and Korean seminarian studying at St. John's University in New York; Angel Ramos, Ph.D., a Puerto Rican Deaf educator; Jean-Pierre Ruiz, S.T.D., Nuyorican Bible scholar.

French, where there are at least a few books worth reading, or, if you are American, try English."[2] If the cyber-storm that erupted in reply is any indication, the editors of *Vanity Fair* severely underestimated the relationship between language and the construction and transmission of identity. The overwhelming response, which included boycotts and death threats, resulted in an explanation and an apology from the editors:

> The backward bigotry of these statements was so far over the line that we felt it could only be taken as satire. In our judgment it was a politically incorrect but blatantly satirical barb directed against anyone who might be unaware of the great contributions Latin people have made and continue to make in every walk of life, here in the United States and around the world. (Note, too, that two sentences later, she insults English-speaking Americans, saying, "If you're American, try [learning] English.")[3]

Lost in the firestorm of opinions ranging from charges of racism to claims of Hispanic hypersensitivity, was the sad reality that what seemed to author and editors as so blatantly satiric unfortunately reflected a slice of vida cotidiana in the United States. The fact that so many did not understand that this column was intended as a work of fiction, and that the writer's attitude was ironic, demonstrates that the bigotry portrayed in the column is still a part of the experience of too many U.S. Latinos/as. Language is not neutral: "Language, after all, is at the heart of an individual's social identity. It is the vehicle through which the songs, folklore, and customs of any group are preserved and transmitted to its descendants" (González 2000: 207).

The significance of language in the navigation of boundaries and in the negotiation of identities within and across generations emerges as a legitimate and necessary locus for theological reflection. For faith communities in particular, the role of language in the process of handing on across generations has pastoral implications. If human identities are formed through "webs of interlocution," then communities of discourse matter, and the process of mutual engagement affects all parties involved, with ramifications for the future (Benhabib 2002: 56).

This chapter is a theological reflection that raises questions regarding the interaction of language and the creation of communal and personal identity. First, I examine the diversity and role of languages within the context of Latino/a lived experiences as this impacts worldviews and self-perceptions of Hispanics, youth in particular. Second, I explore

---

[2]Dame Edna is a drag queen alter ego of Australian comedian Barry Humphries. See Dame Edna, "Ask Dame Edna," *Vanity Fair* (February 2003): 116. Copy of text and the Internet petition available at http:// urbanlegends.about.com/library/bl-dame-edna.htm.

[3] *Vanity Fair* Apology for Dame Edna Racist Column, from *Vanity Fair* editors, (Condé Nast Publications), February 15, 2003, available at http:// www.imdiversity.com/Villages/ Hispanic/arts_culture_media/hav_vanity_fair_apology.asp.

relationships among language, identity, and culture specifically through the concrete experiences of a sector of the U.S. Latino/a community that remains our own marginalized minority: Hispanic Deaf, and the hearing children of Latino/a deaf couples. Third, I propose directions that arise from these encounters, with hopes for further theological reflection that might inform pastoral practice.

Living la Lengua Cotidiana?

Linguistic diversity among U.S. Latinos/as is far more complicated and emotionally and politically charged than bilingual paradigms suggest. Language and the use of language has become a litmus test of one's latinidad. While, ideally, many see the value of maintaining fluency and literacy in more than one language (a hope shared by numbers of Latin American immigrants seeking opportunities in the United States), the implied U.S. cultural norm is conveyed in the monolingual primacy of English. "Language difference, after all, is still a prime marker of identity for Latino communities and is equivocally addressed within the English monoglot terrain of the United States" (Santiago-Irizarry 2001: 474).

Language preferences and abilities, not necessarily predicated by age, range from Spanish dominance to English dominance, with an assortment in between. However, for the most part, the discourse is characterized in binary (Spanish/English) or hybrid terms (*Spanglish*). Spanish has endured through first and second generations, unlike other immigrants' languages, in part because of the ease in maintaining transnational relationships and identities with Latin America. Spanish has secured a visible presence in the United States and it should be noted that the designation "foreign" for Spanish seems odd, considering that its presence in the Americas, for better or worse, predates the arrival of English, and it remains an official and dominant language of Puerto Rico–a part of the U.S. colonial constellation. Spanish carries economic capital and maintains a market influence, as the Condé Nast publishing group certainly learned: "as Californios and Floridians say in Spanglish: Hacer enojar a muchos Latinos con laptops puede ser peligroso."[4] The consumer power of Latinos/as fuels a marketing industry that is "directly involved in the maintenance of latinidad's Hispanic core through its economically driven need to emphasize the permanence of the Spanish language as the basis for Latino/Hispanic identity to ensure and perpetuate its own existence and profitability" (Dávila 2001:411).

---

[4]Loosely translated, "Angering a bunch of Latinos with laptops can be dangerous," from"A Satire, A Protest, Then An Apology, Satire Is A Dangerous Weapon," *Los Angeles Times*, 8 February 2003, available at www.asu.edu/educ/epsl/LPRU/newsarchive/ Art1694.txt.

On the other hand, in the music industry the success and presence in hip-hop of English-speaking Latino rappers cautions against overemphasizing and/or oversimplifying the relationship between language and cultural identity. The preference for English in the raps of a number of second, third, and fourth generation U.S. Latinos reveals both a comfort level with English and a solidarity with the medium's Afro-diasporic roots and fan base.

> Equating the use of English with Anglocentrism negates the appropriation and transformation of the colonizers' language by Afro-diasporic people. Besides, not only are Latinos following Afro-diasporic English-based orality, but use of English also derives from their most immediate communicative experience as young people raised in the United States. Many Latinos/as frequently assert their cultural identity through their particular way of speaking English (Rivera 2002:137–38).

Illustrating the complexity of the U.S. Latino/a relationship with languages, Nuyorican poet Martín Espada borrows an analogy from his friend, another New York Puerto Rican writer, Jack Agüeros: "English and Spanish are like two dogs I love. English is an obedient dog. When I tell him to sit, he sits. Spanish is a disobedient dog. When I tell him to sit, he pees on the couch" (Espada 1998:73–74). While this amusing image expresses differences in command between a first and a second language, the other perros in the litter (the so-called hybrids), are left out. For some, especially in the younger generations, Spanglish[5] offers a voice that holds in creative tension the multiple dimensions of hybrid identities. This linguistic border crossing occurs often in the same sentence. In a "move to trilingualism," Spanglish, in its many forms, demonstrates that today Spanish (and I would add English) is "as elastic and polyphonic as ever, allowing for a wide gamut of voices that goes beyond mere localisms" (Stavans 2003:33). For some, Spanglish is a reaction, a cultural resistance to assimilation in a nation that prizes monolinguality, especially as a ticket to success. For others, "Spanglish también is often an intra-ethnic vehicle of communication, though only in Unaited Esteits...to establish a form of empathy between one another...a result of the evident clash between two full-fledged, perfectly discernible lenguas; and it is not defined by class, as people in all social strata...use it regularly" (Ibid.:43). Neither is it not defined by age, as usage crosses generational lines as well. "One only has to ride the New York City subway...to witness clusters of young Latinos skillfully and

---

[5]"There isn't one standardized Spanglish but many. A type of Domincanish is spoken by Dominican Americans in Washington Heights, and it's different from the Pachuco spoken by Mexicans in El Paso and the Cubonics used by Cubans in Union City." Ilan Stavans, "Spanglish Is Everywhere Now, Which Is No Problema for Some, But a Pain in the Cuello for Purists," *The Boston Globe*, 14 September 2003.

expressively codeswitching among their multilingual and multidialectical speech repertoire without dropping a beat. This linguistic vibrancy evinces how the city's Latino youth have become accomplished linguistic practitioners" (Santiago-Irizarry 2001:474).

As life on the ever-changing linguistic borders illustrates, identities and the networks within which they are created and renegotiated are dynamic and fluid. Vida cotidiana counters what Seyla Benhabib calls the "false assumptions about cultures, their coherence and purity," instead affirming "recognition of the radical hybridity and polyvocality of all cultures; cultures themselves, as well as societies, are not holistic but polyvocal, multilayered, decentered, and fractured systems of action and signification" (Benhabib 2002:25–26). Living la lengua cotidiana reveals power struggles operative in all human interactions and betrays the dichotomy between margins and center, insider and outsider. Language as a turf marker or border establishes who belongs and who does not; it excludes as much as it includes. In the words of Fernando Segovia,

> [We] are a people who live in two worlds, but find ourselves at home in neither one…[w]e share a world of the past, but we do so with many homes, many mixtures, many traditions, and many conceptions of reality. We further share a world of the present, but again, we do so with many faces, many histories, and many visions of God and the world. We are thus not only a bicultural people but a multicultural people, the permanent others who are also in various respects others to one another. (Segovia, 1995:35)

In This Sign: Lo Cotidiano on the Linguistic Margins

In *Freak*, his autobiographically based one-man Broadway show, Latino comedian John Leguizamo introduces his uncle Sanny in his pantheon of characters. Described by Leguizamo as one of his "surrogate moms," Sanny was "a little unconventional…what you'd call a triple threat: Latin, gay, and deaf." Sanny, using his Spanglish ASL,[6] illustrates the deeper complexity of the U.S. communidad latina (Leguizamo and Bar Katz 1997:53). On the linguistic margins, Hispanic Deaf persons and the hearing children of Deaf Latino/a parents nuance an already complicated relationship in the triad of language-identity-culture. By their very existence, Hispanic Deaf people threaten assumptions of homogeneity that ground an understanding of U.S. Deaf culture, and Latino/a assumptions that ground a binary linguistic construction of culture and identity.

---

[6]ASL refers to American Sign Language, a visual-spatial language with its own grammar and syntax used by Deaf people in the United States and in parts of Canada. In the United States, use of ASL is considered a constitutive element in defining Deaf culture.

Living on the margins of Hispanic marginality, this community of Deaf people and the hearing children of Deaf parents bear witness that orality and aurality are unfairly privileged in the construction of communal identity. Sign Language interpreter Maria Izaguirre describes her childhood as one of "growing up as confused, mixed, and multi--cultural as the one Leguizamo acts out in *Freak*."[7] She further elaborates:

> I had a pot-luck kind of early life. Both my parents were deaf. I grew up thinking all parents were deaf. I began using sign language when I was a year old. I learned English backwards. My father was Mexican and my mother Puerto Rican. So I had signing in Spanish, signing in English, the deaf community and the hearing Mexican community, all mixed together. Like John, I had an early self-identity crisis. I had to sort it all out in my adult life.[8]

According to the Census Bureau statistics for 2000, Hispanics are the fastest-growing minority group in the United States, a community marked by its ethnic diversity and the overwhelming youth of its population. Left out of these statistics is the reality that Hispanics also constitute the fastest growing ethnic group among deaf students. A growing number of Latino/a Deaf youth come from Spanish-dominant homes and are among the first generation in their families to attend school and live in the United States. Unlike previous generations of U.S. Deaf, yet like many of their youthful deaf peers, the majority of Hispanic Deaf children are not in residential educational settings but in mainstream programs. However, for Latinos/as the reason appears to be that their parents do not want them far from family, and "do not want to transfer the child-rearing responsibilities to other parties."[9] This emphasis on familia has both positive and negative ramifications: "On one hand their families overprotect them from the dangers of the world. At the same time, they make them feel left out of vital discussions and family decisions."[10]

Immigrant deaf people and the deaf children of Spanish-speaking families face the daunting challenge of learning multiple new languages and cultures in the United States, as well as "Hispanic Deaf culture, which is learned from older students and Hispanic Deaf adults" (Gerner

---

[7]Sign Language interpreter Maria Izaguirre interpreted *Freak* in April 1998 for an audience that included 135 Deaf Latinos/as. Quoted in "Stars, Musicians and Jugglers Entertain TKTS Lines As TDF Celebrates Ticket Booth's 25 Years in Duffy Square," http://www.tdf.org/publications/sightlines/summer-98/summer98sightlines.pdf.

[8]Maria Izaguirre quoted in "Stars, Musicians and Jugglers Entertain TKTS Lines As TDF Celebrates Ticket Booth's 25 Years in Duffy Square."

[9]Gilbert L. Delgado, "Hispanic/Latino Deaf Students in Our Schools," Research Report, April 2001. Available at http://sunsite.utk.edu/cod/pec/ hispanic-deaf.doc.

[10]Gilbert L. Delgado, former superintendent of the New Mexico School for the Deaf, quoted in Robert Waddell, "Deaf Latinos Creating Own Support Network," (April 12, 2000) LatinoLink, available at http://www.egroups.com/group/USA–L_News

de Garcia 1995: 455). Entering school using sign languages unknown by their U.S. teachers, "the school may label these immigrant children as having 'no language,' rather than as using a different language...[*thus*] their language differences are seen as a disability" (Ibid.:456).[11]

Too many Deaf Latino/as, particularly the young, are left straddling multiple worlds of disconnection, with no place on which to stand. As the overwhelming majority of deaf children are born to hearing parents, they are cut off in many ways from the oral tradition in Hispanic cultures expressed through storytelling, dichos, etc., that accompanies the transmission of cultural identity. In other words, Deaf Latinos/as are "immersed in the culture, but not enmeshed."[12] Born of hearing parents and educated in mainstream programs in which hearing students outnumber deaf students, many Deaf Latinos/as navigate their world through interpreters. They become outsiders to the daily interactions most take for granted. In some ways they are removed from experiences of Deaf culture in the United States, a culture in which American Sign Language (ASL) also plays a defining role in the formation and understanding of identity. For Deaf Latinos/as, in the U.S. context the languages of discourse are American Sign Language and English, with an emphasis on its written expression, while the language of home is often Spanish. The intimate relationship of sign languages, identity, and Deaf culture are evident not only in the United States but increasingly in Latin America as well, as members of a linguistic minority shifts the discourse from issues of ability/disability to communication and human rights.

Othercide or Other Side: Lessons in Border Crossings

othercide (oh-THER-sayd), n., m., the elimination of people or attributes different to us or ours. (Stavans 2003:185)

A refreshing feature of theologies emerging from U.S. Latino/a perspectives is a willingness to admit that our reflections are situated and engaged, dependent on and interdependent with "certain communities of discourse, and certain 'webs of interlocution'" (Benhabib 2002:56). At the same time, we recognize that in order to keep "the circle of discourse from degenerating into monologue, cross-contextual conversations can help to prevent the celebration of bias from trapping interpreters in their own ghettos of private meaning" (Ruíz 1995:10). My reflection on the implications of linguistic diversity in la comunidad latina, and some directions it suggests for further theological reflection and pastoral practice, are very much shaped by my own social location. Languages

---

[11]For example, PRSL (Puerto Rican Sign Language), DRSL (Dominican Republic Sign Language), la Lengua de Señas Mexicana, or home signs, i.e. "idiosyncratic signs created for communication with family and friends."

[12]Tomás García Jr., *La Promesa de un Tesoro/The Promise of a Treasure*, available at http://www.cfv.org/caai/nadh70.pdf.

matter to me, they are precious inheritances passed between and across generations. As a second generation U.S. citizen, I struggle to regain the fluency I once had as a child in Spanish, la lengua de mi abuela.[13] Spanish is a living link to my beloved Nana who passed away too early in my youth, and Spanglish characterizes increasingly my daily interactions. ASL is the language I learned in adolescence at the hands of New York's Deaf Catholics, both junior and senior to me, and the dedicated hearing priest who has accompanied this community for over thirty-five years. It remains, like so many youthful explorations, a border crossing with life-altering consequences.

Theological reflection on the implications of linguistic diversity in U.S. Hispanic communities raises broader questions of how we deal with difference and commonality with respect to the networks that form and inform us as individuals and as communities. How do we not sacrifice our differences in attempts to relate on common ground while building alliances across constituencies of marginalization? How do we address the reality that these alliances must also exist entre nosotros? First, painfully, we must admit that marginalized communities can and do marginalize others within their own groups. Reflecting on his experiences as a Deaf Latino, educator Angel Ramos observed:

> People who have been oppressed tend to oppress others, and that is why there is so much oppression even within our own communities. As a Deaf person or as a Hispanic person I just never felt that oppression growing up in NYC. It wasn't until I arrived at Gallaudet that I felt that oppression as a Hispanic, it wasn't until I arrived in Texas that I felt that oppression as a Deaf person.[14]

As communities of faith, how we respond to these questions determines our ability to survive across generations. Do we continue practices of othercide, or do we model the crossings to the other side that ground productive and healthy coalitions?

Intragenerational Traditioning

The significance of intragenerational traditioning is especially evident in Deaf communities because the overwhelming majority of deaf

---

[13]Personally, I identify as Hispanic or hispana. I cite as reference: "the denomination *hispano* in early twentieth-century New York City was widely used as a sign of solidarity among working-class immigrants of Hispanic Caribbean and Spanish descent" (Laó-Montes 2001:5). My mother's parents came to New York City from Spain via Cuba in the early part of the twentieth century. My father, also a first generation New Yorker, was the first in his family of Czech/Slavic immigrants born in the United States. My siblings and I are part of that unique New York hybridity.

[14]Angel M. Ramos, Ph.D., in an electronic conversation with this author 18 November 2003. He is the author of *Triumph of the Spirit* (2003). Gallaudet University, in Washington, D.C., is the only university in the world founded specifically for the mission of providing higher education for the Deaf.

people are born to hearing parents. Therefore, the Deaf "make up the only cultural group where cultural information and language has been *predominantly* passed down from child to child rather than from adult to child" (Baynton 1996:2). This experience increasingly marks vida cotidiana among Hispanic immigrants, deaf and hearing. In the first and 1.5 generations in particular, it is the young who transition each other, influenced by multiple relationships besides family. Attention to transmission within a generation does not mean diminishing the value of transgenerational traditioning. The challenge for theologians is to reflect more intentionally on both means.

Coalitions among Marginalized Communities

Border crossing invites coalition building across marginalized communities in order to secure justice. But frequently solidarity is sacrificed on the altar of compromise to placate the powers that be in order to advance a particular agenda. The familiar refrain, "First we'll get x, then we'll come back for you," has unfortunately marked movements from women's suffrage to civil rights. In the Deaf community, it is manifested in the presence of a growing transcultural population that stretches the boundaries of U.S. Deaf culture.

> [A]s the Deaf Community battles for recognition as bilingual and bicultural, many in the community seem to view multiculturalism as another battle that might divert attention from their own struggle…[I]gnoring the multicultural and multilingual nature of the Deaf Community negatively impacts multicultural members of the Deaf Community, particularly immigrant deaf students. (Gerner de Garcia 1995:463).[15]

Meanwhile, in the Archdiocese of New York, the Deaf community is in danger of losing its church, a victim of reorganization in the face of shifting priorities and dwindling resources.[16] This failure to comprehend the significance of having one's own space should not be lost on Hispanic congregations all too often relegated to the basements of their home churches. The fact that the majority of the Deaf affected by the decision

---

[15]The terms "bicultural" and "bilingual" when used by Deaf scholars are understood in terms of the Deaf and hearing worlds, fluency in ASL and English in spoken and/or written forms. See Padden (1998:79–98). "Multicultural" and "multilingual" reference the increasing transnational and ethnic diversity in the U.S. deaf population, as well as recognition of other national languages–sign as well as written and spoken.

[16]See Daniel J. Wakin, "Deaf Congregation on East Side Fears for Its Future," *The New York Times,* 20 November 2003. This church also serves as a meeting site for Deaf groups, including the Puerto Rican Society for the Catholic Deaf and the Black Deaf Advocates. I am grateful to Msgr. Patrick McCahill, pastor of St. Elizabeth of Hungary, the "home" parish for the Catholic Deaf community in the Archdiocese of New York. Msgr. McCahill patiently taught me Sign Language during my youth and introduced me to this community that remains a personal and professional influence in my life.

are Puerto Rican and Dominican further raises a question: Is this just a Deaf concern, or is it also a Latino/a issue? Will the greater Hispanic community lend its resources in support of our Deaf hermanas y hermanos?

Language, Community, and Resistance

In the public forum, language can serve as a bridge in the construction of identity–collective and personal–or, as a privileging of aural ability and oral expression demonstrate, it can cut others off from conversation. Sensitivity to this dynamic begins with the realization that vocabulary matters too. Carelessness with language is antithetical to coalition-building. For example, constant references to "voice" in justice discourse; the use of deafness, usually in preaching to express a spiritual void; and the assumption of hearing as a precondition for acceptance of the "word" serve to unintentionally create distance.

Language is created by community and in turn also facilitates the creation of community. For example, amidst overwhelming efforts by hearing educators to enforce oralism,[17] religious ministries and Deaf churches played a historic role in preserving Sign Language and in traditioning Deaf youth. Hearing clergy learned at the hands of Deaf sign language masters, and Deaf ministers as well as adult Deaf congregants served as role models for children whose school teachers were predominantly nonsigning hearing people.

> Addressing the Deaf in a public venue like a church demanded a masterful command of Sign Language…The signing ability of ministers aided the preservation of Sign Language in the twentieth century, for most ministers to the Deaf had ample access to preach at state schools…the message was essential to the religious education and the medium unified the culture.[18]
> (Bunch 2000: 339)

From ASL to Spanglish, language creates a discursive space. Ironically, both Spanish and ASL have suffered at the hands of "English Only" protagonists. Yet, they have endured as languages that are more indigenous to the U.S. experience than they are foreign. This power of language to create community also fosters agency.

---

[17]Oralism is used to describe what Deaf culture proponents would label as attempts to assimilate deaf persons by making hearing modalities normative. In education, this would include teaching deaf students to speak and lip read, and a disparagement of Sign Language. The battle between oralists and manualists has raged in various forms for more than a century.

[18]Residential schools for the Deaf, usually state run, played vital roles in the creation of Deaf senses of community and identity. Remarkably, Deaf individuals accomplished this even as many of the institutions sought to eliminate or reduce the use of Sign Language. In schools, usually in the dormitories, ASL was passed intragenerationally by the Deaf children of Deaf parents to the Deaf children of hearing parents.

From this perspective of language as resistance, inclusion rhetoric is a manifestation of assimilation, not border crossing. It signifies loss, not liberation; isolation, not community. "In the name of inclusion in 'the' community, deaf children are frequently denied inclusion in any community. For the sake of an abstraction known as the 'mainstream,' deaf children are denied the solid and tangible fellowship, culture, language and heritage of the deaf community" (Baynton:154). This is a concern shared by constituencies who reside on the margins. "Inclusion touches upon the deepest human yearnings for belonging. But if inclusion means a complete erasure of difference, does it still remain an ideal?" (Schreiter 1997:10). Sometimes as theologians and as people of faith we are tempted to embrace inclusion paradigms naively, believing that only positive interpretations can exist. Careful attention to lo cotidiano reveals alternate perspectives.

In ASL, the sign for mainstreaming presents a visual rendering of what could best be described as mutual integration, left hand down fingers spread moving toward right hand in the same configuration. The result gives an impression of integration, an encounter of mutuality in which each digit and hand still maintains its own integrity. However, the experience of mainstreaming betrays hidden assumptions: "[Once] Deaf people are placed among their hearing peers, they will learn to read and write English fluently, to speak and hear"(Jankowski 1997:89). In response to this experience, another sign was created, in mockery, reflecting not opportunity but oppression, or, as we say in Spanglish, othercide. In this sign only the index finger on the right hand moves toward the open five of the left; this time the image is not one of mutual exchange in the context of integrity, but of "only one Deaf person in the midst of a mass of hearing people, and the Deaf person is subordinately squashed" (Ibid.:89–90). In many ways this image and experience parallels what Ada María Isasi-Díaz calls "one-way traveling" instead of genuine border crossing:

> The lack of knowledge and appreciation of marginalized cultures makes world-traveling mostly a one way affair, because Latinas and Latinos are not allowed to bring into the dominant construction of the world elements from our own culture. It is also a one-way traveling because the few people of the dominant group who travel to our world insist on changing it by acting in the Latina world the way they act in theirs. (2001a:210)

As U.S. Hispanic communities struggle to embrace the complexities of pan-Latino/a diversity, and as the bicultural/bilingual U.S. Deaf community seeks to understand itself in light of a new transnational multilingual reality, a common hope emerges: that one day soon individuals will be able to move back and forth across borders "with a minimum of interference and without the concomitant discomforts of marginality" (Emerton 1998:144).

CHAPTER 34

The Postmodern

Liberation or Language?

■ MANUEL J. MEJIDO COSTOYA

In a well-known Marx Brothers' joke Groucho answers the standard question "Tea or coffee?" with "Yes, please!"—a refusal of choice…[O]ne should answer in the same way the false alternative…: either "class struggle" (the outdated problematic of class antagonism, commodity production, etc.) or "post-modernism" (the new world of dispersed multiple identities, of radical contingency, of an irreducible ludic plurality of struggles). (Zizek 2000b:90)

Lest it be reduced to an ideological moment of the "American way of life," U.S. Hispanic theology may be understood as an attempt to transplant the Latin American theologies of liberation in the U.S. context. Today this means taking the idea of liberation through the postmodern turn to language. But such a task is problematic to the extent that postmodernity imposes the following choice on U.S. Hispanic theologians: "Liberation or language?" The postmodern way of seeing the world is grounded in the linguistic turn, a paradigm shift in the human-social and theological sciences that grants language primordial ontological, epistemological, and methodological status.

The three basic coordinates of postmodern thought—the plurality of particulars, alterity, and difference—emerge in and through the turn to language. One discovers finitude by coming to terms with one another as other, as alter, as revelation (Lévinas 2001:73). Furthermore, it is always a plurality of particular beings that negotiate language. The difference that exists between self and other can either be overcome through conversation or simply be deconstructed. From the positive role of language as *conversation* and its negative role as *deconstruction* emerge the two conceptions of language that have dominated the linguistic turn, namely, the *hermeneutic* and *poststructuralist* conceptions of language.

U.S. Hispanic theologians need to decide which of these two conceptions of language is more appropriate for the task of reconstructing the foundations of the theologies of liberation. These reflections are first an attempt to map out the options and to make the case for the poststructuralist conception of language. Poststructuralism, when it is guided by the idea of psychoanalysis as a critically oriented science, is more suitable for the task of providing a *linguistified corrective* to the Latin American theologies of liberation.

As the latest manifestation of Western idealism, the hermeneutic conception of language is generating the *eclipse of liberation,* reducing the liberationist idea of the transformation of history through social labor to conversation about liberation in the public sphere. It is the hermeneutic conception of language that produces and imposes the choice of either "liberation" or "language." When poststructuralism is grounded in the idea of *psychoanalysis as a critically oriented science,* it unmasks the choice between either "liberation" or "language" as fallacious.

The Hermeneutic and Poststructuralist Conceptions of Language

Hermeneutics still has faith in the universality of the *logos,* which is disclosed and made present by language through the presupposition that everything can be linguistified. This presupposition is valid only if we accept the onto-theological claim that in the beginning was a meta-language that spoke, constituting the being of all beings. Language for hermeneutics functions positively as *presence, disclosure,* and *understanding.* The hermeneutic conception of language emerged in and through Martin Heidegger and Hans-Georg Gadamer's radicalization of that hermeneutic tradition inaugurated by Friedrich Schleiermacher and systematized by Wilhelm Dilthey. But it was Gadamer who secured the onto-theological status for language by claiming, "Language is the universal medium in which understanding occurs," and, "The linguisticality of understanding is the concretion of historically effected consciousness" (1975:389). Gadamer's position came under attack by Jürgen Habermas, whereas Paul Ricoeur attempted to tread a via media between Gadamer and Habermas. Indeed, Gadamer's philosophical hermeneutics, Habermas's early depth hermeneutics[1] and later theory of

---

[1] See Habermas, *Knowledge and Human Interests* (1971).

communicative action,[2] and Ricoeur's hermeneutics of suspicion[3] constituted the debate over hermeneutics from which stems the three chief
variants of the hermeneutic conception of language.

David Tracy clearly articulated the hermeneutic conception of
language with the claim: "We understand in and through language"
(1987:47–65). Tracy situates himself in the linguistic turn, and specifically
labors under the hermeneutic conception of language, positing
"otherness," but excluding the possibility of radical otherness that
undermines "inter-religious dialogue." It is the hermeneutic conception
of language, and specifically the assumptions that all differences can be
liquidated by a "meta-language" and that all particulars are driven by a
"communicative interest" in reaching understanding, that legitimates this
perspective. But not all religious traditions want to communicate. Some,
for example, wish to transform. Indeed, this false universality of "interreligious dialogue" is today generating the historical-hermeneutic
reduction of the critically oriented theological sciences of liberation.[4]

In addition to the hermeneutic conception of language, the
poststructuralist conception of language is an attempt to break with that
idealism that grants onto-theological status to language. It is a critique of
the logocentric metaphysics of presence, a decentering of the knowing
subject, and an attempt to reinsert Western thought in the horizon of
nihilism. Language for poststructuralism no longer functions positively as
presence, disclosure, and understanding, but rather negatively as *lack*,
dissimulation, and *alienation*. Derrida and Lacan are the two most
influential exponents of this tradition.

Derrida takes issue with structuralism for laboring under the classic
way of thinking of the limit of a totality. It is not that there is a totality that
is impossible to master given the finitude of language, but rather that the
lack inherent to finite language excludes the possibility of positing a
totality. It is not that there is always too much that needs to be said; it is
rather that one can never say enough (1967:423). Through the poststructuralist conception of language, Lacan reworks the psychoanalysis
inaugurated by Freud. Language for Lacan expresses the desire of the
subject and is the torturer of being (1981:276). The end of Lacanian
psychoanalysis is to liberate the subject from language, or, stated
positively, to achieve the "Real" beyond language.

Joerg Rieger, like Tracy, situates himself in the linguistic turn.
However, while Tracy understands the linguistic turn from the point of
view of hermeneutics, Rieger understands it from the point of view of
poststructuralism. Language for Rieger does not function positively as

---

[2]See idem, *The Theory of Communicative Action* (1984–1987).
[3]See Ricoeur, "Herméneutique et critique des idéologie" (1986), and *Interpretation Theory* (1976).
[4]See Mejido, "The Real Beyond Language: A Response to David R. Brockman" (2003c).

presence, disclosure, and understanding, as Gadamer, Habermas, and Ricoeur maintain. Rather, along with Derrida and Lacan, Rieger believes that language functions negatively as lack, dissimulation, and alienation. Rieger, like Tracy, grapples with the phenomenon of pluralism. But while Tracy understands pluralism from an integrationist perspective that assumes a harmonious relationship between the plurality of particulars, Rieger understands pluralism from an agonistic perspective that assumes power asymmetries unbalance the plurality of particulars.

Rieger's constructive theology is more consistent with the movement of the problem of knowledge, and with the movement of theology as crisis. Laboring under the poststructuralist conception of language, Rieger is more skeptical about the communicative power of language and takes issue with the hermeneutic assumption that language discloses the *logos*. In this sense Rieger, like Derrida and Lacan, is more consistent with the horizon of nihilism. But Rieger is even more consistent with the movement of knowledge in a more important second way: He does not assume that postmodernity leads automatically to a harmonious plurality of particulars, a harmonious multiculturalism. He does not restrict the problem of postmodernity to the problem of the public sphere. He understands it rather first and foremost as a problem of late capitalism. Indeed, while Tracy's hermeneutic conception of language leads him to equality of all particulars theologies in the public sphere, Rieger's poststructuralism leads him to positively bias those theologies that give pride of place to the problem of exclusion and capitalism.[5]

The Postmodern Eclipse of the Theologies of Liberation

The progressive theologies of Western Europe and North America have, for the most part, understood themselves within the limits of the *historical-hermeneutic sciences,*[6] establishing theological knowledge through the *interpretation* of the meaning of transcendence. This theological knowledge has been possible only to the extent that transcendence has been grasped through the category of *praxis* (i.e., intersubjectivity, interaction, communication). In so far as modern theology has posited praxis as the very conditions of possibility for interpreting the meaning of transcendence, we say it has labored under a practical cognitive interest in the maintenance of mutual understanding.[7]

In the late 1960s theology for the first time understood itself as a *critically oriented science.* The radicalness of Latin American theologies of

---

[5]See Rieger, *God and the Excluded* (2001).

[6]See Mejido, "Theology, Crisis, and Knowledge-Constitutive Interests" (2004a).

[7]This has been the case whether these theologies have situated themselves within the limits of the Kantian horizon of consciousness (i.e., Friedrich Schleiermacher and Joseph Maréchal), the Heideggerian horizon of temporality (e.g., Karl Rahner and Paul Tillich), the Hegelian horizon of becoming (e.g., J. B. Metz and Jürgen Moltmann), or the postmodern hermeneutic conception of language (e.g., David Tracy).

liberation stems from the fact that they were never satisfied with the practical cognitive interest of the historical-hermeneutic sciences, or with the interpretation of the meaning of transcendence grasped through the restricted category of praxis. Latin American theologies of liberation, rather, establish a theological knowledge that is "interested" in the *making* of transcendence, in a theological knowledge that theoretically aims to grasp the invariance that exists between the Kingdom and the socio-historical conditions of misery.

Postmodern style of thought is generating an eclipse of the theologies of liberation, dialectically revealing itself as the *historical-hermeneutic reduction of the critically oriented theologies of liberation*–a reduction that is taking form in and through the postmodern "turn" to language, alterity, and the plurality of particulars. Moreover, this eclipse is manifesting itself as the *liberalization of the liberationist emancipatory project*–a liberalization that is taking form in and through the naturalization of global liberal-democratic capitalism. Today's postmodern condition represents what is arguably the most pernicious environment for theologies of liberation, for while the postmodern turn undercuts the universality of the idea of socio-historical emancipation, the "triumph" of global liberal-democratic capitalism seems to reveal the futility of liberation theology's attempt to realize this emancipation to the extent that such a project historically implied the implementation of real socialism.

The postmodern turn to the particular undercuts the validity of the "meta-narrative" of liberation. This is what we call the historical-hermeneutic reduction of the critically oriented theological sciences of liberation. The category of social labor is now reduced to the category of praxis, understood specifically through the hermeneutic conception of language as reaching understanding in the public sphere. Second, the postmodern naturalization of global-liberal democratic capitalism reveals the futility of liberation theology's attempt to realize liberation to the extent that such a project has implied the implementation of real social-ism. This is liberalization of the liberationist paradigm; the liberationist emancipatory project is now forced to accept the basic coordinates of global liberal-democratic capitalism. This eclipse is being generated from both the "outside" and the "inside." On the other hand, yesterday's "detractors" have become today's "conversation partners." Theologies of liberation are no longer explicitly critiqued and pushed to the periphery, but assimilated into "particular" theologies. By understanding liberation theology as a "local," "contextual," or "public" theology, liberal theologies of the center reduce liberation theology to a historical-hermeneutic science, the work of David Tracy exemplifying this reduction. Liberation theologians are increasingly accepting the basic coordinates of the hermeneutic conception of language. U.S. Hispanic theologians have also contributed to the postmodern eclipse of liberation.

U.S. Hispanic Theology and the Task of Reconstruction

U.S. Hispanic theology has systematically fallen captive to the hermeneutic reduction of the critically oriented theological sciences of liberation. It has failed to realize that such a reduction undercuts the very possibility of U.S. Hispanic theology to the extent that it understands itself as a theology that phenomenologically emerges from a U.S. Hispanic reality that grasps the theological *logos* in the interest of the liberation of U.S. Hispanics. This reduction is the result of *U.S. Hispanic theologians methodically confusing the project of transplanting the critically oriented theological sciences of liberation in the U.S. context with the project of hermeneutically reinterpreting these theological sciences of liberation.* This obfuscation historically manifested itself through the restriction of the concept of *mestizaje* to symbolic-cultural conditions,[8] the *aesthetic turn,*[9] and the eclipse of the question of the relationship between *popular religion and power.*[10] With the emergence of the postmodern linguistic turn, this tendency to hermeneutically reduce the critically oriented theological sciences of liberation is taking the form of a bias in favor of the hermeneutic conception of language.

The task of transplanting the Latin American theologies of liberation (which has historically driven many expressions of U.S. Hispanic theologies) specifically means taking the idea of liberation through the postmodern turn to language. But such a task is problematic to the extent that the postmodern condition is coercing U.S. Hispanic theologians to choose between either "liberation" or "language," that is, between either the socio-historical emancipatory project of making a break with the dialectic of the Americas, on the one hand, or the postmodern turn to language, alterity, and the plurality of particulars, on the other (Zizek 2000b:90–135).

U.S. Hispanic theologians are today choosing language over liberation–that is, choosing as their frame of reference the problem of conversation among the plurality of particular ethnic groups in the public sphere over the problem of the free trade area of the Americas–as the latest moment of the dialectic of Anglo and Hispanic America. An increasing number of U.S. Hispanic theologians understand U.S. Hispanic theology to be a *particular, local, contextual,* or *public* theology, and not a Liberation theology. What is at stake here is nothing more than the radical difference between the historical-hermeneutic theologies of interpretation and the critically oriented theological sciences of

---

[8]See Mejido, "Beyond the Postmodern Condition" (2004b).
[9]See idem, "A Critique of the 'Aesthetic Turn'" (2001).
[10]See idem, "The Illusion of Neutrality" (2002), and "Theoretical Prolegomenon" (1999).

liberation. Today this dynamic is manifesting itself in and through the "inevitability" of the *Free Trade Area of the Americas.*[11]

But the necessity of making a choice between either "liberation" or language" is fallacious: This choice is a product of the postmodern style of thought, the hermeneutic conception of language in particular. Lurking behind this conception of language is the "blackmail" that any radical attempt to push beyond the horizon of liberal-democratic capitalism (i.e., the Free Trade Area for the Americas) will lead ineluctably to "totalitarianism."[12] Indeed, to the question, "Liberation or language?" U.S. Hispanic theologians should answer—"Yes, please!" (Zizek 2000b:90). This "Yes, please!" this refusal of choice, implies a repudiation of the historical-hermeneutic tradition.

U.S. Hispanic theology needs to break with that hermeneutic conception of knowledge exemplified by David Tracy's public theology. With Rieger, it needs to move toward the poststructuralist conception of language. But U.S. Hispanic theology needs to push beyond Rieger's constructive theology, for while Rieger draws on Lacanian psychoanalysis, he, like Paul Ricoeur, understands psychoanalysis as a science of interpretation.[13] In a word, Rieger fails to understand psychoanalysis as a critically oriented science. And in this sense he too, like Tracy and many U.S. Hispanic theologians, falls captive to the hermeneutic reduction of the critically oriented theological sciences of liberation.

The project of reconstructing the foundations of the theologies of liberation in the United States in light of the postmodern condition requires that the U.S. Hispanic theologians take liberation theology's emancipatory cognitive interest through the linguistic turn, but *without reducing it to the hermeneutic conception of language.* The possibility of such a linguistified corrective to the theologies of liberation is found in the *turn to poststructuralism guided by the idea of psychoanalysis as a critically oriented science.* U.S. Hispanic theology needs to turn toward psychoanalysis and not the human-social sciences, because psychoanalysis attempts to overcome symbolic-cultural distortions through the therapeutic power of language. Indeed, psychoanalysis aims to change the world of the patient (Habermas 1971:214–45). U.S. Hispanic theology needs to turn to Lacan and not Freud to the extent that the Lacanian conception of language is more appropriate for grappling with the *mestizo* condition. Indeed, it is in that space opened up by Zizek's reworking of Lacan that U.S. Hispanic theology must contribute to the reconstruction of the theologies of liberation.[14]

---

[11]See Mejido, "The Fundamental Problematic of U.S. Hispanic Theology" (2003a), and "Propaedeutic" (2003b).

[12]See Zizek, *Did Somebody Say Totalitarianism?* (2001).

[13]See Ricoeur, *D'Interpretation* (1965).

[14]See Zizek, *The Sublime Object* (1989), *The Ticklish Subject* (1999), *The Fragile Absolute* (2000a).

Thus the claim that U.S. Hispanic theology needs to turn toward the poststructuralist conception of language guided by the idea of psychoanalysis as a critically oriented science means that U.S. Hispanic theology needs to help rectify the *pathological* state of U.S. Hispanic reality that has been internally and externally corrupted by the dialectic of Anglo and Hispanic America. Toward this end, U.S. Hispanic theology needs to concern itself with the poietic transformation of U.S. Hispanic material-economic conditions in and through *mestizo* labor *and* the praxeological transformation of U.S. Hispanic symbolic-cultural conditions in and through *mestizo* language. As a *system of thought*, U.S. Hispanic theology needs to turn toward *pastoral clinical psychology.* The task of grounding a U.S. Hispanic systematic or constructive theology must be replaced with the task of grounding a U.S. Hispanic pastoral clinical psychology. As a *social movement*, U.S. Hispanic theology needs to turn toward *Latin America* and *Europe*, realizing that Hispanic theologians are not able to open a legitimate space for themselves in the U.S. academy as long as they remain at the mercy of Anglo-American intellectual and economic capital.[15]

---

[15]See Bourdieu, *Méditations*, 1997.

Bibliography

Acuña, Rodolfo. *Occupied America: A History of Chicanos.* San Francisco: Canfield Press, 1972.

Adam, A.K.M. *What Is Postmodern Biblical Criticism?* Minneapolis: Fortress Press, 1995.

Adams, Anna. "Perception Matters: Pentecostal Latinas in Allentown, PA." *A Reading in Latina Feminist Theology: Religion and Justice.* Edited by Maria Pilar Aquino, Daisy L. Machado, and Jeanette Rodríguez. Austin: University of Texas Press, 2002.

Agosto, Efraín. "Paul, Leadership and the Hispanic Church." In *Seek the Peace of the City: Reflections on Urban Ministry.* Edited by Eldin Villafañe. Grand Rapids, Mich.: Wm B. Eerdmans, 1995.

_____. "Paul vs. Empire: A Postcolonial and Latino Reading of Philippians." *Perspectivas: Hispanic Theological Initiative Occasional Papers* 6 (Fall 2002): 37–56.

Alanís, Javier. "Dignity for the Foreigner: A Study of the Doctrine of the Imago Dei from a Lutheran Hispanic/Latino Perspective." Ph.D. diss.: Lutheran School of Theology at Chicago, 2002.

Alcoff, Linda Martin. "Latina/o Identity Politics." In *The Good Citizen.* Edited by David Batstone and Eduardo Mendietta. New York: Routledge, 1999.

Álvarez, David A. *Exposición del Obispo sobre las Razones en el Consentimiento al Canónigo Robinson en la 74ta. Convención General de ECUSA.* St. Just, P.R.: Iglesia Episcopal Puertorriqueña, 2003.

Alves, Rubem. "Las ideas teológicas y sus caminos por los surcos institucionales del protestantismo brasileño." In *Historia de la teología en América Latina.* Edited by Pablo Richard. San José, Costa Rica: CEHILA/DEI, 1981.

Americas, Karl, ed. *German Idealism.* Cambridge: Cambridge University Press, 2000.

Anzaldúa, Gloria. *Borderlands/La Frontera: The New Mestiza.* San Francisco: Spinsters/Aunt Late, 1987.

_____. "Entering into the Serpent." In *Weaving the Visions: New Patterns in Feminist Spirituality.* Edited by J. Plaskow and C. Christ. San Francisco: Harper and Row, 1989.

_____. "Chicana Artists: Exploring Nepantla, el Lugar de la Frontera." In *The Latino Studies Reader: Culture, Economy and Society.* Edited by Antonia Darder and Rodolfo D. Torres. Malden, Mass.: Blackwell, 1998.

Apolinaris, Yamina, and Sandra Mangual Rodríguez. "Theologizing from a Puerto Rican Context." In *Hispanic Latino Theology: Challenge and*

Promise. Edited by Ada María Isasi-Díaz and Fernando Segovia. Minneapolis: Fortress Press, 1996.

Aponte, Edwin David. "Coritos as Active Symbols in Latino Protestant Popular Religion." *Journal of Hispanic/Latino Theology* 2, no. 3 (1995): 57–66.

Aquino, María Pilar. *Our Cry for Life: Feminist Theology from Latin America.* Maryknoll, N.Y.: Orbis Books, 1993.

———. "Theological Method in U.S. Latino/a Theology: Towards an Intercultural Theology for the Third Millennium." In *From the Heart of Our People: Latino/a Exploration in Catholic Moral Theology.* Edited by Orlando O. Espín and Miguel H. Díaz. Maryknoll, N.Y.: Orbis Books, 1999.

———. "Latina Feminist Theology: Central Features." In *A Reader in Latina Feminist Theology: Religion and Justice.* Edited by María Pilar Aquino, Daisy L. Machado, and Jeanette Rodríguez. Austin: University of Texas Press, 2002.

Aquino, María Pilar, Daisy L. Machado, and Jeanette Rodríguez, eds. *A Reader in Latina Feminist Theology: Religion and Justice.* Austin: University of Texas Press, 2002.

Archdiocese of Newark. *Presencia Nueva.* Newark, N.J.: 1988.

Arias, Arturo. "Rigoberta Menchu's History within the Guatemalan Context." In *The Rigoberta Menchu Controversy.* Edited by Arturo Arias. Minneapolis: University of Minnesota Press, 2001.

Armet, Stephan. "Holism and Popular Grassroots Movements." *International Review of Mission* 91, no. 362 (July 2002): 370–81.

Baldwin, Deborah J. *Protestants and the Mexican Revolution: Missionaries, Ministers, and Social Change.* Urbana: University of Illinois Press, 1990.

Balthasar, Hans Urs von. *Seeing the Form,* vol. 1, *The glory of the Lord: A Theological Ethics.* Ft. Collins, Colo.: Ignatius Press, 2002.

Bañuelas, Arturo, ed. *Mestizo Christianity: Theology from the Latino Perspective.* Maryknoll, N.Y.: Orbis Books, 1995.

Basden, Paul, and David S. Dockery, eds. *The People of God: Essays on the Believers' Church.* Nashville: Broadman Press, 1991.

Bastian, Jean Pierre. *Protestantismos y modernidad latinoamericana. Historia de unas minorías religiosas activas en América Latina.* Mexico: Fondo de Cultura Económica, 1994.

Baynton, Douglas. *Forbidden Signs: American Culture and the Campaign Against Sign Language.* Chicago: University of Chicago Press, 1996.

Benhabib, Seyla. *The Claims of Culture: Equality and Diversity in the Global Era.* Princeton: Princeton University Press, 2002.

Bevans, Stephen B. *Models of Contextual Theology.* Maryknoll, N.Y.: Orbis Books, 1992.

Bhabha, Homi K. *The Location of Culture.* London/New York: Routledge, 1994.

Bingemer, Maria Clara, and Ivone Gebara. *Mary, Mother of God, Mother of the Poor.* Maryknoll, N.Y.: Orbis Books, 1989.

Blasi, Anthony J. *Early Christianity as a Social Movement: Toronto Studies in Religion,* vol 5. Bern: Peter Lang Publishing, 1989.

Boff, Leonardo. *Trinity and Society.* Translated by Paul Burns. Maryknoll, N.Y.: Orbis Books, 1986.

_____. *New Evangelization: Good News to the Poor.* Translated by Robert R. Barr. Maryknoll, N.Y.: Orbis Books, 1991.

Bourdieu, Pierre. *Méditations pascaliennes.* Paris: Seuil, 1997.

Brading, D. A. *Mexican Phoenix: Our Lady of Guadalupe, Image and Tradition Across Five Centuries.* New York: Cambridge University Press, 2001.

Brandon, George. *Santeriá from Africa to the New World: The Dead Sell Memories.* Indianapolis: Indiana University Press, 1997.

Brewer, Cynthia, and Trudy Suchan. *Mapping Census 2000: The Geography of U.S. Diversity.* Washington, D.C.: U.S. Government Printing Office, 2001.

Brusco, Elizabeth. *Reforming Machismo: Evangelical Conversion and Gender in Columbia.* Austin: University of Texas Press, 1995.

Burch, Susan. "In a Different Voice: Sign Language Preservation and America's Deaf Community." *Bilingual Reserach Journal* 24, no. 4 (Fall 2000): 339.

Burdick, John. *Looking for God in Brazil: The Progressive Catholic Church in Urban Brazil's Religious Arena.* Berkeley: University of California Press, 1993.

Burgess, Stanley M. *The Spirit and the Church: Antiquity.* Peabody, Mass.: Hendrickson, 1984.

Cardoza-Orlandi, Carlos. "Drum Beats of Resistance and Liberation: Afro-Caribbean Religions, the Struggle for Life, and the Christian Theologian." *Journal of Hispanic/Latino Theology* 3, no. 1 (1995): 50–61.

_____. *Mission: An Essential Guide.* Nashville: Abingdon Press, 2002.

Carr, Anne E. *Transforming Grace, Christian Tradition and Women's Experience.* San Francisco: Harper and Row, 1990.

Carrasco, David. "Jaguar Christians in the Contact Zone." In *Enigmatic Powers: Syncretism with African and Indigenous Peoples' Religions Among Latinos.* Edited by Anthony M. Stevens-Arroyo and Andrés Pérez y Mena. New York: Bildner Center Books, 1995.

Carroll, Robert P. *When Prophecy Failed: Cognitive Dissonance in the Prophetic Traditions of the Old Testament.* New York: Seabury Press, 1979.

Casey, A.L. "Worker Speaks in Spanish." *Christian Evangel* 62 (October 10, 1914): 1–4.

Castillo, Ana. *La Diosa de las Américas: Escritos Sobre la Virgen de Guadalupe.* New York: Vintage Español, 2000.

Castro, Max J. and Thomas D. Boswell. "The Dominican Diaspora Revisited: Dominicans and Dominican-Americans in a New Century." *The North-South Agenda Papers* 53 (January 2002): 1–25.

CELAM. *Pastoral de conjunto.* Bogota, Colombia: CELAM, 1971.

Chávez, Angélico. *Coronado's Friars: The Franciscans in the Coronado Expedition.* Washington, D.C.: Academy of American Franciscan History, 1968.

_____. *My Pentitente Land: Reflections on Spanish New Mexico.* Albuquerque: University of New Mexico Press, 1974.

Chávez Sauceda, Teresa. "Love in the Crossroads: Stepping Stones to a Doctrine of God in Hispanic/Latino Theology." In *Teologia en Conjunto: A Collaborative Hispanic Protestant Theology.* Edited by José David Rodríguez and Loida I. Martell-Otero. Louisville: Westminster John Knox Press, 1997.

Chesnut, Andrew R. *Competitive Spirits: Latin America's New Religious Economy.* Oxford: Oxford University Press, 2003.

Codina, Victor. "Sacraments." In *Mysterim Liberationis: Fundamental Concepts of Liberation Theology.* Edited by Ignacio Ellacuría and Jon Sobrino. Maryknoll, N.Y.: Orbis Books, 1993a.

_____. *Sacramentos de la Vida.* México, D.F.: Ediciones Dabar, 1993b.

Collazo, Luis G. *Espacio para Dios: Desde Albizu Campos hasta Julia de Burgos.* Río Piedras, P.R.: Fundación Puerto Rico Evangélico y Seminario Evangélico de Puerto Rico, 2001.

Colón-Pagán, Nohemí, ed. *Tú sobrepasas a todas: Contribución de las mujeres a la Iglesia Cristiana (Discípulos de Cristo) 1898–1998.* Río Piedras, P.R.: Seminario Evangélico de Puerto Rico, 1999.

Conde-Frazier, Elizabeth. "Hispanic Protestant Spirituality." In *Teología en Conjunto: A Collaborative Hispanic Protestant Theology.* Edited by Jose David Rodríguez and Loida I. Martell-Otero. Louisville: Westminster John Knox Press, 1997.

Cone, James H. *Spirituals and the Blues: An Interpretation.* New York: Seabury Press, 1972.

Conference of Mexican Bishops, *Misal Romano.* 2d edition of the Plegaria Eucaristica. Mexico City, D.F.: Conferencia Episcopal Mexicana, 2001.

Cook, Guillermo, ed. *New Face of the Church in Latin America: Between Tradition and Change.* Maryknoll, N.Y.: Orbis Books, 1994.

Cooke, Bernard. *Sacraments and Sacramentality.* Revised edition. Mystic, Conn.: Twenty Third Publications, 1994.

Corley, Kathleen E. *Private Women, Public Meals: Social Conflict in the Synoptic Tradition.* Peabody, Mass.: Hendrickson, 1993.

Cortese, Anthony. "Moral Development in Chicano and Anglo Students." *Hispanic Journal of the Behavioral Sciences* 4 (1982): 353–66.

Cosío Villegas, Daniel. *Historia General de México,* vols. 1 and 3. México, D.F.: El Colegio de México, 1981.

Costas, Orlando E. *The Church and Its Mission: A Shattering Critique from the Third World.* Wheaton, Ill.: Tyndale House, 1974.

_____. *The Integrity of Missions: The Inner Life and Outreach of the Church.* San Francisco: Harper & Row, 1979.

_____. *Christ Outside the Gates: Mission Beyond Christendom.* Maryknoll, N.Y.: Orbis Books, 1982.

_____. *Liberating News: A Theology of Contextual Evangelization.* Grand Rapids, Mich.: Wm. B. Eerdmans, 1989.

_____. "Evangelism from the Periphery: The Universality of Galilee." In *Voces: Voices from the Hispanic Church.* Edited by Justo L. González. Nashville: Abingdon Press, 1992.

Craddock, Fred B. *Preaching.* Nashville: Abingdon Press, 1985.

Daly, Mary. "Weaving, Context, Creating Atmospheres." In *Weaving the Visions: New Patterns in Feminist Spirituality.* Edited by J. Plaskow and C. Christ. San Francisco: Harper and Row, 1989.

_____. *GynEcology, the Metaethics of Radical Feminism.* Boston: Beacon Press, 1990.

Dávila, Arlene. "The Latin Side of Madison Avenue: Marketing and the Language that Makes Us 'Hispanics.'" In *Mambo Montage: The Latinization of New York.* Edited by Agustín Laó-Montes and Arlene Dávila. New York: Columbia University Press, 2001.

Davis, Kenneth G. "The Hispanic Shift: Continuity Rather Than Conversion?" *Journal of Hispanic/Latino Theology* 1, no. 3 (May 1994): 68–79.

_____, ed. *Misa, Mesa y Musa: Liturgy in the U.S. Hispanic Church.* Shiller Park, Ill.: World Library Publications, 1997.

_____. "Annoying the Sick? Cultural Considerations for the Celebration of a Sacrament," *Worship* 78, no. 1 (January 2004): 35–50.

Davis, Kenneth G., and Jorge L. Presmanes, eds. *Preaching and Culture in Latino Congregations.* Chicago: Liturgy Training Publications, 2000.

Davis, Mike. *Magical Urbanism: Latinos Reinvent the U.S. Big City.* New York: Verso, 2000.

Day, Mark R. "Evangelical Sects Attract U.S. Hispanics." *National Catholic Reporter* 18, no. 20 (March 19, 1982): 1–19.

Deck, Allan Figueroa. *The Second Wave: Hispanic Ministry and the Evangelization of Cultures.* Mahwah, N.J.: Paulist Press, 1989.

De La Torre, Miguel A. *The Quest for the Cuban Christ: A Historical Search.* Gainesville: University of Florida Press, 2002a.

_____. *Reading the Bible from the Margins.* Maryknoll, N.Y.: Orbis Books, 2002b.

_____. *La Lucha for Cuba: Religion and Politics on the Streets of Miami.* Berkeley: University of California Press, 2003.

_____. "The Cuban American Religious Experience." *Introduction to the U.S. Latina and Latino Religious Experience.* Ed. by Hector Avalos. Boston: Brill Academic Publishers, 2004a.

_____. *Doing Christian Ethics from the Margins.* Maryknoll, N.Y.: Orbis Books, 2004b.

_____. "Scriptures." In *Handbook of U.S. Theologies of Liberation.* Edited by Miguel A. De La Torre. St. Louis: Chalice Press, 2004c.

_____. *Santería: The Beliefs and Rituals of a Growing Religion in America.* Grand Rapids, Mich.: William B. Eerdmans Publishing Company, 2004d.

De La Torre, Miguel A., and Edwin David Aponte. *Introducing Latino/a Theologies.* Maryknoll, N.Y.: Orbis Books, 2001.

Derrida, Jacques. "La structure, le signe et le jeu dans le discours des sciences humaines." In *L'Écriture et la Différence.* Paris: Éditions Du Seuil, 1967.

_____. "La différance." In *Marges de la philosophie.* Paris: Les Éditions de Minuit, 1972.

Díaz, Miguel H. "'Dime con quién andas y te diré quién eres': We Walk-with Our Lady of Charity." In *From the Heart of Our People.* Edited by Orlando O. Espín and Miguel H. Díaz. Maryknoll, N.Y.: Orbis Books, 1999.

_____. *On Being Human: U.S. Hispanic and Rahnerian Perspectives.* Maryknoll, N.Y.: Orbis Books, 2001.

Díaz-Stevens, Ana María, and Anthony M. Stevens-Arroyo. *Recognizing the Latino Resurgence in U.S. Religion: The Emmaus Paradigm.* Boulder, Colo.: Westview Press, 1998.

Dolan, Jay P., and Allan Figueroa Deck. *Hispanic Catholic Culture in the U.S.: Issues and Concerns.* Notre Dame, Ind.: University of Notre Dame Press, 1997.

Driver, Juan, *La fe en la periferia de la historia.* Guatemala City: SEMILLA, 1997.

Drogus, Carol Ann. *Women, Religion and Social Change in Brazil's Popular Church.* Notre Dame, Ind.: University of Notre Dame Press, 1997.

During, Simon. "Postmodernism or Post-colonialism Today." In *The Post-Colonial Studies Reader.* Edited by Bill Ashcroft, Gareth Griffiths, and Helen Tiffin. New York: Routledge, 1995.

Durnbaugh, Donald F. *The Believers' Church: The History and Character of Radical Protestantism.* New York: MacMillan, 1968.

Dussel, Enrique. *A History of the Church in Latin America: Colonialism to Liberation (1492–1979).* Translated by Alan Neely. Grand Rapids, Mich.: William B. Eerdmans, 1981.

Dutcher-Walls, P. "The Social Location of the Deuteronomists." *Journal for the Study of the Old Testament* 52 (1991): 77–94.

Dyson, Michael Eric. *Between God and Gangsta Rap: Bearing Witness to Black Culture.* New York: Oxford University Press, 1996.

Ebaugh, Helen Rose, and Janet Chafetz, eds. *Religion and the New Immigrants.* Walnut Creek, Calif.: Altamira Press, 2000.

Eck, Diana L. *A New Religious America.* New York: Harper Collins, 2001.

Ehrlich, Dimitri. *Inside the Music: Conversations with Contemporary Musicians about Spirituality, Creativity and Consciousness.* Boston: Shambala, 1997.

Elizondo, Virgilio. *La Morenita: Evangelizadora de las Américas.* Liguori, Mo.: Ligouri Publications, 1981.

_____. *Galilean Journey: The Mexican-American Promise.* Maryknoll, N.Y.: Orbis Books, 1983, 2000a.

_____. "Popular Religion and Support of Identity: A Pastoral-Psychological Case-Study Based on the Mexican American Experience in the USA." In *Popular Religion.* Edited by Norbert Greinacher and Norbert Mette. Edinburgh: T&T Clark LTD, 1986.

_____. *The Future Is Mestizo: Life Where Cultures Meet.* Oak Park, Ill.: Meyer-Stone, 1988.

_____. "Mestizaje as a Locus of Theological Reflection." In *Mestizo Christianity: Theology from the Latino Perspective.* Edited by Arturo J. Bañuelas. Maryknoll, N.Y.: Orbis Books, 1995.

_____. *Guadalupe: Mother of the New Creation.* Maryknoll, N.Y.: Orbis Books, 1997.

_____. *Christianity and Culture: An Introduction to Pastoral Theology and Ministry to the Bicultural Community.* San Antonio: Mexican American Cultural Center, 1999.

_____. "Hispanic Theology and Popular Piety: From Interreligious Encounter to New Ecumenism." In *Beyond Borders: Writings of Virgilio Elizondo and Friends.* Edited by Timothy Matovina. Maryknoll, N.Y.: Orbis Books, 2000b.

_____. "Our Lady of Guadalupe as a Cultural Symbol." In *Beyond Borders: Writings of Virgilio Elizondo and Friends.* Edited by Timothy Matovina. Maryknoll, N.Y.: Orbis Books, 2000b.

Ellacuría, Ignacio. *Filosofía de la realidad histórica.* El Salvador: UCA, 1990.

Emerton, R. Greg. "Marginality, BiCulturalism, Social Identity." In *Cultural and Language Diversity and the Deaf Experience.* Edited by Ila Parasnis. Cambridge: Cambridge University Press, 1998.

Empereur, James, and Eduando C. Fernández, *La Vida Sacra: A Contemporary Hispanic Sacramental Theology.* Lanham Md.: Rowman and Littlefield, 2006.

Eodice, Alexander R. "Innocence Lost and Found." *Amercan Catholic Philosophical Quarterly* 74, no. 2000 (2001): 299–305.

Escobar, Samuel. "El Poder y las Ideologias en America Latina." In *Los Evangelicos y el Poder Politico en America Latina.* Edited by Alberto Deiros. Grand Rapids, Mich.: William B. Eerdmans, 1986.

_____. "The Church in Latin America after Five Hundred Years: An Evangelical Missiological Perspective." In *New Face of the Church in Latin America: Between Tradition and Change.* Edited by Guillermo Cook. Maryknoll, N.Y.: Orbis Books, 1994.

_____. *Changing Tides: Latin America and World Mission.* Maryknoll: N.Y.: Orbis Books, 2002.

Espada, Martín. *Zapata's Disciple: Essays.* Cambridge, Mass.: South End Press, 1998.

Espín, Oliva. *Latina Healers: Lives of Power and Tradition.* Encino, Calif.: Flor y Canto Press, 1996.

Espín, Orlando O. "Pentecostalism and Popular Catholicism: The Poor and Traditio." *Journal of Hispanic/Latino Theology* 3, no. 2 (1995): 14–43.

_____. *The Faith of the People: Theological Reflections on Popular Catholicism.* Maryknoll, N.Y.: Orbis Books, 1997.

_____. "An Exploration into the Theology of Grace and Sin." In *From the Heart of Our People: Latino/a Explorations in Catholic Systematic Theology.* Edited by Orlando O. Espín and Miguel H. Díaz. Maryknoll, N.Y.: Orbis Books, 1999.

Espín, Orlando O., and Miguel H. Díaz. *From the Heart of Our People: Latino/a Explorations in Catholic Systematic Theology.* Maryknoll, N.Y.: Orbis Books, 1999.

Espinosa, Gastón. "El Azteca: Francisco Olazábal and Latino Pentecostal Charisma, Power, and Faith Healing in the Borderlands." *Journal of the American Academy of Religion* 67, No. 3 (September, 1999): 597–616.

Espinosa, Gastón, Virgilio Elizondo, and Jesse Miranda. "Hispanic Churches in American Public Life: Summary of Findings." *Interim Reports.* Second edition, vol. 2003, no. 2 (March 2003): 1–28.

Estrada Adorno, Wilfredo. *Cántico borincano de esperanza: historia de la distribución de la Biblia del 1898 al 1998.* Bogotá, Colombia: Sociedad Bíblica de Puerto Rico, 1999.

_____. *¿Pastores o políticos con sotanas? Pastoral de la guardarraya en Vieques.* Río Piedras, P.R.: Editorial Guardarrayas and Fundación Puerto Rico Evangélico, 2003.

Feagin, Joe R. "Old Poison in New Bottles." In *Immigrants Out!: The New Nativism and the Anti-Immigrant Impulse in the United States.* Edited by Juan F. Perea. New York: New York University Press, 1997.

Fernández, Eduardo C. *La Cosecha: Harvesting Contemporary United States Hispanic Theology (1972–1998).* Collegeville, Minn.: Liturgical Press, 2000.

Fierro, Alfredo. *The Militant Gospel: A Critical Introduction to Political Theologies.* Translated by John Drury. Maryknoll, N.Y.: Orbis Books, 1977.

Fink, Peter E., ed. *The New Dictionary of Sacramental Worship:* Collegeville, Minn.: Liturgical Press, 1990.

Flores, Juan. *Divided Borders: Essays on Puerto Rican Identity.* Houston: Arte Público Press, 1993.

_____. *From Bomba to Hip-Hop: Puerto Rican Culture and Latino Identity.* New York: Columbia University Press, 2000.

Flores, William V., and Rina Benmayor. "Constructing Cultural Citizenship." In *Latino Cultural Citizenship: Claiming Identity, Space and Rights.* Edited by William V. Flores and Rina Benmayor. Boston: Beacon Press, 1997.

Franciscan Friars of the Immaculate. *A Handbook on Guadalupe.* New Bedford, Mass.: Franciscan Friars of the Immaculate, 1997.

Freedman, David Noel, ed. in chief. *The Anchor Bible Dictionary.* Vol. 6 New York: Doubleday, 1992.

Freston, Paul. *Evangelicals and Politics in Asia, Africa, and Latin America.* Cambridge: Cambridge University Press, 2001.

Fuentes, Carlos. *The Buried Mirror: Reflections on Spain and the New World.* New York: Houghton Mifflin, 1992.

Fukuyama, Francis. *The End of History and the Last Man.* New York: Free Press, 1992.

Funk, A. *Status und Rollen in der Paulusbriefen.* Innsbruck: Tyrolia, 1981.

Gadamer, Hans-Georg. *Truth and Method,* Revised edition. London: Sheed & Ward, 1975.

Galeron, Soledad, Rosa Maria Icaza, and Rosendo Urrabazo, eds. *Prophetic Vision: Pastoral Reflections of the National Pastoral Plan for Hispanic Ministry.* San Antonio: Sheed & Ward, 1992.

García, Alma M. *The Mexican Americans: The New Americans.* Westport, Conn.: Greenwood Press, 2002.

García, Ismael. *Dignidad: Ethics Through Hispanic Eyes.* Nashville: Abingdon Press, 1997.

García, Sixto S. "United States Hispanic and Mainstream Trinitarian Theologies." In *Frontiers of Hispanic Theology in the United States.* Edited by Allan Figueroa Deck. Maryknoll, N.Y.: Orbis Books, 1992.

García-Rivera, Alex. *St. Martín de Porres: The "Little Stories" and the Semiotics of Culture.* Maryknoll, N.Y.: Orbis Books, 1995.

_____. *A Wounded Innocence: Sketches for a Theology of Art.* Collegeville, Minn.: Liturgical Press, 2003.

Garrard-Burnett, Virginia. *Protestantism in Guatemala: Living in the New Jerusalem.* Austin: University of Texas Press, 1998a.

_____. "Transnational Protestantism." *Journal of Interamerican Studies and World Affairs* 40, no. 3 (1998b): 117–25.

Geertz, Clifford. *The Interpretation of Cultures.* New York: Basic Books, 1973.

Gelpí, Juan G. *Literatura y paternalismo en Puerto Rico.* Río Piedras, P.R.: Editorial de la Universidad de Puerto Rico, 1993.

Gerner de Garcia, Barbara A. "ESL Applications for Hispanic Deaf Students." *The Bilingual Research Journal* 19, nos. 3 and 4 (Summer/Fall 1995): 453–67.

Gill, Anthony. "The Struggle to be Soul Provider: Catholic Responses to Protestant Growth in Latin America." In *Latin American Religion in*

Motion. Edited by Christian Smith & Joshua Prokopy. New York: Routledge, 1999.

Goizueta, Roberto S. *"Nosotros:* Toward a U.S. Hispanic Anthropology." *Listening: Journal of Religion and Culture* 27, no. 1 (Winter 1992a): 55–69.

_____. "United States Hispanic Theology and the Challenge of Pluralism." In *Frontiers of Hispanic Theology in the United States.* Edited by Allen Deck. Maryknoll, N.Y.: Orbis Books, 1992b.

_____, ed. *We Are a People! Initiatives in Hispanic American Theology.* Minneapolis: Fortress Press, 1992c.

_____. *Caminemos con Jesús: A Hispanic/Latino Theology of Accompaniment.* Maryknoll, N.Y.: Orbis Books, 1995.

_____. "A Matter of Life and Death: Theological Anthropology Between Calvary and Galilee." *CTSA Proceedings* 53 (1998): 1–20.

_____. "A Christology for a Global Church." In *Beyond Borders: Writings of Virgilio Elizondo and Friends.* Edited by Timothy Matovina. Maryknoll, N.Y.: Orbis Books, 2000.

Gómez Treto, Raul. *The Church and Socialism in Cuba.* Maryknoll, N.Y.: Orbis Books, 1988.

González, José Luis. *El país de cuatro pisos y otros ensayos.* Río Piedras, P.R.: Ediciones Huracán, 1980.

González, Juan. *Harvest of Empire: A History of Latinos in America.* New York: Viking Penguin, 2000.

González, Justo L. *The Spanish Reformers.* Rio Piedras, P.R.: Evangelical Seminary, 1967.

_____. *Story of Christianity: The Early Church to the Dawn of the Reformation.* New York: HarperCollins, 1984.

_____. "Introduction." *Apuntes: Reflexiones Teológicas desde el Margen Hispano* 7, no. 1 (Spring 1987): 23.

_____. *Mañana: Christian Theology from a Hispanic Perspective.* Nashville: Abingdon Press, 1990.

_____, ed. *Voces: Voices from the Hispanic Church.* Nashville: Abingdon Press, 1992.

_____. "Voices of Compassion Yesterday and Today." In *New Face of the Church in Latin America: Between Tradition and Change.* Edited by Guillermo Cook. Maryknoll: N.Y., Orbis Books, 1994.

_____, ed. *Alabadle!: Hispanic Christian Worship.* Nashville: Abingdon Press, 1996a.

_____. *Santa Biblia: The Bible Through Hispanic Eyes.* Nashville: Abingdon Press, 1996b.

_____. Foreword to *Teología en Conjunto: A Collaborative Hispanic Protestant Theology.* Edited by José David Rodríguez and Loida I. Martell-Otero. Louisville: Westminster John Knox Press, 1997.

_____. "Scripture, Tradition, Experience, and Imagination: A Redefinition." In *The Ties That Bind.* Edited by Benjamin Valentín and Anthony Pinn. New York: Continuum, 2001.

González, Justo L., and Zaida Maldonado Pérez. *Introduction to Christian Theology.* Nashville: Abingdon Press, 2002.

_____. *Introducción a la Teología Cristiana.* Nashville: Abingdon Press, 2003.

González Dorado, Antonio. *Los Sacramentos del Evangelio: Sacramentología fundamental y orgánica.* México: CEM, 1993.

Gottwald, Norman K. *The Tribes of Yahweh: A Sociology of the Religion of Liberated Israel, 1250–1050 B.C.E.* Maryknoll, N.Y.: Orbis Books, 1979.

Griswold, Wendy. *Cultures and Societies in a Changing World.* Thousand Oaks, Calif.: Pine Forge Press, 1994.

Guardiola-Sáenz, Leticia A. "Border-crossing and its Redemptive Power in John 7:53–8:11: A Cultural Reading of Jesus and the Accused" In *John and Postcolonialism.* Edited by Mosa W. Dube and Jeffrey L. Staley. London: Sheffied Press, 2002a.

_____. "Reading from Ourselves: Identity and Hermeneutics among Mexican-American Feminists." In *A Reader in Latina Feminist Theology: Religion and Justice.* Edited by María Pilar Aquino, Daisy L. Machado, and Jeanette Rodríguez. Austin: University of Texas Press, 2002b.

Gutiérrez, Ángel Luis. *Evangélicos en Puerto Rico en la época española.* Río Piedras, P.R.: Fundación Puerto Rico Evangélico y Seminario Evangélico de Puerto Rico, 1997, 2001.

Gutiérrez, Félix. "The Western Jurisdiction." In *Each in Our Own Tongue: A History of Hispanic United Methodism.* Edited by Justo González. Nashville: Abingdon Press, 1991.

Gutiérrez, Gustavo. *A Theology of Liberation: History, Politics and Salvation.* Maryknoll, N.Y.: Orbis Books, 1973. (Translated and edited by Sister Caridad Inda and John Eagleson from *Teología de la liberación: Perspectivas.* Lima: CEP, 1971.)

_____. *Las Casas: In Search of the Poor of Jesus Christ.* Translated by Robert R. Barr. Maryknoll, N.Y.: Orbis Books, 1993.

_____. *We Drink from Our Own Wells: the Spiritual Journey of a People.* Maryknoll, N.Y.: Orbis Books, 1997.

Guzmán, Betsy. *Hispanic Population: Census 2000 Brief.* Washington, D.C.: U.S. Census Bureau, 2001.

Habermas, Jürgen. *Knowledge and Human Interests.* Translated by Jeremy J. Shapiro. Boston: Beacon Press, 1971.

_____. *The Theory of Communicative Action.* 2 volumes. Boston: Beacon Press, 1984–1987.

Hackett, David G. *Religion and American Culture: A Reader.* London: Routledge, 1995.

Hamilton, Nora, and Norma S. Chinchilla. "Central American Migration: A Framework for Analysis." *Latin American Research Review* 26, no. 1 (1991): 75–110.

Hanson, M.J., and E. W. Lynch. *Developing Cross-cultural Competence.* Baltimore: Paul H. Brookes Publishing Co., 1993.

Harnack, Adolf. *History of Dogma,* vol. 4. New York: Dove Publications, 1961.

Harris, Max. *Aztecs, Moors and Christians: Festivals of Reconquest in Mexico and Spain.* Austin: University of Texas Press, 2000.

Hayes Bautista, David. *No Longer a Minority: Latinos and Social Policy in California.* Los Angeles: Chicano Studies Research Center, UCLA, 1992.

Heidegger, Martin. *Basic Writings.* New York: HarperCollins, 1977.

Hennelly, Alfred T., ed., *Santo Domingo and Beyond: Documents and Commentaries from the Historic Meeting of the Latin American Bishops Conference.* Maryknoll, N.Y.: Orbis, 1993.

Hernández, Edwin. "Moving from the Cathedral to Storefront Churches." In *Protestantes/Protestants: Hispanic Christianity within Mainline Traditions.* Edited by David Maldonado. Nashville: Abingdon Press, 1999.

Hernández Lozano, David, and Héctor López Sierra, eds. *Impacto cultural de cien años de protestantismo misionero en Puerto Rico.* San Juan, P.R.: Universidad Interamericana de Puerto Rico, Recinto Metropolitano, 2000.

Heron, Alasdair I. C. *A Century of Protestant Theology.* Philadelphia: Westminster Press, 1980.

———. *The Holy Spirit.* Philadelphia: Westminster Press, 1983.

Herrera, Marina. "Who Do You Say Jesus Is? Christological Reflections from a Hispanic Woman's Perspective." In *Reconstructing the Christ Symbol: Essays in Feminist Christology.* Edited by Maryanne Stevens. New York: Paulist Press, 1993.

Hispanic Center. *2002 National Survey of Latinos.* Washington, D.C.:Pew Hispanic Center/Kaiser Family Foundation, 2002.

Hobsbawm, Eric, and Terence Ranger, eds. *The Invention of Tradition.* Cambridge: Cambridge University Press, 1983.

Hollenweger, Walter. *The Pentecostals.* Peabody, Mass.: Hendrickson, 1988.

Hoornaert, Eduardo. *The Memory of the Christian People.* Maryknoll, N.Y.: Orbis Books, 1988.

Hunt, Larry. "The Spirit of Hispanic Protestantism in the United States: National Survey Comparisons of Catholics and Non-Catholics." *Social Science Quarterly* 79, no. 4 (December 1988): 828–45.

_____. "Hispanic Protestantism in the United States: Trends by Decade and Generation." *Social Forces* 77, no. 4 (June 1999): 1601–24.

Huntington, Samuel P. *Who Are We? The Challenges to America's National Identity.* New York: Simon & Schuster, 2004.

Inman, Samuel Guy. *Evangelicals at Havana: Being an Account of the Hispanic American Evangelical Congress, at Havana, Cuba, June 20–30, 1929.* New York: Committee on Cooperation in Latin America: 1929.

Irizarry Mercado, José R. "*Praxis e Identidad*: Discourses and Practices of Puerto Rican Religious Education in the Works of Domingo Marrero and Ángel M. Mergal." Ph.D. diss., Northwestern University and Garrett-Evangelical Theological Seminary, 2001.

Isasi-Díaz, Ada María. "Mujerista Theology's Method: A Liberating Praxis, A Way of Life." *Listening: Journal of Religion and Culture* 27 (Winter 1992): 41–52.

_____. *En la Lucha, In the Struggle: A Hispanic Women's Liberation Theology.* Minneapolis: Fortress Press, 1993, 2004.

_____. *Mujerista Theology: A Theology for the Twenty-First Century.* Maryknoll, N.Y.: Orbis Books, 1996.

_____. "A New Meztizaje/Mulatez: Reconceptualizing Difference." In *A Dream Unfinished: Theological Reflections on America from the Margins.* Edited by Eleazar S. Fernandez and Fernando F. Segovia. Maryknoll, N.Y.: Orbis Books, 2001a.

_____. "Preoccupations, Themes, and Proposals of *Mujerista* Theology." In *The Ties that Bind: African American and Hispanic American / Latino/a Theologians in Dialogue.* Edited by Anthony B. Pinn and Benjamin Valentin. New York: Continuum, 2001b.

_____. "*Lo Cotidiano*: A Key Element of *Mujerista* Theology." *Journal of Hispanic/Latino Theology* 10 (2002): 5–17.

_____. "Christ in *Mujerista* Theology." In *Thinking of Christ: Proclamation, Explanation, Meaning.* Edited by Tatha Wiley. New York: Continuum, 2003.

Isasi-Díaz, Ada María, and Yolanda Tarango. *Hispanic Women: Prophetic Voice in the Church.* San Francisco: Harper & Row, 1988.

Jankowski, Katherine A. *Deaf Empowerment: Emergence, Struggle, and Rhetoric.* Washington, D.C.: Gallaudet University Press, 1997.

Jiménez, Pablo A. "The Bible: A Hispanic Perspective." In *Teología en Conjunto: A Collaborative Hispanic Protestant Theology.* Edited by José David Rodríguez and Loida I. Martell-Otero. Lousville: Westminster John Knox Press, 1997.

Jones-Correa, Michael A. and David L. Leal. "Political Participation: Does Religion Matter?" *Political Research Quarterly* 54, no. 4 (December 2001): 751–70.

Juergensmeyer, Mark. *Terror in the Mind of God.* Berkeley: University of California Press, 2000.

Justin Martyr. "Letter to Emperor Antoninus Pius." In *The Catechism of the Catholic Church*. Washington D.C.: United States Conference–Liseria Editrice Vaticana, 1994.

Keefe, Susan E., and Amado M. Padilla. *Chicano Ethnicity*. Albuquerque: University of New Mexico Press, 1992.

Kiev, Ari. *Curanderismo: Mexican-American Folk Psychiatry*. Toronto: The Free Press, 1968.

Kinder, A. Gordon. *Cassidoro de Reina: Spanish Reformer of the Sixteenth Century*. London: Tamesis Books, 1975.

Lacan, Jacques. *Le séminaire, III, "Les psychoses."* Paris: Éditions du Seuil, 1981.

Ladaria, Luis F. *Introducción a la antropología teológica*. Navarra, Spain: Editorial Verbo Divino, 1996.

Laó-Montes, Agustín. "Mambo Montage: The Latinization of New York City." In *Mambo Montage: The Latinization of New York*. Edited by Agustín Laó-Montes and Arlene Dávila. New York: Columbia University Press, 2001.

LeCompte, Margaret D., and Jean J. Schensul. *Designing and Conducting Ethnographic Research*. Walnut Creek, Calif.: AltaMira Press, 1999.

Lee, Bernard J. *The Catholic Experience of Small Christian Communities*. New York: Paulist Press, 2000.

Leguizamo, John, and David Bar Katz. "Surrogate Moms." In *Freak: A Semi-Demi-Quasi-Pseudo Autobiography*. New York: Riverhead Books, 1997.

Lenski, Gerhard E. *Power and Privilege: A Theory of Stratification*. New York: McGraw-Hill, 1966.

Léon, Luís. "Born Again in East LA: The Congregation as Border Space." In *Gatherings in the Diaspora*. Edited by R. Stephen Warner and Judith G. Wittner. Philadelphia: Temple University Press, 1998.

León-Portilla, Miguel. *La filosofía nahuatl: estudiada en sus fuentes con un nuevo apéndice*. México, D.F.: Universidad Nacional Autónoma de México, 1966.

Lévinas, Emmanuel. *Totalité et infini: essai sur l'extériorité*. Paris: Brodard et Taupin, 2001.

Levitt, Peggy. "Local-Level Global Religion: The Case of U.S.-Dominican Migration." *Journal for the Scientific Study of Religion* 3 (1998): 74–89.

_____. *The Transnational Villagers*. Berkeley: University of California Press, 2001.

Levitt, Peggy, Josh DeWind, and Steven Vertovec. "Transnational Migration: International Perspectives." *International Migration Review* 37, no. 3 (2003): 561–92.

Lints, Richard. *The Fabric of Theology: A Prolegomenon to Evangelical Theology*. Grand Rapids: William B. Eerdmans, 1993.

López, Ediberto. *Para que comprendiesen las Escrituras: introducción a los métodos exegéticos.* Río Piedras, P.R.: Seminario Evangélico de Puerto Rico, 2003.

Lossky, Vladimir. *The Mystical Theology of the Eastern Church.* Crestwood, N.Y.: St. Vladimir's Seminary Press, 1976.

Loya, Gloria Inés. "The Mexican American Woman, a Pastoral Project Based on an Evangelization of Faith and Culture." D.Min. thesis, Graduate Theological Union, 1996.

————. "Considering the Sources/*Fuentes* for a Hispanic Feminist Theology." *Theology Today* 54, no. 4 (January 1998): 491–98.

Lozano, Nora O. "Ignored Virgin or Unaware Women: A Mexican-American Protestant Reflection on the Virgin of Guadalupe." In *A Reader in Latina Feminist Theology: Religion and Justice.* Edited by María Pilar Aquino, Daisy L. Machado, and Jeanette Rodríguez. Austin: University of Texas Press, 2002.

Machado, Daisy L. "A Borderlands Perspective." In *Hidden Stories: Unveiling the History of the Latin Church.* Edited by Daniel R. Rodríguez-Díaz and David Cortés-Fuentes. Decatur, Ga.: AETH, 1994.

————. "Latinos in the Protestant Establishment: Is There a Place for Us at the Feast Table?" In *Protestantes/Protestants: Hispanic Christianity Within Mainline Traditions.* Edited by David Maldonado Jr. Nashville: Abingdon Press, 1999.

————. "The Unnamed Woman: Justice, Feminists, and the Undocumented Woman." In *A Reader in Latina Feminist Theology: Religion and Justice.* Edited by María Pilar Aquino, Daisy Machado, and Jeanette Rodríguez. Austin: University of Texas Press, 2002.

Maldonado, David. "Doing Theology and the Anthropological Questions." In *Teología en Conjunto: A Collaborative Hispanic Protestant Theology.* Edited by José David Rodríguez and Loida I. Martell-Otero. Louisville: Westminster John Knox Press, 1997.

————, ed. *Protestantes/Protestants: Hispanic Christianity Within Mainline Traditions.* Nashville: Abingdon Press, 1999.

Margolis, Maxine. *Little Brazil: An Ethnography of Brazilian Immigrants in New York.* Princeton: Princeton University Press, 1994.

Martell-Otero, Loida I. "Of Satos and Saints: Salvation from the Periphery." *Perpectivas: Hispanic Theological Initiative Occasional Papers* 4 (Summer 2001): 7–38.

————. "Liberating News: An Emerging U.S. Hispanic/Latina Soteriology of the Crossroads." Ph.D. diss., Fordham University, 2005.

Martes, Ana Cristina. *Brasileiros nos Estados Unidos: Um estudo sobre imigrantes em Massachussetts.* Sao Paulo: Paz e Terra, 2000.

Martínez, Felipe. "The Social Thought of Protestant Christians in Puerto Rico in the 1960s: Beginnings of a Puerto Rican theology of Liberation." Ph.D. diss., Drew University, 1997.

Martínez Fernández, Luis. *Protestantism and Political Conflict in the Nineteenth-Century Hispanic Caribbean.* New Brunswick, N.J.: Rutgers University Press, 2002.

Martos, Joseph. *Doors to the Sacred.* Revised and updated edition. Liguori, Mo.: Liguori Publications, 2001.

Marty, Martin E., and R. Scott Appleby, eds. *Fundamentalisms Observed.* Chicago: University of Chicago Press, 1994.

Marx, Karl, and Frederick Engels, *The Holy Family,* Moscow: Progress, 1975.

Mays, James L., ed. *Harper's Bible Commentary.* New York: Harper & Row and the Society of Biblical Literature, 1988.

McBrien, Richard P., gen. ed. *The HarperCollins Encyclopedia of Catholicism.* New York: HarperCollins, 1995.

McCord Adams, Marilyn. *Horrendous Evils and the Goodness of God.* Ithaca, N.Y.: Cornell University Press, 1999.

McGavran, Donald A. *Understanding Church Growth.* Grand Rapids: William B. Eerdmans, 1990.

McGrath-Andino, Lester. *Quo Vadis, Vieques? Ética social, política y ecumenismo.* Río Piedras, P.R.: Seminario Evangélico de Puerto Rico y Fundación Puerto Rico Evangélico, no date.

_____. *Un ministerio transformador: El Seminario Evangélico de Puerto Rico.* Río Piedras, P.R.: Seminario Evangélico de Puerto Rico y Fundación Puerto Rico Evangélico, 1998.

Meier, Matt S., and Feliciano Rivera. *Dictionary of Mexican American History.* Westport, Conn.: Greenwood Press, 1981.

Mejido, Manuel J. "Theoretical Prolegomenon to the Sociology of U.S. Hispanic Popular Religion." *Journal of Hispanic/Latino Theology* 7, no. 1 (August 1999): 27–55.

_____. "A Critique of the 'Aesthetic Turn' in U.S. Hispanic Theology: A Conversation with Roberto Goizueta and the Positing of a New Paradigm." *Journal of Hispanic/Latino Theology* 8, no. 3 (February, 2001): 18–48.

_____. "The Illusion of Neutrality: Reflections on the Term 'Popular Religion.'" *Social Compass* 49, no. 2 (2002): 295–311.

_____. "The Fundamental Problematic of U.S. Hispanic Theology." In *New Horizons in Hispanic/Latino/a Theology.* Edited by Benjamín Valentín. Cleveland: Pilgrim Press, 2003a.

_____. "Propaedeutic to the Critique of the Study of U.S. Hispanic Religion: A Polemic Against Intellectual Assimilation." *Journal of Hispanic/Latino Theology* 10, no. 2 (2003b): 31–63.

_____. "The Real Beyond Language: A Response to David R. Brockman." *Koinonia* 15, no. 1 (2003c): 34–47.

_____. "Theology, Crisis, and Knowledge-Constitutive Interests, or Towards a Social Theoretical Interpretation of Theological Knowledge." *Social Compass* 51, no. 3 (2004a): 389–409.

_____. "Beyond the Postmodern Condition, or The Turn Towards Psychoanalysis." *Liberation Theology: The Next Generation.* Edited by Iván Petralla. Maryknoll, N.Y.: Orbis Books, 2004b.

Miranda, José Porfirio. *Marx and the Bible.* Maryknoll, N.Y.: Orbis Books, 1974. (Translation by John Eagleson from *Marx y la Biblia.* Salamanca: Sigueme, 1972.)

Mirandé, Alfredo. *The Chicano Experience: An Alternative Perspective.* Notre Dame: University of Notre Dame Press, 1985.

Morrill, Bruce. "Initial Consideration: Theory and Practice of the Body in Liturgy Today." In *Bodies of Worship: Explorations in Theory and Practice.* Edited by Bruce Morrill. Collegeville, Minn.: The Liturgical Press, 1999.

Murdoch, Iris. *The Fire and the Sun: Why Plato Banished the Artists.* Oxford: Clarendon Press, 1977.

Museum of Art of Puerto Rico. *Los tesoros de la pintura puertorriqueña/The Treasures of Puerto Rican Painting.* San Juan: Museo de Arte de Puerto Rico, 2000.

Nabhan-Warren, Kristy. *The Virgin of El Barrio: Marian Apparitions, Catholic Evangelizing, and Mexican American Activism.* New York: New York University Press, 2005.

National Conference of Catholic Bishops. *Evangelización: Guiá de Diálogo, Catholic Commission of Hispanic Ministry Region 6 & 7.* South Bend, Ind.: Commission on Hispanic Ministry, 1985(e).

_____. *Hispanic Ministry: Three Major Documents.* Washington, D.C.: USCC, 1995.

Nieto, José C., ed. *Valdés' Two Catechisms: The Dialogue on Christian Doctrine and the Christian Instruction for Children,* Second Enlarged Edition. Translated by William B. and Carol D. Jones. Lawrence, Kans.: Coronado Press, 1993.

Oktavek, Eileen. *Answered Prayers: Miracles and Milagros along the Border.* Tucson: University of Arizona Press, 1995.

Olson, Roger E., and Christopher A. Hall. *The Trinity.* Grand Rapids, Mich.: Eerdmans, 2002.

Padden, Carol A. "From the Cultural to the Bicultural: The Modern Deaf Community." In *Cultural and Language Diversity and the Deaf Experience.* Edited by Ila Parasnis. Cambridge: Cambridge University Press, 1998.

Padilla, C. Rene, ed. *The New Face of Evangelicalism: An International Symposium on the Lausanne Covenant.* Downers Grove, Ill.: InterVarsity Press, 1976.

Pagán, Samuel. *El misterio revelado: Los rollos del Mar Muerto y la comunidad de Qumrán.* Nashville: Abingdon Press, 2001.

Pannenberg, Wolfhart. *Systematic Theology, Vol. 1.* Grand Rapids: William B. Eerdmans, 1988.

Pedraja, Luis G. "Guideposts Along the Journey: Mapping North American Hispanic Theology." In *Protestantes/Protestants: Hispanic Christianity Within Mainline Traditions.* Edited by David Maldonado. Nashville: Abingdon Press, 1999a.

_____. *Jesus Is My Uncle: Christology from a Hispanic Perspective.* Nashville: Abingdon Press, 1999b.

_____. *Teología: An Introduction to Hispanic Theology.* Nashville: Abingdon Press, 2004.

Peña, Milagros. "Border Crossings: Sociological Analysis and the Latina and Latino Religious Experience." *Journal of Hispanic/Latino Theology* 4, no. 3 (February 1997): 13–27.

Perea, Juan, ed. *Immigrants Out!: The New Nativism and the Anti-Immigrant Impulse in the United States.* New York: New York University Press, 1997.

Pérez, Louis A. *Cuba: Between Reform and Revolution.* New York: Oxford University Press, 1995.

Pérez, Zaida Maldonado. "U.S. Hispanic/Latino Identity and Protestant Experience: A Brief Introduction for the Seminarian." *Perspectivas: Occasional Papers* 7 (Fall 2003): 93–110.

Pérez Álvarez, Eliseo. "In Memory of Me: Hispanic/Latino Christology beyond Borders." In *Teología en Conjunto: A Collaborative Hispanic Protestant Theology.* Edited by José David Rodríguez and Loida I. Martell-Otero. Louisville: Westminster John Knox Press, 1997.

_____. *We Be Jammin: Liberating Discourses from the Land of the Seven Flags.* México, D. F.: Publicaciones El Faro, 2002.

_____. *The Gospel to the Calypsonians: The Caribbean, Bible and Liberation Theology.* México, D. F.: Publicaciones El Faro, 2004.

Pérez Rodríguez, Arturo. "Sensual Liturgy as Hispanic Worship." In *Postmodern Worship and the Arts.* Edited by Doug Adams and Michael E. Moynahan. San Jose: Resource Publications, Inc., 2002.

Pérez Rodríguez, Arturo, and Mark Francis. *Primero Dios: Hispanic Liturgical Resource.* Chicago: Liturgical Training Publications, 1997.

Pessar, Patricia. *A Visa for a Dream: Dominicans in the United States.* Boston: Allyn and Bacon, 1995.

Peterson, Anna and Manuel Vásquez. "'Upwards, Never Down': The Catholic Charismatic Movement in Transnational Perspective." In *Christianity, Social Change, and Globalization in the Americas.* Edited by Anna Peterson, Manuel Vásquez, and Philip Williams. New Brunswick, N.J.: Rutgers University Press, 2001.

Pineda-Madrid, Nancy. "In Search of a Theology of Suffering, Latinamente," In *The Ties that Bind: African American and Hispanic American/Latino/a Theologies in Dialogue.* Edited by Anthony B. Pinn and Benjamín Valentín. New York: Continuum, 2001.

Pinn, Anthony B., and Benjamín Valentín, eds. *The Ties that Bind: African American and Hispanic American/Latino/a Theologies in Dialogue.* New York: Continuum, 2001.

Poloma, Margaret. "The Assemblies of God at the Crossroads." In *Religion: North American Style.* Edited by Thomas E. Dowdy and Patrick McNamara. New Brunswick, N.J.: Rutgers University Press, 1997.

Portes, Alejandro, Luis Guarnizo, and Patricia Landolt. "Introduction: Pitfalls and Promise of an Emergent Research Field." *Ethnic and Racial Studies* 22, no. 2 (1999): 217–238.

Pseudo-Dionysius. *Pseudo-Dionysius: The Complete Works.* Edited by John Farina, translated by Colm Luibheid. New York: Paulist Press, 1987.

Quijano, Aníbal. "Colonialidad del poder, cultura y conocimiento en América Latina." *Anuario Mariateguiano* 9, no. 9 (1997): 113–21.

Ramírez, Guillermo. *Introducción al Antiguo Testamento.* Nashville: Abingdon Press, 2003.

Ramos, Angel M. *Triumph of the Spirit: The DPN Chronicle.* Twin Falls, Idaho: R&R, 2003.

Rankin, Melinda. *Twenty Years Among the Mexicans: A Narrative of Missionary Labor.* Cincinnati: Chase and Hall, 1875.

Rappaport, Roy. *Ritual and Religion in the Making of Humanity.* Cambridge: Cambridge University Press, 1998.

Recinos, Harold J. *Jesus Weeps: Global Encounters on our Doorstep.* Nashville: Abingdon Press, 1992.

_____. "Popular Religion, Political Identity, and Life-Story Testimony in an Hispanic Community." In *The Ties that Bind: African American and Hispanic American/Latino/a Theologies in Dialogue.* Edited by Anthony B. Pinn and Benjamin Valentin. New York: Continuum, 2001.

Richard, Pablo, ed. *Materiales Para Una Historia De La Teología En América Latina.* San Jose, Costa Rica: DEI, 1980.

Ricoeur, Paul. *D'Interpretation: essai sur Freud.* Paris: Seuil: 1965.

_____. *Interpretation Theory: Discourse and the Surplus of Meaning.* Fort Worth: Texas Christian University Press, 1976.

_____. "Herméneutique et critique des idéologie." *Du texte à l'action: Essais d'herméneutique, II.* Paris: Seuil, 1986.

Rieger, Joerg. *God and the Excluded: Visions and Blindspots in Contemporary Theology.* Minneapolis: Fortress Press, 2001.

Rivera, Raquel. "Hip Hop and New York Puerto Ricans." In *Latino/a Popular Culture.* Edited by Michelle Habell-Pallán and Mary Romero. New York: New York University Press, 2002.

Rivera-Pagán, Luis N. *Senderos teológicos: el pensamiento evangélico puertorriqueño.* Río Piedras, P.R.: Fundación Puerto Rico Evangélico y Editorial La Reforma, 1989.

_____. *A Violent Evangelism.* Louisville: Westminster/John Knox Press, 1992.

_____. *Los sueños del ciervo: Perspectivas teológicas desde el Caribe.* Quito, Ecuador: Equipo de Historia y Sociología del Protestantismo en Puerto Rico y el Concilio Evangélico de Puerto Rico, 1995.

_____. "Pistas y sugerencias para el estudio del pensamiento protestante puertorriqueño." In *Un ministerio transformador: El Seminario Evangélico de Puerto Rico.* Edited by Lester McGrath-Andino. Río Piedras, P.R.: Seminario Evangélico de Puerto Rico y Puerto Rico Evangélico, 1998.

_____. *Diálogos y polifonías: perspectivas y reseñas.* Río Piedras, P.R.: Seminario Evangélico de Puerto Rico, 1999.

Rivera Rodríguez, Luis R. "Teología puertorriqueña y teología puertorriqueñista." *Casabe: Revista puertorriqueña de teología* 2 (February 1990): 5–7.

Rodríguez, Jeanette. *Our Lady of Guadalupe: Faith and Empowerment among Mexican-American Women.* Austin: University of Texas Press, 1994.

_____. "Sangre llama a sangre: Cultural Memory as a Source of Theological Insight." In *Hispanic/Latino Theology: Challenge and Promise.* Edited by Ada María Isasi-Díaz and Fernando F. Segovia. Minneapolis: Fortress Press, 1996.

Rodríguez, José David Sr., *Introducción a la teología.* San José, Costa Rica: DEI, 1993, 2002.

Rodríguez, José David Jr., *Justicia en nombre de Dios: confesando la fe desde la perspective hispano/latina.* México, D. F.: Publicaciones El Faro, 2002.

Rodríguez, José David, and Loida Martell-Otero, eds. *Teología en Conjunto: A Collaborative Hispanic Protestant Theology.* Louisville: Westminster John Knox Press, 1997.

Rodriguez, Richard. *Hunger of Memory: The Education of Richard Rodriguez.* New York: Bantam Books, 1982.

Rodríguez-Díaz, Daniel R., and David Cortés-Fuentes, eds. *Hidden Stories: Unveiling the History of the Latino Church.* Decatur, Ga.: AETH, 1994.

Rodríguez Juliá, Edgardo. *La renuncia del héroe Baltasar.* Río Piedras, P.R.: Editorial Cultural, 1974.

Roeder, Beatrice A. *Chicano Folk Medicine from Los Angeles, California.* Berkeley, Calif.: University of California Press, 1988.

Rogerson, John, ed. *The Oxford Illustrated History of the Bible.* Oxford: Oxford University Press, 2001:293–355.

Roof, Wade Clark. "Religious Borderlands: Challenge for Future Study." *Journal for the Scientific Study of Religion* 37, no. 1 (March 1998): 1–14.

Rosa Ramos, Moisés. "Teología puertorriqueña." *Casabe: Revista puertorriqueña de teología* 1 (August 1989): 3–4.

Rosaldo, Renato. "Cultural Citizenship, Inequality, and Multi-culturalism." In *Latino Cultural Citizenship: Claiming Identity, Space and Rights.* Edited by William V. Flores and Rina Benmayor. Boston: Beacon Press, 1997.

Rossington, M. "Homi Bhabha." In *The A-Z Guide to Modern Literary and Cultural Theorist.* Edited by Stuart Sim. London: Prentice Hall, 1995.

Ruether, Rosemary Radford. *Sexism and God-Talk: Toward a Feminist Theology.* Boston: Beacon Press, 1993.

Ruíz, Jean-Pierre. "Contexts in Conversation: First World and Third World Readings of Job." *Journal of Hispanic/Latino Theology* 2, no. 3 (February 1995): 5–29.

Ruiz Baia, Larissa. "Rethinking Transnationalism: National Identities among Peruvian Catholics in New Jersey." In *Christianity, Social Change, and Globalization in the Americas.* Edited by Anna Peterson, Manuel Vasquez, and Philip Williams. New Brunswick, N.J.: Rutgers University Press, 2001.

Ruiz, Jean Pierre. "Good Fences and Good Neighbors? Biblical Scholars and Theologians." Paper presented at the 2003 Annual Convention of the Catholic Theological Society of America in Cincinnati.

Rusch, William G., ed. *The Trinitarian Controversy.* Philadelphia: Fortress Press, 1984.

Sáenz, Rogelio, and Clyde S. Greenlees. "The Demography of Chicanos." In *Chicanas and Chicanos in Contemporary Society.* Edited by Robert M. De Anda. Needham Heights, Mass.: Allyn and Bacon, 1996.

Saldarini, Anthony J. *Pharisees, Scribes and Sadducees in Palestinian Society.* Wilmington, Del.: Michael Glazier, 1988.

Sample, Tex. *White Soul: Country Music, the Church and Working Americans.* Nashville: Abingdon Press, 1996.

Sánchez-Walsh, Arlene M. *Latino Pentecostal Identity: Evangelical Faith, Self, and Society.* New York: Columbia University Press, 2003.

Sandín Fremaint, Pedro, and Pablo A. Jiménez. *Palabras duras: homilías.* Ontario, Canada: Ediciones Siembra, 2001.

Sandoval, Moisés, ed. *Fronteras: A History of the Latin American Church in the U.S.A. since 1513.* San Antonio: Mexican American Cultural Center, 1983.

_____. *On the Move: A History of the Hispanic Church in the United States.* Maryknoll, N.Y.: Orbis Books, 1990.

Santiago-Irizarry, Vilma. "Deceptive Solidity: Public Signs, Civic Inclusion, and Language Rights in New York City (and Beyond)." In *Mambo Montage: The Latinization of New York.* Edited by Agustín Laó-Montes and Arlene Dávila. New York: Columbia University Press, 2001.

306 Handbook of Latina/o Theologies

Sauceda, Teresa Chavez. "Love in the Crossroads: Stepping-Stones to a Doctrine of God in Hispanic/Latino Theology." In *Teología en Conjunto: A Collaborative Hispanic Protestant Theology*. Edited by José David Rodríguez and Loida I. Martell-Otero. Louisville: Westminster John Knox Press, 1997.

Scheines, Graciela. *Las metáforas del fracaso. Sudamérica ¿geografía del desencuentro?* La Habana: Casa de Las Américas, 1991.

Schensul, Jean J., and Margaret D. LeCompte, eds. *The Ethnographer's Tool Kit: Using Ethnographic Data, Researcher Roles & Research Partnerships, Analyzing & Interpreting Ethnographic Data, Mapping Social Networks, Spatial Data, (Ethnographer's Toolkit, Vol. 7)*. Walnut Creek, Calif.: AltaMira Press, 1999.

Schmidt, Peter. "Academe's Hispanic Future." *The Chronicle of Higher Education* (November 28, 2003): 8–12.

Schneiders, Sandra M. "Theology and Spirituality: Strangers, Rivals or Partners?" *Horizons* 13 (1986): 253–74.

Schreiber, Alfred. *Die Gemeinde in Korinth: Versuch einer gruppendynamischen Betrachtung der Entwicklung der Gemeinde von Korinth auf der Basis des ersten Korintherbriefes*. Münster: Aschendorff, 1977.

Schreiter, Robert J. *Constructing Local Theologies*. Maryknoll, N.Y.: Orbis Books 1985.

_____. *The New Catholicity: Theology between the Global and the Local*. Maryknoll, N.Y.: Orbis Books, 1997.

Secretariat for Hispanic Affairs. *Prophetic Voices/Voces Proféticas*. Washington D.C.: United States Catholic Conference, 1985.

Segovia, Fernando. "Hispanic American Theology and the Bible: Effective Weapon and Faithful Ally." In *We Are a People: Initiatives in Hispanic American Theology*. Edited by Roberto S. Goizueta. Minneapolis: Fortress Press, 1992.

_____. "Two Places and No Place on Which to Stand: Mixture and Otherness in Hispanic American Theology." In *Mestizo Christianity: Theology from the Latino Perspective*. Edited by Arturo J. Bañuelas. Maryknoll, N.Y.: Orbis Books, 1995.

_____. "Aliens in the Promised Land: The Manifest Destiny of U.S. Hispanic American Theology." In *Hispanic/Latino Theology: Challenge and Promise*. Minneapolis: Fortress Press, 1996.

_____. *Decolonizing Biblical Studies: A View from the Margins*. Maryknoll, N.Y.: Orbis Books, 2000.

Segovia, Fernando, and Mary Ann Tolbert, eds. *Reading from This Place: Social Location and Biblical Interpretation in Global Perspective*. Minneapolis: Fortress Press, 1995.

Sheldrake, Philip. *Spirituality and Theology, Christian Living and the Doctrine of God*. Maryknoll, N.Y.: Orbis Books, 1999.

_____, ed. *The New Westminster Dictionary of Christian Spirituality*. Louisville: Westminster John Knox Press, 2005.

Silva Gotay, Samuel. *Protestantismo y Politica en Puerto Rico, 1898–1930: Hacia una Historia del Protestantismo Evangelico en Puerto Rico.* San Juan: Editorial de la Universidad de Puerto Rico, 1997.

Sinclair, John H. "Research on Protestantism in Latin America: A Bibliographic Essay." *International Bulletin of Missionary Research* 26, no. 3 (July 2002): 110–17.

Slessarev-Jamir, Helene. *Sustaining Hope Creating Opportunities: The Challenge of Ministry among Hispanic Immigrants.* Report prepared for the Annie E. Casey Foundation. Wheaton, Ill.: Wheaton College, 2003.

Smith, Christian, and Joshua Prokopy, eds. *Latin American Religion in Motion.* New York: Routledge, 1999.

Soliván, Samuel. "Hispanic Pentecostal Worship." In *¡Alabadle!: Hispanic Christian Worship.* Edited by Justo Gonzalez. Nashville: Abingdon Press, 1996a.

_____. "Sources of a Hispanic/Latino American Theology: A Pentecostal Perspective." In *Hispanic/Latino Theology: Challenge and Promise.* Edited by Ada Maria Isasí-Diaz and Fernando Segovia. Minneapolis: Fortress Press, 1996b.

_____. *Spirit, Pathos and Liberation: Toward an Hispanic Pentecostal Theology.* Sheffield, Great Britain: Sheffield Academic Press, 1998.

Spradley, James P. *The Ethnographic Interview.* New York: Holt, Rinehart, and Winston, 1979.

Stark, Rodney. *The Rise of Christianity: A Sociologist Reconsiders History.* Princeton: Princeton University Press, 1996.

Stavans, Ilan. *Spanglish: The Making of a New American Language.* New York: HarperCollins, 2003.

Stevens-Arroyo, Antonio M. *Prophets Denied Honor: An Anthology on the Hispanic Church in the United States.* Maryknoll, N.Y.: Orbis Books 1980.

Suárez-Orozco, Marcelo, and Mariela Páez. "Introduction: The Research Agenda." In *Latinos: Remaking America.* Edited by Marcelo Suárez-Orozco and Mariela Páez. Berkeley: University of California Press, 2002.

Sue, Derald Wing, and David Sue. *Counseling the Culturally Different: Theory and Practice,* 3d edition. New York: John Wiley and Sons, 1999.

Suro, Roberto. *Counting the "Other Hispanics": How Many Colombians, Dominicans, Ecuadorians, Guatemalans and Salvadorans Are There in the United States?* Washington, D.C.: Pew Hispanic Center, 2002.

Swete, Henry B. *The Holy Spirit in the Ancient Church.* London: MacMillan, 1912.

Sylvest, Edwin, Jr. "Hispanic American Protestantism in the United States." In *Fronteras: A History of the Latin American Church in the U.S.A. since 1513.* Edited by Moíses Sandoval. San Antonio: Mexican American Cultural Center, 1983.

_____. "Hispanic American Protestantism in the United States." In *On the Move: A History of the Hispanic Church in the United States.* Edited by Moisés Sandoval. Maryknoll, N.Y.: Orbis Books, 1990.

_____. "Bordering Cultures and the Origins of Hispanic Protestant Christianity." In *Protestantes/Protestants: Hispanic Christianity Within Mainline Traditions.* Edited by David Maldonado, Jr. Nashville: Abingdon Press, 1999.

Tamez, Elsa. *The Amnesty of Grace: Justification by Faith from a Latin American Perspective.* Nashville: Abingdon Press, 1993.

Tapia, Andres. "Growing Pains: Evangelical Latinos Wrestle with the Role of Women, Generations Gaps, and the Cultural Divides." *Christianity Today* 39, no. 2 (February 6, 1995): 38–42.

Taylor, Charles. *Varieties of Religion Today.* Cambridge: Harvard University Press, 2003.

Taylor, William B. "The Virgin of Guadalupe in New Spain: An Inquiry into the Social Devotion of Marian Symbolism." *American Ethnologist* 14, no.1 (Feb. 1987): 9–33.

Tillich, Paul. *Systematic Theology.* Chicago: The University of Chicago Press, 1963.

Tracy, David. *Plurality and Ambiguity.* Chicago: The University of Chicago Press, 1987.

Traverzo Galarza, David. "The Emergence of a Latino Radical Evangelical Social Ethic in the Work and Thought of Orlando E. Costas: An Ethico-Theological Discourse from the Underside of History." Ph.D. diss., Drew University, 1992a.

_____. "Towards a Theology of Mission in the U.S. Puerto Rican Migrant Community: From Captivity to Liberation." In *Voces: Voices from the Hispanic Church.* Edited by Justo L. González. Nashville: Abingdon Press, 1992b.

_____. "A Paradigm for Contemporary Latino Thought and Praxis: Orlando E. Costas' Latino Radical Evangelical Approach." *Latino Studies Journal* 5, no. 3 (September 1994): 108–31.

_____. *Orlando E. Costas: Un Hombre en el Camino, Vision y Esperanza Ante lo Eterno.* Rio Piedras, P.R.: Centro Ecumenico de Teología y Pastoral (CENETEPA), 1995.

_____. "Sin: A Hispanic Perspective." In *Teología en Conjunto: A Collaborative Hispanic Protestant Theology.* Edited by José David Rodríguez and Loida I. Martell-Otero. Louisville: Westminster John Knox Press, 1997.

_____. "Historical Roots of the Contemporary U.S. Latino Presence: A Latino Protestant Evangelical Contribution." In *El Cuerpo de Cristo: The Hispanic Presence in the U.S. Catholic Church.* Edited by Peter Casarella and Raul Gomez. New York: Crossroad, 1998.

Trotter, Robert T., II, and Juan Antonio Chavira. *Curanderismo: Mexican American Folk Healing,* 2d edition. Athens, Ga.: University of Georgia Press, 1997.

Trouillot, Michel-Rolph. *Silencing the Past: Power and the Production of History.* Boston: Beacon Press, 1995.

Turner, Kay. "Mexican American Home Altars: Towards Their Interpretation." *Aztlán* 13, no. 1 (Spring 1982): 309–26.

_____. *Beautiful Necessity: The Art and Meaning of Women's Altars.* London: Thames & Hudson, 1999.

Turner, Kay, and Suzanne Seriff. "Giving an Altar: The Ideology of Reproduction in a St. Joseph's Day Feast." *Journal of American Folklore* 100, no. 398 (October-December 1987): 446–60.

Tweed, Thomas A. *Our Lady of the Exile: Diasporic Religion at a Cuban Catholic Shrine in Miami.* New York: Oxford University Press, 1997.

_____, ed. *Retelling U.S. Religious History.* Berkeley: University of California Press, 1997.

United Methodist Church (U.S.). *Hispanic Ministries: Challenge and Opportunity.* Nashville: The Committee on a National Plan for Hispanic Ministry, 1992.

United States Conference of Catholic Bishops. *Encuentro and Mission: A Renewed Pastoral Framework for Hispanic Ministry* (November 13, 2002): 1–28.

Valentín, Benjamin. *Mapping Public Theology: Beyond Culture, Identity and Difference.* Harrisburg, Pa.: Trinity Press International, 2002.

_____, ed. *New Horizons in Hispanic/Latino(a) Theology.* Cleveland: Pilgrim Press, 2003.

Vásquez, Manuel. "Pentecostalism, Collective Identity, and Transnationalism among Salvadorans and Peruvians in the U.S." *Journal of the American Academy of Religion* 67, no. 3 (1999): 617–635.

Vásquez, Manuel, and Marie Marquardt. *Globalizing the Sacred: Religion Across the Americas.* New Brunswick, N.J.: Rutgers University Press, 2003.

Vázquez, Hjamil A. Martínez. "Shifting the Discursive Space: A Postcolonial Approach to U.S. Religious Historiography." Ph.D. diss., Lutheran School of Theology at Chicago, 2003.

Villafañe, Eldin. *The Liberating Spirit: Toward an Hispanic American Pentecostal Social Ethic.* Grand Rapids: William B. Eerdmans, 1993.

Villaseñor, Victor. *Rain of Gold.* New York: Bantam Doubleday Dell, 1991.

Wakefield, Gordon S., ed. *The Westminster Dictionary of Christian Spirituality.* Philadelphia: Westminster Press, 1983.

Warner, Stephen J. "Religion, Boundaries and Bridges." The 1996 Paul Hanly Furfey Lecture. *Sociology of Religion* 58, no. 3 (Fall 1997): 217–38.

Watson, Francis. *Paul, Judaism and the Gentiles: A Sociological Approach.* Cambridge: Cambridge University Press, 1986.

Weaver, Mary Jo. *New Catholic Women: A Contemporary Challenge to Traditional Religious Authority.* San Francisco: Harper and Row, 1988.

Weber, David J. *The Spanish Frontier in North America.* New Haven: Yale University Press, 1992.

Welch, Claude. *Protestant Thought in the Nineteenth Century.* New Haven: Yale University Press, 1972.

Westermann, Claus. *Genesis: A Practical Commentary.* Grand Rapids: William B. Eerdmans, 1987.

White, James F. *The Sacraments in Protestant Practice and Faith.* Nashville: Abingdon Press, 1999.

Williams, Peter W. *America's Religions: From Their Origins to the Twenty-First Century.* Champaign, Ill.: University of Illinois Press, 2001.

Wilson-Kastner, Patricia. *Faith, Feminism and the Christ.* Philadelphia: Fortress Press, 1983.

Wink, Walter. *Homosexuality and the Bible.* Nyack, N.Y.: Fellowship Publications, 1996.

Wittgenstein, Ludwig, G. H. von Wright, and Heikki Nyman. *Culture and Value.* Chicago: University of Chicago Press, 1980.

Wolf, Eric. "The Virgin of Guadalupe: A Mexican National Symbol." *Journal of American Folklore* 71 (1958): 34–39.

_____. *Europe and the People Without History.* Berkeley: University of California Press, 1982.

Zapata, Dominga M. "The Being and Doing of the Church: Pastoral de Conjunto." In *Prophetic Vision: Pastoral Reflections on the National Pastoral Plan for Hispanic Ministry.* San Antonio: Mexican American Cultural Center, 1992.

Zizek, Slavoj. *The Sublime Object of Ideology.* London: Verso, 1989.

_____. *The Ticklish Subject: The Absent Centre of Political Ontology.* London: Verso, 1999.

_____. *The Fragile Absolute—or, Why Is the Christian Legacy Worth Fighting For?* London: Verso, 2000a.

_____. "Class Struggle or Postmodernism? Yes, Please!" In *Contingency, Hegemony, Universality: Contemporary Dialogues on the Left.* Edited by Judith Butler, Ernesto Laclau, and Slavoj Zizek. London: Verso, 2000b.

_____. *Did Somebody Say Totalitarianism?: Five Interventions in the (Mis)use of a Notion.* New York: Verso, 2001.